SLOW TRAVEL

Cambridgeshire & The Fens

Local, characterful guides to Britain's special places

Lucy Grewcock

D1603880

EDITION 1

Bradt Guides Ltd, UK
The Globe Pequot Press Inc, USA

First edition published November 2021
Bradt Guides Ltd
31a High Street, Chesham, Buckinghamshire, HP5 1BW, England
www.bradtguides.com
Print edition published in the USA by The Globe Pequot Press Inc,
PO Box 480, Guilford, Connecticut 06437-0480

Text copyright © 2021 Lucy Grewcock
Maps copyright © 2021 Bradt Guides Ltd; includes map data © OpenStreetMap contributors
Photographs copyright © 2021 Individual photographers (see below)
Project Managers: Anna Moores and Emma Gibbs
Cover research: Ian Spick

ISBN: 9781784777456

British Library Cataloguing in Publication Data
A catalogue record for this book is available from the British Library

Photographs
© individual photographers credited beside images & also those picture libraries credited as follows: Alamy.com (A); AWL Images (AWL); Getty Images (G); Shutterstock.com (S); Superstock.com (SS)
Front cover View towards St Ives (George W Johnson/G)
Back cover Cambridge's skyline (Pajor Pawel/S)
Title page Dating back to the 13th century, Bourn Windmill is one of the oldest surviving mills in the country (pxl.store/S)

Maps David McCutcheon FBCart.S
Typeset by Ian Spick, Bradt Guides
Production managed by Zenith Media; printed in the UK
Digital conversion by www.dataworks.co.in

AUTHOR

Lucy Grewcock lived on the border of Cambridgeshire from the age of ten, attending school a few miles south of Peterborough. Although she now lives in Sussex, her parents and sister have never left East Anglia, giving her two second homes that she regularly returns to – one near Huntingdon and the other on the outskirts of Cambridge. She has been a travel writer and guidebook author for more than a decade, writing for *The Times*, *The Independent*, *The Guardian* and many others.

AUTHOR'S STORY

I moved to East Anglia in the early 1990s, arriving kicking and screaming (quite literally) when my family upped sticks from the hills of Herefordshire and settled in the flatlands of the Cambridgeshire/Northamptonshire border. Reluctant to accept my new home at first, I slowly softened to its charms, lured by its wildlife-filled wetlands, chocolate-box villages and the vast, mysterious Fens. As a family, we would picnic beside the rivers Nene and Ouse, windsurf at Grafham Water, scuba dive near Whittlesey and, dare I say, shop till we dropped in Peterborough. For a special treat, we'd visit Cambridge, which felt like another world, with its posh university, posh shops and posh people. When my sister and I befriended a choir boy at the famous King's College, my mum would drag us along to watch him sing on Sundays. As a kid, I was bored to tears, totally oblivious to the fact that I was witnessing one of the finest choral groups in the world.

Although I left East Anglia for university in Nottingham, and later to settle in Sussex, my parents and sister have stayed put. With my sister living in and around Cambridge for the past 20 years, I have discovered that there's more to this city than the university, that the King's College choristers are anything but boring and that not all Cambridge residents are posh. Researching this book has allowed me to delve deeper into the county's charms and discover the fascinating stories of the Fens: I've discovered Anglo-Saxon embankments, ancient mills and impressively tall hills that I never knew existed. Living more than 100 miles south in Sussex has also given me perspective on what makes the county of Cambridgeshire so unique – the fragments of wild fen at Wicken and Woodwalton are utterly magical, the birdlife at RSPB Ouse Washes is mesmerising, the intricacy of Ely Cathedral is mind-blowing, and I'd challenge anyone to find a more ferocious sunset than those that simmer on the vast horizons of the Fens.

ACKNOWLEDGEMENTS

A big thanks goes to all the Cambridgeshire residents, business owners and all-round enthusiasts who have shared their stories and expertise with me, and have helped to bring this book to life. Sadly, there are far too many to mention but, I can assure you, your efforts have been enormously appreciated.

Another huge thank you goes to the team at Bradt for helping me turn this book into a reality. In particular, I'd like to thank Rachel Fielding for commissioning the book, Anna Moores for her unwavering support, and Emma Gibbs for her excellent edits.

My family deserves a very special thank you for all their help with research and local advice, and for always putting up with me when I turned up for research trips, often at the drop of a hat. Thanks also to my partner Tommy for all his support, to Hudson the dog for his company on the many walks and, most of all, thanks to my Mum, Denise, whose idea this book was in the first place.

FEEDBACK REQUEST & UPDATES WEBSITE

At Bradt Guides we're aware that guidebooks start to go out of date on the day they're published – and that you, our readers, are out there in the field doing research of your own. You'll find out before us when a fine new family-run hotel opens or a favourite restaurant changes hands and goes downhill. So why not write and tell us about your experiences? Contact us on ✆ 01753 893444 or ✉ info@bradtguides.com. We will forward emails to the author who may post updates on the Bradt website at ⟨⟩ bradtguides.com/updates. Alternatively, you can add a review of the book to ⟨⟩ bradtguides.com or Amazon.

CONTENTS

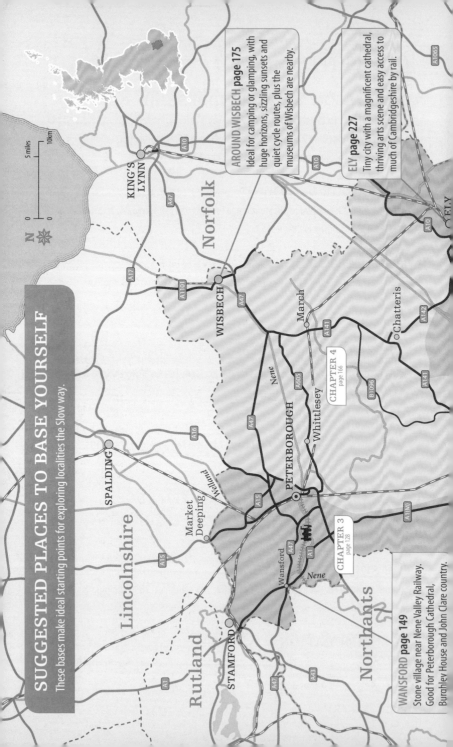

SUGGESTED PLACES TO BASE YOURSELF

These bases make ideal starting points for exploring localities the Slow way.

AROUND WISBECH page 175
Ideal for camping or glamping, with huge horizons, sizzling sunsets and quiet cycle routes, plus the museums of Wisbech are nearby.

ELY page 227
Tiny city with a magnificent cathedral, thriving arts scene and easy access to much of Cambridgeshire by rail.

WANSFORD page 149
Stone village near Nene Valley Railway. Good for Peterborough Cathedral, Burghley House and John Clare country.

CHAPTER 4
page 166

CHAPTER 3
page 128

N

5 miles

10km

KING'S LYNN

Norfolk

WISBECH

March

Chatteris

ELY

Nene

Whittlesey

PETERBOROUGH

SPALDING

Market Deeping

Welland

Nene

Wansford

STAMFORD

Lincolnshire

Rutland

Northants

A10

A47

A17

A1101

A47

A605

A141

A142

A141

B1096

A10

A10

A142

A16

A15

A47

A1

A43

A47

A15

A1(M)

A1139

A605

A16

A1101

CAMBRIDGE page 28
The riverside capital has incredible architecture, urban meadows and one of the world's oldest universities.

LINTON & AROUND page 287
Good for walkers, this area has rolling hills and ancient landscapes. Linton, Hildersham and Balsham are all good options.

HINXTON & DUXFORD page 282
Chocolate-box villages easily reached by bike from Cambridge. Close to Duxford Imperial War Museum.

KIMBOLTON page 117
Smart village with decent cafés and pubs. Home to Kimbolton Castle and close to Grafham Water.

HEMINGFORD GREY page 98
Idyllic riverside village within walking distance of St Ives and Houghton Mill.

CHAPTER 6
page 276

CHAPTER 5
page 220

CHAPTER 1
page 20

CHAPTER 6
page 276

CHAPTER 2
page 70

Suffolk

Essex

Hertfordshire

Bedford

Central Bedfordshire

NEWMARKET

CAMBRIDGE

HUNTINGDON

STEVENAGE

LUTON

Linton

Saffron Walden

Hinxton

Duxford

Royston

St Ives

Hemingford Grey

St Neots

Kimbolton

Great Ouse

Great Ouse

Cam

Cam

GOING SLOW IN

CAMBRIDGESHIRE & THE FENS

Around 8.2 million visitors flock to the city of Cambridge each year but only a fraction stay overnight and very few venture beyond the city centre, let alone explore the rest of the county. Most are day trippers who arrive by the coachload and swarm around the city's historic core before departing a few hours later. To assist these visitors are countless guidebooks and blog posts dedicated to the county's capital, yet there are none I know of (other than this book) that give a comprehensive guide to Cambridgeshire as a whole. For Slow travellers, this makes things easy – by merely reading this book, seeking out a backstreet pub or venturing beyond the county's capital, you'll experience a side to Cambridgeshire that most visitors (and many residents, for that matter) never see. If you're fully committed to the Slow ethos, there's far more to discover: linger longer or travel a little further and you'll find Anglo-Saxon earthworks, wildlife-filled wetlands and historic villages that tell stories of the hermits and horse knockers, earls and adventurers, monks and millers, ice skaters and innovators that make this county so fascinating.

Shaped like a rough-edged diamond, every corner of Cambridgeshire exudes a different identity. In the west, the former county of Huntingdonshire (which has kept its old name) is distinct in its riverside mills and market towns while, north of here, the city of Peterborough has a grand cathedral and is bordered by rolling countryside and honey-coloured villages that line the River Nene. In northeast Cambridgeshire, the pancake-flat fields, vast orchards and remote villages of the Fens feel a world away from the green hills and affluent settlements of southern Cambridgeshire, or the busy streets and grand university buildings of Cambridge itself. It is this diversity that makes the county so appealing

Peterhouse College, Cambridge (SS) ▶

THE SLOW MINDSET

Hilary Bradt, Founder, Bradt Travel Guides

We shall not cease from exploration
And the end of all our exploring
Will be to arrive where we started
And know the place for the first time.

T S Eliot, 'Little Gidding', *Four Quartets*

This series evolved, slowly, from a Bradt editorial meeting when we started to explore ideas for guides to our favourite country – Great Britain. We wanted to get away from the usual 'top sights' formula and encourage our authors to bring out the nuances and local differences that make up a sense of place – such things as food, building styles, nature, geology or local people and what makes them tick. Our aim was to create a series that celebrates the present, focusing on sustainable tourism, rather than taking a nostalgic wallow in the past.

So without our realising it at the time, we had defined 'Slow Travel', or at least our concept of it. For the beauty of the Slow Movement is that there is no fixed definition; we adapt the philosophy to fit our individual needs and aspirations. Thus Carl Honoré, author of *In Praise of Slow*, writes: 'The Slow Movement is a cultural revolution against the notion that faster is always better. It's not about doing everything at a snail's pace, it's about seeking to do everything at the right speed. Savouring the hours and minutes rather than just counting them. Doing everything as well as possible, instead of as fast as possible. It's about quality over quantity in everything from work to food to parenting.' And travel.

So take time to explore. Don't rush it, get to know an area – and the people who live there – and you'll be as delighted as the authors by what you find.

to Slow travellers, who can experience vastly different landscapes, architecture and attitudes within just a few miles.

There is one resounding feature, however, which has shaped this county for centuries. Waterways, both natural and manmade, have defined Cambridgeshire since its earliest days. The city of Cambridge began life as a settlement by the River Cam, while the rivers Nene and Great Ouse were some of the most important transport routes in medieval England. The Fens, meanwhile, were once a drowned world of swamps and marshes, with isolated settlements built on island-like nodules of higher ground. This all changed in the 17th century, when the Great Ouse and Nene were diverted and canalised to drain the fenland swamps and reveal the fertile farmland beneath. Today, the county's network of rivers and drainage channels can be explored by boat or on countryside walks beside their banks that lead to waterside pubs and historic settlements like St Ives, Wisbech and Ely.

Despite being part of Cambridgeshire, the Fens have always been viewed as different. In their pre-drained days, the mist-shrouded swamps were seen as dangerous and impenetrable, navigable only by marsh men who lived by their own laws. Even today, some still believe that only fenlanders can truly understand this region. I'd urge you to shake off this stereotype and set off on an adventure into the deepest darkest Fens. Here, you'll meet welcoming communities who share their home with vast flocks of birds, England's lowest point and fragments of ancient fen that are like nowhere else you've experienced before.

To enrich your explorations in Cambridgeshire, I recommend dipping into some of its literary treasures – this is a region that has inspired writers and poets through the ages, from William Wordsworth to Geoffrey Chaucer who, in the 1300s, immortalised the River Cam in *The Reeve's Tale*. Six centuries later, the poet Rupert Brooke captured the romance of Cambridgeshire village life in *The Old Vicarage, Grantchester* while Sybil Marshall's *Fenland Chronicle*, which is set in a similar era, explores a time in the Fens when men were bent double from turf-digging and houses would get so inundated by water that the beds would often float on the floodwater. *Waterland* by Graham Swift is a another must read. This 20th-century classic delves into 240 years' worth of bleak Fenland lives and dark family secrets. In 1992, it was made into a film starring Jeremy Irons.

There's so much to discover in Cambridgeshire, from historic houses and fascinating museums to cosy pubs and bustling market towns, yet the first thing I do when I visit is hop on my bike or lace up my walking boots and head into the countryside. Here, the skies seem bigger, the birdlife is incredible and the sense of history is palpable. I'd urge you to explore some of rural Cambridgeshire's peaceful and ancient pockets – places like the lonely reserve of RSPB Ouse Washes, the whispering reeds at Wicken Fen and the Iron Age hillfort of Stonea Camp, or the ancient trackway of Devil's Dyke, the bucolic landscapes of John Clare country and the sea of orchards that blankets the northern Fens. By exploring slowly and delving into the stories and histories that have shaped these landscapes, you'll start to get a true sense of Cambridgeshire beyond its capital.

A TASTE OF CAMBRIDGESHIRE

Cambridgeshire has no shortage of great pubs, restaurants, food shops and markets, many of which are champions of Slow food and drink – you can try homemade gin in Grantchester (page 59), local pies at Ely Market (page 230) and scrumptious Chelsea buns from Fitzbillies in Cambridge (page 41), or buy freshly milled flour from Houghton Mill (page 96) or Swaffham Prior (page 263).

Although the county isn't well known for any particular dish these days, it was once the best place in England for eels, which were caught locally and jellied, stewed or baked in pies. Sadly, local eel stocks have plummeted in recent decades and this Cambridgeshire classic has faded from the regional diet. Nonetheless, it is fondly remembered in the city of Ely, which hosts eel-themed artworks and an annual Eel Fayre (page 228), while one restaurant – the Old Fire Engine House (page 235) – still has eel on the menu.

One local speciality to look out for is Cambridge burnt cream: similar to crème brûlée but with a thicker topping of burnt sugar, this decadent dessert was created at Trinity College in 1879 but is often overlooked in favour of its French counterpart. I've seen it on the menu at Sheene Mill (page 313) and at a couple of restaurants in Cambridge. Stilton cheese is another Cambridgeshire foodstuff that has a long history with the area – hailing from Stilton village (page 158), you can enjoy this stinky blue at The Bell Inn (page 159).

You'll find locally produced ales on sale in most Cambridgeshire pubs, while micro-breweries like Wylde Sky Brewing (page 290) and Calverley's (page 42) welcome drinkers to their tap rooms. For brewing on a larger scale, you could visit Elgood's in Wisbech (page 180) which has been making ale since the 1800s. If cider's more your thing, Simon's Cider (page 96) in Godmanchester uses salvaged local apples; if you'd prefer an afternoon quaffing wine, head to Chilford Hall Vineyard (page 290) which produces award-winning reds, whites and rosés in one of the oldest-established vineyards in England.

The best Cambridgeshire produce, however, comes fresh from the soil. Boasting some of the world's richest farmland, the Fens produce a fifth of England's potatoes, a third of our veg and some of the highest-yielding wheat crops on the planet. Much of the UK's celery is grown here and, in 2013, Fenland celery (a British heritage variety) was

A TASTE OF CAMBRIDGESHIRE

Cambridgeshire has some of the world's richest farmland, producing bountiful crops of everything from soft fruits to celery, while its restaurants, pubs and artisan markets showcase this produce at its best.

1 Orchards are a long-standing feature of the Cambridgeshire countryside, with vast fields of apple trees in the northern Fens. **2** Fenland celery is a heritage variety with protected geographical indication (PGI) status. **3** Local markets and farm shops are great places to sample authentic Cambridgeshire produce. **4** Cambridge burnt cream is a decadent dessert, similar to crème brûlée.

LOVECELERY.CO.UK

THRIPLOW DAFFODIL WEEKEND

NATA BENÉS

awarded protected geographical indication (PGI) status. Distinguished by its nutty, bittersweet flavour, this prized vegetable is only available between October and December – look for it in farm shops like Burwash Manor (page 302) and Johnsons of Old Hurst (page 111), or at the farmers' markets in Ely (page 230), St Ives (page 102) and Cambridge (page 29).

Fruit also has a long association with the county. In the mid 19th century, orchards were a defining feature of Cambridgeshire life, with whole villages employed to work in the fruit-growing industry. Histon (page 64) near Cambridge was home to a world-leading jam factory and is still an important jam-making hub today. Huge Bramley orchards were also planted in the Fens, where they're still an important crop – you can see them by following the *Apples & ale cycle route* (page 184), which leads out into the countryside from Wisbech.

HOW THIS BOOK IS ARRANGED

MAPS

The map of Cambridgeshire at the front of this book marks out the areas covered by each chapter. In addition, each of the six chapters begins with a more detailed map of the area, with places numbered to coincide with the text. I have also included a sketch map for each walk or cycle ride that I feel would benefit from one. For more detail, or for routes that I haven't given maps for, OS Explorer maps 208, 209, 225, 226 227, 228 and 235 cover the county.

ACCOMMODATION, EATING & DRINKING

Under the headings of several places in this book, I've listed a few hotels, B&Bs, campsites and self-catering options that have stood out for their Slow ethos and/or atmospheric location. You'll find these listed with their contact information at the end of this book (page 315) and full listings can be found at ⧉ bradtguides.com/camsleeps.

Recommendations for places to eat and drink are listed within each chapter. These include pubs, cafés, restaurants and shops which sell local produce, have a sustainable ethos, or are just so good or atmospheric that I felt they had to be included. That said, a few have made the cut more for their proximity to a particularly important location or landmark.

PRACTICAL INFORMATION & GETTING AROUND

Where possible, I've included contact information and opening hours for the attractions and businesses featured in this book. However, I would always recommend checking opening times (and entrance fees) online, as they are subject to change. I have also listed the main tourist information centres and their websites, all of which are good sources of information and inspiration, and include additional suggestions of places to stay and eat. At the time of writing, there was no county-wide tourist hub or website for the whole of Cambridgeshire – hence the need for this book!

All chapters begin with some information on getting around each area. As a Slow traveller, public transport should always trump driving. As well as cutting carbon, buses and trains allow you to gaze out of the window, soak up the scenery and mingle with the locals. A handy source for route planning is ⊘ transport.cambridgeshirepeterborough-ca.gov. uk, which has a 'journey planner' tool for bus and rail travel.

WALKS & CYCLE RIDES

It goes without saying that travelling under your own steam is the best way for Slow travellers to get about. As one of the flattest counties in England, you'll have few hills to contend with, and those that exist give fantastic, far-reaching views. For extended journeys on foot, you could explore one of the many long-distance walking routes that trail through Cambridgeshire, like the riverside Ouse Valley Way, Nene Way or Fen Rivers Way. Other long-distance routes that pass through the county include the Hereward Way, Three Shires Way and Icknield Way Trail, all of which are waymarked along their routes and highlighted on OS Explorer maps with a diamond symbol. More localised long-distance routes that stick within the Cambridgeshire borders include the 46-mile Pathfinder Long Distance Walk, and the 25-mile Fleam Dyke and Roman Road Walk.

For cyclists, I've mentioned several routes on the Sustrans National Cycle Network (NCN ⊘ sustrans.org.uk) as well as some of my favourite rides around Cambridgeshire's country lanes and wildlife reserves. Cycle-hire centres have been included, although be aware that these are sparse in some areas, except in Cambridge itself (the UK's unofficial 'cycling capital'), where you can't move for bike-hire and repair shops.

EXPLORING BY BOAT

Having been shaped by water more than most counties, Cambridgeshire lends itself perfectly to boat travel and, if you're feeling ambitious, you could plan a multi-day adventure along its network of waterways. The rivers Great Ouse, Cam and Nene are all navigable, as are several of their tributaries, the manmade New Bedford River and Old Bedford River, and some sections of the canal-like lodes in southeast Cambridgeshire. Where appropriate, I've given basic information about boat hire, visitor moorings and marinas but you'll need to do some additional research if planning a big trip – any boat-hire centre will be able to provide this for you. For shorter trips, you can hire boats by the hour, join guided river trips or explore by punt, canoe or paddleboard. Just remember, if launching your own vessel you'll need to get it licensed with the Canal & River Trust – the Cambridgeshire river authorities are notoriously vigilant.

SLOW DAYS OUT IN CAMBRIDGESHIRE

What follows here are some of my favourite days out in Cambridgeshire, from riverside walks and rural cycle rides, to brewery tours and National Trust estates. Whittling them down to just a few was a tough job but hopefully this list will open your eyes to the possibilities this county has to offer, or inspire you to get out there and plan some of your own adventures.

Discover Mill Road & the museums (page 36) A short walk from Cambridge train station, Mill Road is home to the magnificent Cambridge Central Mosque, plus an unusual cemetery and some of the best independent coffee shops and pubs in the city. Later, you could explore Cambridge University Botanic Garden, tour some of the university's free museums, or stay after dark for a bat safari on the River Cam.

Stroll, cycle or punt to Grantchester (page 60) Follow the 2½-mile route from central Cambridge to leafy Grantchester village, stopping off to swim in the River Cam on the way. In Grantchester, you could enjoy a pub lunch or afternoon tea in the Orchard Tea Garden before ambling back through the meadows to Cambridge for a drink in a riverside pub.

Walk between Houghton Mill, the Hemingfords & St Ives (page 106) Ramble between historic Houghton Mill, the market town of St Ives, and the riverside villages of Hemingford Abbots and Hemingford Grey on a five-mile route that leads through open meadows. Along the way, you could visit the National Trust mill, The Manor in Hemingford Grey and the Norris Museum in St Ives. There are several good places to eat and drink en route.

Ride the Nene Valley Railway (page 152) Climb aboard this heritage steam railway at Wansford Station and chug through the countryside to Overton, where you could lay out a picnic at Ferry Meadows. Continue on the train to Peterborough to discover its grand cathedral and the unique Railworld Wildlife Haven.

Explore John Clare country (page 134) Begin your day at John Clare Cottage in Helpston, where you can learn about England's greatest peasant poet and pay your respects at his grave. Next, you could cycle around the villages he loved or head out on foot to discover the landmarks and countryside that inspired him – places like Castor Hanglands and Burghley House estate.

Experience the Holme Posts & Woodwalton Fen (pages 199 and 197) Stand at England's lowest point beneath the historic Holme Posts, then take a walk through the UK's biggest silver birch woodland. You could stop for lunch nearby at the Admiral Wells pub before exploring Woodwalton Fen – one of England's first-ever nature reserves.

Delve into Wisbech's museums & brewery (page 175) The unassuming town of Wisbech is home to beautiful Peckover House, the fascinating Wisbech and Fenland Museum, and the former home of Octavia Hill – one of the founders of the National Trust. You could also admire the Georgian architecture of The Brinks and take a tour of Elgood's Brewery.

Cycle the Lodes Way (page 271) Hire a bike at Wicken Fen and follow the Lodes Way for eight miles past wildlife-filled reed beds and uninterrupted fenland en route to the stately house and gardens at Anglesey Abbey. For the return route, you could loop back through a series of pretty villages, stopping off at the striking twin churches in Swaffham Prior.

Discover Ely Cathedral & markets (pages 228 and 230) One of England's smallest cities, Ely is home to a magnificent cathedral and tranquil riverside, plus the excellent Ely Museum and the former home of Oliver Cromwell. The city also has independent shops and cafés, and is best visited on market days, when farmers' produce and artisan food stalls fill the square.

Wimpole Hall & Bourn (pages 296 and 300) Cambridgeshire's largest stately home, Wimpole Hall spans 3,000 acres and includes a mansion, formal gardens, rare-breeds farm and sprawling parkland which you can explore on foot or by bike. Just up the road is the excellent Willow Tree pub in Bourn village, the Wysing Arts Centre and ancient Bourn Windmill.

Climb Rivey Hill & the Bartlow Hills (page 289) Gazing over the pretty village of Linton, Rivey Hill (367ft) beckons to be climbed. A three-mile loop guides you to the top for panoramic views over Cambridgeshire, while pubs and cafés await in Linton. Nearby, you could stand atop the Bartlow Hills – the largest surviving Roman burial mounds in western Europe.

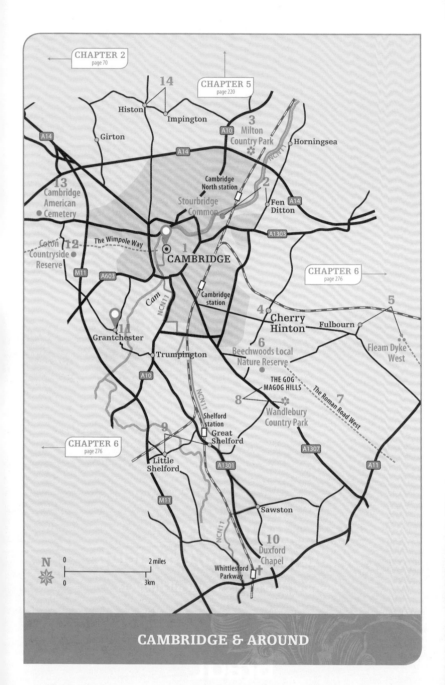

14

Histon

Impington

Girton

A14

A10

3
Milton
Country Park

Horningsea

NCN11

A14

13
Cambridge
American
Cemetery

Cambridge
North station

2

Fen
Ditton

A14

Stourbridge
Common

A1303

Coton
Countryside
Reserve

The Wimpole Way

12

M11

A603

1

CAMBRIDGE

Cam

NCN11

Cambridge
station

5

4

Cherry
Hinton

Fulbourn

11

Grantchester

Trumpington

6
Beechwoods Local
Nature Reserve

Fleam Dyke
West

A10

THE GOG
MAGOG HILLS

The Roman Road West

7

8

Wandlebury
Country Park

NCN11

9

Shelford
station
Great
Shelford

A1307

A11

Little
Shelford

A1301

M11

NCN11

Sawston

10
Duxford
Chapel

Whittlesford
Parkway

N

0   2 miles

0   3km

CAMBRIDGE & AROUND

1
CAMBRIDGE & AROUND

'It fits *all* the stereotypes,' was my partner Tommy's excited reaction when I took him to Cambridge for the first time. Having grown up in the area, I'd barely batted an eyelid at the ornate spires rising above us, the punters on the River Cam, or the university scholars rattling down the cobbled backstreets on rusty old bikes. He'd felt as if the city was putting on a show for us but he was simply witnessing part and parcel of everyday Cambridge life – a storybook scene that shapes most people's first impressions when they visit its historic core. Yet alongside these clichés, as wonderful as they are, Cambridge has many other layers that reveal themselves if you linger a little longer or delve a little deeper. From the haunted bookshop and ancient Leper Church to the cutting-edge technology of Silicon Fen and the backstreet boozers off Mill Road, seeking out these layers is the key to understanding this small city and experiencing more than a tick list of tourist spots.

Going slow in Cambridge is easy when you know how, with urban meadows to picnic in, riverside paths to ramble along and historic streets to explore on foot. Less appealing to Slow travellers are the swarms of tourists that visit the city each summer, but you can avoid the biggest crowds if you visit early or late in the day, or stray away from the city centre to the meadows, villages and nature reserves that surround it.

With footpaths and cycle routes radiating out of the city to the rural fringe, you can easily explore the entire area of this chapter under your own steam. West of Cambridge, you could walk or punt to the tea garden in Grantchester, cycle along the Wimpole Way towards Coton Countryside Reserve and the Cambridge American Cemetery, or ride along the busway route to the pubs of Histon and Impington. East of Cambridge are the lush grasslands of Stourbridge Common and Ditton Meadows, the woodlands and wildlife of Fulbourn Fen, and the Anglo-Saxon embankment of Fleam Dyke. South of the city you can get a whole new perspective of Cambridge from the Gog Magog Hills – a ridge of chalk that gives panoramic views. Nearby, Wandlebury Country Park is steeped in legends, while the ancient Roman Road is best explored by bike.

To enrich your visit, you could time your trip around one of the annual events that infuse Cambridge and its surroundings with arts, culture and eclectic entertainment: head to Fen Ditton in February or May for the biannual Bumps; visit Midsummer Common in June for a double whammy of arts festivals; book your tickets in advance for the folk festival in Cherry Hinton; join the villagers in Grantchester for apple pressing in autumn; or come to Cambridge in December for the Mill Road Winter Fair and the famous King's College carols on Christmas Eve.

GETTING AROUND

Surrounded by a triangle of major roads, Cambridge and its surrounding villages have good links to London and the rest of Cambridgeshire. The M11 skirts the western suburbs, while the A11 flanks the eastern side, and the A14 stretches east–west across the city's northern boundary. However, for getting around the area covered by this chapter, car travel is best avoided as you'll inevitably end up in traffic if you're travelling anywhere near Cambridge.

TRAINS

Cambridge railway station sits southeast of the city centre, a mile or so from the market square. South of the city are the stations at Shelford and Great Whittlesford Parkway, while Cambridge North station is north of Stourbridge Common. You can travel directly between all four stations, and all are linked to Ely (Chapter 5) and London to the south.

BUSES

As you'd expect, bus services are good in and around Cambridge, with lots of options to ferry you around the city, out to the suburbs and to the villages beyond. A comprehensive bus network operated by Stagecoach (⊘ stagecoachbus.com) and GoWhippet (⊘ go-whippet.co.uk) radiates from the city centre, with Drummer Street Bus Station as the main hub. There's also a park and ride scheme

(⌀ cambridgeparkandride.info), which allows car drivers to park on the city's fringe and take a bus to the centre.

For Histon (page 64) and other destinations west of the city, the Guided Busway (⌀ thebusway.info) offers efficient services that aren't affected by road traffic – the buses follow a car-free route along the longest guided busway track in the world, with concrete beams to keep them on track. The network also links up to road sections to reach destinations that sit off the guided tracks.

CYCLING

Dubbed the 'city of cycling', Cambridge has 80 miles of cycle routes that guide you around the city and out into the countryside. New routes are still being created, like the Chisholm Trail which, when complete, will include a two-mile, mostly traffic-free route between Cambridge railway station and Cambridge North station.

Route 11 on the National Cycle Network (NCN) wiggles north–south through Cambridge city centre. From the market place, you could follow it northwards beside the river to Waterbeach (page 47), or south to the DNA Path (page 57), the Shelfords (page 55), and Hinxton (page 284). There's also NCN51, which cuts east–west through Ditton Meadows – heading west, it follows the busway route to Histon (page 64) and Fen Drayton Lakes (page 250); heading east, it takes you to the Swaffhams, Reach and Burwell (pages 262, 264 & 268).

Just outside Cambridge, the cycling trails around Milton Country Park are good for young kids, or you could tackle the ten-mile Roman Road to Horseheath (page 290). For maps and more ideas, visit the cycling section on ⌀ cambridgeshire.gov.uk.

 CYCLE HIRE & MAINTENANCE
Cambridge and its suburbs are bursting with bike shops. I've listed a few below that offer bike hire but you'll find many, many more if you're after parts or servicing only.

Chris's Bikes 2 Thornton Way, Girton CB3 0NJ ✎ 01223 276004 ⌀ chrisbikes.co.uk
◷ Mon–Sat afternoons
City Cycle Hire 61 Newnham Rd, CB3 9EY ✎ 01223 365629 ⌀ citycyclehire.com ◷ Mon–Sat
Grounds Cycle Centre Milton Country Park, Cambridge Rd, CB24 6AZ ✎ 07869 469960
⌀ miltoncountrypark.org ◷ Tue–Sun & bank hols

CAMBRIDGE

Cambridge is one of the UK's most beautiful and historical cities, with ancient colleges and grand architecture, along with green meadows and the tranquil River Cam.

1 King's College was founded by King Henry VI in 1441 and is one of the 31 colleges that make up the University of Cambridge. 2 The Bridge of Sighs spans the River Cam at St John's College and is said to have been a favourite spot of Queen Victoria's.

3 The Sedgwick Museum of Earth Sciences is the University of Cambridge's oldest museum and contains 4.5 billion years' worth of earth science and natural history. **4** Fitzbillies café and bakery was founded in 1920 and is best known for its exceptionally good Chelsea buns. **5** Cambridge University Botanic Garden is home to more than 8,000 plant species and was the brainchild of Charles Darwin's mentor, John Stevens Henslow. **6** Punting past the college backs is a classic Cambridgeshire pastime which became a popular leisure pursuit in the mid-19th century. **7** Full of independent shops, the winding streets and alleyways in central Cambridge are perfect for pottering.

Kingsway Cycles 8 City Rd, CB1 1DP 🔗 01223 355852 🔗 kingswaycycles.com ○ 08.00–17.00 Mon–Fri, 08.00–noon Sat

Outspoken Cycles 140 Cowley Rd, CB4 0DL 🔗 01223 789606 🔗 outspokencycles.co.uk ○ 08.30–17.00 Mon, Wed & Fri, 09.30–16.30 Sat. Walking distance from Cambridge North train station.

Rutland Cycling Grand Arcade, Corn Exchange St, CB2 3QF; CyclePoint, 156 Great Northern Rd, CB1 2FX; 9 High St, Histon CB24 9JD 🔗 01223 307655 🔗 rutlandcycling.com ○ daily

E-SCOOTERS

A new addition to central Cambridge, Voi e-scooters (🔗 voiscooters. com) are available to hire from designated Voi stands. They travel at a maximum of 10mph and, once you've got the hang of it, are good fun and easy to operate. To use one, you'll need to download the Voi app, which allows you to unlock and pay for a scooter. Riders must be at least 18 years old and hold a full or provisional driving licence.

WALKING

As a small city, Cambridge is best explored on foot – particularly the compact centre and the Backs, which are traffic-free and perfect for pottering. Also traffic-free, the riverside footpaths and meadows that fringe the centre are also very pleasant for a stroll – Jesus Green, Midsummer Common and the Mill Pond area are the most central, while Stourbridge Common, Coe Fen and Sheep's Green are further out. For a longer walk, you could follow the river out of the city to rural villages and pubs: the Grantchester Grind (page 60) is a classic route, or you could walk through Stourbridge Common to the riverside pub in Fen Ditton (page 44).

South of the city, you could climb high at the Gog Magog Hills (page 54), explore the farm trails at Coton Countryside Reserve (page 62), discover the Iron Age hillfort at Wandlebury Country Park (page 54) or climb on to the embankment of Fleam Dyke (page 49).

For a bigger challenge, you could tackle the 25-mile Fleam Dyke and Roman Road walk (page 292) over two days, or set off from Cambridge on the 13-mile Wimpole Way – a waymarked walking route that winds west out of Cambridge, past countryside and villages, to reach the magnificent Wimpole Hall. The starting point is one mile northwest of Cambridge's market square, at the junction of Adams Road and Wilberforce Road. If you don't fancy the whole route, you could walk or cycle from Cambridge to Coton (2½ miles) or Hardwick (five miles) and refuel in a pub before returning to Cambridge or catching the bus (Stagecoach 4). For more information about the Wimpole Way and Wimpole Hall, see page 296.

BOATS & PUNTS

Cambridge and its surroundings lend themselves perfectly to explorations by river, with the river meandering through Grantchester Meadows, into the city, and past Stourbridge Common to Fen Ditton and beyond. Punting is a rite of passage in Cambridge, and you can take guided tours of the Backs or try punting yourself upstream to Grantchester. During the peak summer season, it's a good idea to book a punt in advance but, on quieter days, you'll have no problem just turning up. Canoes and kayaks can also be hired.

Riverboats are another option. From Cambridge, you could join a guided cream tea cruise, a Sunday lunch trip to a pub, or an evening bat-spotting safari with on-board experts. If you'd prefer to self-guide, you can hire a boat for the day and tour the Cam at your leisure, or pack your bags for a multi-night trip, exploring the Cambridgeshire waterways and sleeping onboard.

BOAT & PUNT HIRE

Cam Boats ℰ 07706 734763 ⟁ camboats.co.uk. Solar-powered and traditional narrowboats available for self-drive, private tours, hop-on sightseeing cruises and bat-spotting safaris. Most tours depart from Fen Ditton Marina (The Plough, Green End, CB5 8SX) or at Jesus Lock in Cambridge.

Cambridge Boat Hire ⟁ cambridge-boat-hire.co.uk. Narrowboat hire for multi-day, self-guided trips, with a choice of several embarkation points on the Cam.

Cambridge Chauffeur Punts Silver St, CB3 9EU ℰ 01223 354164 ⟁ punting-in-cambridge. co.uk ☉ 09.00–dusk daily. Look for the punts beneath the willows, next to Silver Street Bridge.

Granta Moorings 14 Newnham Rd (outside the Granta pub), CB3 9EX ℰ 01223 301845 ⟁ puntingincambridge.com ☉ May–Sep 09.00–21.00; Oct–Dec & Mar–Apr 10.00–17.00; closed Jan–Feb. Punts and canoes available.

Scudamore's Mill Ln, CB2 1RS; Quayside punting station CB5 8AB; Granta Pl, CB2 1RS ℰ 01223 359750 ⟁ scudamores.com ☉ 09.00–dusk daily. Cambridge's original punt operators have three hire stations, with punts available at Mill Lane (near the Mills Pond area) and Quayside (opposite Magdalene College), plus boats, canoes and kayaks at Granta Place. They also offer themed trips and seasonal bat safaris.

1 CAMBRIDGE

🏠 **Cambridge University Rooms** (page 315), **University Arms** (page 315)

If this is your first visit to Cambridge, don't be surprised if you feel like you've stepped into a film set. Capital of the county, this is a spellbinding city where Gothic towers rise above cobbled streets, the River Cam meanders past ancient colleges and Red Poll cows graze in urban grasslands. If you're a regular visitor or resident, you'll know that, in parallel to this fairy tale is a whole other layer of backstreet pubs, trendy cafés and hidden corners where most tourists rarely wander. This fusion of ancient history, time-old traditions and contemporary quirks creates an eccentric buzz that is quintessentially Cambridge.

For most visitors, the University of Cambridge is an obvious draw, and with good reason. Founded in 1209, it's the second oldest university in the English-speaking world (after Oxford). The university and city are inextricable, having developed side by side over several centuries. As a result, many of Cambridge's most striking buildings and churches belong to the university and are notable for their striking towers, ornate cloisters and beautifully landscaped grounds.

THE CAMBRIDGE COLLEGES

The University of Cambridge is made up of 31 autonomous colleges, which are scattered throughout the city. Having started life as religious institutions, many are several centuries old and have ornate chapels that are some of England's finest. King's College Chapel is the most impressive of these.

When students wish to study at Cambridge University, they apply to an individual college which they are then affiliated to throughout their studies – this is where they sleep, eat, study and socialise. Tutoring sessions, known as 'supervisions', take place within the colleges, while larger classes are held in communal faculty buildings, dedicated to each subject area.

Many of the colleges are open to visitors but each has their own entry conditions – you can visit the halls and chapels of some, while others only grant access to their gardens, and some offer full guided tours. Seasonal visiting hours vary between each one, so it's best to check the college websites before visiting. If you'd prefer to just turn up, you'll usually find public visiting times displayed on boards outside the college gatehouses.

Throughout the year, some colleges also hold events, like gallery openings and the summer Shakespeare Festival (🔗 cambridgeshakespeare.com) where you can lay out a picnic and watch performances in the college grounds.

In parts of Cambridge, the countryside appears to creep into the urban core, with riverside meadows beckoning you to lay out a picnic, dip your toes in the Cam and kick back on the grass with a good book. Cambridge also has an alternative edge, which is at full force on Mill Road – this is the coolest corner of the city, with independent shops, trendy pubs and international restaurants. To delve deeper into the city's bohemian vibes, you could listen to live bands at the Corn Exchange, watch a performance at Cambridge Arts Theatre, or fill your boots with arts and crafts at the annual Strawberry Fair.

THE HISTORIC CORE

Cambridge city centre has one of the best collections of classical architecture in Europe – there are so many stunning buildings and beautiful bridges here that it's impossible to take in every single one. One of the best ways to explore the centre is to simply dive in and get a bit lost – the city's core is easily walkable so, as long as you stick to where the oldest buildings are, you'll never be too far from where you started.

The main market square is a good place to orientate yourself from and is surrounded by cobbled alleyways and university colleges. And there are several city maps dotted around the streets, including 3D versions cast in bronze. If you'd prefer a more methodical approach, you could follow my route below, or there are plenty of operators offering guided walking tours, including several led by Cambridge students (⊘ cambridgealumnitours.co.uk), plus good-value options with the Round Church (⊘ roundchurchcambridge.org/guided-walks), and family-friendly walks with Terrible Tours (⊘ terribletours. co.uk). Alternatively, you could nip into a newsagents and buy a tourist map or pocket guide, or download one of the many online apps offering self-guided walking tours.

"At the geographical and metaphorical heart of Cambridge, the market square is surrounded by many of the city's oldest buildings"

At both the geographical and metaphorical heart of Cambridge, the **market square** (⊙ Market Hill, CB1 0SS) is surrounded by many of Cambridge's oldest buildings, with alleyways leading in all directions to the colleges, riverside and shopping streets. Markets are held in the square seven days a week, and stalls have traded here since the Middle Ages. Today, it's the go-to place to grab anything from fresh juices and

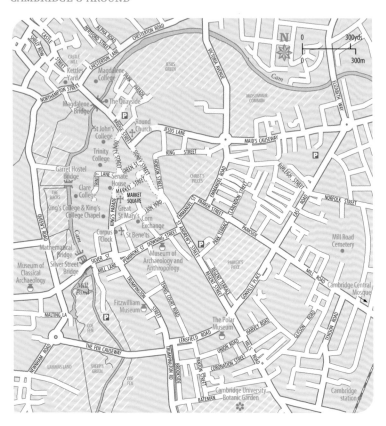

filled bagels to English cheeses and Chinese dumplings. The general market (☉ 10.00–16.00 Mon–Sat) also sells clothes, plants, books and more, while Sundays focus on local crafts and farmers' produce.

Backing on to the west side of market square is the church of **Great St Mary's** (Senate House Hill, CB2 3PQ ⌖ greatstmarys.org ☉ 10.00–17.00 Mon–Sat, noon–17.00 Sun) – the entrance is around the corner on Senate Hill, at the northern tip of King's Parade. A church has stood here since the 13th century, with the current building dating back to the 1400s. For the best view in Cambridge, climb the 123 steps inside the tower and peer down on the city's rooftops. Diagonally opposite the church on King's Parade is King's College and Cambridge's most iconic building, **King's College Chapel**. The chapel was built between 1446 and 1536 under the instruction of five different kings. Inside is

Rubens's *Adoration of the Magi* and the world's largest fan-vaulted ceiling. To take a peek, you can join a guided tour or visit for evensong (17.30 Mon–Sat, 10.30 & 15.30 Sun) – queuing begins 35 minutes before each performance. On Christmas Eve, the Festival of Nine Lessons and Carols is broadcast across the world from this chapel; visitors often queue all day for the chance of a seat.

On the north side of King's College, the Neoclassical white building facing Great St Mary's is **Senate House** (built 1772). The university's graduation ceremonies take place here, with graduates leaving via a side door on to Senate House Passage (right side of Senate House as you face it). If you wander down this passage and veer left when you meet Trinity Street, you'll get a good view of **Clare College**, the university's second oldest surviving college (founded 1326), where the naturalist David Attenborough studied zoology.

North of the market square are lots of independent shops and cafés hidden in the alleyways that branch off Trinity Street and Sidney Street. There are also several more colleges to discover. On the corner of Senate House Passage and Trinity Street is **Gonville & Caius College** (Caius is pronounced 'keys'), where physicist Stephen Hawking studied. Further north on Trinity Street is **Trinity College** (1546), with its castle-like red-brick façade. Founded by Henry VIII, this is Cambridgeshire's largest and wealthiest college, previously attended by Prince Charles, Lord Byron, Alfred Tennyson and Isaac Newton.

Continuing north, Trinity Street leads into St John's Street. At the merging of these two streets is All Saints Garden, which hosts a popular Saturday craft market. Opposite the garden, **St John's College** boasts a Victorian chapel with one of the tallest towers in Cambridge. Founded in 1511 by Henry VIII's grandmother, St John's was attended by poet William Wordsworth and slave trade abolitionist William Wilberforce. At the end of St John's Street is the **Round Church** (⌂ roundchurchcambridge.org ⊙ 11.00–16.30 Tue–Sat) – the second oldest building in Cambridge. Built by crusaders in 1130, it was modelled on the church of the Holy Sepulchre in Jerusalem and is one of only four round churches in England. Inside, the visitor centre has an exhibition of Cambridge's story, from Roman times to the present day.

From the Round Church, you can walk northwest along Bridge Street to the quayside and **Magdalene College** (pronounced 'maudlin'), where diarist Samuel Pepys studied in the 17th century. A short walk (around

300yds) northeast of the quayside, **Castle Hill** sits just off Castle Street, behind The Castle Inn. This is where the original settlement of Cambridge was founded – an information board at the base tells you more, and it's an easy climb to the hill's 82ft summit for views across the city. Southeast of the quayside, Bridge Street leads back past the Round Church to the market square via Sidney Street and Market Street.

In the southeast corner of the market square, Perry Cury Street leads to Lion Yard – a multi-level mall of high street shops and places to eat. In the southwest corner of the market square is Peas Hill, with some intriguing alleyways branching off it – St Edward's Passage, for example, is home to the 13th-century church of **St Edward King and Martyr** and the 18th-century **Haunted Bookshop** (9 St Edward's Passage, CB2 3PJ ☉ 10.00–17.00 Mon–Sat), which is renowned for supernatural sightings – the shop been occupied by a specialist in children's and illustrated books since the 1990s but the previous owner asked that the shop kept its original name, owing to the eerie figures seen floating up the stairs. Also on St Edward's Passage is the main entrance to the excellent **Cambridge Arts Theatre** (6 St Edward's Passage, CB2 3PJ ✎ 01223 503333 ⬦ cambridgeartstheatre.com), which was founded in 1936 by the economist John Maynard Keynes. The theatre claims to have launched some of the UK's most celebrated actors, including Emma Thompson and Sir

"In the southwest corner of the market square is Peas Hill, with some intriguing alleyways branching off it"

Ian McKellen, both of whom performed here when they were students at Cambridge. It's a great place to see top-quality theatre productions that include world premieres and long-running classics. At the bottom of Peas Hill, Wheeler Street leads east, where you'll find **Cambridge Corn Exchange** (3 Parson's Court, Wheeler St, Cambridge CB2 3QE ✎ 01223 357851 ⬦ cambridgelive.org.uk) – a great place for live music, I have many a happy memory of seeing bands here as a teenager. Having started life as a 19th-century corn exchange, selling farmers' produce, it began transitioning into a community and arts venue in the early 20th century, and was properly converted into a concert hall in the 1970s. It has since hosted everyone from the Royal Philharmonic Orchestra, David Bowie and Queen to Take That, Radiohead and the Arctic Monkeys. Opposite Wheeler Street, Bene't Street (short for Benedict) leads west off Peas Hill and boasts Cambridge's oldest building – the

11th-century tower of **St Bene't's Church**. The church was founded in 1020 and, while the main building was altered in the 13th, 14th and 19th centuries, the tower remains unchanged.

Bene't Street leads southwest to the junction of King's Parade and Trumpington Street, where you'll find the **Corpus Clock** – unveiled in 2008 by Stephen Hawking, this sculptural timepiece features a mythical Chronophage (time eater) that stings each hour to death. From here, Trumpington Street leads south past several more colleges, including Corpus Christi (the only Cambridge college founded by townspeople), Pembroke (where comedian Eric Idle studied in the 1960s) and Peterhouse – the university's oldest college (founded 1284), with an alumni that includes comedian David Mitchell and film director Sam Mendes.

CAMBRIDGE – THE BACKSTORY

In the 1st century BC, Cambridge started life as an Iron Age settlement on Castle Hill, which sat on the edge of the Fens next to a crossing point on the River Cam. This position gave the settlers fish, eels and wildfowl from the swampy, pre-drained Fens, along with access to the river, which provided a navigable artery through the marshes and out to the coast. When the Romans arrived, they built a fort on the hill and established a bridge across the river. The Saxons and Normans later occupied the site and expanded the settlement further – the Normans built St Bene't's Church (see above) in 1086, a castle on Castle Hill (1088) and the Round Church (page 31) in 1107.

The university's first colleges were founded in the 1200s and Cambridge continued to grow, although it was a very different place than it is today. It was seen as a dirty place, 'infected' by the fenland swamps – the damp, low-lying land was a breeding ground for plague-carrying rats that brought severe bouts of the Black Death. In the 1600s, the city made a big step in tackling this issue, installing a clean watercourse known as Hobson's Conduit. Cambridge also held an important role at the start of the English Civil War (1642–51), with a parliamentary base established here and control of the town given to Oliver Cromwell, who hailed from nearby Huntingdon (page 90) and was educated at Cambridge.

The 18th and 19th centuries saw periods of growth in the city, with Addenbrooke's Hospital established in 1766 and the London–Cambridge railway line opening in 1845. At the dawn of the Victorian era, Cambridge was a wealthy town, with a host of new industries and colleges. Moving into the 20th century, the university's buildings escaped the worst of the World War I and II air raids, and in 1951 the town was granted city status, becoming one of just 18 English cities that doesn't have a cathedral.

THE BACKS & MILL POND

When people talk about **The Backs**, they're referring to a strip of land by the River Cam where six colleges (St John's, Trinity, Trinity Hall, Clare, King's and Queens') back on to the banks. This riverside vantage point gives a whole different perspective of the university colleges, with their ancient buildings rising above the water and their landscaped grounds rolling down to the banks. Most impressive is the view of King's College Chapel, which dwarfs Clare College next door.

However, unless you've paid to enter the college grounds, you can't simply stroll along the Backs and take it all in as much of the riverside is on private college land. Instead, the best way to experience the Backs is from the river itself – punting is the traditional method of transportation but you could also canoe, kayak or paddleboard. All punting companies (page 27) offer guided trips, enriched with stories of Cambridge folklore and college antics.

If you don't fancy punting, there are a few places where you can glimpse the Backs on foot, without having to enter the college grounds. **Silver Street Bridge** (next to the Anchor pub on Silver St) allows you to gaze upstream to Queens' College and **Mathematical Bridge** – designed by William Etheridge in the 1740s, this bridge follows a sophisticated design that makes it look as though it's built from long pieces of timber but it is, in fact, made from lots of shorter pieces. Further downstream, **Garret Hostel Bridge** (next to the Jerwood Library on Garret Hostel Ln), gives glorious views upstream to the grounds of Trinity Hall and the stone arches of Clare Bridge (part of Clare College), and downstream to Trinity College and Trinity Bridge. Set back from the river, the footpath that runs parallel to Queen's Road gives a fantastic view of the back of King's College.

If all that punting or elbowing your way across bridges for a glimpse of the Backs has left you hankering for some breathing space, then a short wander south of Silver Street Bridge takes you to the **Mill Pond** area, where a patch of countryside has sneaked into the city. Here, at the southern end of the Backs, the river splits and meanders into calm pools that are flanked by grassy meadows. It's a lovely place to stroll or spread out a picnic in the long grass – just beware of cow pats, as well as actual cows, which have grazed here since medieval times. You could have a decent leg stretch too, with the riverside footpath extending south through the meadows to Coe Fen and Sheep's Green (page 39), which sit across The Fen Causeway (A1134).

PUNTING

Punting along the Backs is a rite of passage, and the clunk and splash of punters is part of the city's soundtrack. For anyone unfamiliar with the term, 'punting' involves propelling a flat-bottomed boat along the river, using a pole to push off the riverbed. Originally a means of transport, it was taken up as a leisure activity in the 1860s.

If you fancy giving it a go, you could either hire a punt and steer yourself, or opt for a chauffeur (usually a university student) who will do the work for you. There are several places where you can hire punts, the most obvious spots being Magdalene Bridge and Silver Street Bridge – within a few feet of either location, you'll be accosted by well-spoken students wearing deck shoes and waving clipboards, who will eagerly arrange your punt trip for you. You can also book in advance (page 27), which is a good idea on busy summer weekends.

A chauffeured tour of the Backs takes around 45 minutes. Among the highlights, you'll see the Mathematical Bridge, King's College Chapel and the ornate Bridge of Sighs at St John's College. If you're doing it yourself, then I'd allow at least an hour – you'll need more time to get to grips with the punt and take breaks (it's thirsty work)!

If you're feeling more adventurous, you could punt upstream to Grantchester (page 57) for a cream tea or pub lunch. The trip takes around 90 minutes each way, and you'll need to hire your punt from one of the upper river stations (not Magdalene Bridge or Silver Street Bridge). It's best to check in advance with the punting company you plan to hire with.

THE EAST-SIDE PARKS

To the north and east of the marketplace, several parklands carpet the city. The smallest but most central of these is **Christ's Pieces**, less than ten minutes' walk from the market square and next to Drummer Street Bus Station. I'm rather fond of this leafy park, which has mature trees and a rose garden dedicated to Princess Diana, but my brother-in-law (a local resident) bemoans that it's a magnet for daytime drinkers.

South of Christ's Pieces, the wide lawns of **Parker's Piece** are a popular place for games of cricket, rounders and, most importantly, football – it was here that the rules of modern football were confirmed, with Cambridge students committing them to paper in 1848. You can read the rules in the east corner of the park, where they're inscribed on a concrete monument. Parker's Piece is also known for its striking central lamppost – Reality Checkpoint – which is said to mark the boundary between the university 'bubble' of central Cambridge and the real world beyond where everyday Cambridge folk live.

THE UNIVERSITY MUSEUMS

One of the best things about Cambridge is its museums, many of which are owned by the university and are free to visit. If you're searching for a rainy day activity, then this is it – pick one or two that appeal and take yourself on a tour. Each February, the museums host 'Twilight at the Museums', where you can enter each one after dark. To find out more about this and other museum events, visit ⊘ museums.cam.ac.uk.

Fitzwilliam Museum Trumpington St, CB2 1RB ⊘ fitzmuseum.cam.ac.uk ⊙ 10.00–17.00 Tue–Sat, noon–17.00 Sun & bank hols. The don of Cambridge's museums, this vast site has more than half a million artefacts and artworks across the ages, from Egyptian coffins to Monet paintings.

Kettles Yard Castle St, CB3 0AQ ⊘ kettlesyard.co.uk ⊙ 11.00–17.00 Wed– Sun. This is the former home of Tate Gallery curator Jim Ede (1895–1990). You can explore his house and view his collection of British modern art, which includes works by Henry Moore.

Museum of Archaeology & Anthropology Downing St, CB2 3DZ ⊘ maa.cam.ac.uk ⊙ 10.00–17.00 Tue–Sat, noon–17.00 Sun. Come to see ancient artefacts like samurai armour, a Roman skeleton, 500-year-old potatoes, and instruments from Captain Cook's voyages.

North of Christ's Pieces are the sprawling meadows of Jesus Green and Midsummer Common, which flank the River Cam and are bisected by Victoria Avenue. There's always plenty going on in **Jesus Green**, which has grass tennis courts, a skatepark, a barbecue area and a 1920s lido, Jesus Green Swimming Pool (⊘ better.org.uk/leisure-centre/ cambridge/jesusgreenlido ⊙ May–Sep 07.00–19.00 daily) which, at almost 300ft, is one of Europe's longest. West of the lido, Jesus Green Lock is an embarkation point for river cruises (page 27). East of Jesus Green, **Midsummer Common** feels wilder, with long grass and a herd of Red Poll cattle in spring and summer. Each June, it hosts Midsummer Fair (an ancient travellers' fair which has been held here since 1211) and Strawberry Fair – an arts festival with performers, music and crafts, the latter began life in 1974 and has been fuelling Cambridge's alternative edge ever since with craft workshops, world cuisine, vegan food stalls, and live music that ranges from folk, rock and reggae to punk, ska and techno.

MILL ROAD

A mile-long hub of hipster cafés, international restaurants and independent shops, Mill Road is the coolest corner of Cambridge. This

Museum of Classical Archaeology Sidgwick Av, CB3 9DA ⏚ www.classics.cam. ac.uk/museum ☉ 11.00–14.00 Tue–Fri, 14.00–17.00 Sat. Home to one of the largest plaster cast collections in the world, including the largest surviving collection of plaster cast Greek and Roman statues.
Museum of Zoology Downing St, CB2 3EJ ⏚ www.museum.zoo.cam.ac.uk ☉ 10.00–16.30 Tue–Sat, noon–16.30 Sun. Two floors of birds, mammals and aquatic life, perfectly frozen in time. Highlights include a 68ft fin whale and the skeleton of a dodo.
The Polar Museum Lensfield Rd, CB2 1ER ⏚ www.spri.cam.ac.uk/museum ☉ 10.00–16.00 Thu–Sat. Trace the stories of polar exploration through Arctic and Antarctic artefacts and explorers' possessions, including Shackleton's snow goggles and Scott's camera.
Sedgwick Museum of Earth Sciences Downing St, CB2 3EQ ⏚ sedgwickmuseum. org ☉ 10.00–12.30 & 14.00–16.30 Thu–Sat. The university's oldest museum explores 4.5 billion years of earth sciences, from the birth of the planets to the first geological map.
Whipple Museum of the History of Science Free School Ln, CB2 3RH ⏚ whipplemuseum.cam.ac.uk ☉ 14.00–15.30 Mon–Thu, 14.00–15.30 Fri. Discover historical and rare scientific instruments, like Charles Darwin's microscope.

foodie enclave branches southeast of the city centre between Parker's Piece and the A1134. Perfect for Slow visitors, it's far enough from the city centre to filter out the tourist hordes but is only ten minutes' walk from the train station. Alongside the cafés and restaurants are eclectic shops offering everything from vintage clothes to organic meats. If you're as addicted to rummaging through charity shops as I am, then this is the place to come – and if smashed avocados, flat whites and craft ales are among your favourite things, you should probably consider moving here.

Mill Road runs through two neighbourhoods: Petersfield (on the city centre side) and Romsey Town (southeast end). A bridge over the railway tracks marks the border between the two but the whole area is known collectively as Mill Road. There's a real sense of community here, which is reflected in the busy calendar of local events, which includes music gigs, yoga classes and mental health talks in the cafés. **Mill Road Winter Fair** (⏚ millroadwinterfair.org), one of Cambridge's annual highlights, is held on the first Saturday in December when the road closes to traffic and becomes filled with food stalls, local crafts and open-air performances. In 2021, there were plans to switch to three smaller fairs, held on Saturdays in October, November and December, so it's best to check the website for the latest details.

A much-loved urban sanctuary on the Petersfield side is **Mill Road Cemetery** (*⊘* millroadcemetery.org.uk). The main entrance is between 43 and 45 Mill Road, which leads into the cemetery along a walkway of lime trees. Consecrated in 1848 by the Bishop of Ely, the cemetery was designed by the first curator of Cambridge University Botanic Garden. Today it's a haven of plants, wildflowers and wizened trees, which grow around listed monuments, war graves and art installations that were inspired by local birdlife. In the centre of the cemetery is the footprint of a 19th-century chapel, which was demolished in 1954.

"It's a haven of plants, wildflowers and wizened trees, which grow around listed monuments and art installations"

On the Romsey Town side of Mill Road is **Cambridge Central Mosque** (309–313 Mill Rd, CB1 3DF *⊘* cambridgecentralmosque.org), which opened to the public in 2019. Europe's first eco-friendly mosque, this contemporary masterpiece has an intricate timber structure that features a vaulted, octagonal lattice roof. Huge glass windows and skylights maximise natural light; grey water and rainwater are used to flush the toilets and irrigate the gardens, and other energy needs are met through local sustainable sources. Led by an architect firm that was responsible for the London Eye, the mosque was designed with the help of Professor Keith Critchlow, a world-leading expert in sacred architecture and Islamic geometry. Visitors can enjoy the peaceful garden and on-site café, or book a guided tour of the building.

CAMBRIDGE UNIVERSITY BOTANIC GARDEN

1 Brookside, CB2 1JE *⊘* botanic.cam.ac.uk ⊙ Feb, Mar & Oct 10.00–17.00 daily, Apr–Sep 10.00–18.00 daily, Nov–Jan 10.00–16.00 daily

Five minutes' walk west of the train station (or 15 minutes' walk south of the town centre), is Cambridge University Botanic Garden. There are two entrances: Station Road Gate (on Hills Rd, opposite Station Rd) is nearest the train station; or Brookside Gate (Trumpington Rd/A1134) is on the west side.

The garden was initiated in the 1820s by Charles Darwin's mentor, John Stevens Henslow, who convinced the university to move its original plant collection to a larger site, where it could be developed into a centre for learning. Created with the help of garden curator Andrew Murray, the current site opened in 1831 and began welcoming the public in 1846. Laid out to blend aesthetics with scientific research, one of the first features was the Systematic Beds, which are organised in botanical sequence, so that similar species can be compared and classified. Lakes, trees and walkways were added, and by the end of the 1800s the garden had amassed the rarest tree collection in the country.

Today the garden has around 8,000 plant and tree specimens in different zones that range from the woodland garden to the tropical hot house. You could follow the Main Walk past giant redwoods that were grown from the first seeds brought to England, or you could walk along the Rising Path and peer down on the historic Systematic Beds. You can also learn about everything from climate change and endangered plants to the first potatoes brought over from South America in Tudor times. There are seasonal highlights too, like the winter snowdrop trail, summer music concerts and autumn colours tours.

COE FEN, SHEEP'S GREEN & LAMMAS LAND

Half a mile's stroll west of the Botanic Garden, Coe Fen and Sheep's Green are neighbouring water meadows that were traditionally grazed by sheep (Sheep's Fen) and cows (Coes), with the latter still a common sight in summer. At the northern end, the grasslands extend across The Fen Causeway (A1134) to meet the Mill Pond area (page 34), near the city centre.

Cut through by the Cam, Coe Fen and Sheep's Green have a long history as outdoor swimming hubs. Before the days of municipal swimming pools, this is where Cambridge folk came to swim and socialise. Throughout the 19th and much of the 20th century, diving boards and wooden bathing sheds stood in the meadows, and swimming lessons and competitive events were often held. A reminder of these days can be found at the southern tip of **Coe Fen**, which lines the river's east bank. Here,

"Cut through by the Cam, Coe Fen and Sheep's Green have a long history as outdoor swimming hubs"

a little stone building sits in a walled garden, with stone slabs lining the riverbank. This is Hodson's Folly, a late 19th-century summerhouse built by Pembroke College butler John Hodson to keep an eye on his daughter as she swam in the river – back then, the area next to the folly was a designated women's bathing place, with changing sheds built opposite the folly. The folly can be accessed from the river (look out for it as you're punting past) or via a gate from Coe's Fen, where you'll also find an information board.

A few feet north of the folly, a bridge leads across the river to **Sheep's Green**, which lines the west bank. Here, you'll find Sheep's Green Learner Pool, which has served the city for several decades. West of the pool, another bridge leads across a tributary to **Lammas Land**, which was once another area of grazing land – the name 'Lammas' refers to the Lammas rights, which allowed commoners to graze their livestock here between Lammas Day (12 August) and 6 April. Today, this grassland is a public park with mown grass, a summer paddling pool and a kids' play area. Bordering Lammas Land and Sheep's Green to the west is Paradise Local Nature Reserve – a patch of riverside woodland, where boardwalks lead over swampy ground beneath a canopy of trees.

¶¶ FOOD & DRINK

I've cherry-picked some of my favourite Cambridge cafés and restaurants, along with those that are particularly historic or have scenic riverside settings. For take-away coffees, snacks and lunches, the stalls in the **market place** (◷ 10.00–16.00 daily) are an excellent option, with hot food offered alongside artisanal breads and picnic items. It's also worth noting that several of the city's pubs are run by Greene King brewery so, while many are full of history and have scenic settings, their menus are all the same and rather bog-standard. With this in mind, I haven't listed them below but, if you're just after a drink, it's worth seeking out The Anchor (Silver St), which overlooks Silver Street punting station, The Eagle (Bene't St), which has a ceiling scrawled with the names of RAF and US airmen who frequented the pub during World War II, and Fort St George (Midsummer Common), which has a fantastic setting beside Midsummer Common and the River Cam.

The historic core

Aromi 1 Bene't St, CB2 3QN; 3 Peas Hill, CB2 2PP; 30 Fitzroy St, CB1 1EW ⬧ aromi.co.uk. This family business serves handcrafted Sicilian dishes, pizzas and bakes. They have three shops in Cambridge.

Bread and Meat 4 Bene't St, CB2 3QN ◷ 11.30–20.30 daily. A slow food champion serving gourmet sourdough sandwiches with British meats, alongside other homemade dishes created with local ingredients. To wash it down, choose craft ales, organic coffees or Suffolk cream milkshakes.

Cambridge Wine Merchants 31–32 Bridge St, CB2 1UJ ✐ 01223 568989
⌂ cambridgewine.com ⊙ 10.00–21.00 Sun–Thu, 10.00–22.00 Fri & Sat. Named as one of
the UK's top 25 wine bars and best independent retailer, this wine shop and bar has one of
the world's largest collections of wines, spirits and cigars, including some from Cambridge
colleges. Their Bridge Street premises sits by the river and has views of Magdalene College.
They also have a shop and bar on King's Parade (✐ 01223 309309 ⊙ 10.00–20.00 Mon–
Sat, 11.00–19.00 Sun).

Fitzbillies 51–52 Trumpington St, CB2 1RG ⌂ fitzbillies.com ⊙ 08.00–18.00 Mon–Fri,
09.00–18.00 Sat & Sun. Founded in 1920, this cake shop and café is legendary for its Chelsea
buns – actor Stephen Fry once described them as 'peerless'. They have a second café on
Bridge Street (number 36) next to Magdalene Bridge. They also offer pre-order picnics and
afternoon teas.

Michaelhouse Café Trinity St, CB2 1SU ⊙ 09.00–17.00 Mon–Sat, noon–16.00 Sun. Just
off the market square, this converted church is breathtakingly beautiful, with most of the
old features retained. Serving breakfasts and lunches that prioritise local produce, it's a
wonderful sanctuary from the hubbub of city life.

Midsummer House Midsummer Common, CB4 1HA ✐ 01223 369299
⌂ midsummerhouse.co.uk ⊙ 12.30–13.30 & 18.00–19.30 Wed–Sat. This acclaimed
restaurant occupies a Victorian villa on Midsummer Common and holds two Michelin stars.
The seasonal menu focuses on English produce – think Suffolk tomatoes with English basil,
grass-fed Yorkshire beef, and Cambridgeshire strawberries with ewe's yoghurt.

The Old Bicycle Shop 104 Regent St, CB2 1DP ✐ 01223 859909 ⌂ oldbicycleshop.com
⊙ 10.00–23.00 Mon–Sat, 10.00–17.00 Sun. After 173 years of trading, Britain's first bike
shop (Charles Darwin is said to have bought a bike here in the 1800s) closed its doors.
Luckily, the new owners embraced the old shop, with everything from bike-part artworks
to cycle-themed cocktails in their trendy café/restaurant. The menu ranges from vegan
brunches to cod with dashi seaweed but my favourite is the 'Tandem' platter with jackfruit
nuggets and sweet potato hummus.

Restaurant Twenty Two 22 Chesterton Rd, CB4 3AX ✐ 01223 351880 ⌂ restaurant22.
co.uk ⊙ noon–13.30 Wed, noon–13.30 & 18.00–20.45 Thu–Sat. Set in a Victorian house
with stained-glass windows, this fine-dining restaurant is committed to local suppliers.
Come for the set lunch or evening tasting menu, and savour the likes of chalk stream trout
with caviar, or lamb with summer herbs.

The Varsity Hotel & Spa Thompson's Ln (off Bridge St), CB5 8AQ ✐ 01223 306030
⌂ thevarsityhotel.co.uk ⊙ seasonal hours (see website). The roof terrace at Varsity is the
ultimate place to sip a cocktail or tuck into a burger with panoramic city views. It's only open
in summer (see website for opening times) but there's another bar and brasserie one floor
down, which is open year-round and also has good views.

Mill Road

Mill Road has way too many good cafés and eateries to list them all. I've pulled out some of my favourites but I'd urge you to keep your eyes peeled for more. And it isn't just Mill Road itself you should check out – hidden in the residential streets are a smattering of other highlights, including some of Cambridge's best pubs.

Bedouin 98–100 Mill Rd, CB1 2BD ✐ 01223 367660 🖰 bedouin-cambridge.com. With a Bedouin tent draped across the ceiling, this atmospheric restaurant transports you to North Africa, serving tasty Moroccan tagines and grilled meats.

Calverley's 23A Hooper St, CB1 2NZ ⊙ 17.00–22.30 Thu & Fri, 11.00–22.30 Sat. It's well-worth seeking out this backstreet micro-brewery, which serves craft beers from their tap room. Food trucks often make an appearance, and you can buy draught take-outs by the bottle.

The Cambridge Blue 85–87 Gwydir St, CB1 2LG ✐ 01223 471680 ⊙ Wed–Sun. Festooned with beer pump badges and memorabilia, this CAMRA winner dubs itself 'Cambridge's Real Ale Paradise'. It offers a fantastic choice of ales, keg beers and one of the largest whisky collections in Cambridge. The rear garden backs on to Mill Road Cemetery, and the food is mostly Pieminister pies.

Culinaris 88 Mill Rd, CB1 2BD ⊙ daily. This artisanal food store and deli sells goods from acclaimed international producers, along with home-baked breads and fresh sandwiches. Expect a personal service, and ask them for recipe suggestions.

Empress Pub 72 Thoday St, CB1 3AX ✐ 01223 247236 ⊙ from 16.00 daily. Famous for its annual excessive display of Christmas decorations, this backstreet pub has an eccentric vibe – the newspaper clippings on the wall tell you about the pub's former pig. It has a traditional interior and a pizza menu.

Hot Numbers Dales Brewery, 5–6 Gwydir St, CB1 2LJ. This local institution occupies a former Dales Brewery building – it's easy to spot, with the old brewery sign rising above the surrounding buildings. Coffee snobs will be in seventh heaven – you can specify your espresso shot by the millilitre, and the responsibly sourced beans are roasted in small batches. The brunch menu includes smashed avocado on sourdough with burnt lime and chilli.

Limoncello 212 Mill Rd, CB1 3NF ✐ 01223 507036 🖰 limoncello.co.uk ⊙ 09.00–23.00 Mon–Thu, 09.00–midnight Fri & Sat, 10.00–17.00 Sun. This Italian deli serves lunch and dinner which focus on antipasti and traditional Italian pizzas. You can also buy everything from artisanal pasta to speciality oils and wine. There's a garden at the back, but I prefer the pavement seating, where you can people-watch with an espresso or Aperol Spritz in hand.

Live and Let Live 40 Mawson Rd, CB1 2EA. Alongside its regularly changing local ales, this backstreet boozer has one of the most impressive rum selections you'll find anywhere – the list includes white, dark and spiced rums, along with tasting notes and information about their distilleries. It's won several CAMRA awards, including Pub of the Year (2020).

The Old Norfolk Street Bakery 89 Norfolk St, CB1 2LD ⌂ norfolkstbakery.co.uk
⌚ 07.30–17.30 Mon–Fri, 08.30–14.00 Sat. Norfolk Street runs along the north side of Mill Road Cemetery. Here you'll find another pocket of pubs and cafés, which includes this little bakery. Established in 1868 and reopened in 2012, they bake breads, cakes and Portuguese delicacies. They have a sister bakery and café near Cambridge train station (7 Station Rd, CB1 2JB).

The Petersfield 2 Sturton St, CB1 2QA ✆ 01223 306306 ⌚ 17.00–23.00 Mon–Fri, 11.00–23.00 Sat, noon–21.00 Sun. This friendly little pub has a colourful interior with local artworks, plus an intimate courtyard garden. The regularly changing menu ranges from burgers and crab sandwiches to pan-seared scallops and celeriac katsu curry.

Relevant Records 260 Mill Rd, CB1 3NF ✆ 01223 244684 ⌂ relevantrecordcafe.co.uk
⌚ 09.00–17.00 daily. Serving coffees and light lunches, this licensed café includes an underground vinyl-only record store, and the café doubles as a gig venue – see the events page on their website.

Vanderlyle 38–40 Mill Rd, CB1 2AD ⌂ vanderlyle-restaurant.com. This intimate restaurant allows its menu to be driven by the seasonal and ethical ingredients supplied by local farmers and producers, which means that many of the dishes are vegetarian. Book a seat at the pass and watch the chefs create your tasting menu of Cambridge salad, confit turnip and celeriac semifreddo, with each dish presented like a work of art.

Near the train station

The Botanic Garden has a good café serving breakfasts and light lunches, or you could wander towards the train station for independent places to eat on Hills Road and Station Road.

The Old Ticket Office Cambridge railway station, CB1 2JW ✆ 01223 859017
⌂ oldticketoffice.com ⌚ noon–22.00 Mon–Sat, noon–18.00 Sun. Next to the train station, this former ticket office has been tastefully transformed into a traditional pub, serving craft ales, artisan coffee, toasties and sharing boards.

Smokeworks 1–3 Station Rd, CB1 2JB ✆ 01223 631627 ⌂ smokeworks.co.uk ⌚ noon–14.30 & 16.30–21.00 Tue–Thu, noon–21.00 Fri, 10.00–21.00 Sat, 10.00–15.00 Sun. Housed in a former pub, this restaurant and tap room specialises in craft ales, bourbon and slow-cooked food, like 14-hour brisket, smoked ribs and smoked halloumi bites. They also do weekend brunches and have a second site near the city centre (2 Free School Ln, CB2 3QA).

Stem & Glory 50–60 Station Rd, CB1 2JH ✆ 01223 757150 ⌂ stemandglory.uk
⌚ 08.00–23.00 Mon–Fri, 09.00–23.00 Sat–Sun. Contemporary vegan restaurant that serves adventurous plant-based cuisine such as kimchi pancakes, tofu yakitori and vegan fudge brownies.

STOURBRIDGE COMMMON TO FLEAM DYKE

Northeast of the city centre, the green expanse of Stourbridge Common flanks the southern bank of the River Cam, which flows out of the city to Fen Ditton village. South of here, you could seek out the Cherry Hinton chalk pits, the ancient moat in Fulbourn Fen or the Anglo-Saxon earthwork of Fleam Dyke.

2 STOURBRIDGE COMMON & FEN DITTON

🏠 **The Crown and Punchbowl** (page 315) ⛺ **Gayton Farm** (page 315)

One of the city's glorious green lungs, **Stourbridge Common** is a rugged flood meadow, grazed by cattle (Apr–Oct). With long grass and uneven ground, it feels as if a piece of the countryside has been sliced off and plonked in the city's suburbs. A footpath circumnavigates the common, and the River Cam flows along its northern boundary, where narrowboats and rowers float past.

Today the common is a bucolic place for a picnic or walk but it was once the site of the largest fair in medieval Europe, Stourbridge Fair. In 1211, King John granted a three-day fair to support the work of the local leper hospital and its chapel. With easy river access, the fair drew large crowds, while traders brought shellfish, timber and other goods along the Cam. It began as a two-day event but, by 1589, had been extended to more than a month and included entertainment like theatre performances and wrestlers. A lively and drunken event, John Bunyan used the fair as inspiration for Vanity Fair – the unholy festival in *Pilgrim's Progress*.

"Today the common is a bucolic place for a picnic but it was once the site of the largest fair in medieval Europe"

However, with the decline of river travel in the late 18th century, the fair began to lose momentum and finally petered out in 1933.

The leper hospital which instigated the fair is long gone but its chapel, which still stands, is thought to be the oldest complete surviving building in Cambridge – the **Leper Chapel of St Mary Magdalene** (Barnwell Junction, Newmarket Rd/A1134, CB5 8JJ) was founded c1125 as a centre of worship for leprosy sufferers, and later became a free chapel (not attached to a parish). Worship ceased in the 18th century but, with Stourbridge Fair still going strong at the time, it was used as a storage space and makeshift pub.

Restored by the Cambridge Preservation Society, the chapel is now used for worship on the first Sunday of each month. The grounds are always open but the doors are usually locked. To see inside, you could visit for worship or during one of the local events (see ⌀ cambridgeppf.org), like the September medieval fair, where you can learn about the chapel and its history. It's worth mentioning that the chapel sits next to a busy road and there is no parking here, so you'll need to arrive on foot or by bike.

The grassland meets a trainline at the east end of Stourbridge Common, which you can cross via a footbridge to **Ditton Meadows** – interwoven with drainage channels, these flood meadows extend east to **Fen Ditton village**. Walking to this pretty village (one mile from the western end of Stourbridge Common, or three miles from central Cambridge) is a popular local pastime. The village itself, which has some lovely old thatches and a 13th-century church, is the setting for the university's biannual Bumps races, which go directly past the riverside pub – the village's long-established affiliation with rowing is echoed in the church weather vane, which features a rowing boat. If you fancy making a base in the area, neighbouring **Horningsea** village (1½ miles northeast) has a couple of good accommodation options and pubs.

THE BUMPS

⌀ cucbc.org/bumps

Cambridge University's 'bumping races' were established in the 1820s when the rowing clubs realised that the twists and turns of the Cam made it tricky to race side by side. The races now take place twice a year: the Lents are held in late February/early March (Lent term) and the May bumps are in early June (at the end of the May term). The May bumps attract more rowers, bigger crowds and, typically, better weather.

At the start of the races, crews line up on the river with 1½ boat lengths of water between them – their position is based on their finishing order the previous year. When the starting cannon is fired, the crews row upriver, aiming to bump the boat in front of them. The following day, their positions are reset and the chase begins again. The ultimate goal is to achieve 'head of the river' at the front of the pack.

The course runs along the River Cam, from Baits Bite Lock (downstream of Fen Ditton) to just past the railway bridge at Stourbridge Common. You can watch the races from the riverbanks but the best place to spectate is the garden of The Plough pub (page 46).

FOOD & DRINK

The Green Dragon 5 Water St, CB4 1NZ ☎ 01223 363506 ⌂ greendragoncambridge.
co.uk ◷ 15.00–21.00 Mon & Tue, noon–21.00 Wed, noon–22.00 Thu–Sat, noon–18.00
Sun. At the far west end of Stourbridge Common, the Green Dragon is thought to be the
oldest pub in Cambridge – it once welcomed Oliver Cromwell and J R R Tolkien. There's a
riverside garden, blackened timbers inside and, at the time of writing, food supplied by
artisan food trucks.

Other Syde The Engineer's House, Riverside, CB5 8HN ☎ 07761 049353 ⌂ othersyde.co.uk
◷ Tue–Sun. With a fantastic setting next to Cambridge Museum of Technology, this café/
bar/restaurant sits in the gap between Stourbridge Common and Midsummer Common,
in the grounds of the city's old pumping station. They have terraced outdoor seating
which overlooks the river, and there's a cocktail bar and pizzeria inside. Expect craft beers,
handmade pizzas, local ice cream and English sparkling wine.

The Plough Green End, Fen Ditton CB5 8SX ☎ 01223 293264 ⌂ theploughfenditton.co.uk.
A former paper mill and coaching inn, this posh pub/restaurant has a huge riverside garden,
which is the best place to watch the University's bi-annual Bumps races from. It attracts a
smartly dressed crowd for its seasonally inspired menu, featuring dishes like rotisserie pork
belly and scallops, or seared sea bass with pickled watermelon.

3 MILTON COUNTRY PARK

Cambridge Rd, Milton CB24 6AZ ⌂ miltoncountrypark.org

A mixture of woods, lakes and meadows, this country park is sandwiched
between Milton (a village just off the A10) and the River Cam. This was
once a working quarry, with sand and gravel extracted until the 1960s.
Today, it's a 95-acre public park with walking trails, picnic spots and
kids' play areas. It's also has a bike-hire centre and family-friendly tracks
that lead around the park and link up with NCN51 and NCN11 – the
latter follows the River Cam to Cambridge (four miles southwest) and
Waterbeach (three miles northeast).

The park has an impressive calendar of events, which range from bike
maintenance and bushcraft workshops to outdoor yoga and mindfulness
sessions. Anglers can buy day tickets for the two main lakes, there's a
community orchard, and you can learn how to paddleboard or canoe.
They also run open water swimming sessions, which my brother-in-law
Felix regularly attends, even when there's frost on the ground. To join
him, you'll need to book a slot online. In autumn, the park hosts an
annual festival with apple pressing, campfire crafts, canoe safaris and
live music.

Cambridge to Waterbeach on NCN11

❋ OS Explorer map 209 *Cambridge* and 226 *Ely & Newmarket*; start: Market St, Cambridge
📍 TL449584; 6 miles; easy (flat all the way)

Mostly traffic free, this scenic linear ride follows NCN11 through Stourbridge Common and alongside the River Cam between Cambridge and Waterbeach.

From Cambridge market square, head east on Market Street, then left on to Sidney Street, following it north to Bridge Street. The NCN11 signs direct you right on to Thompson's Lane, then right on to Richmond Terrace to Jesus Green. Stick to the riverside path as you ride east through Jesus Green, Midsummer Common, and past Cambridge Museum of Technology to Stourbridge Common. When the path splits in Stourbridge Common, follow signs for St Ives and cross the bridge over the river to the Green Dragon pub.

From the pub, NCN11 directs you right along Water Street. At the end, turn right on to Fen Road cycle path and head northeast for a few yards. When you see the river on your right, join the riverside path and follow it for 3½ miles to the road bridge at Clayhithe. Just before the bridge, NCN11 leads left on to a wooded path – you could then exit the path on to Clayhithe Road, where you'll find the riverside Bridge pub (page 260) or you could continue half a mile west to the cafés and pubs in Waterbeach (page 259). Once you've rested and refuelled, retrace your route to Cambridge or catch the train back to Cambridge from Waterbeach station.

4 CHERRY HINTON

In Cambridge's southeast corner, the suburb of **Cherry Hinton** was named after the abundance of cherry trees grown here from the 1500s. The roads can get busy round here, and much of the area is residential but there are a couple of landmarks that make it worth visiting. On the western edge (city side) is **Cherry Hinton Hall Park**, a 30-acre parkland and woodland, with a kids' paddling area and a chalk stream. This is also the site of the Cambridge Folk Festival (⊘ cambridgelive.org.uk/folk-festival), which attracts thousands of music fans each year.

In the centre of the park is Cherry Hinton Hall – a Grade II-listed house, built in 1839 by a surgeon, John Okes, who laid out the original parkland. Much of Okes's vision, which included a walled garden, two orchards and exotic plants, is now gone but the area directly in front of the house has been planted in a similar style. The hall itself is owned by Cambridge City Council and is currently leased to a school.

A walking/jogging path runs around the park's tree-lined edge, and the eastern tip of the grounds have been given over to nature. Forty-eight of the park's most impressive tall trees are labelled and numbered, creating a tree trail that starts with the Beech (number 1) near the parking area and finishes at the Elm (48). You can download a Tree Trail map from ⌀ cambridge.gov.uk. The chalk stream – Cherry Hinton Brook – runs through the eastern side of the park, where excavations have revealed evidence of medieval watermills – there's an information board by the water to tell you more. The stream runs northwest towards Cambridge, and there's a walking/cycling path that leads for a mile beside the stream to the cafés and pubs on Mill Road (page 42).

Southeast of the park is **Cherry Hinton Chalk Pits** (Limekiln Rd, CB1 8NQ) – a set of chalk and lime quarries that supplied building materials for Cambridge colleges until the 1980s. On the east side of Limekiln Road, East Pit is now a Local Nature Reserve and SSSI, while West Pit (across the road) is less accessible. East Pit feels surreal, with footpaths weaving through patchy grassland beneath white cliffs that were formed around 95 million years ago. Metal staircases allow you to climb higher up the chalky banks for panoramic views over the pits, while wildflowers like milkwort, harebell and rare moon carrot grow within the grassland. Adjacent to East Pit, Lime Kiln Close Local Nature Reserve is the oldest of the three chalk pits and is covered in a woodland of ash, field maples and cherry trees that are descendants of Cherry Hinton's namesakes.

It's worth mentioning that access to East Pit and Lime Kiln Close Local Nature Reserve is only possible on foot or by bike – there are bike stands by the main entrance but no car parking area or even any lay-bys nearby. The other option is to park further east, on the corner of Ainsdale and Fulbourn Road, where a gate leads to the eastern tip of Lime Kiln Close Reserve.

5 FULBOURN & FLEAM DYKE WEST
🏠 **The Old Chapel** (page 315)

Three miles east of Cherry Hinton is **Fulbourn**. On the west side, this village is crowned by Fulbourn Windmill, the county's largest surviving smock mill. This handsome Dutch landmark can be seen for miles, standing on an outlier of the Gog Magog Hills (page 54). Erected in 1808, it ground wheat for more than 100 years until it was struck by lightning in 1933 and further damaged by a storm in 1936. Restoration began in the 1970s and it is now cared for by a local group who aim to throw open its door on the first Saturday of each month (see ⌀ fulbournwindmill. org.uk for upcoming dates). North of the mill is Fulbourn Hospital, which started life as the 'Pauper Lunatic Asylum' in 1855 and went on to become a pioneering centre for mental health care.

At the eastern end of Fulbourn, the old village curves around the church of St Vigor's and Fulbourn Manor. Here, tucked between modern buildings, are listed timber-framed houses, photogenic thatches and classic Cambridgeshire cottages built from yellow gault bricks. Some of my favourite buildings include the old flint cottages on ancient Impetts Lane, and the row of neo-Gothic almshouses (built 1864) on Church Lane. The short high street has a handful of independent shops, which include an antiques store, an excellent butchers (the sausage rolls are delicious) and a little fruit shop in the old village forge. St Vigor's Church has a 13th-century tower and 14th-century nave. It once shared its graveyard with a second church (All Saints), which was pulled down in the late 1700s. Next to the church, Fulbourn Manor (on Manor Walk) has been owned by the Townley family for more than 200 years. Rebuilt in 1901, this is the last occupied site of the 'five manors of Fulbourn' that stood here in Norman times. Take a peek through the gates, if they're open, to see a listed statue of William of Orange in the forecourt.

Bordering the village to the east is **Fulbourn Fen** – this former marshland is a unique nature reserve with a 150-year-old woodland and ancient grasslands that have never been ploughed. Grazed by livestock to hold back the scrub, the grasslands range from dry meadows with ancient oak trees to wet meadows with rushes and water mint – boardwalks cross this soggy ground, which is kept artificially wet by raising the water table. The reserve also harbours a medieval mound and moat that belonged to one of Fulbourn's former manors.

At the northeast corner of Fulbourn Fen, the Harcamlow Way footpath leads east to **Fleam Dyke** – a three-mile-long Anglo-Saxon embankment that strikes southeast towards the village of Balsham (page 291). In places, it stands almost 50ft above sea level – an elevation which, in Cambridgeshire, gives far-reaching views. Walking along all or part of this route is a highlight of the area, even if you only visit the western tip near Fulbourn, where a wooden staircase leads to the top and an information board fills you in on its history. If you fancy walking the full length (roughly 5½ miles between Fulbourn and Balsham), it's a good idea to start at the Balsham end as you can then take the bus (Stagecoach 16A) back to Balsham in the afternoon. The eastern end of Fleam Dyke is covered in more detail on page 292, and you can use OS Explorer map 209 *Cambridge* for route planning.

Fulbourn offers several more options for countryside explorations. Heading south of the old village, you could walk or cycle for 1½ miles on Babraham Road (which is more like a rural lane) to the Roman Road (see opposite). Or, heading north and northeast of the village, you could follow Caudle Ditch and Little Wilbraham River to the villages of Great and Little Wilbraham, which have thatched cottages and a 16th-century pub. For more ideas, the booklet *A Walking Guide to the Fulbourn Area* is a good source of inspiration. You can buy a copy in Fulbourn Library (Haggis Gap, CB21 5HD).

¶¶ FOOD & DRINK

Of Fulbourn's three pubs, the **Six Bells** (9 High St, CB21 5DH ✎ 01223 880244) has the most convenient location in the old village. This 16th-century pub serves British cuisine and has a huge garden with mature trees. Inside, there are cosy nooks, old timbers and historical village photos.

If you're walking to the Wilbrahams, the **Hole in the Wall** (2 High St, Little Wilbraham CB21 5JY ✎ 01223 848616 ⟡ holeinthewalldining.co.uk ⊙ Wed–Sun) is a 16th-century pub with low ceilings and a woodburner in the snug. It takes its name from the days when locals bought ale through a hole in the building's wall. The gastro-pub menu includes things like torched halloumi, confit duck leg and tofu tikka skewers.

SOUTH OF THE CITY

Burst free of the city's southern fringe and the countryside awaits in all its glory. Just a short bus ride or bike ride from Cambridge city centre are the arboreal depths of Beechwoods Nature Reserve and Wandlebury Country Park, the heights of the Gog Magogs and the rare chalkland habitats of the ancient Roman Road.

6 BEECHWOODS LOCAL NATURE RESERVE

Worts' Causeway, CB22 3FB

This mature beech plantation is a tranquil spot for woodland walks – I particularly love it in autumn, when fingers of sunlight beam between the trunks and illuminate the carpet of ginger leaves. Originally planted in the 1840s, it was expanded in 1992 and now covers around 25 acres. A network of footpaths leads through the wood, with information boards to put you on the right track – despite this, I still managed to get lost when I first visited, as all the paths look pretty similar. As you explore/get lost, seek out the wizard's face carved into a tree and, in summer, look for white helleborine orchids – also known as 'poached egg plants', this declining species has white flowers with a yellow lip. You may also hear the drumming of woodpeckers and, in the evening, see pipistrelle bats darting overhead.

The nearest bus stop is Babraham Road (Stagecoach PR4, park & ride), or there's a lay-by opposite the entrance for cars. If you've cycled from the city centre (roughly five miles), there's a bike lock stand just inside the entrance.

7 THE ROMAN ROAD WEST
Worts' Causeway, CB22 3FB

Less than half a mile east of Beechwoods LNR, just off Worts' Causeway, is the western end of the Roman Road – a ten-mile track that you can explore by foot or bike. The county's longest surviving stretch of Roman road, this ancient trackway once connected Cambridge to the Icknield Way. After the fall of the Roman Empire, it became a busy route for Suffolk wool merchants.

To allow surface water to drain into ditches on either side, the centre of the road was built up and, in places, you can still make out this cambered profile. With this hardpacked surface being too difficult to farm, the track has never been ploughed, so its fringes are home to ancient chalk grasslands – in summer, you can see blue harebells, purple knapweeds and wild basil along with butterflies, grasshoppers and skylarks. You may even spot a common lizard or two, lying on the track and basking in the sun.

"Its fringes are home to ancient chalk grasslands – in summer, you can see blue harebells, purple knapweeds and wild basil"

There's a small parking area (a large lay-by) at Worts' Causeway, with access to the track. From here, you could cycle the full length of the road to Horseheath village. To plan a route, use OS Explorer maps 209 *Cambridge* and 210 *Newmarket & Haverhill*. You can read about the eastern end of the Roman Road in Chapter 6 (page 290).

BEYOND THE CITY

Surrounding Cambridge are pretty villages, country parks, peaceful woodlands and unique visitor attractions, all within a bike or bus ride of the city centre.

1 Wandlebury Country Park is home to an Iron Age hillfort, sheltered by woodland. 2 Duxford Chapel dates back to medieval times and consists of a single room, built of flint and cobble. 3 Milton Country Park has lakes for wild swimming, cycle tracks for family bike rides, plus a bike-hire centre and café. 4 Cambridge American Cemetery is the UK's only American World War II cemetery. It has an excellent visitor centre which explores Britain's relationship with the US.

If you fancy a bigger challenge, you could combine the Roman Road with Fleam Dyke for a 25-mile walking route. You'll find details about this in Chapter 6 (page 292), or you could visit the Friends of the Roman Road and Fleam Dyke website ⊘ frrfd.org.uk.

8 THE GOG MAGOG HILLS & WANDLEBURY COUNTRY PARK

Two miles south of the city centre, the **Gog Magog Hills** are Cambridge's mountains – this is where city folk come to climb high, fly kites and, in winter, go sledging. Straddling Babraham Road (A1307), these chalk hills rise to a mere 246ft but, surrounded by lowlands, they feel far higher. The area includes a golf course and two public reserves – Magog Down and Wandlebury Country Park – but when locals refer to the Gog Magog Hills (or, more simply, 'the Gogs') they are usually talking about Magog Down.

On the southern side of Babraham Road, **Magog Down** (car park off Haverhill Rd, CB22 5FX) is a magnet for anyone craving elevation, with Little Trees Hill as its centrepiece. It's a short stroll to the summit, and the reward is one of the best views in Cambridgeshire – fields and farms roll on for miles, and the northern aspect gives a fantastic view of the city, with Addenbrooke's Hospital dominating the foreground. Beneath Little Trees Hill, a network of trails wiggles through the reserve's woodland, wildflower meadows and fields.

On the northern side of Babraham Road, **Wandlebury Country Park** (CB22 3AE) has its own bus stop on the Cambridge–Haverhill service (number 13), and a cycle path leads here from the city centre (roughly 4½ miles). The park has two main draws: an 18th-century estate and an Iron Age hillfort, Wandlebury Ring. My favourite place for an autumn walk, the hillfort features a sunken concentric ditch and footpath, sheltered by wooded banks. Come October, the inner ditch is carpeted with russet-coloured leaves, while medusa-like roots twist up the banks. Spring is good too, with pretty wildflowers and woodpeckers drumming in the trees. Setting off from the car park, it's less than a mile's walk around the inner ring, which has a fairy-tale stone part-way round. The park also has a designated viewpoint area where, on clear days, you can glimpse Ely Cathedral.

The 18th-century estate sits in the centre of the park and has a grand stable block where the Arabian stallion Godolphin Arabian was stabled

GOGS MYTHS & LEGENDS

The Gogs are steeped in folklore and have been popular with occultists since the 1960s. Most tales are based around the mythical giants of Gog and Magog, who are said to slumber in the hills. Other stories are more sinister, like the tale of a ghostly rider who, on moonlit nights, challenges anyone who calls 'knight to knight, come forth'. In the early 20th century, local children believed that gods were buried here. This story grew legs when archaeologist T C Lethbridge carried out excavations and, after much poking around, claimed to have uncovered a solar god and a three-breasted female riding a chariot. His 'finds' and unorthodox methods caused controversy, and many believed he had simply mistaken a set of natural features in the ground.

– Godolphin was the best-known of three historic stallions from which most modern thoroughbreds are descended. Once you've paid your respects at Godolphin's grave, the estate's gardens are a lovely place to lay a picnic or sip a hot drink from the pop-up weekend café.

FOOD & DRINK

The Gog Farm Shop Heath Farm (just off the A1307), Shelford Bottom CB22 3AD. Next to Wandlebury Ring, this award-winning collection of small shops includes a butchery, deli, café and gift shop. It's a good place to pick up seasonal Cambridgeshire veg, local organic meats, freshly baked bread, homemade pies and more.

9 THE SHELFORDS

South of Cambridge and a mile or so west of the Gog Magog Hills are the suburban villages of Great Shelford, Little Shelford and Stapleford. Further south are Sawston and Whittlesford. These sought-after settlements are a short cycle or train ride from Cambridge city centre but, unless you're interested in tracing Obama's family roots (see box, page 56), they don't really register on the tourist radar. Having said that, the NCN11 cycle route links all five, so you may find yourself riding through if you're exploring on two wheels. If so, the church of St Mary's (Church St, Great Shelford) is worth a wander – above the chancel arch is an impressive 15th-century Doom painting. You could also seek out the pre-Norman architecture of All Saints Church (Church St, Little Shelford), the tile maze in the flint church of St Andrew's (Mingle Ln, Stapleford), and the 20th-century wall painting at St Mary and St Andrew (Church Ln, Whittlesford).

¶¶ FOOD & DRINK

All five villages have pubs and cafés where you can quench your thirst or grab a bite. **Shelford Deli** (8A Woollards Ln, Great Shelford CB22 5LZ ⌂ shelforddeli.co.uk ☉ Tue–Sat), which was listed by *The Independent* as one of the 50 best delis in the UK, is an excellent café-bistro and grocery store. Another good café is **East Roast Coffee** in Sawston (8 Mill Ln, CB22 3HZ ☉ Mon–Sat), which has a reputation for top-notch coffees and cakes. For pubs, **The Tickell Arms** (North Rd, Whittlesford CB22 4NZ ✆ 01223 833025 ⌂ thetickellarms.co.uk) is a gastro-pub with two gardens, real fires and an orangery overlooking the pond. 'Highly recommended' by the *Michelin Guide*, they serve gastro cuisine with home-grown veg.

10 DUXFORD CHAPEL

Station Rd, Whittlesford CB22 4NL; English Heritage

Step off the train at Whittlesford Parkway train station (ten minutes from Cambridge) and you're steps away from **Duxford Chapel**. Built of flint and cobble, there's something rather charming about this simple medieval building. Its early history is hazy but it's likely to have started life as a hospital, serving travellers that arrived at the adjacent priory. However, features like the *piscina* (where the priest washed his hands) in the south wall confirm that it was being used for worship by the 14th century. It's a unique little place but there isn't a lot to see – inside is an austere room with exposed roof timbers. The door is unlocked during daylight hours, so you're free to wander in and look around.

Next to the chapel, the Red Lion pub stands on the site of the medieval priory. The current building is mostly 16th/17th century but it includes

OBAMA'S FAMILY ROOTS

In 2009, Great Shelford hit the headlines when Barack Obama's family tree was traced to the village. American genealogists discovered that 17th-century residents Thomas and Ann Blossom were ancestors of the 44th President of the United States. They left the UK in the 1620s, boarding the second *Mayflower* voyage to the New World, where they joined many other Puritans and settled in Salem, Massachusetts.

When the residents of the Shelfords heard the news, they wasted no time in inviting Obama to the annual Shelford Feast (⌂ shelfordfeast.co.uk). In preparation, a local curry house created the 'Barak O'bhuna' curry, Shelford Deli made a 'Yes We Can' flan, and The Gog Farm Shop crafted a stars and stripes cheese platter. And while Obama's political engagements meant that he couldn't attend the feast, his family connections have since laced the Shelfords with international fame.

The DNA Path

❄ OS Explorer map 209 *Cambridge*; ⚲ TL459541

If you cycle between Addenbrooke's Hospital and Great Shelford on NCN11, you'll find yourself on a mile-long strip of 10,257 coloured stripes. This is the DNA Path, created in 2005 to celebrate the 10,000th mile of the National Cycle Network and to raise awareness of Cambridgeshire's pioneering DNA research.

Each stripe represents two things: one mile of the NCN, and one of the four bases that make up the human gene *BRCA2*, which was decoded at the Wellcome Trust Sanger Institute (page 284). The DNA Path represents the gene's 10,257 colour-coded bases in their exact order. If one stripe in the sequence is different, a person's risk of breast cancer could increase.

BRCA2 is just one tiny piece of the human genome (the complete genetic content of a human). If your entire genome was laid out at the same scale as the DNA Path, it would circle the Earth ten to 15 times and take around four years of cycling to complete. The start of the DNA Path is marked by a double helix sculpture that is 750,000,000 larger than real life.

some beautiful 13th-century timber beams that were carved by the priory's monks. Over the years, the priory transitioned into a coaching inn, welcoming James I in 1619. More recently, an international hotel chain (Holiday Inn Express) teamed up with the pub and built a modern hotel in its grounds, which is rather at odds with the site's ancient fabric. Nonetheless, the pub is a pleasant place to enjoy a drink, either beneath its ancient beams or on one of the benches by the chapel.

GRANTCHESTER & THE WEST

West of Cambridge is one of the county's most romantic villages – Grantchester and its glorious tea garden can be reached from the city centre by walking, cycling or punting along the river. North of here is the impressive American Cemetery and the suburb of Histon with its long history of jam making.

11 GRANTCHESTER
🏠 **The Blue Ball Inn** (page 315)

A couple of miles southwest of Cambridge, this leafy village is chocolate-box pretty, with thatched cottages and a honey-coloured church. On its

BARREL ROLLING & APPLE PRESSING

Every Boxing Day, Grantchester's villagers take to the streets for the annual Barrel Rolling Race. This eccentric fundraiser sees huge barrels being rolled down Coton Road, cheered on by the crowd. The villagers also get together each October to press the thousands of apples that fall in and around the village. It's an industrial-sized process, involving a variety of apple-pressing paraphernalia, with countless apples being pulped and juiced. You can find out about this and other local events on ⊘ grantchester.org.uk.

eastern periphery, the Grantchester Meadows roll back from the river and are the perfect setting for picnics on the grass or wild swimming in the river, which is permitted (or 'tolerated') on this stretch. It's worth mentioning that the river between Grantchester and Silver Street Bridge in Cambridge is sometimes called the Granta, although many people call it the Cam, and the two names are used interchangeably.

Along with its idyllic setting, Grantchester is known for its legacy of famous residents – current villagers include the sculptor Helaine Blumenfeld OBE and the novelist and former politician Jeffrey Archer. The village also claims the world's highest concentration of Nobel Prize winners, thanks to the number of Cambridge academics who have lived here.

A charming High Street meanders through the village, which has the church of **St Mary and St Andrew** at its heart. The church is mostly 14th and 15th century, although some sections have been dated to AD1100. It acts as a mini tourist information point, displaying information about village life and its many claims to fame – Grantchester is the setting for the TV detective series *Grantchester*, and was also the subject of the Pink Floyd song *Grantchester Meadows*, which is based on band member David Gilmour's experiences of growing up here. Cambridge University's Corpus Christi College has been patron of the church since 1380 and you'll find the college's coat of arms – an image of a pelican pecking its breast – on the mosaic floor in front of the altar.

Grantchester's most famous resident was the Edwardian poet Rupert Brooke (1887–1915). A graduate of King's College, Brooke lived at Orchard House, and later at the Old Vicarage (where Jeffrey Archer now lives). He was part of the Grantchester Group – a community of artists and intellectuals that included economist John Maynard Keynes and novelists Virginia Woolf and E M Forster. The group would meet to discuss the arts, host parties and swim naked in Byron's Pool. Brooke reminisced about this idyllic life in his poem *The Old Vicarage, Grantchester* (1912). When World War I broke out, he joined the Royal Naval Division and wrote an acclaimed set of war sonnets, based on his experiences, that express idealism in the face of death – the most famous being *The Soldier*. Brooke died of septicemia in 1915 and became epitomised as the symbol of a lost generation. You can see original photos of Rupert Brooke at the Orchard Tea Garden (page 62).

Byron's Pool

Still in the dawnlit waters cool
His ghostly Lordship swims his pool,
And tries the strokes, essays the tricks,
Long learnt on Hellespont, or Styx.
The Old Vicarage, Grantchester (1912) by Rupert Brooke

Less than a mile upstream from Grantchester is Byron's Pool – the old mill pool where poet Lord Byron (1788–1824) bathed when he was a student at Trinity College. Rupert Brooke, who also swam here, drew on Byron's legend in his poem *The Old Vicarage, Grantchester*.

It's fair to say that the romance of the pool has faded somewhat over the years, thanks to the introduction of metal railings, a concrete weir and distant traffic noise from the M11. Nonetheless, it's still a lovely spot, and the pool is surrounded by grassland, woods and riverside footpaths. As you wander, look for kingfishers and great spotted woodpeckers, a wealth of autumn fungi, or wildflowers, butterflies and damselflies in summer.

FOOD & DRINK

The Blue Ball Inn 57 Broadway, CB3 9NQ ✐ 01223 846004 ✐ blueballgrantchester.co.uk. My favourite of Grantchester's three pubs, this cosy 18th-century free house is the village's oldest drinking hole. It's also home to the HQ of Grantchester Cricket Club. Expect real ales, a log fire and a pretty courtyard at the back. Their menu is refreshingly simple and good value, with lunchtime baguettes and home-cooked classics, like shepherd's pie.

Cambridge Distillery 20 High St, Grantchester CB3 9NF ✐ 01223 751146 ✐ cambridgedistillery.co.uk ☉ 11.00–16.00 daily. This gin distillery captures the English seasons by using local botanicals, including some from Grantchester Meadows. They've won several awards as one of the world's most innovative distilleries. You can buy and sample

The Grantchester Grind

OS Explorer map 209 *Cambridge*; start: Market Sq, Cambridge ♀ TL449584; 2½ miles; easy (flat all the way)

Nicknamed the 'Grantchester Grind', this classic linear route leads beside the River Cam (or River Granta as this section is sometimes known) between central Cambridge and Grantchester. It can be enjoyed on foot or by bike and is a route that has been trodden by everyone from Charles Darwin to Elizabeth I. You could also punt or canoe along the river, rewarding your efforts at Grantchester's pubs, gin distillery or famous tea garden.

1 Exit Cambridge market square on St Mary's Passage, which brings you to King's Parade. Turn left, passing King's College on your right, and head south along King's Parade, which turns into Trumpington Street.
2 Turn right off Trumpington Street on to Silver Street, and then left along Laundress Lane. Exit on to Mill Lane, turn right to reach the River Cam and go through the metal gate to cross the cobbled footbridge over the weir.
3 Turn left and follow the riverside path south to the A1134 (The Fen Causeway). Cross the road and continue south on the riverside path for around 160yds.
4 Where the path splits, stay close to the river and go through the metal gate, passing Sheep's Green Learner Pool on your right. Follow the path as it bends right (away from the river) to a metal bridge.
5 Cross the bridge, turn left, and follow the sign for 'Riverside Walk Grantchester 1½'. Go through the gate to Paradise Local Nature Reserve and follow the path through the reserve.
6 Exit the reserve through the gate and turn left on to a lane, following the 'Riverside Walk Grantchester' sign (sometimes obscured by nettles). Turn left on to Grantchester Meadows street and follow this to reach a narrow track, which leads you past a field (on your left) called Skaters' Meadow (an information board tells you about this former ice-skating ground).
7 At the end of the track, go through the metal gate into meadow – you are now in Grantchester Meadows (a series of grassy meadows). To cross the meadows, either continue straight ahead on the surfaced 'top path' (best for cyclists) or use the more scenic riverside path to your left (better for walkers). These paths run parallel to each other, and you can cross between the two.
8 After a mile on either path, you'll see the first few houses of Grantchester village ahead. If you're on the riverside path, turn right before the gated fence to join the top path, then turn left. From the top path, you can turn right for the Red Lion pub (follow the huge sign), or take the narrow path straight ahead to the High Street, church and The Orchard Tea Garden.

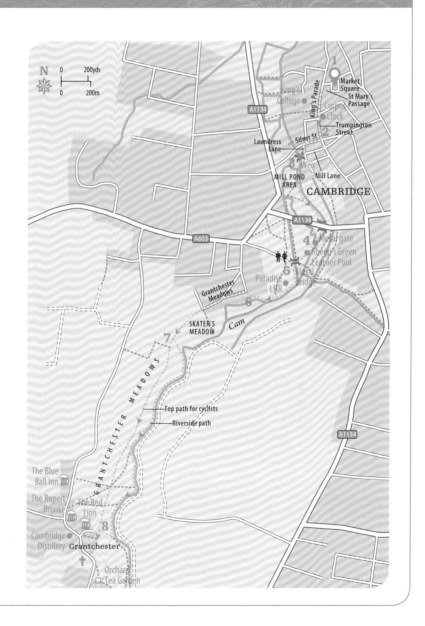

N

0   200yds
0   200m

Market
Square
King's
College
King's Parade
St Mary's
Passage
Corpus
Clock
Trumpington
Street
Laundress
Lane
Silver St
Well
MILL POND
AREA
Mill Lane
CAMBRIDGE
A1134
A1134
A603
Metal gate
Sheep's Green
Learner Pool
Paradise
LNR
Meal
Bridge
Grantchester
Meadows
SKATER'S
MEADOW
Cam
GRANTCHESTER MEADOWS
Top path for cyclists
Riverside path
The Blue
Ball Inn
The Rupert
Brooke
The Red
Lion
Cambridge
Distillery
Grantchester
Orchard
Tea Garden

gins or book tastings and masterclasses. They also have a shop and classroom in central Cambridge (10 Green St, CB2 3JU).

The Orchard Tea Garden 47 Mill Way, CB3 9ND ✆ 01223 840230 ⏛ theorchardteagarden. co.uk ⊙ summer 10.00–18.00 daily, winter 10.00–16.00 Wed–Sun. Taking tea in this heritage apple orchard is a tradition that began in the 1800s. It's a lovely place to recline in a deckchair and indulge in a 'Rupert Brooke' or 'Maynard Keynes' afternoon tea. They also do light lunches, as well as beers and cocktails. If visiting in late summer/autumn, be prepared for wasps – they're fans of the fallen apples.

12 COTON COUNTRYSIDE RESERVE

Nr Coton CB23 7PZ (car park access from Barton Rd A603)

⅄ Highfield Farm Touring Park (page 315)

Two miles northeast of Grantchester, Coton Countryside Reserve is a 300-acre site of pastures, woodland and farmland. The reserve is looked after by local charity Cambridge Past, Present & Future, who acquired the land in the 1930s to protect it against city sprawl. Both a refuge for wildlife and a working farm, it is farmed under the Countryside Stewardship Scheme, using a wildlife-friendly approach.

Waymarked footpaths weave through the reserve, and you can download a leaflet of suggested routes at ⏛ cambridgeppf.org. The Viewpoint Walk leads to Red Meadow Hill, which gives fantastic views over Cambridge – you can see Cambridge University Library tower, King's College Chapel and several other towers and spires. The reserve also has an orchard where you can lay your packed lunch on a picnic table. It's worth noting, however, that the reserve is close to the M11, so you're likely to hear some road noise.

Half a mile north is the small village of Coton, with its village pub and garden centre. A signed footpath/cycle track leads here from Cambridge (2½ miles each way), following the same route as the Wimpole Way (page 297).

ⴼ FOOD & DRINK

Coton Orchard Garden Centre Cambridge Rd, CB23 7PJ. This large farm shop, café and garden centre is part of Coton Orchard, which was planted in 1922. The farm shop is a good place for picnic supplies, with a deli counter and freshly baked goods (including buns from Fitzbillies in Cambridge; page 41), and the café serves fresh coffees, cakes and lunches.

The Plough 2 High St, CB23 7PL ✆ 01953 210489 ⏛ theploughcoton.co.uk ⊙ Tue–Sun. Visit this smart gastro-pub for a posh meal or casual beer in the garden. After a 'family recipe G&T', choose from seasonal dishes like chalk stream trout, Newmarket sausages, or chateaubriand sharing steaks. The pub claims to offer 'the largest selection of wines by the glass anywhere in Cambridge'.

13 CAMBRIDGE AMERICAN CEMETERY

⌂ **Crafts Hill Barn** (page 315)

A1303 (Madingley Rd), Coton CB23 7PH ☉ 09.00–17.00 daily

The UK's only American World War II cemetery, this 30-acre site is quite something. As well as a peaceful place for remembrance, it showcases some impressive craftsmanship and tells the story of Britain's relationship with the US during World War II through interactive displays.

Fringed by ancient woodland, the landscaped grounds are the resting place of 3,812 Americans who gave their lives in the Battle of the Atlantic, the strategic bombing campaign over Europe, or during training exercises on British soil. A further 5,127 souls whose bodies were never recovered are remembered on the Wall of the Missing. Among them is the jazz musician Glenn Miller (1904–44).

The flag near the main entrance is raised each morning before 09.00; bells are chimed and songs are sung at 10.00 and noon; and the flag is lowered at 16.40 (or 15.30 in winter), followed by more chimes and songs. The visitor centre guides you through the story of the war through videos, photos and memorabilia. You can hear the stories of Americans

SILICON FEN

A global hotspot of science and innovation, Cambridge and its suburbs are nicknamed 'Silicon Fen' after California's Silicon Valley. The area is home to more than 1,500 science and technology companies, many of which are global leaders – this is the home of Microsoft's European research lab and Astra Zeneca's international R&D. Google, Spotify, Apple and Toshiba are also here, alongside hundreds of enterprising start-ups.

This cluster of software, electronics and biotech companies began taking shape in the 1950s when Cambridge emerged as a leader in mathematical, computer and human DNA research. Cambridge Biomedical Campus (now Europe's largest centre of medical research) began developing in the south of the city in the 1960s, and Britain's first official science hub – Cambridge Science Park – was launched on the northeast fringe in the 1970s. By the early '90s, the Wellcome Sanger Institute in Hinxton (page 284) was being established as an ideas factory, and it is now a world leader in DNA and genome research.

who bonded with Cambridgeshire communities, found romance and made the county their home, and see the treats they brought over to England, like Wrigley's chewing gum and Lucky Strike cigarettes.

The site also has a memorial building with huge teak doors, adorned in artworks of tanks and ships. Inside are decorative military maps, a stunning ceiling mosaic, a small chapel and a stained-glass panel for every American state.

A mile and a half northwest of the cemetery is the pretty village of **Madingley**, surrounded by woodland. This is the home of Madingley Hall, where the University of Cambridge's Institute of Continuing Education (the oldest department of its kind in the UK) is based. Alongside undergraduate and postgrad courses for adults, the institute offers public lectures and talks. As a visitor, you can admire the hall's 16th-century Baroque architecture, and walk around the gardens which were designed by Capability Brown in the 1750s. Much of Brown's vision remains and, as you wander around the sloping lawns, passing statues, formal gardens and a lake, you can take in the sweeping views that he so expertly framed.

¶¶ FOOD & DRINK

There is no café at the American Cemetery but good food and drink aren't far away. The café at **Coton Orchard Garden Centre** (page 62) is half a mile southeast, or there are two good options in Madingley village.

Madingley Hall Café CB23 8AQ ⊘ madingleyhall.co.uk ⊙ 09.00–16.00 daily. Set within the main building, the café at Madingley Hall serves cakes and light lunches. There's also a relaxed evening dining venue – Terrace Bar Restaurant (⊙ from 17.00 Mon–Sat) – which does burgers, salads and fish and chips.
The Three Horseshoes High St, Madingley CB23 8AB ✆ 01954 210221
⊘ threehorseshoesmadingley.co.uk ⊙ Tue–Sun. This thatched country inn has a fireplace and lovely garden, and serves fine wines and gastro-pub food (such as smoked cod pâté and chicken panzella).

14 HISTON & IMPINGTON

Northwest of Cambridge, the merged suburban villages of Histon and Impington are best known for two things: pubs and jam – this area was once the home of Chivers & Sons (see box, opposite), one of Europe's leading jam producers in the 19th and 20th centuries. Unwins seeds (still

PRESERVING HISTORY

Local boy Stephen Chivers saw an opportunity when the railway came to Histon in 1847: he bought an orchard and began transporting the fruit to London and the north. By the 1870s, the family business was flourishing and they decided to give jam making a whirl, opening a factory in the village. They expanded into marmalade, mincemeat, lemonade, and the first clear commercial dessert jelly (1889). By 1895, Chivers had become Europe's first large-scale commercial canners and a world leader in preserve production, with a pioneering factory that had the finest canning machinery in Europe. Chivers & Sons employed more than 3,000 people by the 1930s and were the largest canner of fruit and veg in England.

After the war, the company lost momentum and their factories were sold to Schweppes. The original factory was demolished in the 1980s and a multi-million-pound replacement was built. Jam is still made in Histon today and, although the name on the jars is now Hartley's, the company proudly associate themselves with the Chivers story. The Chivers brand, meanwhile, was sold to the Boyne Valley Group, who make jams under the Chivers name in Ireland. Within Histon and Impington, the Chivers legacy lives on through street names like Chivers Way. Even the stained glass in the east window of St Andrew's Church (21 Percheron Cl, Impington CB24 9YX) remembers Histon's entrepreneurs – the apples and pears commemorate the Chivers family, while the sweet peas are for the Unwins, who are now a household name for packaged seeds.

sold in garden centres across the UK) also started life here, when Histon lad William Unwin started selling sweet pea seeds in the early 1900s.

Quiet and quaint these villages are not, but ale enthusiasts may be tempted to visit for the plethora of pubs, and there's a handful of other highlights, including a heritage orchard, some decent coffee shops, and the only Gropius building in Britain – Grade I-listed **Impington College** (New Rd) was designed in 1938 by the founder of the Bauhaus movement, Walter Gropius. The guided busway route (see below) leads directly past the villages, and you could easily cycle here from central Cambridge (four–five miles), following the traffic-free cycle route (NCN51) that leads beside the busway.

A pub & heritage tour

While researching Histon and Impington, I turned to my cousin and Histon resident Andrew, who guided me around the local landmarks and pubs, some of which have stood here for centuries – today, the villages share six pubs but at one time they had closer to ten. I've tweaked Andrew's route to create a circular walking tour that starts and finishes at the guided busway stop – you could walk the full route in less than an hour but you'll need longer if you're planning to stop off for a pint or two.

Starting at the Histon and Impington guided busway stop, you're a few steps from **The Railway Vue** (163 Station Rd). Serving customers since 1853, this pub originally overlooked the railway line, which was converted to the busway route between 2007 and 2011. Head north on Station Road and you'll spot glimmers of the past in the old thatches that are dotted between modern buildings. Number 117 was once the Chequers pub, and further up is the much-loved **Geographer** café and shop, followed by Histon Baptist Church – this striking church was built in 1899 with donations from Stephen Chivers. Opposite is another former pub – number 73 was once the Black Horse, built by the landlady of the Railway Vue.

Just after the Baptist church, you'll come to a road junction with the war memorial straight ahead on a patch of grass. Turn right, then left on to Water Lane, which once had a watercourse running along its length – apparently, many a pubgoer would wobble into this stream on their way home. The contemporary gate on your right is the entrance to Homefield Park, a little patch of urban woodland. Continue north along Water Lane, passing houses built of Cambridgeshire's yellow gault bricks – numbers 15 to 25 were once workers cottages, built by Stephen Chivers in the 1890s. As you approach the village green, you'll see the **Rose & Crown** (2 Glebe Way) up ahead. More than 450 years old, this is one of the villages' oldest buildings.

Cross to the village green, passing the pond on your right and Histon Smokehouse (which occupies another former pub) on your left. Pass the village sign (which features the Histon Giant) on your left and the village pump on your right. Keep straight and you'll arrive at **The Boot** (1 High St), which occupies a 300-year-old L-shaped (or boot-shaped) building. Next to The Boot, the **Barley Mow** is an 18th-century beer house now owned by Greene King, and further up the High Street is the 19th-century **Red Lion**.

North of the Red Lion, the High Street merges into School Hill. Follow this road to the grassy island, then veer right on to Windmill Lane, where you'll pass longstanding butchers, the Histon Chop Shop.

Bear left at the butchers on to Church Street and the 17th-century **King William IV**, known locally as the King Bill. Wander northwest of here on Church Street and you'll arrive at **St Andrew's Church**, where the graveyard has a memorial to the Histon Giant (see box, below). Inside the church are some of Cambridgeshire's finest Early English transepts.

To return to The Railway Vue, you could retrace your footsteps to The Boot, then turn right on to Station Road and follow it half a mile south. Alternatively, you could make your way via the busway footpath by exiting St Andrew's churchyard in the southeast corner, where a footpath leads southeast to Bell Hill. Turn left on to Bell Hill, left again on to Park Lane, then a fourth left on to St Audrey's Close, which leads south to the busway via a pedestrian cut-through. When you pop out on to the busway, cross to the walking/cycling path and turn left to walk southeast. After 330yds or so, you'll pass the entrance to **Histon and Impington Community Orchard Project** (CB24 9JS) on your left. Established in 2011 to celebrate the villages' fruit growing heritage, it grows apple varieties like 'Lord Burghley' from Burghley House (page 147), and 'Chivers Delight', which was raised by Stephen Chivers in the 1920s. Annual events are sometimes held at the orchard, like the Winter Wassail, when locals sing songs and toast the trees with mulled drinks to wake them up from their winter slumber – for dates and details, visit ⌀ hicop.info. The Railway Vue is just over half a mile's walk southeast of the orchard along the busway.

THE HISTON GIANT

Histon's village sign features a curious character holding a boulder above his head. This is Moses Carter (1801–60), the Histon Giant, who was said to weigh more than 23 stone and measure over seven feet tall – a real BFG, especially when the average height of a male was around 5ft 5ins at the time. Loved by local children, there was talk of him carrying two or three under each arm as he walked around the village. Other stories tell of him eating enormous beefsteak puddings and defeating every opponent at the Stourbridge Fair wrestling matches (page 44). His best-known feat involved heaving a boulder across the village to 'Boot corner' – the boulder still sits in the garden of The Boot pub.

When Carter passed away in 1860, aged 59, he was buried at St Andrew's Church in Histon. A memorial was unveiled in the churchyard in 1998 to mark the 138th anniversary of his death – look for the plaque dedicated to Moses Carter, with the inscription: 'Affectionately known as the Histon Giant.'

⅋⅋ FOOD & DRINK

Any of the pubs I've already mentioned are worthy of a visit but, if you only have time for one, it has to be **The Red Lion** (27 High St, CB24 9JD ✆ 01223 564437 ⌖ theredlionhiston. co.uk ⊙ 16.00–23.00 Mon–Thu, noon–23.00 Sat, noon–21.00 Sun). An alehouse since the early 1800s, this local institution serves an impressive array of beers that range from local ales to Belgian and German beers on draught. Outside, a mock blue plaque remembers the pub's years as a 'mobile free zone', while the interior is adorned with flagons, tankards and retro advertising boards. The menu focuses on home-cooked pub classics, and they have annual beer festivals in Easter and September.

If you're after a special meal with cocktails and fine wine, head to **The Boot** (1 High St, CB24 9LG ✆ 01223 209010 ⌖ boothiston.com ⊙ 11.00–23.00 Mon–Sat, noon–22.00 Sun). Set in a Grade II-listed building, The Boot was transformed from an old boozer to an upmarket brasserie with the help of celebrity chef Raymond Blanc. Now it's the sort of place people pop open bottles of Lanson Père and savour pan-fried stone bass or boeuf bourguignon.

There are two very good coffee shops: **The Geographer** (103 Station Rd, CB24 9NP ⌖ thegeographer.uk) is a café and store selling artisan food, craft beers and travel-inspired gifts, and **Stir** (Unit 1, 10 School Hill, CB24 9JE ⌖ stircambridge.co.uk ⊙ 07.30–17.00 Mon–Fri, 08.00–17.00 Sat, 08.00–16.00 Sun) serves brunches, homemade pastries and their own sourdoughs. For something different, you could try **Histon Smokehouse** (20 The Green, CB24 9JA ✆ 01223 491174 ⊙ 09.00–22.00 Tue–Thu, 09.00–23.00 Fri & Sat, 09.30–17.00 Sun), where they use local and sustainable ingredients to create smoked dishes like brick-cooked chicken, smoked tofu and brunches.

FOLLOW US

Tag us in your posts and share your adventures using this guide with us – we'd love to hear from you.

⬛ BradtGuides   🐦 BradtGuides
📷 bradtguides   ▶ bradtguides

A mindful journey through Britain's special places

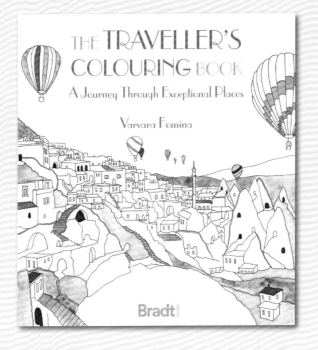

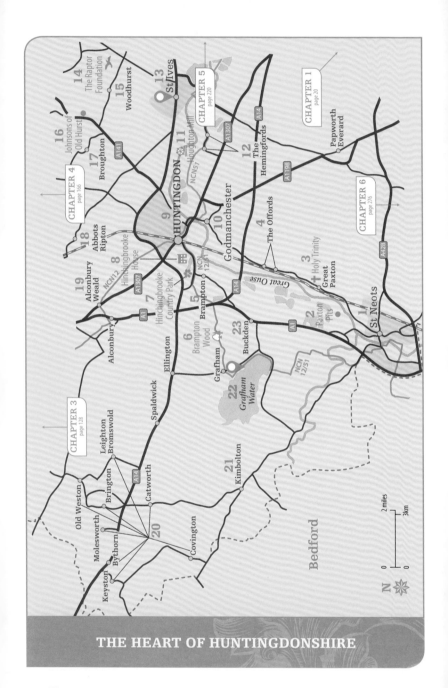

THE HEART OF HUNTINGDONSHIRE

2

THE HEART OF HUNTINGDONSHIRE

Welcome to west Cambridgeshire and the district of Huntingdonshire – an ancient county that clung to its historical title when it was merged, kicking and screaming, with Cambridgeshire in 1974. This chapter focuses on the district's central and southern heartland, from Keyston and Kimbolton in the west to St Ives and the Hemingfords in the east, and from St Neots in the south to Alconbury. The official Huntingdonshire boundary, however, reaches north of Alconbury to Wansford (Chapter 3) and northeast beyond Ramsey (Chapter 4). Here, in southern and central Huntingdonshire, the River Great Ouse arrives from Bedfordshire and winds lazily past bankside settlements and ancient water meadows (including one of England's largest). This meandering stretch of the river is the most natural in the county, before it reaches the Fen Edge and becomes dramatically engineered. A key navigational route, it was this great river – the fourth longest in the UK – that allowed medieval trade to flow between central England, East Anglia and the coastal ports at The Wash. It gave rise to powerful abbeys, lucrative mills, bustling river ports and one of the biggest fairs in England. With the dawn of railways and motorcars, river trade was quietened but the towns remained, along with a handful of mills which you can still see today. The Ouse Valley Way footpath provides a bucolic link between each one, as does the river itself, which you can explore by boat, paddleboard or by taking a dip. Flanking the River Great Ouse are lakes and lagoons at Hinchingbrooke Country Park, Paxton Pits and Godmanchester Nature Reserve – former gravel pits which have been given over to wildlife. West of the river is Grafham Water, Cambridgeshire's biggest lake; walking or cycling around it is a Cambridgeshire rite of passage.

History abounds in Huntingdonshire. This is Cromwell country – Oliver Cromwell, who ruled the British Isles between 1653 and 1658, was born and schooled in Huntingdon. He later moved to Ely and became a local MP. A century earlier, Catherine of Aragon (the first wife of Henry VIII) spent her final days in Kimbolton Castle after a spell at Buckden Towers. The diarist Samuel Pepys also hailed from these parts, and some say his buried treasure still lies in the village of Brampton. Nearby, Hinchingbrooke House was the family home of the Montagues and the many Earls of Sandwich – the fourth of which created the eponymous lunchbox staple. Other intriguing and notable past residents have included the Eynesbury Giant, the St Neots' assassin and the author Lucy Boston.

In the north and west, away from the water, riverside towns and crenellated manors give way to scattered villages, farms and acres of open countryside. This landscape made an ideal setting for a host of World War II airbases, although, with military functions now scaled back, you're more likely to hear the screech of red kites and the honking of greylag geese than the reverberations of a Lancaster Bomber.

GETTING AROUND

West Cambridgeshire sits at the crossroads of two major highways: the north–south A1 and the east–west A14. The UK's longest numbered road, the A1 runs between London and Edinburgh and connects St Neots and Huntingdon with Peterborough. Slicing through the A1 near Huntingdon and Brampton, the A14 links the Northamptonshire border with Cambridge and Newmarket. It's tempting to zoom along these arteries, ticking off the market towns as you go, but doing so misses out on the essence of historic Huntingdonshire, with its pretty villages and gentle pace of river life. If you're travelling by car, ignore the A-roads and instead make your way along scenic B-roads and empty rural lanes: it's far more rewarding. If using the A14, be aware that it underwent major restructuring in 2020/2021, so older maps will be out of date.

TRAINS

St Neots and Huntingdon are your two options for rail travel in this area. As little as eight minutes apart, both are served by the East Coast Main Line, which runs between London and Edinburgh via Peterborough. Trains to Peterborough take around 15 minutes from Huntingdon or just over 20 minutes from St Neots.

HISTORIC HUNTINGDONSHIRE

As you tour around west Cambridgeshire, you'll notice a profusion of 'Huntingdonshire' signage, honing the point that this district was once a county in its own right. This is a status that some insist still stands.

Huntingdonshire's (rather hazy) early history has been traced back to around AD920 when it's thought that Edward the Elder (son of Alfred the Great) cast the then Danish occupiers out of the region and established the shire. Henry II declared the entire county a royal forest in 1154, although much of this woodland had been cleared for farming by the 1700s. Adding to the district's heritage is its glut of famous residents, from Oliver Cromwell to Samuel Pepys, while the bustling market towns and historic mills that flank the River Great Ouse give it a landscape and character that is distinct from the rest of Cambridgeshire.

This unique history and sense of identity was diluted when the county merged with Cambridgeshire in 1974 and became the district of Huntingdon – a label which local councillors quickly changed to Huntingdonshire. Today, Huntingdonshire Day is celebrated on Cromwell's birthday (25 April) and the old county has an official flag that has a green background and features a golden hunting horn (a reminder of its royal forest days). It's hard to ignore the affinity that some people have with the old shire, many of whom feel they have a different heritage from those in other parts of Cambridgeshire and the Fens. Despite this, it seems unlikely that county status will return any time soon. As one journalist put it, 'Huntingdonshire is not so much a county as a state of mind.'

BUSES

Huntingdon, St Neots and St Ives are the hubs of the bus network, with services run by Go Whippet, Stagecoach and Dews Coaches. As you would expect, travel between and around these towns, as well as to/from Cambridge and Peterborough, is faster and more frequent than to the surrounding villages – some of which only see one bus a day. Huntingdon and St Ives are on the busway network (⊘ thebusway.info; page 254), with links to Peterborough and Cambridge. These buses use both roads and purpose-built tracks. Smaller settlements, including Alconbury, Godmanchester and Houghton are also on this network.

For Grafham Water (page 119), the bus stops in Perry and Grafham are served by Go Whippet 400, which also stops at Hinchingbrooke County Park (page 89). The Raptor Foundation (page 108) can be visited on request (ask the driver) on Busway D. For Johnsons of Old Hurst (page 111), the Huntingdon to Ramsey (Stagecoach 30) and Huntingdon to March (Stagecoach 35) buses both stop in Old Hurst village.

1

THE HEART OF HUNTINGDONSHIRE

Huntingdonshire is a former county that became part of Cambridgeshire in 1974. Here, the River Great Ouse meanders past villages, nature reserves and market towns like St Ives, St Neots and Huntingdon – the birthplace of Oliver Cromwell.

1 Godmanchester is bordered by the River Great Ouse and backs on to one of England's largest water meadows.

2

PETER HIGGER/PAXTON PIT MILL

ALAN COPSON/AWL

2 Paxton Pits Nature Reserve includes a series of former gravel pits that were flooded in the 1980s and given over to wildlife. 3 St Ives is a charming market town on the banks of the River Great Ouse. 4 Hemingford Abbots is one of Cambridgeshire's prettiest villages, with historical houses and thatched cottages. 5 The Cromwell Museum in Huntingdon has the most extensive collection of Cromwell artefacts in the world. 6 St Neots is the largest town in Cambridgeshire, with a riverside setting and 12th-century marketplace.

MARTIN CHARLES HATCH/S

THE
CROMWELL
MUSEUM

Cambridgeshire
County Council
Education
Libraries
& Heritage

ST. NEOTS

CYCLING

Grafham Water is a hub for off-road cycling, with a lovely ten-mile loop (page 120) that skirts the water's edge. This reservoir is also the endpoint of the 49-mile **Three Shires Way**, which begins in Buckinghamshire – the final 25 miles of this bridleway enter Cambridgeshire at Covington and pass through Spaldwick before taking a celebratory loop around the lake.

National Cycle Network Route 12, which starts in north London, runs through St Neots and alongside Grafham Water before heading to Brampton and Huntingdon. From the latter, you can continue to The Alconburys, or switch to **Route 51** for Godmanchester, The Hemingfords and St Ives.

The quiet country roads west of Grafham Water and north of the Great Ouse are also good for cycling. If planning your own route, use OS Explorer map 225 *Huntingdon & St Ives*; avoid crossing the A14 and A1 at ground level – there are several bridges and underpasses where you can cross more safely, including those at Catworth, Spaldwick, Brampton, Godmanchester and Alconbury.

 CYCLE HIRE

Rutland Cycling Grafham Marlow Car Park, Grafham Water PE28 0BH ✆ 01480 812500 ⌖ rutlandcycling.com/pages/rutland-cycling-grafham.aspx ☉ 09.00–17.30 daily

WALKING

The most varied routes in this part of Cambridgeshire are by the water. The 142-mile **Ouse Valley Way** (⌖ ldwa.org.uk) follows the course of the River Great Ouse from source to sea, starting in Northamptonshire and passing through six counties en route to The Wash. The 16 or so miles that track through this chapter are Cambridgeshire's most varied, with the route passing through St Neots, Paxton Pits, Brampton Mill, Godmanchester, Houghton Mill and St Ives, before continuing to the emptier landscapes of the Fens. In addition, there are many other unnamed footpaths skirting river and lakes, and linking towns and villages. Two of my favourite routes are the five-mile circular between St Ives, The Hemingfords and Houghton Mill (page 106), and the ten-mile circumnavigation of Grafham Water (page 120).

Away from the water, networks of countryside footpaths provide a perfect way to appreciate the beating heart of rural Huntingdonshire.

The paths between Broughton and Abbots Ripton (page 113) connect two of the area's best pubs for foodies, while the western leg of the **Pathfinder Long Distance Walk** also runs through this region, between Broughton and The Offords (19 miles). You could also explore the Green Corridor of grasslands which runs through the centre of St Neots, go on a family stroll around Hinchingbrooke Country Park, enjoy a woodland ramble through Brampton Woods, stride out across Portholme Meadow or keep your eyes peeled for birdlife as you stroll around Paxton Pits Nature Reserve.

BOAT

Gliding along the River Great Ouse by boat is a fantastic way to tour waterside towns, villages and countryside. The Huntingdonshire stretch of the river has plenty of free moorings, where you can pull up for a picnic or visit riverside pubs, like **Brampton Mill** and **The River Mill** in St Neots.

There are several good options for hiring self-drive riverboats by the hour, day or half-day, and some also offer narrowboats and cruisers for overnight holiday hire. Boating is suitable for first-timers, and you don't need a licence – you'll receive full instruction, river information, safety briefings, lock guidelines and route maps.

 BOAT HIRE

All Aboard Boat Hire The River Mill, School Ln, Eaton Socon PE19 8GW ⌀ 07765 846145 ⌀ allaboardboathire.co.uk

Lazy Days Boathire The Av, Huntingdon Boathaven, Godmanchester PE29 2AF ⌀ 07951 785305 ⌀ lazydays-boathire.co.uk

Purvis Marine The Riverside Car Park, Hartford Rd, Huntingdon PE29 3RP ⌀ 01480 453628 ⌀ purvismarine.co.uk (website undergoing maintenance). Overnight hire available.

ALONG THE GREAT OUSE

Here in the southwest corner of Huntingdonshire, the River Great Ouse enters Cambridgeshire for the first time. A cluster of towns and settlements take advantage of the higher ground along its initial 15-mile stretch through the county, before the river descends across the low-lying Fens and heads northeast towards Norfolk and The Wash. The castles, monasteries and mills that were built along this historic trade route led to the development of three key market towns: St Neots, Huntingdon and St Ives. While the monasteries and castles are gone, a handful of mills remain, including the impressive examples at Houghton and Brampton. Between these towns and mills lie pretty villages and bucolic water meadows.

1 ST NEOTS

The largest town in Cambridgeshire, St Neots does well to retain its community vibe and distinct local identity. This is largely thanks to the town's quirky history, buzzing little arts scene and verdant riverside setting, all of which give Slow travellers an excuse to visit. Slicing the town in two, the River Great Ouse tempers the pace of urban life and is flanked by the Green Corridor – a lush swathe of parks and meadows that runs through the town's length. The east and west riverbanks are linked by foot, cycle and road bridges, the most impressive of which is **Willow Bridge** – a 1135ft car-free bridge that skims over the floodplain in the southernmost districts of Eaton Socon and Eynesbury.

Along with the River Great Ouse, St Neots's identity has been shaped over the centuries by monks, markets and the Great North Road. The original settlement developed around a riverside monastery, which later became St Neots Priory. Home to the allegedly stolen bones of the Cornish Saxon monk St Neot, the priory attracted pilgrims and, with them, trade. The monks established a thriving market, which continued to prosper after the monastery was destroyed during the Dissolution (in the early 1500s). The town grew further when the river was dredged for navigation in the 18th century, and further still with the arrival of stagecoaches and the Great North Road (page 149) – the original route of which still runs through the western part of St Neots and is signed as Great North Road.

Before 1965, the river formed a county boundary with Bedfordshire that halved the size of St Neots. On the eastern riverbank (Cambridgeshire side), were the settlements of St Neots and Eynesbury. On the western bank (Bedfordshire) were Eaton Socon, Eaton Ford and Crosshall. When a decision was made to shift the county boundary further west, the five settlements became one and were named after the largest. A tell-tale sign that St Neots was once several settlements are its three churches, all with the same name (see box, page 80). Today, these five former settlements are relatively indistinct, yet Slow travellers that are

THE EYNESBURY GIANT

James Toller was born in the village of Eynesbury (now in southeast St Neots) in 1798. His parents were of average height but young James quickly surpassed them. By the age of ten he was 5ft tall, and by 18 had grown a further three feet. News of the 'Eynesbury Giant' spread far and wide, and Toller rose to fame. Locals say that he would stroll past the pubs and swing the signboards with his hand, and that he could walk along the street and chat with people through their bedroom windows. In 1815, he was exhibited in London and presented to the King of Prussia and the Emperor of Russia.

James Toller passed away in 1818, at 8ft 1½ins and just 21 years of age. Fearing that his body would be taken by body-snatchers for scientific research, he was buried inside Eynesbury Church – one of the few buildings he could enter without bowing his head.

willing to dig beneath the surface will find intriguing pockets of history in each one – a good way to explore each settlement is via the series of local heritage trails produced by the Eatons Community Association (ESCA). You can pick up a booklet of trails at St Neots Museum (page 80) or the library (Priory Ln, PE19 2BH).

Market Square & around

One of the largest and oldest of its kind, St Neots's marketplace dates back to the 12th century. In the centre of the square is one of the largest Day Columns in England, made of cast iron and erected in 1822 by local brewer John Day. The statues of monks that stand around the Day Column are a reminder of the town's original 12th-century stallholders.

On the ground in the northwest corner is a mosaic of the 9th-century King Alfred Jewel. Believed to have been made for the Saxon king, this teardrop-shaped jewel features a man's face that is thought to be St Neot – the town's namesake and a friend of King Alfred's. The jewel itself is housed at the Ashmolean Museum in Oxford. At the opposite end of the square is the 19th-century **Paine & Co brewery building** with its original carriageway arch built during the stagecoach era. To experience the Market Square in full swing, visit on a Thursday for the weekly market, or come on the second or fourth Saturday of the month for the farmers' market. On non-market days, the square is used as a car park.

Running along the northern edge of Market Square is the High Street. Tucked between the chain stores are some excellent independent shops, cafés and restaurants. Some of the most intriguing are hidden

ST MARY'S MANY CHURCHES

Confusingly, St Neots has three churches that are all called St Mary's – a reminder of the days when the town was a collection of independent villages. As you wander around St Neots, you'll often find yourself under the watchful gaze of a 130ft tower that earned its church the nickname 'the Cathedral of Huntingdonshire'. Slap bang in the town centre, this is the largest of the three St Mary's, standing head and shoulders above the other two. Listen out for the toll of its ten bells, or step inside to discover the Norman font, Victorian woodwork and carvings on the roof timbers. The other two St Mary's are in Eaton Socon and Eynesbury. Step inside the latter to discover the 'Eynesbury Zoo' – a collection of animal sculptures, carved into the 500-year-old pews.

in backstreets and courtyards like **Priory Lane** and **Cross Key Mews**: you can create your own coffee blend at St Neots's first micro-roastery, **Bohemia Roasts** (16 Cross Key Mews, PE19 2AR ☏ 01480 216540 ⊕ bohemiaroasts.com), or buy craft beers, Ely gin and British cheeses at **Shumë** (3 Cross Key Mews, PE19 2AR ☏ 01480 214747 ⊕ shume. co.uk). At the rear of the mews, a little alleyway pops out by **The Smiling Grape Company** (Unit 1, Priory Chambers, Priory Ln, PE19 2BH ☏ 01480 403100 ⊕ smilinggrape.com ⊙ 10.00–18.00 Tue–Sat), an award-winning, family-owned wine merchant. On New Street is the quaint **St Neots Museum** (8 New St, PE19 1AE ☏ 01480 214163 ⊕ stneotsmuseum.org.uk ⊙ 11.00–16.00 Tue–Sat), where you can enter the town's original prison cells, learn about local quirks like the Bank of St Neots, and delve deeper into the history of St Neots Priory. To find the site of the priory, head back to the Smiling Grape and walk through Priory Lane car park, where you'll find several information boards that map out the priory grounds. Around the corner, just past the Priory Centre on Priory Lane (notice the theme here!) are the remains of an 18th-century brewery, with its beautifully restored **Oast House**.

The Green Corridor

Flanking the River Great Ouse on both banks, a series of parks, flood meadows and pockets of ancient woodland creates a strip of green through the length of St Neots, which the council has christened the Green Corridor. On the western bank, just across the bridge from the Market Square, the landscaped lawns of **Riverside Park** include a mile of waterside frontage, a skate park, a miniature railway and a network of paths and cycle routes. In summer, the park hosts live bands on Sunday afternoons (May–Sep 14.30–16.30, weather dependent), with brass, swing and jazz playing free of charge in the open air. To make the most of it, bring a picnic and a blanket. For details and dates, see ⚲ visitstneots.co.uk. To the north, **Regatta Meadow** hosts the annual **St Neots Regatta** in July, with around 1,500 rowers descending on the meadow for a weekend of rowing and camping – or, as one reporter put it, for 'boats, burgers and beer'. Further north still are the wilder grassy meadows of **St Neots Common**, where some locals still hold the right to graze livestock on Lammas Meadow and Islands Common.

The Ouse Valley Way passes through the Green Corridor, providing a continuous waymarked walking route from Eaton Socon in the south to Paxton Pits Nature Reserve (page 83), just north of St Neots. Information boards in the Riverside Park map show a nine-mile loop, which you could start at any point in the Green Corridor.

Eaton Socon

Tucked against the Bedfordshire border in southwest St Neots, Eaton Socon welcomes the River Great Ouse into Cambridgeshire. It also boasts the earthworks of a 12th-century motte and bailey castle but, sadly, these are now hidden in the grounds of a private house. Of the town's five merged settlements, Eaton Socon seems to have been the most successful in retaining some of its former village identity, particularly around St Mary's Church and the village green. Next to the green on School Lane is the 19th-century **village lock-up**. Used to detain troublemakers, 'The Cage' was considered impregnable until an Irish criminal escaped in February 1858. The lock-up is open to the public during the annual May Day weekend, when Eaton Socon residents celebrate local history and gather on the green for live music, dance, food and the crowning of the May Queen. Further down School Lane is the 19th-century **River Mill** (now a pub and restaurant; page 83) where the current owners have been hailed for catapulting water power into the 21st century with their pioneering hydro-power scheme. The first of its kind in the world, the mill's VETT (Venturi-Enhanced Turbine Technology) project was launched in 2017 and is said to generate enough electricity to power the pub and 32 homes. Next to the mill is **River Mill Marina** (School Ln, PE19 8GW ✆ 01480 473456), which offers short-term moorings – handy if you're exploring the county by boat.

During the **Great North Road** coaching era (page 149), Eaton Socon was a busy staging area. The modern-day road that bears the same name traces part of the original London to York route and retains several former coaching inns, including The Old Sun, The Waggon and Horses, The Eaton Oak and the 13th-century **White Horse Inn** (⬧ thewhitehorseeatonsocon. co.uk). Outside the last, a blue plaque commemorates the pub's heyday and lists some of the travellers that stopped by – the likes of Samuel Pepys, the Queen of Norway and Charles Dickens, whose characters dine at 'Eton Slocombe' in his novel *Nicholas Nickleby*.

🍴 FOOD & DRINK

St Neots embraces the Slow Movement rather well, with a scattering of independent restaurants, community hubs and family-owned cafés tucked between high street chains and hidden away on backstreets. Without too much effort, you'll find local makers, bakers and brewers selling everything from Cambridgeshire craft beers to locally roasted coffee.

Art & Soul 7 New St, PE19 1AE ✎ 01480 216167 ⬧ artandsoul.cafe ⊙ 10.00–16.00 Tue–Thu & Sun, 10.00–17.00 & 18.30–23.00 Fri, 09.00–17.00 Sat, 10.00–16.00 Sun. This café, gallery and creative space places a strong emphasis on connecting with others and nurturing the soul – be it through homemade food, creativity, or simply someone to talk to. My favourite space is the upstairs room, which doubles as an arts venue (see the online schedule for art classes and yoga). Come for an all-day 'big brunch bagel', try the tasty salads (trust me, they're good), homemade soups, vegan tacos or charcuterie boards, or stop by for fresh cakes and house-blend coffee from local roasters.

THE ASSASSIN

John Bellingham, the only person to have assassinated a UK prime minister, hailed from St Neots. A failed businessman, Bellingham was arrested in Russia for financial debt and imprisoned for five years. Furious with the government for refusing to help him, he developed a dangerous grudge. In May 1812, Bellingham entered the House of Commons and lay in wait for the former Russian ambassador, Lord Leveson Gower. When a figure approached, Bellingham shot him from behind with a duelling pistol, only to discover that he'd accidentally killed the prime minister, Spencer Perceval. Making no attempt to escape, he was hanged at Newgate Prison.

Fast-forward a couple of centuries and one of Bellingham's descendants – Henry Bellingham – became a Conservative MP (for North West Norfolk), with a seat in the very same building that the assassination of the prime minister took place.

Bohemia on The Square 20 Cross Key Mews, PE19 2AR ✆ 01480 716265
🖥 bohemiastneots.com ◷ 08.00–17.00 Mon–Thu, 08.00–midnight Fri–Sat, 09.00–15.00
Sun. A local favourite, this café, bar and restaurant serves breakfast, brunch and lunch, plus
evening meals on Fridays and Saturdays. Much of their seasonal produce is locally sourced,
with coffee beans prepped at their own micro-roastery. The evening menu features modern
world tapas – think Welsh rarebit, Mongolian beef skewers and Caribbean sweetcorn fritters.
They also have a café/bistro at Alconbury Weald (page 114).

Poppy's Vintage Tea Room 17 Church Walk, PE19 1JH ✆ 01480 215932
🖥 poppysvintagetearoom.com ◷ Mon–Sat. Tucked down an alleyway, this charming tea
room is infused with 1920s memorabilia. Expect homemade cakes and lunches served with
a smile: traditional ploughman's, freshly made quiche or high tea with warm scones. Outside
seating in summer.

The Refill Shop 40 St Mary's St, Eynesbury PE19 2TA ◷ Tue–Sun. A recent addition to
Eynesbury, this plastic-free refill shop and café dispenses everything from pasta and spices,
to shampoo and peanut butter fresh from the machine. You can also stop by for homemade
vegan cakes and coffees (bring your own mug for take-aways).

The River Mill School Ln, Eaton Socon PE19 8GW ✆ 01480 219612 🖥 therivermillpub.
co.uk. Set in a Grade II-listed converted watermill (page 81), this pub/restaurant is open for
breakfast, lunch and dinner. Information boards tell you more about the building's history
and pioneering hydro-power project. Riverside picnic tables outside.

2 PAXTON PITS NATURE RESERVE

High St, Little Paxton PE19 6ET 🖥 paxton-pits.org.uk

A watery reserve on the edge of Little Paxton village, these former gravel
pits were flooded and given over to wildlife in the 1980s. Unusually,
part of the site is still an active quarry, which you can glimpse as you
explore the half-dozen lakes and riverside. Parking is free, and the
nearest bus stop (you'll need the number 66) is a few minutes' walk
away in Little Paxton.

Nightingales and cormorants are star species here, along with
nationally important numbers of wildfowl. Visit in spring or early
summer to hear the nightingales' song, which reaches its peak in May
(dawn and dusk near Kingfisher Hide can be good). Summer is also the
time to see cormorant and heron chicks venturing out of their nests –
June mornings at Hayden Hide are a good bet. Other summer sightings
include kingfishers, muntjac deer and up to 18 species of damsel- and
dragonflies. Autumn and winter can also get exciting, with thousands of
rooks, jackdaws and hundreds of cormorants roosting at dusk.

To guide your explorations, two waymarked routes lead from the car park: the Meadow Trail (1½ miles) and the Heron Trail (two miles). Bikes are permitted but the reserve is best explored on foot. You can also follow the Ouse Valley Way (page 76) south to St Neots (around three miles to Market Sq). Over the next decade, plans are afoot for expanding the reserve from 190 acres to more than three-and-a-half times its current size. The aim is to create new lakes, reed beds and wet woodland, plus an area of scrub for nightingales, and a network of paths and cycleways. Drop into the volunteer-run visitor centre to find out more, as well as to report any wildlife sightings after your ramble.

"The aim is to create new lakes, reed beds and wet woodland, plus an area of scrub for nightingales"

3 CHURCH OF THE HOLY TRINITY
Church Ln, Great Paxton PE19 6RG

The little village of **Great Paxton** sits across the railway tracks and river from Paxton Pits. It is best known for its unique **Church of the Holy Trinity**. While the exterior isn't anything special, it has an unusually high nave which is quite breathtaking. This is one of only three surviving Anglo-Saxon aisled churches in England, with a north transept arch that, according to the church, is the highest unsupported Anglo-Saxon arch in Europe. Pevsner described the arch as being 'thrown across at a height unparalleled in Early English architecture'; 2020 marked 1,000 years since construction of the church started. The church is usually locked but there is often someone working in the churchyard who can let visitors in. Otherwise, contact the vicar Annette Reed on ✆ 01480 211048.

⑪ FOOD & DRINK

The Bell 48 High St, PE19 6RF ✆ 01480 700107 ⊗ mybellpub.com. Friendly village pub with beer garden and annual events that include gin and rum festivals plus darts and pétanque games that are open to all. The menu includes homemade burgers, butcher's choice sausages, veggie lasagne and gluten-free puddings.

Great Paxton Community Shop 48a High St, PE19 6RF ✆ 01480 218624 ⊗ greatpaxtoncommunityshop.co.uk. Opened by volunteers in 2017, this charming little shop sits in the car park of the Bell Inn. Its Cambridgeshire and Bedfordshire produce ranges from meat, dairy and veg to filled rolls and fresh salads. They also sell ice cream made in the village, and honey from Great Paxton bees.

4 THE OFFORDS

A mile and a half north of Great Paxton and a stone's throw from the Great Ouse, The Offords (or simply 'Offord' as some road signs say) refers to the neighbouring villages of **Offord Cluny** and **Offord D'Arcy**. There isn't a whole lot here to warrant coming out of your way but it's a pretty place to stop if you're passing through on the Ouse Valley Way footpath (page 76), which skirts the villages to the west, or spending a night at **Buckden Marina** (⌂ buckdenmarina.co.uk), which offers visitor berths for Great Ouse explorers. A three-minute walk from Offord Cluny, this marina should surely be called 'Offord Marina', as Buckden (page 122) is three times as far away to the west.

The Offords' riverside location, shared pub (The Horseshoe; see below) and network of local footpaths makes this a good area for pub walks. Crossing points over the railway tracks and weirs lead you to the Ouse Valley Way on the west bank. From here, you could follow the river north for roughly 2½ miles to Brampton Mill (page 87) or south for two miles to Paxton Pits Nature Reserve (page 83). Footpaths also lead west across the fields for a couple of miles to Buckden.

"The overgrown churchyard has become a haven for wildlife – look for tawny owls, sparrowhawks, bats and woodpeckers"

In Offord D'Arcy, look for a wooden post signed 'Historic Church', just off the High Street (B1043); the private track opposite Graveley Road will lead you to St Peter's Church. Frozen in time, this redundant, Norman-era church is cared for by the Churches Conservation Trust. It closed in the late 1970s when All Saints in Offord Cluny became the sole parish church. Today, it's used for occasional services, craft fairs and events, while the overgrown churchyard has become a haven for wildlife – an information board encourages you to look for tawny owls, sparrowhawks, bats, woodpeckers and other wildlife. To see inside the church, ask for the key at The Limes (back up the track) or book a tour through the website ⌂ stpetersofforddarcy.co.uk.

FOOD & DRINK

The Horseshoe 90 High St, Offord D'Arcy PE19 5RH ✆ 01480 810293 ⌂ theoffordshoe. co.uk. Known locally as 'The Shoe', this family-owned village pub places high priority on sourcing East Anglian produce. Sunday roasts are very popular (you'll need to book).

5 BRAMPTON

⅄ Willows Park & Marina (page 316)

Two miles southwest of Huntingdon, this large village is neither grand nor quaint, and there's no sign of the River Great Ouse from the main village itself. Despite this, I've always found Brampton rather appealing, with its jumble of architectural styles and little-known link to the diarist Samuel Pepys. For many years, RAF Brampton played a central role in community life, with a large base at the southern end of the village. This ended in 2012 when the base was disbanded and the site became a housing development.

Without a nudge in the right direction, you could easily miss out on Brampton's biggest claim to fame: **Pepys House**. Passed down to Pepys from his father, this timber-framed cottage became his country retreat, rental property and the site of his buried treasure (see box, below). Set at the edge of Brampton on the B1514 (Huntingdon Rd), you can stroll here from the main village to peer down the driveway of number 44 – there's a plaque outside to reassure you that you've got the right house but do be aware that this is a private home. Once you've had a peek, head back towards the main village on Huntingdon Road, passing the **ancient waymarker** which directs travellers 'to Thrapston' (in Northamptonshire) and 'to London' but, surprisingly, not to Brampton. Luckily, the modern-day signage does this job.

Entering the village on Church Road, notice the Gothic tower of the church of **St Mary Magdalene** looming ahead. The expansive interior is really quite stunning, largely thanks to the impressive collection of Kempe & Co stained glass. Parts of this church date back to the 13th

BRAMPTON'S BURIED TREASURE

In June 1667, amid a threat of invasion by the Dutch Navy, the diarist Samuel Pepys instructed his wife and father to bury some of his fortune in the garden of their Brampton home. 'Pray God give them good passage, and good care to hide it,' Pepys wrote in his diary. Returning to Brampton in October, he dug up his gold under the cover of night and was furious at how poorly they'd buried it: 'But good God! to see how sillily they did it, not half a foot under ground, and in the sight of the world from a hundred places.' Worse still, he was 25 sovereigns short. The mystery of this missing gold has never knowingly been uncovered – the remains of Pepys's hoard may still be buried in Brampton today.

century, with the tower added in 1635. In the sanctuary are three choir stalls with beautifully carved 13th-century misericords that were praised by the art historian Nikolaus Pevsner. The curtain behind the altar was part of a hanging used for Queen Elizabeth II's 1953 coronation in Westminster Abbey.

 Brampton's oldest pub – the 16th-century **Black Bull** (see below) – stands next to the church. Pass the pub on your left, turn right on to the **High Street**, and prepare for a rollercoaster of architectural styles, from the handsome 19th-century Institute and the unusual Round House to modern brick homes, thatched cottages and a low-rise 1960s strip of shops. Whenever I've visited this eclectic array and popped into the handful of independent shops on the High Street (which include a butcher's, gift shop and teeny tiny florists), I've noticed a real sense of local pride. Don't just take my word for it: on the wall of the Community Centre are three plaques for 'Best Kept Village' and 'Large Village of the Year' – you'll find them above a bench that is dedicated to 'The Village Sweeper'.

 Continue to the end of the High Street and the prettiest part of Brampton: the **village green**. Among the hodgepodge of buildings here are tiny thatched cottages, the 1889 Methodist church and The Hare on the Green – the green's oldest building, it was built as a cottage in 1824 and is now a café, bar and community hub.

FOOD & DRINK

The Black Bull 25 Church Rd, PE28 4PF ℘ 01480 457201 ⬛ TheBlackBullBrampton. Reputed as one of Pepys's local haunts, this 16th-century coaching inn is Brampton's oldest. The pub grub menu includes a selection of 'famous' homemade pies. The large garden is perfect for lazy summer days.

Brampton Mill Bromholme Ln, PE28 4NE ℘ 01480 459758 ⬧ thebramptonmill.co.uk. Located a mile outside the village (accessible from Brampton via footpaths), this expansive former mill has a superb riverside setting. Following a makeover, the interior combines modern artwork and furniture with traditional beamed ceilings. The menu ranges from steaks and fresh fish to plant-based burgers, washed down with house cocktails, such as raspberry mules or blood orange and passionfruit collins.

Hare on the Green 40 The Green, PE28 4RH ℘ 01480 413592 ⬧ hareonthegreen.co.uk. A family-run, hare-themed café, pub and restaurant with a kids' area and games. The varied menu, which uses locally sourced produce where possible, includes take-away options. Roasts on Sundays.

WALKS & RIVER TOURS
FROM BRAMPTON MILL

Bromholme Ln, Brampton PE28 4NE ❄ OS Explorer map 225 *Huntingdon & St Ives;*
♀ TL225706

A 500-year-old mill turned pub/restaurant, Brampton Mill makes a good base or pit stop for **Great Ouse walks**. One mile east of the main village, it sits at the end of a track, just off Huntingdon Road (B1514). From the car park, the Ouse Valley Way leads east across Portholme Meadow to Godmanchester (1½ miles), or southwest to Buckden Marina (2½ miles). If you're starting in Brampton village, a footpath leads from the rear of the churchyard, past the back of Pepys House and across the fields to the mill (less than a mile).

To explore the river by boat, the volunteer-run **Great Ouse Ferry** runs almost daily (weather and river conditions permitting) between Brampton Mill and the Chinese Bridge in Godmanchester. During the half-hour trip, Captain Tim is happy to share his knowledge of the Great Ouse. All he asks for is a small donation towards the ferry's upkeep. To arrange a trip call (✆ 07999 799401) or email (✉ greatouseferry@gmail.com).

Another option is a **SUP safari** with Jonti watersports (✆ jonti.co.uk) who offer guided hour-long river 'safaris' on stand-up paddleboards (SUPs), with all equipment provided. The circular route from the mill includes a couple of portages (getting out and carrying your board). Jonti's SUP safaris also take place at St Neots (best for beginners) and Huntingdon rowing club.

6 BRAMPTON WOOD NATURE RESERVE
Car park off Brampton Rd, west of A1 at PE28 0DB

A mile and a half west of Brampton village, this patch of ancient woodland is more than 900 years old and, set in England's least-wooded county, is one of Cambridgeshire's largest at 326 acres. As you stroll along two miles of grassy rides, you'll be walking past oak, aspen, ash, field maple and birch. Those in the know may spot the wood's more unusual and stand-out trees: veteran oaks, wild cherries, rare service trees (near the visitor centre) and two impressive wild pear trees (on the southwest edge). In spring, it's blessed with bluebell displays, and in summer the woodland comes alive with orchids, devil's-bit scabious, water purslane and hairy St John's Wort. This is also one of the best places in the UK to see the elusive black hairstreak, one of Britain's rarest butterflies. Other rare wildlife includes the hazel dormouse – in 1992, Brampton Wood was one of the first reintroduction sites in England for this species.

7 HINCHINGBROOKE COUNTRY PARK
PE29 6DB

Once part of the Hinchingbrooke House estate (see below), this wildlife haven was a commercial gravel pit before it became a public park in 1989. Today, all three species of British woodpecker can be seen, along with nuthatch, marsh tit, otter and kingfisher. A network of walking trails leads between grassland, wildflower meadows, woodland and lakes. There's also a boating area, fishing platforms and mountain bike section. Bring a picnic or barbecue food (fixed stands available), and don't forget your wellies if the weather's wet. The park also has an apiary, which is cared for by Huntingdonshire Beekeepers' Association (HBKA). During the warmer months (Apr–Sep/Oct) the viewing gallery is open daily; head inside to learn about beekeeping and peer through the glass window to see the bees buzzing around their 14 hives, all of which are different. On Sunday afternoons, you can watch the beekeepers at work and see frames of honey and eggs being removed from the hives. To step the other side of the glass, contact the HBKA (⊘ huntsbka.org.uk) to ask about courses and taster sessions.

8 HINCHINGBROOKE HOUSE
Brampton Rd, Huntingdon PE29 3BN ⊘ hinchhouse.org.uk ⊙ guided tours Jun–late Aug 14.00–17.00 Sun

You can't help but notice this manor's many chimneys and crenellated turrets poking above the old stone wall on your way into or out of Huntingdon on the B1514. The walls of Hinchingbrooke House have many a story to tell. Some of these stones once formed the walls of a 13th-century nunnery, which was dissolved in 1536 during the Reformation. Two years later, in March 1538, Henry VIII presented the house to Richard Cromwell, who began converting it into an Elizabethan country house with huge bow windows and a medieval gateway taken from Ramsey Abbey (page 201).

The Cromwells had a penchant for lavish spending and entertaining royalty, which included Queen Elizabeth in 1564 and King James in 1603. As Hinchingbrooke passed through the generations, the Cromwells' debts mounted and, in 1627, Sir Oliver Cromwell (uncle of Oliver Cromwell, Lord Protector) was forced to sell Hinchingbrooke to Sir Sidney Montague. In 1660, the house passed to his son Edward Montague (the first Earl of Sandwich) who carried out elaborate extensions and alterations, which included two additional storeys to the western range of the property, a kitchen in the north wing, a new staircase and an iconic garden wall. This era was well documented by Samuel Pepys (the earl's cousin, secretary and protégé) who noted on 13 October 1662, 'I am sorry to think of the money at this time spent therein.'

Hinchingbrooke stayed in the Montague family until 1962, passing through a successive line of earls, the most renowned of which was John Montague, the fourth Earl of Sandwich, famed for creating the sandwich as a mobile supper that he could eat while gambling. He was also known for funding Captain Cook's voyages of exploration – to express his gratitude, Cook named several islands in his honour, including Hinchinbrook and Montague islands, just off the east coast of Australia. Cook also named many other discoveries after the earl, including the South Sandwich Islands near South Georgia. Eventually, Hinchingbrooke House was sold to Huntingdon County Council in 1962/63 and served as a hospital and police control centre before becoming the sixth-form centre of Hinchingbrooke School.

Today, summer tours of the state school's historic building and grounds are given by the sixth-form pupils themselves, who share stories of ghostly sightings as they guide you through the rooms. A highlight is the bone cupboard, which houses the remains of two individuals found in stone coffins beneath the stairs. As part of the tour, tea and cakes are served in the old dining room or on the terrace overlooking the croquet lawn. Each October, the school hosts 'The Horror at Hinchingbrooke House' – a critically acclaimed, theatrical Halloween attraction that invites you to walk through dark rooms, mazes and woodland while being hunted by 80 or so actors dressed as killer clowns, chainsaw maniacs and demonic creatures. It often sells out, so book in advance at ⊘ enterifyoudare.co.uk.

9 HUNTINGDON

⌂ **The Old Bridge Hotel** (page 316)

The birthplace of Oliver Cromwell, home of Huntingdon Castle and an important staging post on the Great North Road (page 149), you'd be forgiven for getting excited about this Georgian market town – which was also the seat of Conservative MP John Major, who served as Prime Minister between 1990 and 1997. But, unless you lower your expectations, you're likely to be disappointed. Huntingdon has long been overshadowed by prettier and more prosperous Cambridgeshire towns, and even the locals I spoke to agreed that it's lacklustre. It does, however, have two saving graces: The Old Bridge Hotel and the Cromwell Museum – both of which make it worth visiting. The latter is housed in the former Huntingdon Grammar School building where both Cromwell and Samuel Pepys went to school. As you wander around town, you'll notice that everything from pubs to street names are dedicated to the pair.

At the heart of the town is **Market Hill**, with its cluster of historic landmarks and weekly markets (Wed & Sat). In the centre of the square is the **Thinking Soldier** war memorial, created by Lady Kathleen Scott, widower of Scott of the Antarctic. Behind this is Huntingdon's oldest pub, the **Falcon Inn** – poke your nose inside and time travel back to the 16th century. Cromwell used this pub as a Civil War headquarters and is said to have recruited his New Model Army here, addressing his troops in the square from the pub's upstairs window. Also in the square is **All Saints' Church**, where the body of Mary Queen of Scots spent the night of 6 October 1612 on its procession from Peterborough Cathedral to Westminster Abbey. Opposite the church is the **Cromwell Museum** (Grammar School Walk, PE29 3LF ⚭ cromwellmuseum.org ☉ 11.00–16.00 Tue–Sun & bank hols). Oliver Cromwell was born in Huntingdon in 1599 and became MP of the town in 1628, so it makes sense that the world's most extensive collection of Cromwell artefacts should be housed here. Reopened in 2021 after a major refurbishment, the museum tells Cromwell's life story through portraits, items of clothing, armour, death masks, surgical instruments and historical documents. You could spend several hours here delving into his early days as a schoolboy in this very building and following the development of his political career, through to his role in the English Civil War and his time as Lord Protector, ruler of England, from 1653 to 1658. Cromwell is one of the most controversial characters in English history, so the museum aims to present facts and thoughts about him, leaving visitors to make their own judgements. Run by an independent charity, entry is free but donations are very welcome.

Diagonally opposite the museum (on the corner of George and High sts) is **The George Hotel**. A significant Great North Road posting house, the modernised interior is underwhelming but it has a fantastic Jacobean courtyard where a prominent clock face once timed the coaches.

Open-air Shakespeare productions have been held here in summer since 1959 (⌀ satg.org.uk). Further up the High Street (northwest end) is **Cromwell House**, where a plaque remembers the Lord Protector's birth here in 1599, while his family coat of arms hangs above the door.

At the opposite end of the High Street, where the pedestrianised section ends, is **Cowper House**, home to the nature poet William Cowper between 1765 and 1767. Further down, opposite St Mary's Church, **Castle Hill House** was the wartime HQ of the RAF Pathfinder Force (page 98). This end of town is where the High Street meets the river, with the Great Ouse forming Huntingdon's eastern boundary. A six-arched **medieval stone bridge** hops over the river to Godmanchester (see opposite), with a converted Victorian mill (once a World War I military clothing depot) on the Godmanchester side and the ivy-clad **Old Bridge Hotel** on the Huntingdon side. This grand Georgian townhouse was once the home of the prosperous Veasey family. Now one of Cambridgeshire's favourite hotels, it's well worth stopping by at the lounge bar/café, restaurant or wine shop.

Upstream and directly behind the Old Bridge Hotel is **Huntingdon Castle Hills** – a Norman motte and bailey site, where you can climb the biggest mound for views over the Great Ouse and an information board. A few minutes' walk downstream, between the river and the B1514, is **Riverside Park**. This is a pleasant-enough spot for a picnic or stroll; a footpath leads through it to the old village of **Hartford** (roughly one mile from the Old Bridge), which merges into the Huntingdon fringe. If you'd prefer to paddle this stretch, contact **Jonti** watersports (⌀ jonti.co.uk) for stand-up paddleboarding, who offer guided stand-up paddleboarding safaris.

If you're a fan of flea markets, one Huntingdon gem worth seeking out is **Cambs Lock Antiques & Collectables** (1 St Mary's St, PE29 3PE). In a town that isn't known for its independent shops, this eclectic emporium is an exception. The ultimate snooper's paradise, it's chock-full of everything from 18th-century cowbells to butter churns, 1960s fur coats, retro card tables and garden furniture. Don't be surprised if you find yourself absorbed in the warren of multi-level rooms for far longer than you'd anticipated.

For a more detailed tour of the town, pop into the Town Hall on Market Hill and pick up a Town Trail map or download one from ⌀ huntingdonfirst.co.uk.

FOOD & DRINK

Huntingdon doesn't have a huge amount to offer the Slow Movement in terms of food and drink. My favourite place is **The Old Bridge** (1 High St, PE29 3TQ ✆ 01480 424300 ⌂ huntsbridge.com), mostly for its relaxing atmosphere and setting – with a sunny terrace and a roaring fire in winter, it is easily the best place to relax and refuel in Huntington. Oenophiles will also appreciate the hotel's in-house, award-winning **Old Bridge Wine Shop** (✆ 01480 458410), which has a wine list that has been declared 'the UK's best in every major competition'. With 24 fine wines opened daily, the help-yourself wine tasting set-up is a fantastic, and rather dangerous, way to quaff an afternoon away. Prices are at both extremes – you can buy a bottle for less than a tenner or just shy of a grand.

10 GODMANCHESTER

One mile south of Huntingdon, this large riverside village has a long history and a spectacular setting beside Portholme Meadow – submerged in winter and strewn with wildflowers in summer, the sight of this vast expanse is reason enough alone to visit the village. As you gaze across the meadow, try to imagine Victorian skaters pirouetting on the ice, horses galloping over the green, and some of England's earliest aircraft taking flight; more on this shortly.

Travel further back in time and Godmanchester was once the site of **Durovigutum** – a walled Roman town that controlled an important river crossing and road junction on Ermine Street (a major Roman road, which connected London with Lincoln and York). Decades' worth of excavations have revealed that Durovigutum was a wealthy settlement with a tax office, bathhouse and marketplace. The map outside the Town Hall reveals where the Roman walls once stood. To find out more, visit the Godmanchester Museum website (⌂ godmanchester.co.uk); this volunteer-run charity collates the town's history and shares its findings online, as well as during open days, Roman re-enactments and hands-on history events. Plans are also afoot to open a permanent museum in the church of St Mary (Chadley Ln, PE29 2AW).

A marvellous, mid 18th-century Georgian house, **Island Hall** (Post St, PE29 2BA ✆ 01480 459676 ⌂ islandhall.com) sits almost too modestly on Post Street, opposite the historic Black Bull coaching inn and the war memorial. This is the private home of Christopher and Lady Linda Vane Percy – the seventh generation of the family to live here. Behind its façade, the hall's English-Baroque interior (which was restored by the current owners) includes original carved panelling and many of the Vane Percy's possessions, collected since the family acquired the hall in 1800. Outside, three acres of gardens lead down to the Great Ouse where a replica of an original 18th-century Chinese bridge connects to the hall's namesake: an ornamental island in the river. The bridge was built just after the peak of the late 18th-century 'Chinoiserie' phase, when Asian-style art and design became popular in the UK. Informal tours of the hall and grounds are given by family members who also offer 'croquet teas' on the lawn, lunches in the stone-flagged hall and candlelit suppers. Bookings can be made through the Historic Houses website (⊘ historichouses.org) but prices are steep unless you're visiting as a large group.

The western edge of Godmanchester skirts Portholme Meadow and traces the course of the Great Ouse. With a beautiful view across the millpond and out to the meadow, **The Causeway** is where you'll find most of the village shops, many of which occupy timber-framed Tudor buildings. Where The Causeway meets the Town Hall on Post Street, you'll find the village's second (and largest) **Chinese Bridge** – it may seem odd that such a small settlement has two Chinese-style bridges but it's likely that the first inspired the second. The second bridge was first built in 1827 but, after falling into disrepair, was removed and replaced with a replica in 1960. This process was repeated in 2010, so the bridge you see today is the third incarnation of the original. A prominent local landmark, its pretty white arch of Chinese Chippendale latticework crosses the river and links the village streets to Portholme. If you cross the bridge and turn right along the river, you'll arrive at the site of **Godmanchester Mill** and the Mill Yard (now a free car park on Post St). The earliest records of a mill date back to 1499, when the lease included a clause that forbade the miller's wife from interfering with the machinery. Sadly, the watermill ground its last kernel of corn in 1884 and was demolished in 1927.

Portholme Meadow

One of the largest ancient water meadows in England, Portholme is a rare example of a forgotten landscape, formed over hundreds of years by silt deposits from the seasonal Great Ouse floods. The first time I visited in winter, I was shocked to find a vast lake lapping at the village – it was as if Godmanchester had been transported to the seaside. For the locals, this is nothing unusual – when the river floods, Portholme simply does its job of soaking up the excess. Summer paints a different scene, with couples strolling across the grassland, livestock grazing and fishermen sitting patiently on the banks. The meadow is managed as a traditional Lammas Land, which means that hay is grown in summer and harvested on Lammas Day (a traditional festival at the beginning of August that marks the first wheat harvest of the year), followed by grazing until April for commoners.

Life here hasn't always been this tranquil. Portholme was once an enormous seasonal ice rink, which attracted skaters and spectators from far and wide. The flooded meadow would freeze in winter and the locals would drop everything to skate, race, and play 'bandy' (page 245) – a highlight of the year. When the ice melted, other pursuits would take over. Horseracing became popular in the 18th century and Portholme Races was one of the most fashionable events in the racing calendar. Flying came next – the huge expanse of flat, open ground was ideal for the tentative early days of aviation and, in 1910, one of England's first pilots, James Radley, took flight here.

19 April 1910 was a great day locally. This was the day that James Radley made the first-ever flight from Portholme and virtually the whole of Godmanchester and Huntingdon turned out to watch. He flew circuits of the meadow – 16 miles in 23 minutes in a Bleriot monoplane to the cheers of the spectators. Subsequently, the crowds flocked to see other early aviators trying out the flying machines here.
Patrick Hull, godmanchester.net

A year later, Radley and fellow aviator Will Rhodes-Moorhouse began building aircrafts in Huntingdon. Portholme became a Royal Flying Corps training station during World War I and in the 1930s the meadow was visited by Sir Alan Cobham's famous flying circus.

Today, the meadow is an internationally important wildlife haven, with rare marshland and meadow plants. In summer, the meadow is alive with dragonflies, damselflies and a host of other bugs, birds and beasts. In winter, the floodwaters welcome Bewick's swans, greylag geese and golden plover. Since World War II, more than 95% of wildflower-rich meadows like this have disappeared in England, which makes Portholme all the more special. Walking is the best way to enjoy it, with the Ouse Valley Way striking southwest from Godmanchester to Brampton Mill (about one mile each way).

🍴 FOOD & DRINK

A true Cambridgeshire champion, **Simon's Cider** (Unit 2, Roman Way Industrial Park, London Rd, PE29 2LN ⌂ simonscider.co.uk ⊖ every other Fri & Sat) makes ciders and perries using Cambridgeshire-only produce, much of which is saved from rotting away in local gardens; his tap room is a little out of town but worth it. Other than that, Godmanchester has plenty of places to fill a hole or quench your thirst but doesn't have much of an affiliation towards Slow food. On The Causeway, you can choose between the pub, café, Indian take-away, and fish and chip shop, or there's a bakery, Chinese/Malaysian restaurant and a pub on Post Street. Back from the river, **The White Hart** (2 Cambridge Rd, PE29 2BW ✆ 01480 414050 ⌂ whitehart-godmanchester.co.uk) has the best reputation in town, serving up decent gastro-pub food.

11 HOUGHTON MILL

🏠 **Eagle Mill** (page 316) 🏕 **Waterclose Meadows Campsite** (page 316)
PE28 2AZ ✆ 01480 301494 ⊖ mill: Mar–Oct via guided tour (booking essential); tea room: Mar–Oct daily, Nov–Feb Fri–Sun (but check website for changes); National Trust

Set on an island above tranquil water meadows, this working watermill is a strong contender for Cambridgeshire's most idyllic – unsurprisingly, it has inspired countless artworks over the centuries, some of which you can see inside. The experience during the guided tours is hands-on. Visitors can watch, hear and smell three floors' worth of 18th-century cogs, wheels and millstones in action. You can control the model locks, hoist sacks of grain on the Victorian pulley systems, and use a hand quern to mill your own flour. The ground floor has an interactive virtual tour, making the mill accessible to those unable to climb the stairs.

A mill has stood on this spot for more than 1,000 years. During the Victorian era, it was one of the most important in the area, producing large quantities of flour. You can try some of Houghton's stone-ground wholemeal flour for yourself by tucking into a scone, cake or savoury bake in the tea room, or by buying a bag of flour from the mill shop. A two-minute walk from the centre of Houghton village, the mill has its own campsite, which makes a bucolic base for exploring more of the area. The historic town of St Ives (page 101) lies two miles to the east, and the village of Hemingford Abbots (page 100) is half a mile southwest across the meadow – see the box on page 106 for a circular walking route that visits both.

North of the mill, the adjoining villages of **Houghton** and **Wyton** are well worth a wander, with their thatched, whitewashed and Georgian

HOUGHTON MILL CANOE TRAILS

With easy launching at the millpond, Houghton Mill is a good place to set off on a canoe or paddleboard adventure. The National Trust website suggests two good trails: the three-mile Trout Stream Loop (about an hour) takes you on a bucolic circumnavigation of Houghton Meadow; or the 5½-mile route to St Ives (an hour each way) gives you the option to moor up and discover the town's cafés, pubs and historic sites (page 101). Alternatively, you could plan your own route using OS Explorer map 225 *Huntingdon & St Ives*. For boat hire, try Houghton Boats (07759 316260).

buildings. The hub of these villages is the 'green' (more of a paved square), with its community store, antiques shop, smart village pump and unusual **thatched clock tower**. In the southeast corner is a marble **statue of Potto Brown** (1791–1871), a successful Houghton miller, philanthropist and Nonconformist who built the village school and chapel. He also helped to fund the St Ives Free Church (page 103) and Huntingdon Free Church.

Wyton is also the name of an RAF airbase, 1½ miles north of the villages. Established in 1915, **RAF Wyton** became a World War II bomber base and, in 1942, was the home of the Pathfinder Force – an elite unit of the RAF Bomber Command, which was tasked with the dangerous and lonely role of target-marking. Today, the force is remembered with the waymarked Pathfinder Long Distance Walk and annual Pathfinder March (page 98), which sets off from RAF Wyton. The airfield was decommissioned in 1995 but the base remains active for intelligence support.

FOOD & DRINK

If you're visiting the mill, **Houghton Mill Tea Room** is the obvious choice for refreshment but the village itself shouldn't be overlooked. On Houghton and Wyton village green, little **Houghton Tea Room** (PE29 2AZ) does very good cakes, and the **Houghton & Wyton Community Shop** (hwcommunityshop.org Wed–Sun) is a shining example of a village hub, with local fare that often includes Brampton pies, Grafham fish and Houghton flour. Also on the green is the **Three Horseshoes** (threehorseshoesinnhoughton.co.uk), while just around the corner is **The Three Jolly Butchers** (3 Huntingdon Rd, PE28 2AD 01480 463228 3jbs.co.uk). Both pubs serve a wide choice of pub grub but the The Three Jolly Butchers is generally seen as the better option for foodies serving British classics such as battered cod, steak and ale pie, and pan-fried liver and bacon.

THE PATHFINDER MARCH

This annual, 46-mile challenge is held on the Saturday nearest to midsummer day, in memory of the RAF Pathfinder Force. Starting and finishing at RAF Wyton, the route links war memorials and former Pathfinder stations as it loops through the Cambridgeshire countryside. Previous years have seen up to 300 participants from across the globe walking or running the entire route, or entering as relay teams. With a time limit of 20 hours to complete the course, walkers set off at 04.00 and runners get going at 08.00, with eight checkpoints to pass through along the way. You can enter online at ⊘ pathfindermarch.co.uk.

The route is permanently waymarked, so you can tackle the whole loop or smaller sections at any time of year. To plan a section, use OS Explorer map *225 Huntingdon & St Ives* and use the Pathfinder signposts to keep you on track.

12 THE HEMINGFORDS

🏠 **The Lodge at Hemingford Grey House** (page 316) ⚑ **Quiet Waters Caravan Park** (page 316)

If you dream of moving to a quintessential English village, Hemingford Grey and Hemingford Abbots should both be on your radar. Once part of the Ramsey Abbey estate, these affluent neighbours are connected by a riverside footpath that leads across the meadows and are adorned with historic houses, thatched cottages and a storybook manor. Both Houghton Mill and St Ives are within walking distance (page 106), so you could base yourself here and enjoy a weekend of countryside strolls, local history and good food. A highlight of the Hemingfords' calendar is the annual regatta (⊘ hemingfordregatta.blogspot.com) which, after more than a century, claims to be England's oldest village rowing regatta.

Hemingford Grey

The larger of the two villages, Hemingford Grey has a beautiful riverfront footpath which gives access to the village's two major draws: **The Manor** and the **Church by the River** (aka the church of St James). The latter has the most picturesque setting of any church I know: for a spellbinding view, approach from the south on the riverside footpath or, even better, by boat from Hemingford Abbots. The 'crown' atop the church tower is the base of the former spire, which blew down during the 1741 hurricane, causing a large stone to crash into a windowpane at Hemingford Grey House next door. Branching east off the riverside is the High Street, where you'll find Hemingford Stores, The Cock inn and some beautiful thatched cottages, including The Old Bakehouse and 16th-century Glebe Cottage.

One of the oldest continuously inhabited homes in Britain, the 12th-century moated **manor** (PE28 9BN ℘ 01480 463134 ⊘ greenknowe. co.uk ☺ garden: 11.00–17.00 daily; house tours: May–Dec by appointment) was made famous by the *Green Knowe* children's books by Lucy Boston (1892–1990), who lived here for more than 50 years. Boston featured real-life settings and objects from the house and garden in her books. Her son Peter illustrated the series, which has been translated into several languages and made into various TV and radio productions.

The house is now owned by Boston's daughter-in-law, Diana. Visiting out of season, I called ahead to arrange an informal tour. A world away from a museum, the house feels alive and lived in (which it is) from the moment you step through the door. A fantastic storyteller herself, Diana and her dog took me on a magical journey through their home, bringing each ancient room to life with fact and fiction. After sitting at the table where Lucy wrote her books and learning about The Manor's history, we went upstairs to the bedrooms where Diana showed me the original *Green Knowe* illustrations (drawn by her late husband) and some of the patchworks Lucy loved to create in her spare time. These patchworks are some of the world's most famous, being the only complete collection that was made in the same place they are displayed in. Next, we walked 'through a wardrobe' to the 900-year-old music room where we listened to haunting music on an enormous 1929 horned gramophone. Above the music room, Diana led me up a fantastically steep little staircase; 'I love watching the children's eyes light up when I take them up to Tolly's room,' she told me, opening the door to the attic bedroom where Tolly – the main character in the *Green Knowe* books – keeps his toy box and other treasures. Almost everything you see at The Manor was featured in Boston's books, from African masks and birdcages to the views of the Great Ouse through the windows.

The moated gardens are also open to the public and can be accessed without booking. Just enter through the garden gate on the riverside path and put a contribution in the honesty box. Lucy Boston laid out these four acres of gardens herself, planting more than 200 trees and shrubs. As you explore, look for her beloved yews, herbaceous perennials and the hidden garden. You can also visit The Manor for talks and ghost stories in the music room. For dates, see the website or paper schedule, pinned outside the house.

> 'I'm glad this house is stone,' said Tolly. 'It smells of stone. When you come back to any house that you know, it has such a special smell. Do you think when they built this they put some magic somewhere to make it last?'
> Lucy M Boston *An Enemy at Green Knowe* (1964)

More than a century before Lucy Boston moved in, The Manor had another claim to fame. In the early 1700s, it was home to the 'Beautiful Miss Gunnings'. Sisters Maria and Elizabeth Gunnings were considered to be two of the most beautiful women in Europe – the nature poet William Cowper, who lived in Huntingdon for a while, described them as 'two nymphs adorned with every grace'. News of the siblings' beauty soon reached London, where they were invited to prestigious balls and were mobbed when they promenaded in the park. Originally from very humble beginnings, their rags to riches story saw both girls married into some of England's most aristocratic families.

Hemingford Abbots

Grey's little sister, Hemingford Abbots is chocolate-box pretty, although it lacks the literary clout of its neighbour. In the village centre, near the 500-year-old pub, a map highlights the most historic buildings. These include the Old School House with its charismatic clock tower, and the smart Manor House on Church Lane. Opposite is the Grade I-listed church of St Margaret of Antioch, much of which originates from the late 1300s. Note the striking stained-glass windows, created by local engraver David Peace. Among the village's quirks and landmarks are the 'Swap Box' (an honesty library in a traditional red phone box), the 250-year-old village stone on Rideaway, and the remains of the medieval village cross on the corner of Royal Oak Lane.

⊪ FOOD & DRINK

Axe and Compass High St, Hemingford Abbots PE28 9AH ⌀ 01480 463605
⌀ axeandcompass.co.uk ⊙ kitchen Tue–Sun. A 15th-century thatched pub with a garden and children's play area beneath the church spire. The menu includes pub classics, burgers and sharing platters. Bike stands for cyclists.

The Cock 47 High St, Hemingford Grey PE28 9BJ ✆ 01480 463609 🖥 thecockhemingford. co.uk. Serving villagers since 1767, this award-winning pub was chosen in 2021 by *The Good Pub Guide* as one of its top ten pubs . My favourite room is the back bar room with its tiny window, low ceiling and timber beams (taller individuals will need to duck). With a big emphasis on local produce, the modern British menu includes fresh fish and the pub's own sausages (a must), served with Hemingford horseradish mash. They also serve 'Cromwell' cider, which is brewed by a man down the road (light, sparkling and dangerously drinkable).

13 ST IVES

As I was going to St Ives,
I met a man with seven wives,
Each wife had seven sacks,
Each sack had seven cats,
Each cat had seven kits,
Kits, cats, sacks, and wives,
How many were going to St Ives?

Locals believe that this ancient riddle, first published in 1730, was written about a man going to the Great Fair in St Ives, Cambridgeshire. Those in the southwest, however, are convinced that it's about St Ives in Cornwall. Written by an anonymous author around 300 years ago, it's unlikely we'll ever be 100% sure either way. This riddle isn't the only source of confusion between these Cambridgeshire and Cornish counterparts – search for 'St Ives' on Google or a SatNav and, almost without fail, you'll end up in Cornwall which, it seems, takes digital precedence over Cambridgeshire. To avoid a navigational nightmare, the postcode 'PE27' will keep you in the right county.

There's a lot to like about this ancient riverside town, from its unusual Bridge Chapel and the Old Riverport to the independent shops and historic Monday market. St Ives is a place to delve into Huntingdonshire history, potter around its shops and cafés, and soak up the Great Ouse views.

Originally known as 'Slepe', the settlement was renamed 'St Ives' in AD1001 when a ploughman discovered a stone coffin buried in a field. The Abbot of Ramsey Abbey (who happened to be the landlord) decided that the bones inside belonged to St Ivo, a Persian bishop. This announcement led to the founding of St Ivo's Priory. Pilgrims came, the river was bridged and trade boomed. Before long, Ramsey Abbey's biggest source of local income was the St Ives Fair: one of the four largest

MARKET MANIA

In 1110, Henry I granted a royal charter for the St Ives Fair, which grew to become one of England's largest. Held every Easter, the Great Fair was best known for its wool and textiles but everything from fish and spices to shoes and beer were also sold. Weekly markets followed when King John granted a charter for a regular Monday market in 1200. Livestock was sold on The Broadway (known then as Bullock Market) for around 700 years, with up to 12,000 cattle being shown on market day. This brought big business to the town's inns – during the Victorian era, St Ives had around 70 pubs and several 'bawdy houses' (brothels). But by the late 19th century, things were getting out of control with the filth and mayhem caused by thousands of unruly beasts becoming a health hazard. In 1884, the cattle market was moved to a more contained site on the present-day Market Road. The market site is now home to the town's main bus station but you can still see some of the metal bars from the old cattle pens. At the entrance is the town crest, which features four bulls' heads – a reminder of just how significant the cattle markets were.

St Ives continues to host a weekly Monday market, plus a Friday market on Market Hill. Mondays are the busiest, especially on bank holidays. An award-winning farmers' market takes place at Sheep Market (opposite the old cattle market) on the first and third Saturday of each month. Each October, the Michaelmas Fair dominates the town centre, as it has done for hundreds of years.

wool fairs in England. While markets and fairs are still an important part of the town's identity, all that remains of St Ivo's Priory is the wall of a 14th-century barn on Priory Road – look for the information plaque on the old stone wall that skirts 'The Priory' office building.

The Old Riverport

Before the development of railways and roads, the River Great Ouse was East Anglia's major transport route, and St Ives was one of England's busiest riverports. The Quay would have been a hive of activity, with merchant ships unloading their cargo, riverside inns bursting at the seams, and rows of barges and fen lighters (flat-bottomed boats) jostling for space, and young 'horse-knocker' boys tending the horses that pulled these flat-bottomed boats along the river. In 2014, in recognition of this rich heritage, St Ives officially named its town centre and quayside 'The Old Riverport'.

Most of the Riverport's shops and cafés are clustered along **Market Hill** and **The Broadway**. Once part of the medieval fairground and market site, this linear strip has a good dose of historical charm. Many of the grander buildings here were once busy coaching inns or the homes of prosperous millers and brewers.

Looming over Market Hill, the Gothic-style **Free Church** (built 1863–64) is one of the oldest Nonconformist churches in England and was largely funded by Potto Brown of Houghton (page 97). Nip upstairs to appreciate the stunning worship space, or stay downstairs for the fair trade shop. Outside the church is an impressive bronze **statue of Oliver Cromwell** with a very stern gaze. Although Cromwell lived in St Ives for a while during the 1630s, the statue was originally intended for his hometown of Huntingdon. When Huntingdon failed to raise enough funds or local interest, St Ives stepped in – a reminder of the town's history of nonconformity. Unveiled in 1901, the statue commemorates Cromwell's 300th birthday.

On The Broadway, **Queen Victoria's Memorial** was built to mark her Diamond Jubilee. Don't believe the inscription on the side that says it was presented on Edward VII's coronation day, 26 June 1902. Edward was ill, so the coronation and unveiling of the memorial were postponed until August but the inscription was never changed. At the far end of The Broadway is the excellent **Norris Museum** (PE27 5BX ✆ 01480 497314 🖑 norrismuseum.org.uk ⊙ 10.00–16.00 Mon–Sat, May–Sep also 13.00–16.00 Sun). Free to enter, the museum started life in 1933 as the natural history collection of St Ives local Herbert Ellis Norris and was reopened in 2017 after a £1million revamp. You can immerse yourself in an interactive pocket history of Huntingdonshire's early days, told through Stone Age flint tools, 160-million-year-old Jurassic fossils, Roman pottery and Victorian relics. Some of Norris's original collection is displayed in a recreation of his study, as well as a fantastic exhibit about the magic of fenland skating (see box, page 244) – listen to the video stories of Cambridgeshire locals skating under moonlight, and see an original 'bandy' stick and a pair of fen runners (ice skates). Beyond the museum is **The Waits** – a riverside strip with moorings. From here, a cut-through leads to **All Saints Church**, the only church in England to have been hit by an aeroplane – a student pilot collided with the spire in 1918. Another quirk of this parish church is the carved rabbits that disappear and emerge on the west door, though no-one seems to know why. To the west of the church is the entrance to Holt Island Nature Reserve on Church Street.

A DEVIOUS PLAN FOR A PORT

Far from a happy coincidence, the success of St Ives as a medieval riverport was a strategic decision made by the landowners at Ramsey Abbey. The River Great Ouse was a hugely important medieval trade route, allowing goods from Europe and the east coast to flow to and from central England via King's Lynn in Norfolk. Recognising an opportunity to establish St Ives as the river's major port and highest point of navigation, the abbey built large watermills at Hemingford, Houghton and Hartford throughout the second half of the Middle Ages. These mills blocked navigation upstream to Huntingdon so that, past St Ives, goods had to be transported by road or unloaded and carried over the mill dams. As a result, trade in St Ives boomed and, by the late 13th century, Huntingdon was crippled. It wasn't until the early 17th century that inland navigation beyond St Ives became possible through dredging the river and building locks around the mills.

The narrow streets of Merryland and Crown Street link Market Hill with The Broadway and form a T-junction with Bridge Street, which leads to **St Ives Bridge**. Built in the 1420s to replace the earlier wooden bridge, this is one of only four bridges in England that incorporates a **Bridge Chapel**. The chapel has had a chequered history as a toll house, a place of worship, a pub, a surgery, a private residence and, allegedly, a brothel. For a peek inside, ask for the key at the Norris Museum.

Down on **the Quay**, look up at the bridge and notice how four of its six arches have pointed tops, while the other two are rounded. During the 1645 Civil War, the bridge was partially blown up by the Roundheads to prevent King Charles's troops crossing the river. The rounded arches were part of the rebuild in 1716. From the Quay, you should also have a good view across the river to the seven-storey **Old Mill**, which was built as a steam-powered corn mill in 1845 and later became a factory, then flats. At the eastern end of the Quay, on the corner of Wellington Street, the Masonic Lodge was built as a grain store in the 17th century, while the houses along Wellington Street were once home to local watermen.

Holt Island Nature Reserve

Church St, PE27 5BY ⬦ holtisland.org ⊖ Apr–Sep (& Oct, weather permitting) 10.00–16.00 Sat, Sun & bank hols

A nine-acre river island, this secretive reserve is tucked away behind All Saints Church, to the west of the town centre. When the gate is unlocked, cross the footbridge and follow the raised boardwalks to discover wet woodland, reed beds and riverside wildlife. This tranquil haven is home to warblers, herons, kingfishers, cormorants, badgers, foxes and more. If conditions are suitable out of season, the Norris Museum can give you a key.

Before its life as a nature reserve, the island was used in the 1700s as a 'holt' – a place where osier willows are grown commercially for the basket-making industry. Back then, it was named 'Ingle Holt' after its owner, George Wright Wright Ingle (that's right, two 'Wrights'). Bequeathed to the town council in 1934, the island ran wild for 20 years before it became a reserve. In 1913, a river-fed swimming pool was dug in the island. Closed in 1949, the pool is now used for Sea Scout moorings.

 ## RIVER CRUISES

St Ives Electric Riverboat Co Quay pontoon, Old Riverport ✆ 07906 257308 🖋 electricriverboat.co.uk ☺ Apr–Oct. From St Ives, you can cruise the Great Ouse on a chauffeured electric boat, without the disturbance of engine noise. Hourly trips depart (weather permitting) for Hemingford lock, with detailed commentary. To reserve a seat, put your name on the booking board on the Quay or call to pre-book. Private hire also available.

 ## FOOD & DRINK

St Ives has a decent selection of pubs, cafés and restaurants, most of which are on or around Market Hill, The Broadway and Bridge Street.

J Wadsworth Wines 34 The Broadway, PE27 5BN ✆ 01480 463522 🖋 wadsworthwines. co.uk. This drinks emporium is a site to behold, with more than 900 wines, 400 whiskies and hundreds of other spirits, liqueurs and brews. These range from Cambridgeshire ales and affordable wines, to 50-year-old Talisker Secret Stills priced at an eye-watering £1,100. The company was started in 1869 by John Wadsworth, a former Mayor of St Ives.

River Terrace Café Manor Mews, Bridge St, PE27 5UW ✆ 01480 468098 🖋 riverterracecafe.co.uk. The coolest café in town: expect your tea in a glass pot and your salads with kale, halloumi and freekah. The cakes are excellent, and they run regular tapas evenings and other themed nights. Set in a beautiful Grade II-listed building next to St Ives Bridge, with views of the Great Ouse and riverside seating outside.

Tom's Cakes 19 Market Hill, PE27 5AL 🖋 tomscakes.co.uk. Housed in the original toll house for St Ives's sheep market, this local institution is famous for its homemade cakes and bakes that reflect the seasons, from summer lavender to autumnal apple. Provenance is taken seriously, with free-range Cambridgeshire eggs and fresh veg from the Fens.

St Ives, The Hemingfords & Houghton Mill

✳ OS Explorer map 225 *Huntingdon & St Ives*; start: Queen Victoria memorial, St Ives
📍 TL312713; 5 miles; easy (flat all the way)

T his classic St Ives circular leads to Houghton Mill and the picture-postcard Hemingfords. You could start at any point and walk in either direction but this anti-clockwise route gives the best views of the breathtaking Church by the River. You'll pass two pubs and a tea room, plus more options in St Ives.

1 Start in the town centre at the Queen Victoria Jubilee Memorial. Turn your back on Crown Street and Merryland and walk northwest along The Broadway. Continue to the Norris Museum and, just past it, The Waits riverside path. Where The Waits bends right and merges into Ramsey Road, turn left on the cut-through to All Saints Church. Keep the church on your right as you walk around the churchyard and exit through the first gate on to Church Street. Pass the entrance to Holt Island on your left and follow the footpath signs for the Ouse Valley Way and The Thicket Path.

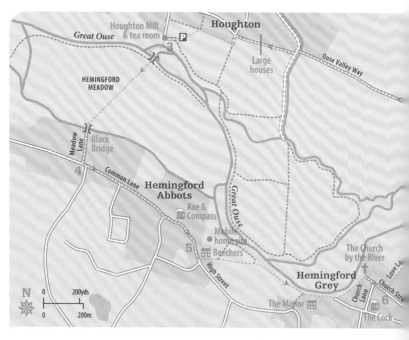

2 Take the surfaced path through The Thicket (a patch of woodland) and continue straight for about 875yds. Just after the path crosses a stream, follow it round to the left, then stay right on the surfaced track. Continue straight, passing large houses on your right at the edge of Houghton village. Just before the first house on the left, follow the public footpath sign left, then right. This track shortly leads to a kissing gate at the back of Houghton Mill car park. Cross the car park to Houghton Mill and tea room.

3 Walk directly through the mill and cross the bridge over the Great Ouse. Follow the surfaced path through Hemingford Meadow and cross the river at Black Bridge to reach Hemingford Abbots village. Continue straight on Meadow Lane.

4 At the end of Meadow Lane, turn left on to Common Lane. Continue straight as it merges into the High Street, passing the Axe and Compass pub on your left. Where the High Street snakes right, you'll pass a timbered and thatched cottage (Beechers) on your left. Immediately after the house, turn left down a track, following the footpath sign for Hemingford Grey.

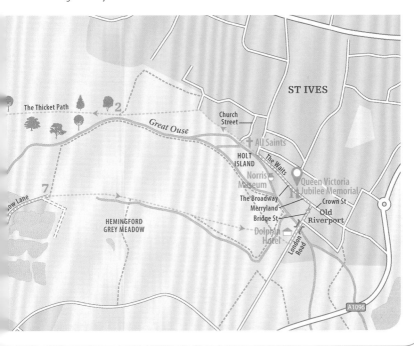

St Ives, The Hemingfords & Houghton Mill (continued)

5 Stay on the path as it passes a mobile home site and small meadows, leading to a gate. Go through the gate and continue on a riverside path with the river on your left. You are now in Hemingford Grey village. Pass the garden gate to The Manor on your right and look ahead for a picture-postcard view of The Church by the River. Where the footpath meets a dead-end road, keep left to rejoin the riverside path, which skirts the churchyard and emerges by the church gate.

6 Turn right on to Church Street and walk past a row of historic cottages. (To detour to The Cock pub, take the first right at Lodge Cottage on to Church Lane. The pub is a few paces away at the end of the lane. Retrace your steps to return to the route.)

Continue along Church Street, passing Cleveland Cottages on your right. Opposite number 22, turn left on to Love Lane. Keep left and straight when the path emerges on to a cul-de-sac and continue on the footpath. At the end of the path, cross to Meadow Lane, following the footpath sign for St Ives. At the end of the lane, where it narrows to a path, follow the footpath sign through the central metal gate and into Hemingford Grey Meadow.

7 Cross the meadow on the path, with views of St Ives ahead. The path leads through the southern part of the meadow but can sometimes be difficult to make out – look for the flattened grassy track and aim to the right of the furthest church spire in St Ives. The path leads to a gate and into the car park of the Dolphin Hotel. Cross the car park, exit on to London Road and turn left. Cross the bridge to the Old Riverport and continue straight on Bridge Street into the town centre. A left turn on to Merryland will bring you back to the Queen Victoria memorial.

WOODHURST TO KEYSTON

North of the Great Ouse, Cambridgeshire appears to be all fields, farms and pretty villages, with nothing much going on at all. Don't be deceived. Local landowners have put all this space to ingenious use. Between the cows and crops lie crocodiles and constrictor snakes, while the skies are roamed by serpent eagles and sparrowhawks, and the country pubs are some of Cambridgeshire's finest. In summer, don't be surprised if you hear the foot stamping of festivalgoers, or the thud of feet on the annual Pathfinder March.

14 THE RAPTOR FOUNDATION

The Heath, St Ives Rd, Woodhurst PE28 3BT ☏ 01487 741140 ☽ raptorfoundation.org.uk

Meander along the backroads north of St Ives and you'll spot little brown signs with an icon of an owl dotted around the countryside.

Follow one of these and you'll arrive at a pioneering sanctuary that helped to advance the understanding of raptor rehabilitation back in the early '90s. When Stewart and Liz McQuillan started caring for raptors in 1989, they discovered that few vets had any experience in working with birds of prey. One, however, was able to help. Vet and raptor enthusiast John Cooper shared his knowledge with the couple and, by 1991, the McQuillans' sanctuary had become a training centre for Royal Veterinary College students in Glasgow, Edinburgh and London.

The Raptor Foundation now cares for around 190 birds of prey, from common buzzards and kestrels, to serpent eagles, snowy owls and sparrowhawks – all of which you can meet during a visit. Some of the birds you'll see are more than 20 years old and one – Benjamin the golden eagle – was born in the early '70s. There are reptiles and meerkats to meet, plus daily flying displays where the raptors swoop over visitors' heads. You'll also learn about the centre's work, which involves rescuing, rehabilitating and releasing wild birds, taking in abandoned chicks and providing 24-hour care for injured raptors.

The first time I visited the foundation, a friend who was working here gave me a behind-the-scenes tour and an introduction to the life of a falconer. One of my jobs involved preparing a pile of dead chicks for the raptors' supper – an experience that confirmed I'm far too squeamish to look after my own bird of prey. However, budding falconers with stronger stomachs could book on to one of the centre's training courses which cover everything from handling to health care.

15 WOODHURST

A mile or so west of the Raptor Foundation is Woodhurst – one of the UK's best-surviving examples of an Anglo-Saxon ring village. It's thought that the shape of this village has been more or less unaltered since it was founded, with the settlement arranged along a roughly mile-long oval-shaped road. There is evidence of Roman occupation here – archaeological digs have uncovered pots, coins, a burial urn and several skeletons, one of which had its head chopped off. Sadly, many of the oldest buildings were destroyed by fire in the 1800s and, like many small villages, the days of the butcher, baker and blacksmith have gone. Nonetheless, Woodhurst has a close-knit community that includes heritage enthusiast Shirley Firth, who collates local history at woodhurst-cambs.com. What follows are the highlights of her historical village walk; guiding you past several former pubs, this would have made for a very wobbly pub crawl if you could time-travel back to the 1900s.

Start halfway along Church Street at the church of **St John the Baptist**, with its pepperpot bell turret; the church's oldest part is the 12th-century north wall. Walking east along Church Street you'll pass the white frontage of St John's House on your right – pub number one,

"Just past the bus shelter is the old village shop, which still features the Woodhurst General Stores sign"

it was known as **The Travellers Arms** and was particularly popular with RAF Wyton during World War II. In 1968, it was the last of Woodhurst's half-dozen pubs to close. Continuing along Church Street, the old **village pump** sits at the end of St John's Close. Just past the bus shelter is the old **village shop**, which still features the Woodhurst General Stores sign. Skirting a pond at the east end of the village, the white thatched cottage on your left was the much-loved **Three Horseshoes** pub (1799–1922). The hooks at the front were used to pull down burning thatch and, unique to Woodhurst, parts of the pub ceiling were made from Norfolk reed and manure. The other white thatch overlooking the pond is **Swan Weir**, a 16th/17th-century cottage that's thought to be the oldest surviving house in the village.

Following the pavement as it curves right on to South Street, you'll pass the stone manor of **Holdich Farmhouse** (c1760). Further along South Street, the simpler **Fullards Farmhouse** is recognisable by its green front door and window frames, and was home to the prominent Fuller family throughout the 18th century. Continue past the Willows and **Pear Tree Cottage** (18th century), walking on the verge until the pavement kicks back in at the western end. When you rejoin Church Street, the first house on your left is the 200-year-old Cherry Tree House, which was once **The Sun** pub. You're no longer in the conservation area now, so you'll pass modern houses on the way back to the church. Just before the church on your right, Harradine House was the old **Half Moon and Stars** pub and, next door, Church View was the **Farmer's Boy**. A drink at these neighbouring inns would have made a perfect end to our walk but, sadly, the landlords pulled their last pints more than 100 years ago. Today, parched villagers have to walk a 1½ miles across the fields to the nearest pub in Pidley (footpath off Wheatsheaf Rd).

16 JOHNSONS OF OLD HURST

Old Hurst PE28 3AF ✆ 01487 824658 ♲ johnsonsofoldhurst.co.uk ☺ Tue–Sun

A 35-stone crocodile isn't the first thing you'd expect to come across on a Cambridgeshire farm. And it's not alone: there were 15 crocs in residence when I visited, along with a royal python, a green-winged macaw, several iguanas and a mob of meerkats.

Johnsons of Old Hurst is a ten-minute drive north of both Huntingdon and St Ives, but it feels like another world. This working farm has been in the Johnson family since 1899 but it wasn't until the current Johnson, Andy, took over that he let his passion for reptiles run wild. Supported by conservation experts, he converted a cattle shed into a temperature-controlled tropical house and started to grow and share his collection of endangered species, working with expert conservationists that include Zoological Society of London fellow Ken Sims. There's also a children's play area and a walking trail around the farm. All the attractions are free of charge but it's a rare few that manage to resist the temptations of the tea room, steak house or vast farm shop. Everything operates with sustainability and waste reduction in mind – leftovers from the farm shop's butchery get fed to the crocodiles.

¶¶ FOOD & DRINK

True to their slogan, Johnsons is a real 'farm to fork' sort of place, with many of their ingredients produced locally or on the farm itself. In **The Eccentric Englishman Tea Room**, I tucked into a very reasonably priced steak baguette with a view of the farm's own cattle through the window – if that's a little too close to the bone, there are plenty of good veggie options too. Across from the tea room, the **Steak House** serves lunches, evening meals and a cracking Sunday carvery in a seriously impressive converted barn, complete with a life-sized bronze sculpture of a lion.

Opposite the café is the **farm shop**, where you can easily buy all of your weekly groceries and more. Much of the meat in the butchery is produced on the farm, they bake their own breads and pastries on site, and you can buy fenland fruit and veg, small-batch gins and beers, and UK cheeses.

17 BROUGHTON

A couple of miles northwest of Old Hurst is Broughton. This ancient farming village developed around a moated manor that was an important meeting place for the Abbots of Ramsey and owned by the Cromwells from 1570. Today, all that's left of the manor is a grassy mound off Illings Lane – you can access it via the waymarked Pathfinder footpath. Thankfully, more is left of the village itself. At its heart is the Crown Inn and the church of All Saints. Parts of the church date back to the 1100s but much of the structure is 13th and 14th century, built with Barnack stone (se box, page 146). Restoration work in the 19th and 20th centuries revealed a 15th-century Doom Painting on the chancel arch, which you can see along with two paintings of Adam and Eve.

After a nosey around the church, take a wander around the village's early 17th-century houses. Diagonally opposite the church on School Road, the Elizabethan rectory is thought to have been built by Sir Oliver Cromwell (uncle of the Lord Protector) around 1600. Just around the corner on Bridge Road, the Flemish bonding and Dutch gables at Bridge Farm are a reminder of the Dutch engineers who settled here when they came to drain the Fens (see box, page 168). Closer to the church on Bridge Road is the Old Brewhouse (now a converted barn) and, east of the pub on Causeway Road, the little brick hut next to the village sign is a 19th-century lock-up. A plaque on the wall introduces some of the village's former characters.

¶¶ FOOD & DRINK

The Crown Inn PE28 3AY ✐ 01487 824428 ⊘ thecrowninnrestaurant.co.uk ⊙ Tue–Sun. A popular gastro-pub with an idyllic village setting, The Crown is often hailed as having one of the best restaurants in the area. They focus on local, seasonal and sustainable produce, and cater well for vegan, gluten-free and dairy-free diners. Choose from pub classics or modern mains, such as pan-fried basil polenta or lamb with capers and balsamic.

18 ABBOTS RIPTON

🏠 **The Elm** (page 316)

As far as quaint Cambridgeshire villages go, Abbots Ripton (five miles west of Broughton) does an excellent job of adhering to the English idyll, with its thatched cottages, cosy pub, primary school, historic church, well-kept green and traditional village shop. Way out in the Cambridgeshire countryside, surrounded by open fields, woodlands and other thatched villages, it's a good base for pub walks. All this space and serenity also lends itself to another pleasure-seeking pastime: festivals. On the village's southeast fringe is **Abbots Ripton Hall** on the de Ramsey estate, owned by the Fellowes family since 1737. Here, eldest son Freddie Fellowes (heir to the title Baron de Ramsey) launched the Secret Garden Party in 2014. Set in the landscaped gardens of the family's Georgian farmhouse, the festival hosted around 30,000 revellers each year, including Prince Harry in 2014. Secret Garden Party threw its final wild weekend in 2017, with the new We Out Here festival taking over the site in 2019. I'm sure it won't be the last.

Abbots Ripton & Broughton pub walks

The open countryside around Abbots Ripton and Broughton is ripe for a ramble, with wildlife-rich hedgerows, ancient woodland and the rolling grounds of Abbots Ripton estate, plus two of Huntingdonshire's best pubs for foodies. From The Crown in Broughton, you could follow the waymarked Pathfinder footpath west to Kings Ripton (1½ miles) and then zigzag across the fields to The Abbot's Elm (2½ miles). Northeast of Abbots Ripton, public footpaths skirt ancient Wennington Wood and the de Ramsey's estate before following the field edges eastwards back to Broughton. Use OS Explorer map 225 *Huntingdon & St Ives* to plan a circular walk through the villages and estate (roughly eight miles) or a shorter stroll from either pub. Keep your eyes peeled for red kites, brown hares and, in late summer, hedgerow blackberries.

 FOOD & DRINK

Abbots Ripton Village Stores Station Rd, PE28 2PA. A true village shop that sells a bit of everything, including fresh coffees, artisan breads from the local baker, and fresh pastries baked on site. Other local produce includes Cambridgeshire honey, sausages and small-batch sloe gin. The picnic benches out front are a welcome sight for cyclists and ramblers.

BARONS DE RAMSEY

The Fellowes family have long and important links with Huntingdonshire and Ramsey Abbey (page 201). Coulson Fellowes, who represented Huntingdonshire in the House of Commons from 1741 to 1761, bought Ramsey Abbey House and the site of the former abbey in 1737. The Ramsey estate then passed through generations of Fellowes, as did the family tradition of representing Huntingdonshire. In 1887 Edward Fellowes was made the first Baron de Ramsey — a title which passed to William Henry Fellowes in 1887, followed by his son Ailwyn Edward Fellowes (third Baron de Ramsey) in 1926. Ailwyn vacated the residence at Ramsey and moved the family seat to Abbots Ripton Hall, where it remains today. Ailwyn's son, John Fellowes, became the fourth Baron de Ramsey in 1993, with his son Freddie next in line to take over.

The Elm Moat Ln, PE28 2PD ✐ 01487 773773 ⌂ the-elm.co.uk. After a devastating fire in 2010, this thatched country inn was restored by Lord and Lady de Ramsey. The menu includes pub classics and seasonal specials, such as summer vegetable broth or venison with aubergine and pine nuts. Game and veg is taken from the de Ramsey estate, fish is sourced locally and several ingredients are foraged. Enjoy the crackling fire in winter or the beautiful garden in summer.

19 ALCONBURY WEALD

If the name 'Alconbury' sounds familiar, you may be thinking of RAF Alconbury. East of the A1, this former airbase was occupied by the United States Air Force (USAF) during World War II and the Cold War. Flying ceased in 1995 and USAF activities were scaled back. With a vast area of land lying unused on the outskirts of Huntingdon, it was only a matter of time before a major housing development took hold. This started to take shape in 2009, with the vision for Alconbury Weald – a 1,400-acre settlement of homes, schools, leisure facilities and business spaces, it has become the largest new residential development scheme under construction in Britain and is expected to take around 20 years to complete.

Unless you have a penchant for urban planning, you're probably wondering what a massive housing development is doing in a Slow guide. Bear with me. Amid its 5,000-plus new homes, Alconbury Weald aims to embrace its military past, restore its listed buildings and create a Heritage Area at its heart. The first of these repurposed sites is an **RAF Watch Office**, built in 1940–41 – this World War II relic is among the few of its kind remaining in the UK. Now open as a café/bistro serving brunch, lunch and world tapas (The Boulevard, PE28 4XA ✐ 01480 716262 ⌂ bohemiaalconburyweald.com ◷ 08.00–17.00 Mon–Thu, 08.00–noon Fri–Sat 09.00–15.00 Sun), you'll find it near to the Club building, which itself is home to a library and heritage space. Other heritage buildings to be developed include a Cold War Avionics Building and U2 Spy Plane Hangar. The line of the former runway will form part of the Heritage Area, with the original flight strip becoming a 'Runway Park' of trees, water features and memorials at key take-off points where pilots left and never returned. Much of this heritage work is yet to take place but new

"Alconbury Weald aims to embrace its military past, restore its listed buildings and create a Heritage Area"

elements are regularly being added. Private tours can be arranged via ✎ 01480 413141 or ✉ info@alconbury-weald.co.uk.

20 THE NORTHAMPTONSHIRE BORDER VILLAGES

West of the A1, where the county rubs against the Northamptonshire border, the spaces between settlements widens, with farms, fields and villages scattered either side of the A14. There isn't a whole lot here to draw the visitor other than cycle rides or Sunday drives, perhaps stopping off for a drink or bite in a village pub – for Slow travellers, this probably sounds ideal.

Venture down the unmarked roads west of Alconbury and the A1 to discover sleepy settlements like **Leighton Bromswold**, where the traditional village pub makes a good pit stop for cyclists. Wander towards the village church and you'll find a curious sight: two benches sitting ceremoniously around a lump of stone. This is the Leightonstone – an ancient marker where taxes were collected and criminals tried.

Wiggle your way northwest towards the B660 and you'll reach the nostalgic Swan pub in **Old Weston**, with the 300-year-old cottages in **Brington** sitting two miles to the south. The pretty village of **Molesworth** sits 1½ miles west of Brington, and another two miles west is **Bythorn** with its 500-year-old church, which can be hard to spot, owing to its lack of spire – after leaning to one side, the spire was removed in the '60s and replaced with a copper cap.

"Keyston has an interesting village hall in a converted threshing barn, plus a 15th-century Grade I-listed church"

A hop across the busy A14 (walkers and cyclists should use the footbridge) brings you to **Keyston**, which has an interesting village hall in a converted threshing barn, plus a 15th-century Grade I-listed church with fine spire and elaborate west porch. Covered with a cloth at the back of the church is a rare oaken cadaver – a wooden skeleton memorial from a 15th-century tomb, radiocarbon tests have given an estimated carving date of c1415. To access the church, contact the vicar (✎ 01832 710881) for the key.

Three miles southeast of Keyston, **Covington** lays claim to historic Huntingdonshire's highest point – but don't hold your breath: at 265ft, Huntingdonshire (when it was an official county) claimed the lowest county highpoint in England. The summit sits unmarked, one mile northwest of the village centre, in the aptly named **Boring Field** (also

WEST COUNTRY CYCLE RIDES

The quiet country roads in the far west are perfect for exploring on two wheels, with the majority of heavy traffic sticking religiously to the A14. That said, there are no cycle paths here, so do be aware of farm vehicles and commuters. The Cambridgeshire County Council website (⬧ cambridgeshire.gov. uk) has a good 23-mile or 14-mile loop to download, which include all of the villages I've mentioned in this section, and more. To find it, search for 'cycle routes and maps', scroll through the Huntingdonshire cycle rides section and select 'Spaldwick & Keyston'. If planning your own route, use OS Explorer map 225 *Huntingdon & St Ives*. Please note that there are two footbridges to safely cross the A14 — one at Bythorn and the other near Catworth — so there is no need to risk your life.

known as Bush Ground). From Covington, footpaths and country roads lead northeast to **Catworth**, where the prettiest part of the village (on Church Rd) has 300-year-old cottages and a 13th-century church. Spaldwick, which sits 2½ miles west via footpaths boasts a 17th-century village pub and the tallest church spire in Huntingdonshire.

🍴 FOOD & DRINK

The George Inn 5–7 High St, Spaldwick PE28 0TD ✆ 01480 890293 ⬧ thegeorgespaldwick.co.uk. A mere hop off the A14, it's far nicer to stop for a coffee or bite at The George than at Spaldwick services, 400m down the road. Expect a revamped 17th-century coaching inn with modern décor, old beams and an open fireplace. The menu focuses on local, free-range, organic and bio-dynamic produce.

The Green Man 39 The Av, Leighton Bromswold PE28 5AW ✆ 1480 890238 ⬧ greenmanleightonbromswold.co.uk. A proper village inn, this was one of the first English pubs to be licensed as an ale and gin house (27 January 1650). They serve hearty grub with locally sourced ingredients. In their own words: 'we are stuck in a time warp but often the old ways are normally the best, when it comes to running a pub anyway!'

The Pheasant at Keyston PE28 0RE ✆ 01832 710303 ⬧ thepheasantatkeyston.co.uk ◔ Wed–Sun. Reflecting its rural surroundings, this award-winning pub has a true country feel, with open fires, oak beams and paintings of rural scenes on the walls. With a reputation for good food, the menu changes daily and focuses on seasonal and local produce, with dishes like asparagus and poached egg, 24-hour pork belly with black pudding mash and rhubarb crumble with ice cream.

The Swan Main St, Old Weston PE28 5LL ✆ 01832 293400 ◔ kitchen closed Mon, Tue & Thu. A real step back in time, everyone should experience The Swan at least once. Don't expect anything fancy, just honest food and beer. There's a simple main bar and restaurant, plus a games room with Northamptonshire skittles. Wednesday is fish and chips night; it's best to book ahead so the chef can order enough in.

GRAFHAM WATER & THE WEST

🏕 **Grafham Water Caravan Club Site** (page 316)

England's third-biggest reservoir and the largest lake in Cambridgeshire, Grafham Water is a 20th-century creation, carved out of the landscape to provide water for a wave of urban development in the 1960s. In a county that lacks mountains, beaches and big forests, Grafham is a magnet for outdoorsy folk who come here to walk, cycle, sail, windsurf, paddleboard and picnic.

Catherine of Aragon would have experienced a very different landscape several centuries ago when she arrived in Huntingdonshire and was held in nearby Buckden and Kimbolton.

21 KIMBOLTON

🏠 **The Warren House** (page 316)

Kimbolton owes its fame to its crenellated 'castle', but this well-heeled village is worth a visit in its own right – which is just as well, as the castle (now a private girls' school) only opens to the public once or twice a year. Colourful façades line the wide main street, which is framed at one end by the castle and at the other by the church – for a striking first impression, arrive on the High Street from the western end. Kimbolton has a feeling of yesteryear, with a traditional hardware store, pharmacy and post office, and pretty backstreets lined with quaint cottages. It's not surprising that house prices here are among the highest in Huntingdonshire. Behind the church, a little alleyway called 'Carnaby' leads over the meandering River Kym to a pristine cemetery, where a plaque reads 'Best Kept Village 1989'. It's fair to say that Kimbolton has maintained its high standards ever since.

From Norman castle to public school, **Kimbolton Castle** (🖱 kimbolton.cambs.sch.uk/castleopen ☉ annual open days or by appointment) – actually a fortified mansion – has a long and colourful history, yet its fame rests on a bite-sized period of the 16th century. In 1534, Catherine of Aragon, Henry VIII's first wife, was exiled to the castle and lived out her days here until 1536. Her body was carried to Peterborough Cathedral (page 134) in a two-day procession that attracted a whole troop of priests, maids and mourners. Some believe that she still haunts the castle hallways.

Another of Kimbolton's former residents (and alleged ghosts) is Sir John Popham. The judge who trialled Guy Fawkes, Popham lived at the castle 70 years after Catherine's death and is said to have murdered his baby daughter here. In 1615, the Montagues (the Earls and Dukes of Manchester) moved in and the castle remained with the family for 335 years. During this time, the renowned 18th-century architect Sir John Vanbrugh undertook an extensive phase of rebuilding and added the battlements to reflect the mansion's early days as a Norman castle. Venetian artist Giovanni Antonio Pellegrini carried out a series of commissions and his paintings still adorn some of the walls and ceilings. In 1950, the house was sold to Kimbolton School. On open days, you can tour the State Rooms, marvel at Pellegrini's murals, learn more about the castle's history and stroll around the wooded grounds. You can also stay at the Warren House – the former home of the estate's gamekeeper, which is now a self-catering cottage owned by the Landmark Trust (page 316).

Even if you're not interested in churches, I'd urge you to step inside **St Andrew's** (standrew-kimbolton.org.uk) or arrange a guided tour – you can do so through the website. There's lots to see, as I found out when a Kimbolton resident kindly showed me around. 'Let me show you something that you wouldn't expect in a church,' he said, pointing to the far corner of the south aisle where a stone carving gazed back at me between a pair of spread-eagled legs. He went on to show me the bullet holes 'from Cromwell's day' in the oak church door, along with the ancient breastplate that hangs above it – 'there used to be a pair of crossed swords until someone stole them'. As we walked through the north aisle, he paused solemnly beside a memorial plaque dedicated to the 379th Bombardment Group (USAF) who served at Kimbolton airfield during World War II. Next, we entered the north chapel where he pointed out another garish grotesque, 'I think the stonemason was having some fun'. But the real secrets of this chapel, I discovered, lay beneath my feet. 'The Earls and Dukes of Manchester are buried in a vault where you're standing,' he told me. 'They were all members of the Montague family who lived at Kimbolton Castle.' Monuments to the Montague family dominate St Andrew's, and one of the best is found in

THE TIFFANY WINDOW

At the back of St Andrew's Church is a stained-glass window that seems brighter, bolder and more striking than the others. This is the Tiffany Window, a memorial to the twin daughters of the Duchess of Manchester, who lived at Kimbolton Castle and outlived them both. Both twins died of tuberculosis, the first aged 16 and the second five years later, aged 21. In their memory, the twins' mother commissioned the American designer Louis Comfort Tiffany to create a stained-glass window. A leader of America's Art Nouveau movement and the son of the Tiffany & Co jewellery founder, Louis also created works for Mark Twain and the US president. Created in 1901, the window's southern aspect allows it to beam with sunlight. There are many Tiffany windows in the USA but this is one of just a handful in England, and the only one in a parish church.

the south chapel. Here, young twins are commemorated in the Tiffany Window. For the full effect, he told me to face the window and take a few steps back so that I had both the twins' window and a marble bas-relief dedicated to their mother in my line of sight. 'The positioning of these two dedications is no accident,' he explained.

FOOD & DRINK

There's a good choice of places to eat and drink on Kimbolton High Street, from 'proper pubs' like **The Saddle** (⏂ 01480 860408) to independent cafés, **Crawfords** (⏂ 01480 861000 ◷ Mon–Sat) and **Olivers Café** (⏂ 01480 860217 ◷ Mon–Sat).

22 GRAFHAM WATER

Grafham Water Visitor Centre, Marlow Park, PE28 0BH ⏂ 01480 812154
⏂ anglianwaterparks.co.uk/grafham-water ◷ visitor centre & café: 11.00–15.00 Mon–Fri, 11.00–16.00 Sat & Sun; bike hire: 09.00–17.30 daily

I've lost count of the number of times I've cycled, strolled and windsurfed at Grafham Water. Growing up nearby, it was a go-to spot for family bike rides, sponsored school walks and birthday barbecues. Created in the 1960s, Grafham was one of the first UK reservoirs to combine water supply with recreation. It was colonised with wildlife from the outset, and the sailing club, trout fishery and nature reserve were opened by Prince Philip on the same day as the water treatment works.

This manmade lake has wide appeal, loved as it is by locals and visited by sailors from far and wide. At almost three miles long and just under 1½ miles wide, it's large enough to sail across or circumnavigate, yet not too big to intimidate. A track follows the shoreline for almost ten miles – perfect for a big walk or half-day bike ride (see box, below). It's the county's best sailing spot for dinghy sailors and windsurfers, with the flat Cambridgeshire landscape providing relatively few obstructions to the wind. Another trump card is the lake's seclusion: a road traces the eastern shoreline between the little villages of **Perry** and **Grafham**, but the western edge is traffic-free, offering a rare slice of waterside tranquillity.

You've got a choice of two main hubs for parking and amenities. **Marlow Park** (PE28 0BH) on the northeast shore is the main base for families and cyclists. Here, you'll find the visitor centre, café and bike

Cycle ride: Grafham Water circular

✳ OS Explorer map 225 *Huntingdon & St Ives*; start: Marlow Park ♀ TL165681; 10 miles; easy (flat all the way)

With a gravelly track circumnavigating the reservoir, walking or cycling around Grafham Water is a delight at any time of year. The cycle-hire shop at Marlow Park (PE28 0BH) is the obvious place to start pedalling and most people tend to ride in an anti-clockwise direction, but there are no real rules. Walkers and bikers use the same path for much of the way, except at Grafham village where the footpath avoids the village and sticks to the water's edge. The cycle route is flat, mostly off-road and easy to follow, so there's no real need for a map.

1 Cycle northwest out of Marlow Park, riding beside the water's edge with the lake on your left. After half a mile, turn right on to Church Hill, following the sign for National Cycle Network Route 12.

2 At the T-junction, turn left on to Church Road (coming off NCN12) and follow it through Grafham village, all the way to the end where the road meets the lakeside track, just past Hill Farm on your left.

3 Stay on the lakeside track (the route is obvious) for four miles as it leads through fragments of ancient woodland and the nature reserve to arrive at Mander Park (you're roughly halfway at this point, so you could stop for a snack at the café, or continue to the Wheatsheaf in West Perry a little further on).

4 Where the cycle track ends at Mander Park, turn left on to the B661 and follow the road through West Perry, passing The Wheatsheaf on your right. After the pub, use the cycle track beside the B661, which leads through East Perry.

hire (rutlandcycling.com/pages/rutland-cycling-grafham.aspx), plus big grassy stretches for outdoor games. On the south shore, **Mander Park**'s (PE28 0BX) fishing lodge and café sit next to **Grafham Water Park**, which provides RYA watersports courses and taster sessions at the sailing club. Less than a mile to the east, **Plummer Park** has parking but no other facilities.

Only accessible by foot, bike or boat, the quieter western end has the nature reserve and bird sanctuary, along with pockets of ancient woodland and wildflower meadows. Position yourself in a bird hide and spy on rare and scarce species like the grey phalarope and, if you're lucky,

5   Stay on the cycle path as it bends left, away from the B661, just before the 'Treatment Works' sign. Follow the cycle track beside the lake, passing a dam and 1960s water tower at the east end. Stick to the track as it bears left and arrives back at Marlow Park, where ice cream or hot chocolate awaits in the café.

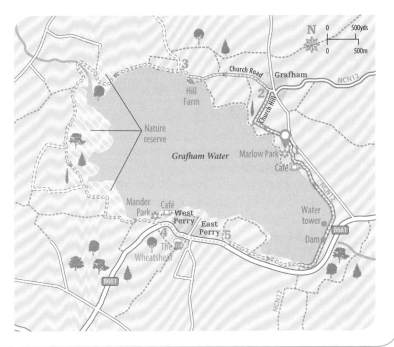

the great northern diver. Visit in spring for avocet and bullfinches, or come in summer for mute swans. Autumn sees sandpipers, dunlin and other waders, followed by winter waterbirds and huge flocks of gulls.

¶¶ FOOD & DRINK

To make the most of this waterside setting, it's best to bring a picnic or use the fixed barbecue stands at Marlow Park or Mander Park. Otherwise, the cafés at both parks offer hot and cold food – Marlow Park's café is in the visitor centre, and the Harbour View Café Bar (✐ 01480 812110) at Mander Park has a balcony over the water. Back from the reservoir, **The Wheatsheaf** in West Perry (✐ wheatsheafperry.com) has a reputation for good food. A mile and a half north of Marlow Park, the 14th-century **Mermaid** in Ellington (✐ themermaidellington.com) has a regularly changing menu that includes the likes of seasonal partridge from the local gamekeeper.

23 BUCKDEN

🏠 **The George** (page 315), **The Lion Hotel** (page 315)

Roughly one mile east of Grafham Water and one mile west of the River Great Ouse, this fine historical village has an air of superiority, with its crenellated 'palace', designer womenswear shop (✐ annefurbank.co.uk) and elegant Georgian houses. The first time I visited, I had a distinct feeling that Buckden was checking me out to see if I'd fit in. Thankfully, my unease was unwarranted, as the people I met here couldn't have been more welcoming.

Dominating the High Street are two former coaching inns: the modernised 18th-century **George Hotel** and the 15th/16th century **Lion Hotel**, which retains more of its original charm. They sit directly opposite each other at the heart of the village, on what was once the Great North Road – as with many Cambridgeshire villages, Buckden owes its early prosperity to this major north–south route. Back then, the village would have been busy with royal guests visiting Buckden Palace, and a stream of Great North Road travellers making use of the village's 13 or so coaching inns. Today, it's a popular place to stop for coffee or lunch. It also makes a good base for an overnight stay and, although small, is the sort of place that Slow travellers may be inclined to linger.

Rising above Buckden High Street are the turrets of **Buckden Towers** (High St, PE19 5TA ✐ fobt.org.uk), formerly known as Buckden Palace. For 650 years, this red-brick fortress was home to the powerful Bishops of Lincoln. Since 1956, Buckden Towers has been used by the Claretian

Missionaries, who have carried out much restoration work and now use the site as a retreat centre. The gardens and grounds are open for the public to explore at leisure, but to learn more and hopefully see inside you'll need to visit on one of the Heritage Open Days in September, or arrange an hour-long tour through the Friends of Buckden Towers (⏍ fobt.org.uk/aboutTowers.html).

Sealed behind a wall, moat and outer bailey, the manor harks back to an era when bishops were wealthy lords who held military roles. The original building that stood on this site was the home of St Hugh, Bishop of Lincoln between 1186 and 1200. Destroyed by fire in 1291, only the foundations of the original building remain. The most extensive period of rebuilding took place in the 15th century, with Bishop John Russell credited for completing the striking features that stand today. The iconic gatehouse and Great Tower are the very same that Catherine of Aragon would have seen when she arrived in 1533. Exiled from court by Henry VIII, she was held at Buckden before being transferred to Kimbolton Castle (page 117). Catherine was just one of Buckden's many royal visitors. Others included Henry VIII himself and his fifth wife Catherine Howard, as well as Henry III (1248) and James I (1619). The palace fell into disrepair in the 17th century and was seized by Parliament during the Civil War (1642–51), before being returned to the See of Lincoln following the Restoration of the monarchy in 1660. In the 18th and early 19th centuries the palace found itself in a prime position on the Great North Road, and its visitors stayed at grand coaching inns, such as The Lion. By the mid 1800s, the importance of the palace had diminished and parts of the buildings were demolished. The moat was filled in and a Victorian house was built on the site in 1872. It later served as a World War I Red Cross hospital and a shelter during the Blitz.

When you visit, be sure to enter the grounds from the High Street for the most striking vista. Walk through the original gatehouse to the main courtyard, where you'll be greeted by a statue of St Hugh and a modern (rather ugly) Roman Catholic church. Climb the steps to the battlements on the raised wall to your right and peer down on the replica Tudor knot garden. Started in 1992 to commemorate Catherine of Aragon, the garden is planted with culinary, medicinal and dye-making herbs which would have been used during Catherine's lifetime. The garden is usually locked but you can ask for a key from the main house on weekdays. The rest of the grounds include well-kept gardens with a large

1

CAMBRIDGESHIRE WATERWAYS

Waterways have always been a defining feature of the Cambridgeshire landscape, from the ancient trade routes on the rivers Nene and Great Ouse, to wildlife-rich wetlands and a vast network of drainage ditches that help to drain the Fens and keep floodwaters in check.

1 Raised footpaths, like those at Wicken Fen, help you to keep your feet dry when the rivers are in flood.

2

SS

3

2 The Ouse Washes is the largest area of washland in the UK, attracting thousands of ducks and whooper swans in winter. 3 March is popular with narrowboaters, with the old course of the River Nene running through the town centre. 4 Experiencing Cambridgeshire by boat is a popular pastime and competitive sport, with regular rowing races taking place on the Cam and Great Ouse. 5 A grid pattern of drainage ditches cuts through the Fens and helps to manage the risk of flooding. 6 Konik ponies are used to graze semi-wild patches of fenland, like the water meadows at Wicken Fen.

PETER MOULTON/S

4

5

SS

6

ANDY335

pond and, next to the towers, the medieval church of St Mary with its 13th-century porch and 15th-century nave. If you've booked a guided tour, you'll receive a detailed history of the grounds and, when they're not in use, a tour of the church and its chapels, plus a peek inside the King's Room in the tower itself – occupying the entire ground floor of the tower, this stately room has a timber-beamed ceiling and large stone fireplace where Catherine of Aragon would have warmed herself.

FOOD & DRINK

Day's of Buckden 28 High St, PE19 5XA ☏ 01480 810272. Traditional family butcher selling locally sourced meat, veg, groceries and deli items. Highly recommended by locals.

The George 39 High St, PE19 5XA ☏ 01480 812300 ⌕ thegeorgebuckden.com. Modernised 18th-century coaching inn with a wine bar, brasserie and private dining room. The breakfast menu ranges from full English to smashed avocado, moving on to falafel or pulled pork sandwiches for lunch, and aged sirloin or cauliflower steaks for supper. They also serve coffees and cream teas.

The Lion 44–46 High St, PE19 5XA ☏ 01480 810313 ⌕ thelionbuckden.com. Former coaching inn with impressive inglenook fireplace, panelled walls and wooden beams. The Ivy Room at the back has a beautiful 'star spangled' ceiling adorned with fairy lights. The à la carte menu includes British classics, such as liver and bacon, lamb shank, jam roly-poly and Eton mess.

The award-winning Slow Travel series from Bradt Guides

Over 20 regional guides across Britain.
See the full list at bradtguides.com/slowtravel.

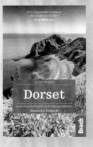

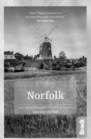

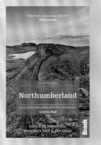

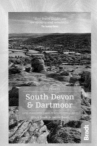

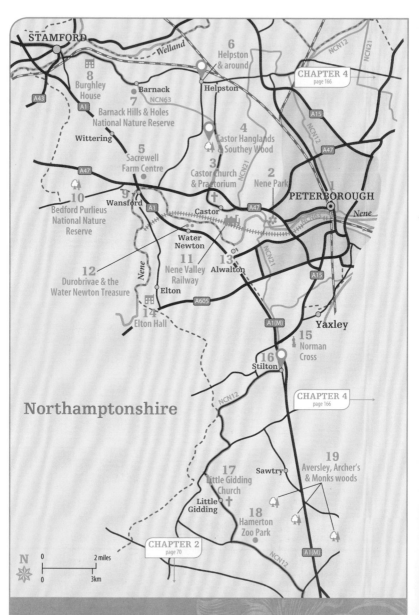

STAMFORD

Welland

6
Helpston
& around

Helpston

CHAPTER 4
page 166

8
Burghley
House

Barnack

7
Barnack Hills & Holes
National Nature Reserve

NCN63

4
Castor Hanglands
& Southey Wood

Wittering

5
Sacrewell
Farm Centre

3
Castor Church
& Praetorium

2
Nene Park

PETERBOROUGH

Nene

10
Bedford Purlieus
National Nature
Reserve

9
Wansford

Castor

12
Durobrivae & the
Water Newton Treasure

Water
Newton

11
Nene Valley
Railway

13
Alwalton

Nene

Elton

14
Elton Hall

A605

A1(M)

Yaxley

15
Norman
Cross

16
Stilton

Northamptonshire

CHAPTER 4
page 166

19
Aversley, Archer's
& Monks woods

17
Little Gidding
Church

Sawtry

Little
Gidding

18
Hamerton
Zoo Park

NCN12

CHAPTER 2
page 70

N

0   2 miles

0   3km

THE UPPER NENE VALLEY & GREAT NORTH ROAD

3
THE UPPER NENE VALLEY & GREAT NORTH ROAD

The Upper Nene Valley boasts one of the prettiest stretches of river in the county. Here, the River Nene (pronounced 'neen' like 'keen' in these parts, or 'nen' like 'pen' further south) performs dramatic loops past sleepy villages, golden fields and the fen-edge city of Peterborough, before it becomes channelised and joins the great fenland drainage system to the east. Peterborough itself holds limited Slow appeal, save for its magnificent cathedral – a Norman masterpiece that is one of England's finest.

The rural villages northwest of Peterborough are a complete contrast to the city and hold a wonderful rural charm. Castor's striking church sits atop the second-largest excavated Roman palace in England, while Helpston was the home of England's greatest peasant poet John Clare (1793–1864), whose childhood home is now a museum dedicated to him. Nearby, the ancient quarry at Barnack provided stone for the great fenland monasteries and the colleges of Cambridge University; today it's a fairy-tale landscape, rich in rare orchids. A few miles west, spilling over into Lincolnshire, is Burghley estate, home to England's greatest Elizabethan house.

Charging through west Cambridgeshire, the A1 (England's longest numbered road) bores south towards Huntingdon. This north–south artery is a successor to Britain's earliest public highway – the Great North Road – which heralded in the golden era of coaching. You can still see glimmers of this heyday, with two Cambridgeshire villages evoking its spirit particularly well: Wansford's wide street is dominated by the historic Haycock coaching inn, while the Bell Inn at Stilton still rides on the fame of its stinky cheese. The days of the Great North Road were numbered with the arrival of the first railways – a period you can travel back to by riding a heritage steam train along the Nene Valley Railway, which chugs past the lakes and meadows of Nene Park and continues into Peterborough, within walking distance of the cathedral.

GETTING AROUND

The A1 is northwest Cambridgeshire's major highway, connecting Huntingdon and St Neots with Peterborough and bypassing pretty villages along the way. Past Peterborough, it veers northwest to Stamford (Lincolnshire), while the A47 heads east to the Fens and west to Leicester. The A1 is the fastest way to get around but I'd urge you to avoid it where possible – there's far more charm on the cycle routes, heritage railway and river.

TRAINS

Peterborough sits on the East Coast Main Line between London and Edinburgh. From Peterborough station, you can travel to Cambridge in less than an hour (⊘ crosscountrytrains.co.uk), and direct to Huntingdon (14 minutes) or St Neots (24 minutes) with Thameslink (⊘ thameslinkrailway.com). Other local destinations from Peterborough include Whittlesey (seven minutes), March (15 minutes) and Ely (around 30 minutes). The Nene Valley Railway (page 152) runs a regular programme of heritage trains between Yarwell Junction, Wansford Station, Ferry Meadows and Peterborough (⊘ nvr. org.uk).

BUSES

Peterborough's Queensgate Bus Station is a hub for both local buses and long-distance coaches. For local travel, the villages nearest to Peterborough receive the best services, with Stagecoach (⊘ stagecoachbus.com) and Delaine buses (⊘ delainebuses.com) covering most routes. Some villages and attractions can also be accessed via the CallConnect on-demand minibuses (⊘ lincsbus. info/callconnect). Villages further south are better connected to Huntingdon than Peterborough, using Dews Coaches and Go Whippet – The Giddings and Hamerton Zoo Park are on the Huntingdon–Leighton Bromswold Go Whippet 401.

CYCLING

Peterborough Green Wheel is a network of cycle routes that connects villages and attractions via waymarked cycle paths, quiet roads and urban cycle lanes, which link up with the National Cycle Network

TOURIST INFORMATION

Peterborough Town Hall, Bridge St, PE1 1HG ✆ 01733 452336 �online visitpeterborough. com

(NCN). Green Wheel routes fan out from central Peterborough but it's better to avoid the city itself and stick to the village routes – there's little joy to be had in pedalling through suburbs like Bretton. The route that follows NCN63 is the exception – this traffic-free section weaves between Nene Park (page 137) and the city, linking with NCN12 which takes you directly to the cathedral.

For family-friendly rides, cycling around Nene Park is by far your best option. More confident riders should check out the suggested routes on ⌂ travelchoice.org.uk/cycling/peterborough-routes, or plan longer rides – NCN12, for example, runs through several villages between Peterborough and Hamerton Zoo.

CYCLE HIRE

Brompton Bike Hire Dock #4287, Station Rd, Peterborough PE1 1QL ✆ 0203 474 0700 ⌂ bromptonbikehire.com

Rutland Cycling Summer: Nene Outdoor, Lakeside Activity Centre, Ferry Meadows, PE2 5UU ✆ 01733 236103 ⌂ rutlandcycling.com/pages/cycle-hire-ferry-meadows ⏱ 10.00–16.00 weekends, bank hols & school holidays, winter: Ham Ln, PE2 5UU ✆ 01733 371013 ⏱ 11.00–16.00 Tue–Sun, plus Mon during school holidays & bank hols

WALKING

The Nene Valley has plenty of variety for walkers, with woodlands, nature reserves and glorious open countryside, along with pretty villages and atmospheric pubs. Nene Park gives you lots of options, while the waymarked routes around Castor Hanglands (page 141) are magical on sunny days, as are the footpaths around ancient Bedford Purlieus wood (page 151). To add history to your ramble, you can follow in John Clare's footsteps at Helpston (page 142), seek out the deserted church near Stilton (page 160), or join a guided Roman relics walk from Castor (see box, page 139). The long-distance Nene Way also tracks through this chapter, wiggling for ten miles between Yarwell Junction and Peterborough, and the Hereward Way meets the Nene Way at Sibson and follows the river to the city.

THE UPPER NENE VALLEY &
GREAT NORTH ROAD

The Upper Nene Valley boasts a beautiful stretch of river, which meanders past villages, wildlife-rich countryside and the city of Peterborough. It is also home to relics of the old Great North Road, with former coaching inns still standing where this ancient trackway once passed.

JASON BALLARD/A

3

1 At the heart of Nene Park are watersports lakes, wildlife areas and perfect picnic meadows. 2 Peterborough has one of the finest Norman cathedrals in England, with a wooden ceiling that is the only one of its type surviving in Britain. 3 Barnack Hills and Holes is a unique nature reserve that was once one of England's most important medieval quarries. 4 The smart village of Wansford sits by the River Nene and was largely designed by the 19th-century architect Samuel Sanders Teulon. 5 The Bell Inn in Stilton was one of the most famous coaching inns on the Great North Road and is the original home of Stilton cheese. 6 Helpston is home to John Clare Cottage – a museum that pays homage to England's greatest peasant poet, who grew up in the village.

PETERBOROUGH & CLARE COUNTRY

Peterborough and many of its surrounding villages lie within a unitary authority that's both part of Cambridgeshire and an entity all of its own. The northwest corner of this region, where the county rubs against the borders of neighbouring Northamptonshire and Lincolnshire, has a unique character, with soft undulations and charming honey-coloured villages that are in sharp contrast to the flat, stoneless Fens that border Peterborough to the east. This is Clare country, where the 19th-century poet John Clare lived, roamed and wrote.

1 PETERBOROUGH

The county's biggest city, Peterborough is larger than Cambridge itself. As a teenager living nearby in the '90s, I spent most of my pocket money here, thanks to the vast city centre mall – Queensgate Shopping Centre – which was part of Peterborough's 'New Town' expansion plan in the 1960s and '70s. To be honest, the city holds limited appeal for Slow travellers, other than as a convenient point of entry if you're arriving into Cambridgeshire from the north. There are, however, a handful of draw cards that warrant it a place in this book: the cathedral and the unique Railworld attraction, plus the eastern terminus of the Nene Valley Railway, which puts a fantastic Slow spin on getting here, and away.

The ancient heart of the city, Cathedral Square hosts Peterborough's most celebrated sites. Standing proud is **Peterborough Cathedral** (PE1 1XZ ⌂ peterborough-cathedral.org.uk ⊙ 09.00–17.15 Mon–Fri, 09.00–15.00 Sat, noon–15.15 Sun). The first stones were laid here in 1118, making it one of England's finest Norman cathedrals, with its triple-arched frontage and asymmetrical appearance (one of the towers is incomplete). One of the Fen Five monasteries (see box, page 188), it would have been a formidable feature in the medieval landscape, rising above the waterlogged Fens, which lapped the settlement to the east. The cathedral has witnessed the birth of two princesses, Blanche (1392) and Philippa (1394); the imprisonment of King Charles I (1646); and the burial of two queens – Catherine of Aragon (1536) and Mary Queen of Scots (1587).

The original monastic buildings that stood on this site saw their fair share of invasions. Founded in AD655, they were sacked by Viking warriors and famously raided by fenland hero Hereward the Wake (see box, page 175), before being burnt to the ground in 1116. Construction of the replacement cathedral began two years later and, to help fund the new building, a market area was established to the west of the monastic precincts. The monks went on to develop new commercial streets around the cathedral site, and Peterborough's urban street plan started to take shape. The next few centuries saw the Becket Chapel and ornate wooden ceiling constructed, although much was damaged when Cromwell's troops ravaged the city during the Civil War (1642–43).

> ...he did most miserably deface the Cathedrall Church, breake downe the Organs, and destroy the glasse windowes, committing many other outrages on the house of God...
> The Royalist newsbook *Mercurius Aulicus* (1643–45)

Today, the cathedral's restored Gothic façade gives a show-stopping first impression; inside, the 13th-century hand-painted wooden ceiling is the only one of its kind that survives in Britain. You'll find Catherine of Aragon's grave near the High Altar in the north aisle, and a plaque commemorating Mary Queen of Scots on the opposite side – her body was removed by her son (James I) and reburied at Westminster Abbey in 1612. The Anglo-Saxon Hedda Stone behind the altar commemorates the destruction of the early monastery when it was attacked by Vikings in 864.

To dig deeper into the cathedral's past, it's worth timing your visit around one of the themed events held throughout the year, which range from Catherine of Aragon talks to candlelit tours and guided walks by 'Old Scarlett' the Tudor gravedigger. The Tower Tour is another highlight – join a guided climb for spellbinding views towards Ely Cathedral (page 228), and to get up close with the intricate ceiling, nave roof and giant Gothic vaults.

A few paces from the cathedral's main entrance is the **Guildhall**. This fine, open-sided building was built in 1670–71 to celebrate the Restoration of the monarchy. Today, its position by McDonald's means that the hall's ancient steps are a popular place for eating burgers and chips. Next to the Guildhall, the striking church of **St John the Baptist** rests just below ground level. It was built between 1402 and 1407 using materials from an earlier church and the nave from the cathedral's Becket Chapel. In 1881, a gale sent part of the tower crashing through

CATHERINE OF ARAGON

Queen of England from 1509 to 1533, Catherine of Aragon lived out her final years in Cambridgeshire – she was banished to Buckden (page 122), held at Kimbolton (page 117) and finally buried at Peterborough Cathedral. During her lifetime, she oversaw the English victory at the Battle of Flodden (1513) and commissioned a controversial book on women's rights to education.

Despite these achievements, it's her ill-fated marriage to Henry VIII which has sealed her place in the history books. Catherine, the first of his six wives, refused to stand down as queen when Henry sought to annul their marriage. Banished from court, she died at Kimbolton Castle. Her ill health was blamed on the unsavoury fenland climate but it was more likely due to cancer. Meanwhile, Henry took supremacy over religious matters, married a second wife and set the wheels in motion for the English Reformation and the Dissolution of the Monasteries.

the aisle roof, initiating a two-year phase of restoration. The church took on its Perpendicular style under the direction of Gothic architect J L Pearson (who designed Truro Cathedral).

A few minutes' walk southwest of Cathedral Square, **Peterborough Museum and Art Gallery** (Priestgate, PE1 1LF; free entry ⊙ closed Mon) houses one of the finest collections of Jurassic marine reptiles in the world. It's also home to a replica of the Water Newton treasures (page 154) and displays arts and crafts produced by Napoleonic prisoners at The Norman Cross (page 157). You can also learn about the modern development of Peterborough and experience an original Victorian operating theatre, which is one of the last surviving period operating theatres in the country (the museum building was once an infirmary).

Also signposted south of the square (an eight-minute walk from the cathedral) is the award-winning **Railworld Wildlife Haven** (Oundle Rd, PE2 9NR ✆ 01733 344240 ⊘ railworld.net ⊙ varies, see website). Here, you'll discover full-scale salvaged locomotives which include the famous RTV31 hovertrain (page 248), alongside wildlife habitats that welcome bees, bats and newts. Next to Railworld is the eastern terminus of the Nene Valley Railway (page 152).

Longthorpe Tower & Thorpe Hall

A couple of miles west of the city centre (bus number 2) Longthorpe village is home to the 14th-century **Longthorpe Tower** (Thorpe Rd, PE3 6LU ✆ 01733 234193 ⊙ Mar–Oct 10.00–16.30 Sat, Sun & bank hols; English Heritage). You can climb inside the tower, built by Robert Thorpe in 1290–1300, to marvel at one of the most important sets of 14th-century domestic wall paintings in northern Europe. Also in Longthorpe village is the 17th-century **Thorpe Hall** (Thorpe Rd, PE3 6LW). One of few mansions built during the Commonwealth era, it was created largely from the ruins of the Bishop's Palace at Peterborough Cathedral. The hall is now a hospice with tranquil grounds and Victorian-era gardens that are open to the public.

¶¶ FOOD & DRINK

It goes without saying that there are endless places to eat and drink in Peterborough, from independents to national chains, although few are fully on board with the Slow food ethos. On the top deck of a floating Dutch barge, **Charters Bar** (Town Bridge, PE1 1FP ♪ 01733 315700 ⬧ charters-bar.com) is a real-ale emporium, specialising in local Oakham Ales; on the lower deck is the award-winning **East Restaurant** (♪ 01733 315702 ⬧ east-restaurant.co.uk), which serves pan-Asian cuisine. Diehard ale fans could also detour south of the river to the **Palmerston Arms** (82 Oundle Rd, Woodston) which has an open view of the cellar. For decent coffee, try the in-house roasted beans at **Bewiched** (25 Bridge St, PE1 1EH). At the cathedral, **Sundays at the Cathedral** (♪ 07919 916529 ⊙ 09.30–16.30 Tues–Sat, 10.00–16.00 Sun) in Becket Chapel is a good option, known for their daily roast lunches and roast dinner rolls.

2 NENE PARK

⚐ **Nene Park Campsite & Caravan site** (page 316)
Ham Ln, PE2 5UU ⬧ nenepark.org.uk

Two-thousand-acre Nene Park sprawls beside the river between Peterborough and Wansford, encompassing meadows, lakes, woods and farmland. The vast park is the local go-to for picnics, watersports and family bike rides, and is zoned into different sections, with the lakes and grassland of **Ferry Meadows** (the main recreational hub) at its heart – this is also where you'll find the visitor centre, cycle-hire centre and outdoor activity hub. You could learn to sail or windsurf, join the wild swimming group, hire a paddleboard, go fishing and birdwatching, or fire up a barbecue. In the park's eastern zone is **Woodston Reach** (good for woodland walks) and **Thorpe Meadows** (rowing lake and sculpture park). The west has the **Rural Estate** – an ancient landscape threaded with footpaths and bridleways that lead to the villages (and pubs) of Castor and Sutton.

The park started taking shape in the 1970s, when the area was used for gravel extraction to build new roads. The gravel pits were then flooded to form a series of artificial lakes. Cycle routes and footpaths were added to create a much-needed local breathing space, which has remained popular ever since. It's worth mentioning that the area around the outdoor activity hub, cycle-hire centre and visitor centre can get busy in peak periods, but you don't have to wander far beyond this to find plenty of green space to spread out in.

There are lots of traffic-free routes to explore by bike – just be aware that cycle paths are shared with walkers, so take care around busy sections. Maps are available from the cycle-hire centre. You could also use the Green Wheel and National Cycle Network paths to continue on beyond the park to Alwalton (less than two miles from the visitor centre), Castor (2½ miles) or Peterborough Cathedral (around four miles).

Suggested **walking routes** include the 1½-mile Ham Mere Trail and the 2½-mile Bluebell Trail (best in spring) – you can buy pocket maps in the visitor centre or download a trail map at ⌀ nenepark.org.uk/storage/Ferry-Meadows-pdf-map.pdf.

¶¶ FOOD & DRINK

Nene Park has picnic sites, barbecue stands, pubs and cafés. **Lakeside Kitchen & Bar** (⌀ lakesidekitchenandbar.com) has the best setting – next to Gunwade Lake in Ferry Meadows – with a terrace and big glass windows overlooking the water. They serve sandwiches, burgers, salads and homemade cakes. On Overton Lake, **Ferry Meadows Café** (⌀ lakesidekitchenandbar.com/ferry-meadows-cafe) does jacket potatoes, toasties and snacks.

3 CASTOR CHURCH & PRAETORIUM

Stocks Hill, Castor PE5 7AX ⌀ castorchurchtrust.co.uk

Just off the A47, Castor village has a double hit of history. Perched on a hill above thatched and brick homes, the Grade I-listed church of **St Kyneburgha** is one of England's most important churches, with its marvellous three-tiered Norman tower. The other stonework is a blend of Roman and Norman with Saxon carvings. Inside, the church has a medieval altar, 14th-century wall painting and beautiful roof adorned with angels.

Entwined in the church's history is the discovery of a **praetorium** (Roman palace) that once stood on the same site. Excavations, which began in the early 19th century, revealed Britain's second-largest known

CASTOR & WATER NEWTON ROMAN WALKS

The best way to discover the Nene Valley's Roman past is by joining a guided walk with a local historian. The St Kyneburgha Building Preservation Trust (⌀ castorchurchtrust. co.uk/tour) offer tours on request, with the option to explore Roman Castor and the church, or nearby Durobrivae and Normangate near Water Newton (page 154). Alternatively, you could try the self-guided Castor Roman Trail (1.8 miles) on ⌀ castorromans.co.uk – an impressive resource, created by the local primary school.

Roman building (after Fishbourne, West Sussex). The palace was built around AD230 and you can still see the foundations beside the road on Stocks Hill – look for growth-like stones coming out of the wall. The man to thank for the discovery of the praetorium is Edmund Tyrell Artis (1789–1847), who is buried near the south porch.

The framework of St Kyneburgha's began more than 200 years after the Romans left England and abandoned the praetorium. In AD650, a Saxon convent was founded among the praetorium ruins by St Kyneburgha (daughter of the heathen King Penda of Mercia) and her sister. When she died, St Kyneburgha's shrine became a place of pilgrimage. The convent was later raided by Vikings and rebuilt by the Normans, who added the famous tower, nave and most of the transepts. Castor's is the only church in the world dedicated to St Kyneburgha, although her remains were moved to Peterborough Cathedral in the 11th century.

⫴ FOOD & DRINK

Castor has several pubs and cafés on Peterborough Road, which is just down the hill from the church. The thatched **Royal Oak** (24 Peterborough Rd ⌀ 01733 380217 ⌀ royaloakcastor.com) specialises in hand-stretched pizzas, cocktails and gins. The other 'proper pub' is **The Prince of Wales Feathers** (38 Peterborough Rd ⌀ 01733 380222 ⌀ princeofwalesfeathers.co.uk), which offers pub grub and has a covered seating area at the back. Both pubs serve Castor's own beer. Between these two, **The Chubby Castor** (34 Peterborough Rd, PE5 7AX ⌀ 01733 380801 ⌀ thechubbycastor.com) is a Michelin Plate restaurant in a historical pub setting – expect the likes of beef tartare and hand-picked crab lasagne. Book ahead for the set lunch, the seven-course tasting menu or afternoon tea.

Continue northwest on Peterborough Road and Castor merges into the village of Ailsworth, where you'll find **The Coffee House** (107A Peterborough Rd ⌀ 01733 380093 ⌀ castorcoffee.co.uk), which serves breakfasts, lunches, cakes, tray bakes and milkshakes. The best seating is across the road, beneath the willows.

4 CASTOR HANGLANDS & SOUTHEY WOOD

🏠 **The White Hart** (page 316) 🏡 **Pea Cottage** (page 316) ⛺ **The Nest** (page 316)
Southey Wood parking area, Langley Bush Rd, PE6 7BF

The Hanglands walk

✽ OS Explorer map 235 *Wisbech & Peterborough North*; start: Southey Wood, Langley Bush Rd, PE6 7BF 📍 TF110023; 3 miles; easy (flat all the way)

The best way to explore Castor Hanglands and see the ponds is to follow the Hanglands Walk. Waymarked with yellow markers, the trail is easy to follow but finding the start point requires a nudge in the right direction. The best place to start is the Southey Wood parking area on Langley Bush Rd (the postcode PE6 7BG will get you in the rough area).

1 From Southey Wood parking area, turn your back on the entrance to the wood, cross the road and follow the signposted bridleway on to a wide track. Follow this until you come to a large yellow post at a fork in the track.

2 Turn left at the yellow post, following the arrow along a path. Continue to a gate at the edge of a woodland. From here, a series of blue arrows directs you through two more gates. The sign at the second gate directs you 'To Hanglands Walk'.

3 You can now follow the yellow waymarkers, which takes you in a full loop around the reserve. At the end of the loop, retrace your footsteps to the parking area.

For a longer walk, you could combine this with the waymarked Heath Walk, or you could plan a pub walk through Southey Wood to/from the White Hart in Ufford.

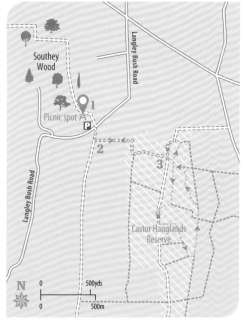

North of Nene Park and the A47, **Castor Hanglands** is a mosaic of ancient woodland, grassland and wetland, where the water table lies just below ground level. Once part of the ancient forest of Nasborough, this nature reserve features a number of ponds, including the most wildlife-rich pond ever surveyed in the UK. The main pond in the wetland area has been monitored since the early '70s, with more than 100 aquatic and 120 invertebrate species recorded in a single year – double the amount found in a typical pond. Star species include great crested newts and stoneworts (plants that have been around since the Jurassic period).

"This is a fantastic place for a walk, with trails that lead beneath the trees, through the heath and past the ponds"

This is a fantastic place for a walk, particularly in summer, with trails that lead beneath the trees, through the heath and past the ponds. Tread quietly in the scrubland where blackcaps, nightingales and whitethroats sing; and listen for tawny owls, treecreepers and nuthatch in the oak, ash, maple and hazel woodland. In the northwest corner, the open grassland has historical ridge and furrow cultivation patterns. From here, a footpath heads west to meet Langley Bush Road and the car park for **Southey Wood** – a working Forestry Commission woodland with oak, beech and pines, as well as more exotic giant fir, western hemlock and lawson cypress. The wood is a good option for a picnic spot, with benches available next to the fire road, a couple of minutes' walk from the parking area.

FOOD & DRINK

The White Hart Main St, Ufford PE9 3BH ✆ 01780 740250 ⌾ whitehartufford.co.uk. Ufford is walking distance from Southey Wood (less than a mile southeast). The 17th-century village pub has garden seating, local memorabilia in the bar area, and country décor in the restaurant. There's also a woodburner and an orangery. The menu ranges from venison with pickled blackberries to Ufford burgers and chalk-stream trout. Steaks are sourced from nearby Willow Brook Farm.

Willow Brook Farm Shop & Granary Tea Room Scotsman Lodge, Stamford Rd, PE6 7EL ✆ 01733 749483 ⌾ willowbrookfarmshop.co.uk. The Granary Tea Room is one of my favourite places for coffee or lunch, particularly in summer when tables are set up in the meadow. Breakfasts, lunches, roast dinners and cakes are all made using produce from the farm shop (a butchers that also sells veg, eggs and chutneys). The Granary also opens for occasional theme nights and sausage-making classes.

5 HELPSTON & AROUND

🏠 **The Bluebell** (page 316)

Two miles north of Castor Hanglands, **Helpston** village was the home of 'England's greatest peasant poet', John Clare (1793–1864). It's this claim to fame that draws most visitors, as Helpston boasts John Clare's memorial, museum and grave. Clare was renowned for his long rural walks, using the local countryside as his muse – although much-changed, you can still explore 'Clare Country' via scenic footpaths, bridleways and cycling routes.

The thatched and whitewashed **John Clare Cottage** (12 Woodgate, PE6 7ED ⌖ clarecottage.org ⊙ summer 11.00–16.00 Fri, Sat & Mon, winter 11.00–15.00 Fri, Sat & Mon) is now a museum dedicated to the poet and offering a window into the rural life of the 1800s. Run by the John Clare Trust, the cottage has been restored using traditional materials; some of the rooms have been recreated in 19th-century style, and the gardens are planted with flowers and shrubs that were typical of Clare's time. You can read his poetry, find out more about his life and learn about past and present approaches to mental health. There's also a shop and a café, which are open to all.

Around 210yds north of the museum, the **John Clare Memorial** stands at the junction of Glinton Road and Church Lane. **Clare's gravestone** is just off Church Lane, in the churchyard of St Botolph's.

East of Helpston is the large village of **Glinton**, where Clare attended school in St Benedict's Church. Glinton was the home of Clare's childhood sweetheart, which led him to write a poem dedicated to Glinton's famously slender spire. North of Helpston, **Maxey**'s most striking sight is the church of St Peter (High St, PE6 9EJ), which sits surrounded by fields on the village's western edge and is home to the Sweeting Museum – a collection of local artefacts compiled by the Reverend Sweeting in the late 1800s. The finds include a 17th-century tobacco pipe, Italian marble from Peterborough Cathedral, and the fossilised tooth of a 'hairy elephant'.

The best way to experience the landscapes and landmarks that influenced Clare's poetry is via the local footpaths and cycle routes – whichever way you wander, you're likely to be walking in his footsteps. John Clare Cottage has a selection of **walking routes**, which you can buy in the shop or download from ⌖ clarecottage.org/13/poems/walks-in-clare-country. One of these, Swaddeywell, is a lovely 6½-mile route that starts and finishes in Helpston, and covers the poet's favourite places. For **cycling routes**, ⊘ travelchoice.org.uk has mapped trails which lead through Helpston and the surrounding villages from Peterborough – Route 3: Cycling John Clare Country is an 11-mile circular route mostly on quiet roads and lanes. You could adapt the route according to your preferred start point, or you could plan an alternative using the Green Wheel (page 130) and NCN21.

Torpel Manor Field & The Torpel Way

At the western end of Helpston, next to the junction of the B1443 and Langley Bush Road, a footpath sign directs you into a lumpy bumpy field, often grazed by Hebridean sheep. This is Torpel Manor Field, a Scheduled Ancient Monument that contains the earthworks of what is thought to have been a Norman manor. Look carefully and you can see evidence

ENGLAND'S GREATEST PEASANT POET

John Clare (1793–1864) was born into a peasant family in Helpston, where he lived for much of his life. Widely regarded as one of England's greatest nature poets, his genius was only fully recognised 100 years or so after his death, when new editions of his works were released. Today's literary experts position him alongside Wordsworth and Coleridge.

Poetry was Clare's passion but he worked as an agricultural labourer to make ends meet. He wrote about nature and rural life at a time when the countryside was being transformed by enclosures and new farming techniques, and his first poems saw great success, outselling John Keats. But, as Clare's work fell out of fashion, he began to struggle with mental health and he checked into an asylum in Essex. When he discharged himself, he walked some 90 miles home, sleeping rough – the **John Clare Walk** (⊘ clarecottage.org/5/the-john-clare-walk), which roughly follows his route, has now become a pilgrimage to the poet. Shortly after his walk home, Clare was committed to Northampton Lunatic Asylum where he saw the final 23 years of his life before dying of a stroke. Buried in Helpston, his gravestone remembers him as 'the Northamptonshire peasant poet' – Clare's nickname before Helpston became part of Cambridgeshire.

Hill-tops like hot iron glitter bright in the sun,
And the rivers we're eying burn to gold as they run;
Burning hot is the ground, liquid gold is the air;
Whoever looks round sees Eternity there.
From *Autumn* by John Clare

of the house, ditches and defensive walls. The manor, created by the de Torpel family in the 12th century, was surrounded by a 60-acre deer park.

Today, the area is managed as both a heritage and wildlife site. You're free to wander around the site, but take care as you do so and keep dogs on leads. Research into the site's history is ongoing as part of the Torpel Project (⌀ torpel.com) while also signed across the field is the **Torpel Way** – an 18-mile walking route between Peterborough and Stamford in Lincolnshire.

¶¶ FOOD & DRINK

Most villages in the area have at least one pub, and many enjoy a good reputation. Those local to Helpston include the following, as well as the aforementioned **Granary Tea Room** and the **White Hart** in Ufford (page 141).

Helpston, Maxey & Glinton Spire – a circular cycle tour

❋ OS Explorer map 235 *Wisbech & Peterborough North*; start: John Clare Memorial, Helpston
♀ TF121054; 7½ miles; easy (flat all the way)

1 From the John Clare Memorial on Glinton Road, cycle north on Church Lane, passing St Botolph's Church on your right. At the junction with Maxey Road, turn left, cycle over the level crossing and head north along Maxey Road with open countryside either side. Continue towards Maxey church (St Peter's), with views of the church tower ahead.

2 At the church, turn right on to Maxey High Street and cycle into the village. Continue towards the Blue Bell pub.

3 Just before the pub, turn right on to Woodgate Lane, which becomes an off-road track. Continue as it leads over a bridge, turns a sharp left and meets a road (there's a good view over wildlife-filled lakes towards the end of the track). Turn left at the road, then right on to a surfaced track, following the Green Wheel signpost for Glinton.

(If your tyres aren't suitable for the off-road track, you can instead cycle past the Blue Bell in Maxey and continue along the High Street, out of Maxey and into the countryside. Then take the first right, signposted 'Etton 1', and continue for less than a mile until you reach a Green Wheel and NCN21 signpost directing you left to Glinton.)

4 The track to Glinton leads through open countryside, a set of tunnels and scrub (when you emerge from the scrub, look to your right for fine views of Glinton's church spire) until it meets a road.

The Blue Bell 10 High St, Glinton PE6 7LS ☎ 01733 252285 🖥 thebluebellglinton.co.uk
☺ Wed–Sun. Large pub/restaurant with contemporary garden room and patio, plus
a dining room and bar with roaring winter fires. The modern menu includes things like
lunchtime ciabattas, bavette steak and pan-seared cod with artichoke purée.

The Bluebell 10 Woodgate, Helpston PE6 7ED ☎ 01733 252394 🖥 bluebellhelpston.co.uk
☺ kitchen Wed–Sun. A traditional community pub with a nod to John Clare – order a pint
at the Poet's Bar and sup it by the fire in the Clare Snug. The seasonal menu features local
meat, game and Helpston veg. You can also try their homemade Woodgate gin and buy a
book about the pub's history and favourite recipes.

The Golden Pheasant 1 Main Rd, Etton PE6 7DA ☎ 01733 252387
🖥 goldenpheasantetton.com ☺ Tue–Sun. Pub/restaurant with a grand exterior and large
outdoor area with kids' playthings. The posh pub grub receives rave reviews, particularly the
locally sourced meats.

5 At the road, turn right, following the Green Wheel signpost and NCN21 for Glinton & Peakirk, then immediately left (signed again for Glinton & Peakirk). This takes you on a tarmacked cycle track through the fields. After half a mile, turn right to stay on NCN21, following the Green Wheel signpost for Glinton. Continue to Glinton village to reach the

church at the T-junction of North Fen Road and the B1443/High Street.

6 Turn right at the T-junction, passing Glinton's Blue Bell pub on your left. At the end of the road, make a right and then an immediate left to cycle up Helpston Road, following the sign for 'Village College'. At the end of this cul-de-sac, walk your bike over the footbridge which crosses the A15.

7 The footbridge leads you down to the B1443. Bear right (heading west) and use the shared cycle-/footpath to return to the John Clare Memorial.

6 BARNACK HILLS & HOLES NATIONAL NATURE RESERVE

Barnack PE9 3EX; parking on Wittering or Walcot rds

Head west of Helpston, via Ufford or Bainton, and you'll arrive in **Barnack** – a chocolate-box village that is famous for its quarried stone, which was extracted over several hundred years. When the quarry was exhausted, it left a lumpy landscape of lime-rich rubble that became colonised by wildflowers. Now a nature reserve, **Barnack Hills and Holes** is a miniature world of peaks and troughs that always reminds me of Teletubbyland.

A mere 50 acres, this storybook landscape boasts half of Cambridgeshire's surviving limestone grassland. Eight species of orchid bloom here, along with the rare pasque flower (April/May). Other lime-loving plants include rockrose, wild thyme, quaking grass and ox-eye daisy. The site also nurtures nationally scarce insects and uncommon butterflies. The little mounds dotted around the site are the nests of yellow meadow ants and, on summer nights, the twinkle of glow worms adds to the magic.

Once you've explored the reserve, it's worth taking a potter around Barnack itself. You can see the quarried stone in full glory at the Grade I church of **St John the Baptist** (Main St) – the oldest parts of the building are the lower stages of the Anglo-Saxon tower (notice the decorative stonework). Two hundred yards south of the church on Bishops Walk is the striking Kingsley House, a 16th-century rectory where Charles Kingsley wrote *The Water Babies* (1863).

BARNACK STONE

Peterborough Cathedral, Ely Cathedral, Ramsey Abbey, much of Norwich Cathedral, some of the grandest houses in East Anglia and several Cambridge colleges were built using Barnack's prized oolitic limestone.

Extraction began in Roman times and, by the Middle Ages, blocks were being hauled by oxen and shipped along the Nene to build the fenland's great abbeys. The stone was so sought after that the monasteries fought over the rights to it – some historians cite it as the most important quarry in medieval England.

The best stone had been worked out by the start of the 16th century but secondhand supplies became available after the Dissolution of the Monasteries (1536–40) – it was this repurposed stone that built the Cambridge colleges. Quarrying of lower-quality stone continued until the 18th century and was used to surface the Great North Road.

🍴 FOOD & DRINK

The Millstone Inn Millstone Ln, Barnack PE9 3ET ✆ 01780 769979
🖥 themillstonebarnack.co.uk ⊖ closed Mon, food served Wed–Sun. Recently refurbished, this village pub has modern décor alongside original beams and old stone walls. They serve lunchtime sandwiches and modern British fayre, such as saddle of venison with stilton scone and blackberries, seared cod loin with wild mushrooms, and pumpkin and sage ravioli with chive sauce.

7 BURGHLEY HOUSE

PE9 3JY 🖥 burghley.co.uk ⊖ House: Mar–Oct 10.30–17.00 closed Fri; gardens 10.30–16.30; parkland 07.00–18.00

Grazing the Lincolnshire border, Burghley dubs itself 'England's Greatest Elizabethan House'. It's a bold claim but entirely warranted with a manor this grand. The main roof is almost an acre in size and, on the ground and first floors, there are 35 major rooms and 80 lesser rooms, along with endless bathrooms and an enormous Tudor kitchen with a 260-piece copper cookware set.

The ancestral home of the Cecil family, Burghley was largely designed by William Cecil – Queen Elizabeth I's Lord High Treasurer (1555–87) and the first Lord Burghley. Today, the house is owned by Michael Cecil (the eighth Marquess of Exeter, 17th Earl of Exeter and 18th Baron Burghley) who carried out a decade's worth of restoration work. Michael now resides in Canada and his cousin manages the estate.

Much of what you see inside was collected over the centuries by the Cecils. John Cecil (1648–1700) amassed his fine art collection during four Grand Tours of Italy in the 1600s. Other treasures include Japanese ceramics, a mother-of-pearl pagoda and one of the finest collections of Chinese snuff bottles in the Western world. There's also the stunning Pierre Gôle furniture in the Blue Silk Bedroom, and the alarming Verrio murals in the Hell Staircase. Equally impressive are the estate's gardens and deer park. The 18th-century parkland was laid out by Lancelot 'Capability' Brown (see box, page 252), and the oak trees and limes in the South Gardens were planted by Queen Victoria and Prince Albert. The park is roamed by fallow deer and open to the public but you'll need an admission ticket to access the Sculpture Garden and Garden of Surprises with its mirrored maze and swivelling Caesar busts.

You can explore the house and gardens at your leisure or by guided tour. Families may be tempted by Beastly Boring Burghley – a 'horrible history' tour for seven to 12 year olds. Burghley also has a busy calendar of events, from food markets and lectures to country shows and car rallies. My favourite is the annual Burghley Horse Trials (⊘ burghley-horse.co.uk); established in 1961, this three-day equestrian event is part of the Grand Slam of Eventing, alongside Badminton Horse Trials, and is held in September.

⏚ FOOD & DRINK

Burghley House has two places to eat. **The Orangery** serves breakfasts, lunches and afternoon teas – which include the 'Cecil', 'Elizabeth' or 'Champagne', all with homemade miniature cakes. **The Garden Café** offers salads, sandwiches and 'famous' chocolate brownies. Alternatively, you could hop across the Lincolnshire border for a wide choice of pubs and cafés in the lovely town of Stamford.

8 SACREWELL FARM CENTRE

Great North Rd, Thornhaugh PE8 6LB (signed on the A47 and A1) ⊘ 01780 782254
⊘ sacrewell.org.uk

Sacrewell is a heritage farm and agricultural education charity that specialises in rare breeds, just off the A47, southwest of Hanglands. Farming has taken place here since Roman times, with excavations revealing villas, a corn dryer and more. Over the centuries, Sacrewell has adapted to almost every agricultural development and key event in British history, from the Industrial Revolution to large-scale milk production, battery hen farming and the Women's Land Army.

Here you can meet Suffolk Punch horses, endangered Landrace pigs and rare Lincoln Longwool sheep, plus lambs in spring. There's also a restored 18th-century watermill built from Barnack stone and powered by a spring-fed millpond – watch the waterwheel turning, then venture inside to learn about the original Victorian miller as you explore four floors of creaking wooden machinery; you'll find sacks of wheat grain on the top floor and can watch as grain travels down the chute to be ground by the millstone.

Other bygone farming equipment includes a 1950s tractor and horse-drawn carts. The rabbits in the petting area and ducklings in the hatchery always go down well with young children. There's also a resident woodcarver, plus seasonal sheep shearing and honey harvesting, and a programme of rural craft workshops such as blacksmithing and herbal tincture making.

A good way to make the most of everything here is to camp on site and buy a weekend ticket that allows you to dip in and out of the activities and attractions. The farm's café serves coffee and cakes, as well as hot meals and sandwiches. The on-site shop sells local produce, ethically sourced coffee, preserves and fresh eggs. You're also welcome to bring a picnic.

THE GREAT NORTH ROAD & AROUND

South of the A47, the spirit of the old Great North Road is captured in villages like Wansford and Stilton, which sit either side of the A1. Glimmers of the past can also be found in patches of ancient woodland where highwaymen once preyed on unsuspecting travellers. The countryside between these woods and villages is blissfully quiet – ideal for rambling, cycling or simply taking in the views from tranquil spots like Little Gidding church.

9 WANSFORD

🏠 **Haycock Manor Hotel** (page 316)

Wansford-in-England, as it's playfully referred to (see box, page 150), exudes an air of importance with its wide main street and smart stone buildings. This affluent appearance harks back to its prosperous past as a river crossing, trade hub and key staging post on the Great North Road.

THE GREAT NORTH ROAD

One of England's earliest and greatest public highways, the Great North Road ran for 409 miles between London and Scotland. It was carved by feet, hooves and wagon wheels in the 1600s, following old Roman roads and the natural topography of the land. Travelled by everyone from bishops and beggars to Cromwell's army and kings and queens, the route was fraught with danger and rife with highwaymen, including the legendary Dick Turpin. With road improvements made in the 18th century, faster travel made way for the 'golden age of coaching', with grand inns providing food, lodgings and stables. The road was quietened in the 19th century by the coming of the railways, and the last mail coaches departed in the 1840s. Today, the A1 – Britain's longest numbered road – parallels much of the original highway, although it bypasses the towns, villages and coaching inns that made the old route so famous.

A village of two halves, Wansford sits on both banks of the River Nene, linked by the 17th-century Old Wansford Bridge (a Scheduled Ancient Monument), which was once one of England's most expensive toll bridges. Part way across this bridge is the old boundary stone between Northamptonshire and Huntingdonshire – the village was divided between the two until 1965, when it became part of Cambridgeshire. The church of St Mary's sits northwest of the river, with the shops and pubs southeast of the river. As you wander along the wide main street, notice the similarity of the buildings inscribed with the letter 'B'. Their distinct style is the work of 19th-century architect Samuel Sanders Teulon (1812–73), who developed the village for the first Earl of Bedford. The best example of Teulon's style is the gatehouse of Stibbington House (southern end of Elton Rd), with its latticed windows, bargeboard gables and tall pinnacle, which mimics the spire of St Mary's. Other examples of Teulon work include the row of terraces numbered 1–11 Elton Road and, on the opposite side of the road, numbers 2, 4, 13 and 15.

Wansford does well to maintain its independent vibe, with a traditional post office and a couple of quirky shops: the vintage clothing specialist, Boheme Clothing (⌂ bohemeclothing.com) makes for fascinating window shopping, even when closed; the same goes for New Colinette Yarn Shop – a wool specialist which, last time I visited, had ice-cream sundae yarn sculptures in the window. Outside Boheme Clothing, notice the homemade take on a blue plaque, dedicated to a former Wansford resident. It reads: 'Tom Guy Stood Here 1996–2011.'

Looming over the main street, the 16th-century **Haycock Manor Hotel** was once one of the finest establishments on the Great North Road. Although recently refurbished, you can still imagine the stagecoaches arriving after a long and weary journey, their passengers

WANSFORD-IN-ENGLAND

Above the entrance to the Haycock is an illustrated sign with a man on a hay bale (or 'haycock') and the words 'What Wansford in England?' written beneath. Barnaby, the main character from the 1638 *Barnabæ Itinerarium* (*Barnabee's Journal*) by Richard Brathwait, is said to have fled from Wansford during the plague and fallen asleep on a haycock which rolled away and floated downriver. On waking, he asked a passer-by where he was. When they answered 'Wansford', he cried 'what, Wansford in England?' and the name stuck.

alighting in the stable yard, which could hold up to 150 horses – some of the original tethering rings still hang on the walls. Among its many visitors, the Haycock welcomed Mary Queen of Scots en route to her execution in Northamptonshire.

For several centuries, Wansford also enjoyed a booming river trade. From the 17th century, riverside wharves, jetties, mills and warehouses would have been busy with fen lighters (flat-bottomed boats) transporting Barnack stone and other goods to inland destinations or out towards the Fens. Many of Wansford's riverside buildings are former warehouses that hark back to this era.

FOOD & DRINK

If you'd prefer a pub, walk south on London Road to **The Paper Mills** (✆ 01780 782328 ⊕ paper-mills.com). This revamped old stone pub serves local ales and a seasonal menu.

Haycock Manor Hotel ✆ 01780 782223 ⊕ haycock.co.uk. This refurbished hotel is home to fine-dining restaurant Prévost (⊕ Wed–Sat for lunch & dinner), which is set in the modernised conservatory area and offers a three-, five- or eight-course tasting menu of innovative dishes, such as carrot tartar, dry aged duck with blackberries, and Cornish cod with clams and roe. Alternatively, you could dine at the more informal Haycock Kitchen (⊙ daily for breakfast, lunch, afternoon tea, dinner) – a brasserie which serves the likes of native lobster and pork tomahawk steak.

The Wansford Lounge 2A London Rd, PE8 6JB ✆ 01780 593022 ⊕ wansfordcountrylounge.co.uk ⊙ 09.00–16.00 Mon–Sun & some evenings. Opened in 2017 to rave reviews, this family-run café offers brunches, lunches and three-course meals with wine. Expect a trendy interior with brick walls and filament light bulbs. The window seats have views of the Haycock's grand façade. Their commitment to local produce includes eggs 'from Farmer John', and bread from the local bakery. 'Have you tried their steak pie?' one local asked me, 'it's to die for!'

10 BEDFORD PURLIEUS NATIONAL NATURE RESERVE

Nr Wansford, PE8 6NN (unmarked road off A47 – follow 'Farm Access' sign for Cross Leys Farm. Parking is 100yds on your left)

A couple of miles west of Wansford is England's most flower-rich wood and the largest patch of ancient woodland in Cambridgeshire. Bedford Purlieus is a fragment of Rockingham Forest, once a royal hunting ground and major Saxon woodland. The name harks back to an era when the woodland was owned by the Duke of Bedford as part of his Wansford estate. While most ancient woodlands contain around 260 different plant species, Bedford Purlieus has close to 500. There's history here too: the Romans quarried this area for iron ore and, in 2008–09, Channel 4's *Time Team* uncovered the equivalent of a Roman industrial estate.

There's a network of trails to wander, plus a wonderful wildflower meadow near the parking area. As you walk deeper into the woodland it feels truly magical with lush undergrowth and towering trees – expect oak, ash, hazel and birch. If you're here in summer, look for bellflowers, fly orchids, herb paris and clouds of butterflies. In spring, you can spot newts, nesting birds, bluebells and stinking (quite literally) hellebore; in autumn, find berries and crab apples; and in winter seek out spurge laurel and roosting owls.

11 NENE VALLEY RAILWAY (NVR)

Wansford Station, Old Great North Rd, PE8 6LR ✐ 01780 784444 (office), 01780 784404 (talking timetable) ⬙ nvr.org.uk ☺ trains operate every weekend & sometimes midweek; check website for special events

At Nene Valley Railway (NVR), you can hop on a steam or diesel train and travel back in time on a preserved section of Peterborough's first railway line. A glorious way to explore the Nene Valley, this heritage railway chugs through the countryside between Yarwell Junction (2½ miles south of Wansford) and Peterborough. Wansford Station is the main hub – this is the starting point for most people's journeys and is where you'll find the café and NVR office. It's also where most trains are stationed and repaired. Just be aware that Wansford Station is located 1½ miles from the village of Wansford itself.

The original tracks, between Peterborough and Blisworth in Northamptonshire, opened in 1847. As the network expanded with links to Cambridge, Norwich and the Midlands, Wansford Station became an important East Anglian junction. This heyday came to an end in the 1960s when Dr Beeching axed a third of the British rail network. Passenger trains ceased but the line continued carrying freight until 1972. Happily, the closure was relatively short-lived, with engine enthusiasts at Peterborough Railway Society reopening a section of the line in 1977. Today, their 7½-mile stretch has become one of the UK's premier historic railways, used to film everything from Agatha Christie television adaptations (*The Mystery of the Blue Train* and *Murder on the Orient Express*) to Bond movies *Octopussy* (1983) and *GoldenEye* (1995). The NVR can accommodate both British and continental engines, making it unique in Europe.

From Wansford Station, services operate west towards Yarwell and east to Ferry Meadows (Overton and Orton Mere stations) and Peterborough. It takes 30 minutes to ride the full length of the line (Yarwell to Peterborough) but almost all visitors start their journeys at Wansford Station and explore the line in both directions from there. Many people hop off for a picnic at Ferry Meadows – from here, you could catch the train back or return on foot, following the Nene Way or Hereward Way (it's around six miles from Orton Mere to Wansford Station). Special events and themed rides take place throughout the year, from Thomas the Tank Engine celebrations to 'Santa Specials' which, based on the amount of mulled wine I was plied with last time, is as exciting for adults as it is for kids. All tickets, whether for standard journeys or themed events, need to be booked in advance through the website.

Even if you don't fancy a train ride, watching the locomotives arrive and depart at Wansford Station is an experience in itself – you can't help but feel a tingle of excitement when you hear the whistle of a steam train echoing through the tunnel. As the train nears the platform, you'll be met with a whoosh of white steam, a belch of black smoke and an ear-splitting grinding of steel. Once the flat-capped controllers have hurried their passengers into carriages, the doors are shut with a satisfying clunk before the train pulls away, building momentum with a chugaddy-chug-chuggaddy-chug as it disappears down the track.

Next to the Nene Valley Railway is something completely different – Adventure Rutland operates a **watersports hub** at Sibson Lake Marina

THE ORIGINAL THOMAS THE TANK ENGINE

Even non-enthusiasts will recognise a certain blue train that resides at NVR. 'Thomas' was named by Reverend W Awdry, author of the *Thomas the Tank Engine* series, who lived in Cambridgeshire for several years. Before it found fame, the little blue engine worked for the British Sugar Corporation factory in Peterborough until diesel engines started to replace steam. Purchased by the Peterborough Railway Society and moved to NVR in 1973, Thomas can be seen here at his home in Wansford Station most of the year.

(Great North Rd, PE8 6LS ☏ 07818 226565 ⌖ adventurerutland.com). Here, you can hire kayaks and paddleboards (including an 18ft mega-SUP for groups) to use on the lake, or you can book on to a guided trip along the River Nene. They also host regular wild swimming sessions at the lake.

⑪ FOOD & DRINK

Turntable Café Old Great North Rd, PE8 6LR. Located at Wansford Station, this friendly café serves breakfasts, burgers, snacks and hot meals with views of the locomotives through the windows.

12 DUROBRIVAE & THE WATER NEWTON TREASURE

🏠 **River Nene Cottages** (page 316)

Travel three miles south of Wansford on the A1, turn off on to Old North Road (a nod to the former route of the Great North Road) and you'll arrive in **Water Newton**. This little hamlet stands on what was once the Roman garrison town of **Durobrivae**, built on Ermine Street, just across the river from Castor's palace (page 138), with the industrial suburb of Normangate in between. You can walk between Water Newton and Castor by following the footpath that crosses the river and leads one mile northeast.

I had a cup of tea in Water Newton with local resident and history enthusiast, Tony Capon, who opened my eyes to the village's monumental local history. Excavations began here in the 1800s but the 'eureka' moment came in 1975 when archaeologists uncovered the world's earliest known mass of Christian silver, shedding light on a period of Christianity that experts knew almost nothing about. The 'Water Newton Treasure', which includes 27 items of silver tableware, is now in the British Museum, with replicas at Peterborough Museum.

Despite this monumental discovery, there is no visitor centre in Water Newton and, to the untrained eye, the site of Durobrivae (which sits opposite Mill Lane) is nothing more than an empty field. To bring it to life, Tony showed me aerial photographs that revealed parts of Durobrivae, and the embossed line of Ermine Street, running almost parallel to the A1. To see more, he recommended joining one of the local history walks from Castor (see box, page 139). You could also plan your own walk to Castor or Wansford along the Nene Way.

'While you're out walking,' Tony added, 'you may well find yourself a memento'. Durobrivae was a production centre for Nene Valley Colour Coated Ware (or Castor Ware), which was produced between the 2nd and 4th centuries, and as a result the countryside is riddled with Roman pottery. Keep your eyes peeled for fragments of cups and flagons that, having been dipped into coloured liquid clay, may have a brown, orange, green or black tinge. There are other remains here too – Tony told me that he once stepped out of his house to find a Roman coin sitting on top of a molehill in his garden.

Water Newton's church (St Remigius) is 11th century and has an idyllic setting by the river. The best views of the church, and the rest of Water Newton for that matter, are from the river – you can get your fill by following the riverside footpath or, if you have your own vessel, from a boat or paddleboard. Back in 2013, the church was threatened with closure so the locals launched a summer festival to raise funds. The music festival has been held almost every year since, with around 500 revellers attending the one-day event in late August. Find out more at ⌂ waternewtonvillage.co.uk.

13 ALWALTON

⌂ Lynch Lodge (page 316)

This quaint little village sits a few hundred yards off the route of the former Great North Road (the A1). The heart of the old village (the pretty bit) is around Church Street, where the pub sits opposite the thatched village stores. Further down Church Street is the church of St Andrew's, parts of which date back to the 12th century. Inside, you'll find a stone tablet dedicated to Sir Henry Royce (1863–1933), the co-founder of Rolls-Royce cars, who was born and buried in the village.

Next to St Andrew's is Alwalton Hall (⌂ alwaltonhall.com), a Georgian manor built for the fourth Earl Fitzwilliam. Today, it's a luxury day spa offering all manner of pamper packages. Just after the hall, Church Lane splits at a grassy island. Take the right-hand fork and you'll pass the Old School and School House, which bears another dedication to Henry Royce by its front door – the mill where Royce was born is no longer standing, so the plaque was placed here instead. Where Church Lane ends, the striking Jacobean building on your right is Lynch Lodge. Available to rent as a holiday home (page 316), this was once a grand gateway building at the entrance drive of nearby

Milton Park (the largest private house in Cambridgeshire), which was then owned by the Fitzwilliam family. A surfaced footpath to the left of Lynch Lodge leads to the River Nene and Ferry Meadows Country Park (just over a mile).

⍾ FOOD & DRINK

Alwalton Post Office, Stores & Café 18 Oundle Rd, PE7 3UP ⊙ 09.30–16.30 Mon–Fri, 09.30–15.30 Sat & Sun. A step back in time, this three-in-one shop has the post office and stores downstairs, and a tea room decorated with teddy bears upstairs. Come for coffee, light lunches or afternoon tea.

The Cuckoo 20 Oundle Rd, PE7 3UP ⌀ 01733 239638 ⊘ vintageinn.co.uk. Originally a stable building, this large pub has long been part of village life, with low beams and lots of seating in the garden. As part of the Vintage Inns group, the Cuckoo offers a standard menu of steaks, pub classics and seasonal specials.

14 ELTON HALL

⌂ **The Crown Inn** (page 316) ⌂ **The Arc Cabin** (page 316)
PE8 6SH ⌀ 01832 280223 ⊘ eltonhall.com ⊙ 14.00–17.00 selected days May–Aug (see website)

Elton village's baronial hall – a part-Gothic manor that has been in the Proby family for 400 years – rises castle-like over landscaped parkland. The 15th-century tower is the oldest part but most of what you see today is down to extensive additions and alterations, carried out by the Probys over the centuries. The first Proby to arrive in Elton was Sir Peter, who bought a lease of the Manor of Elton in 1595 and went on to become Lord Mayor of London (1622). His grandson, Sir Thomas, incorporated the medieval chapel and original gatehouse to create an impressive residence, and the hall was Gothicised in the 18th century by John Proby, Earl of Carysfort. The current Probys – William and Meredyth – undertook a huge amount of restoration work when they arrived in 1980.

Inside, you can discover the medieval chapel (still used for family christenings), the richly furnished drawing room and the library, which includes Henry VIII's Prayer Book – a present from his sixth wife, Katherine Parr. The hall's fine art collections include several Old Masters, and you can also see the State Coach that was used by the Probys to attend Queen Victoria's Diamond Jubilee celebrations. Outside, the restored gardens are based on a 1911 design by A H Hallam Murray, father-in-law to Sir Richard Proby, who died in 1979. Highlights include the Gothic orangery, ornate topiary and Wisteria Walk.

You can pay to enter both the hall and gardens, or the gardens only. If you fancy recreating the Elton look in your garden back home, chat to the experts at the neighbouring **Bosworth's Garden Centre**.

⑪ FOOD & DRINK

Elton village has several good places to eat and drink, all within walking distance of Elton Hall.

The Black Horse 14 Overend, PE8 6RU ✆ 01832 280591 ⌂ theblackhorseatelton.co.uk. Characterful old pub with revamped interior, open fires and garden. The menu includes the likes of Black Horse fried chicken peanuts, wild mushroom and stilton crumble, braised blade of beef, and roast cod with spiced cauliflower, plus wraps, salads and pub classics.

The Crown Inn 8 Duck St, PE8 6RQ ✆ 01832 280232 ⌂ crowninnelton.co.uk ⏰ kitchen Tue–Sun. This cosy pub is one of the village's older buildings. There's an open fire in winter and a garden at the back. Food includes homemade burgers, local bread, free-range pork belly and vegan options. Be sure to try the Crown Inn Ale.

Loch Fyne The Old Dairy, PE8 6SH ✆ 01832 280298 ⌂ lochfyneseafoodandgrill.co.uk. Housed in an old dairy, this restaurant is part of the Loch Fyne chain. Scottish seafood is the focus but meat and veggie dishes are also on the menu.

Mulberry Café Bosworth's Garden Centre, PE8 6SH ✆ 01832 343104 ⏰ 09.00–16.30 Mon–Sat, 10.00–16.30 Sun. The café at the garden centre next to the hall serves 'Elton Breakfasts', afternoon teas, and lunches.

15 NORMAN CROSS

PE7 3TB

South of Peterborough, on the A15, stands a tall column topped with a bronze eagle. Marking the former site of the world's first purpose-built prisoner-of-war camp, this memorial commemorates the 1,770 men who died at Norman Cross. There's little to see, however, apart from the memorial column, which was unveiled just a few days before World War I broke out.

Norman Cross PoW camp was constructed in 1797 as a 42-acre wooden site that housed French and Dutch prisoners during the Napoleonic Wars. The camp was intended as a model depot for the humane treatment of prisoners, who slept in tiered hammocks across four barracks. At its busiest, this 'small town' housed 7,000 prisoners and 500 guards. The prisoners could take part in educational classes and crafts, such as carving and marquetry; some of the most talented prisoners received commissions for their work and were allowed to sell their crafts at the prison gates. Disease, however, was rife, and is largely responsible for the deaths commemorated by the memorial.

The prisoners were repatriated in 1814, following Napoleon's defeat, and the camp was dismantled. The camp's few remaining brick-built buildings are now private houses, while the former stables is an art gallery (normancrossgallery.com 11.00–16.00 Sat).

16 STILTON

🏠 **The Bell Inn** (page 316)

This is indeed the very village that gave its name to England's famous smelly blue – a cheese so sought-after that turophiles have been travelling here for centuries to taste it. So where are all the cheese shops and Stilton-themed cafés? Alas there are none. Even the annual cheese rolling festival saw its final wooden cheese bounce down the street in 2018.

To see Stilton in its prime, you need to travel back to the days of the Great North Road (see box, page 149). Stilton was about as far as you could ride by horse from London in a day, making the village a popular hub for thirsty travellers. At its height, there were more than a dozen pubs in Stilton, with the mighty Bell Inn at its heart – it was this pub's longstanding landlord, Cooper Thornhill, who sold the famous cheese.

The arrival of railways saw the buzz of the Great North Road decline but, with the dawn of the motorcar, Stilton thrived once again, with

THE STILTON SAGA

Folks have argued for decades over the true home of Stilton cheese. While it's agreed that Stilton village and The Bell Inn gave name and fame to the crumbly blue, it's thought that the cheese may have been made in Leicestershire and only sold in Stilton. Seizing an opportunity, Leicestershire applied for PDO (Protected Designation of Origin) status in 1996, which effectively banned Cambridgeshire from making the cheese. New evidence has since suggested that the cheese was in fact made in Stilton village. Historian Richard Landy discovered a recipe for 'Stilton' cheese written in 1722, with the letter's author describing a delicious cheese produced and sold by the Stilton landlord Cooper Thornhill. In celebration, The Bell Inn mounted a plaque declaring it 'the birthplace of Stilton Cheese'. The PDO is yet to be lifted but Cambridgeshire continues to battle for the paperwork that allows the cheese to be made here.

garages, guesthouses and tea rooms doing a roaring trade. This finally came to an end in 1958 when the A1 bypass turned the High Street into a dead-end road and extinguished the passing trade. Businesses collapsed overnight and the fabric of the village changed forever. Today, with the unusually wide High Street standing quiet, and the enormous pub sign of The Bell creaking in the breeze, it almost feels as if Stilton is waiting for the rumble of stagecoaches to return.

While Stilton's fame certainly surpasses it, a visit to the village isn't entirely wasted. The 16th-century **Bell Inn** is still going strong(ish), the huge sign that hangs outside a replica of the original which, at the time, was so heavy, it was held up by a post. Opposite, The Angel was The Bell's great rival (the stone outside was a mounting block for Great North Road travellers) and, further up the road, The Talbot has replaced its original coaching arch with a window. Stilton isn't a pretty village, however, so don't come here expecting chocolate-box cottages. 'It's always been a village of the common man,' Kelvin Davis, a resident and local history buff told me. 'It never had a grand estate or Duke pouring money into it, like Wansford.' Instead, the tombstones at the church of **St Mary Magdalene** tell stories of the down-to-earth characters who have shaped the village over time: people like Thomas Lunn, a night coachman who served 30 years on the Great North Road; Jean Habart, a PoW at Norman Cross (page 157) who became landlord of The Talbot; and of course, Cooper Thornhill, landlord of The Bell Inn and the originator of Stilton cheese.

FOOD & DRINK

Dominating Stilton high street, **The Bell Inn** (PE7 3RA ✆ 01733 241066 ⌂ thebellstilton. co.uk) is the most atmospheric of Stilton's pubs, with old stonework and timber beams. The bar and restaurant serve Stilton-themed dishes, such as Stilton pâté, beef stew with Stilton dumplings, and Stilton veggie burgers. Diagonally opposite, **The Talbot** (PE7 3RP ✆ 01733 240291 ⌂ talbotstilton.co.uk) also offers Stilton-laced pub grub.

17 LITTLE GIDDING CHURCH

PE28 5RJ ⌂ littlegiddingchurch.org.uk

The Giddings are a string of quiet villages along a two-mile stretch of country road. Great Gidding is the largest and Steeple Gidding is the most southerly but it's the teeny tiny hamlet of Little Gidding, sitting between the two, that is best known. In the early 1600s, this was the home

Stilton circular

❄ OS Explorer map 227 *Peterborough*; start: The Bell Inn, Stilton PE7 3RA ♀ TL162893; 6 miles; easy (flat all the way)

S tarting and finishing at The Bell Inn, this circular walk guides you along part of the original Great North Road and over open farmland and countryside, past a deserted church and through a medieval village site. It was kindly shared with me by the Stilton Stumblers walking group (⟁ stumblers.stilton.org/lets-stumble) as their favourite local route.

1 With your back to the pub, turn left (south) along the High Street. Pass Stilton Pavilion on your right, then go through the gate ahead and continue along the surfaced road (this was the route of the original Great North Road).

2 At the end of the road, turn right on to a footpath that leads between hedges and across a golf course. Cross a wooden bridge into a field, turn left and follow the path with the field boundary on your left, passing through three kissing gates. Continue on this path until it reaches a surfaced track.

3 At the track, turn right and follow the road to Denton. Look for the ruined church on your left (a carol service is still held here at Christmas) and follow the road as it bears right through the village and continues to Caldecote, where you'll come to a T-junction.

4 At the T-junction, turn left and then head immediately left across the road to the cul-de-sac. Follow this road as it bears left, then turn right on a bridleway in front of a stable block with a clock tower, passing to the left of the stables. Turn left at the trees and then right over a wooden bridge into the copse. You'll pass a large fish pond on your left before continuing up a slight incline and over a stile. You are now at the site of a medieval settlement, with the remains of a motte and bailey on your right (see the information board).

5 When the path meets Washingley Lane, cross and continue ahead on the signed bridleway, with the field boundary on your right. Soon you'll pass another medieval village information board on your right. Cross a small bridge and continue ahead, up the hill. At the top, turn right over a wooden bridge, then left to follow the track around a copse to your right. Continue on the track with a brook on your right. When you reach a fence, turn left and follow it uphill. At the top of the hill, turn right through a gate and follow the bridleway through two more gates. This brings you to The Paddocks (a cul-de-sac) in Folksworth.

of Nicholas Ferrar (1592–1637), who established an Anglican religious community which harboured the King of England and inspired the poem *Little Gidding* (1942) by T S Eliot, as quoted in the box on page 10.

6 Follow The Paddocks to Elm Road and turn left, passing the duck pond on your right and a converted Victorian schoolhouse on your left. At the Fox pub, turn right on to Manor Road, then right again to follow Washingley Road through the village. Turn left on to Townsend Way and look for the path on your right between the houses. This path leads you through a gate and into a field.

7 Follow the path diagonally left across the field, through a gate and into a pasture. You are now coming down Caldecote Hill into Stilton. Go through a kissing gate to meet Caldecote Road at the edge of Stilton.

8 Turn left along Caldecote Road and into Stilton. Turn right at the T-junction on to St Mary's Road, which veers left and becomes Church Street. Continue past St Mary's Church to reach The Bell Inn.

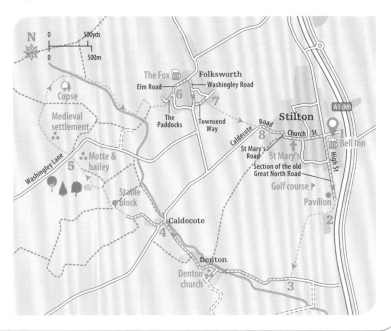

Ferrar (who was ordained a deacon in 1626) and his family (around 30 of them) devoted themselves to God and led simple Christian lives at a time of religious and political unrest – the era between the English

ALEXEY FEDORENKO'S

1

HISTORY & HERITAGE

Cambridgeshire has a unique and fascinating history of medieval monasteries, Fenland drainage, fearless rebels and civil war stories.

1 Ely Cathedral started taking shape in the 11th century but its story began some 400 years earlier when Etheldreda (an East Anglian princess) founded a monastery here.

2

ROBERT COOKE'S

ENGLISH HERITAGE

KEVIN EAVES/S

JO LERPINIERE/GRE

2 Houghton Mill is a working mill on the River Great Ouse that has stood here for centuries. **3** Longthorpe Tower boasts some of the most important 14th-century domestic wall paintings in northern Europe. **4** Ramsey Abbey Gatehouse is all that still stands of what was one of the richest monastic buildings in medieval England. **5** Great Chishill Windmill dates back to the 19th century and is the only open trestle post mill in England with a fantail. **6** Stretham Old Engine is the last of Cambridgeshire's steam-powered pumping stations.

J AND S PHOTOGRAPHY/S

Reformation and Civil War. The Ferrars nursed the sick, wrote books (some of which are now in the British Museum) and walked three times a day to the tiny church of St John the Evangelist. They also held short hourly services in the manor house they lived in, from six in the morning until eight at night. King Charles I stayed with the Ferrars on three occasions – the third was in 1646 (after Nicholas Ferrar's death), when he was fleeing the Battle of Naseby.

Damaged during the Civil War and rebuilt in 1714, the tiny chapel is unique in a county of grand medieval churches and soaring spires. It's an incredibly peaceful place, with fantastic views over west Cambridgeshire. Inside is Nicholas Ferrar's original panelling, brass tablets, lectern and brass font – the lid of which is twisted after being thrown in a pond during Cromwell's raid in 1646. To find the church, follow the unnamed, dead-end road signed for Little Gidding – as the church website puts it: 'Little Gidding Church is difficult to find, but unforgettable when found.'

¶¶ FOOD & DRINK

Fox & Hounds 80 Main St, Great Gidding PE28 5NU ✆ 01832 293298 ⊘ thegiddings.org. uk/community/fox-and-hounds-pub ⊙ 17.00–midnight Tue–Fri, 11.00–midnight Sat & Sun. Grade II-listed pub with inglenook fireplace and sheltered garden. Menu focuses on Thai curries.

18 HAMERTON ZOO PARK

PE28 5RE ✆ 01832 293362 ⊘ hamertonzoopark.com

A few miles south of the Giddings on winding country roads, **Hamerton Zoo Park** describes itself as 'probably the most environmentally responsible zoo in Europe'. The park, which opened its doors to rare and unusual breeds in 1990, is now striving to become completely carbon-neutral by powering itself with wind turbines, solar panels and biomass boilers.

It's home to around 100 different types of animals, from lynx and lemurs to white tigers, bears and wolves. Unique for British zoos, there's also a wombat enclosure and walk-through 'Outback Aviary'. My mum often brings the grandkids here, and I think she enjoys riding the toy train past the animals as much as they do. The animal collection is ever-changing, so there will no doubt be some new faces by the time you visit.

19 AVERSLEY, ARCHER'S & MONKS WOODS

East of Hamerton Zoo and the Giddings, the A1 is flanked by patches of ancient woodland that were, no doubt, once part of a great forest. West of the A1, **Aversley Wood** and **Archer's Wood** are pleasant spots for a stroll, and the former has 'armed' ponds that were once used by cattle drovers – unique to Cambridgeshire and Suffolk, these ponds were dug in a star shape with arms extending from a central area. Half a mile southeast of Aversley, Archer's Wood was a legendary highwaymen's haunt in the golden days of the Great North Road – the notoriety of this woodland meant that it was cut back to within an archer's bow-shot to safeguard travellers. Today, you're more likely to hear the drumming of a great spotted woodpecker than 'stand and deliver'.

East of the A1, **Monks Wood** (PE28 2LR; no official car park, use lay-bys around the perimeter) is the largest woodland and the best for exploring. A smorgasbord of ancient trees, rare flora, and weird and wonderful fungi, Monks Wood hosted the largest Nature Conservancy research station between 1961 and 2009. Using the woodland for its research, the station played a leading role in conservation initiatives and gained international recognition for its work on the impact of DDT and pesticides on birds of prey. It also developed important wildflower meadow recreation methods, and it became a national depository for mapping the distribution of British flora and fauna. Today, this 388-acre lowland wood is a National Nature Reserve with a network of public footpaths and grassy rides.

As you explore, you'll be brushing past hazel, blackthorn and dogwood, beneath a canopy of oak, ash and field maple. Keep your eyes peeled for rare wild service trees and billions of beetles (more than 1,000 species). Expect rich colours in autumn and a sea of bluebells in spring; pack a picnic in summer and bring wellies in winter.

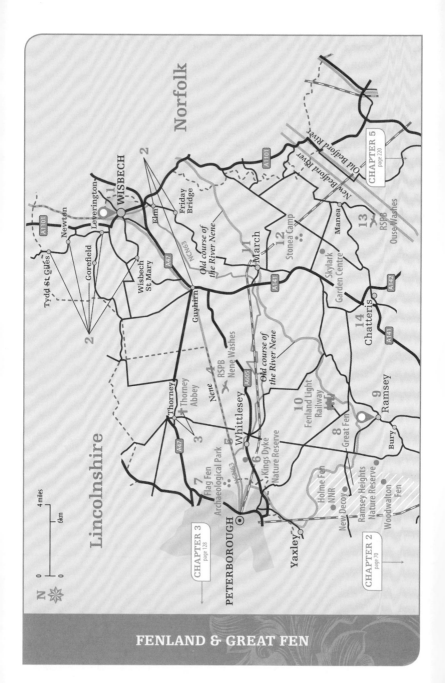

FENLAND & GREAT FEN

4

FENLAND & GREAT FEN

Home to England's lowest point, the country's biggest washland and some of the richest farmland in the world, there's nowhere quite like the Cambridgeshire Fens. With vast fields, straightened rivers and a grid pattern of drainage channels, almost every inch of this landscape has been engineered to prevent it from flooding. Despite this, the Fens can feel wild in their remoteness, with huge flocks of birds and enormous skies where sunsets sizzle in cinematic intensity. This chapter covers the northern half of the Fens – the least-populated area of Cambridgeshire, where life is dominated by arable farming and feels far removed from the rest of the county. To explore, you could cruise along quiet waterways, cycle along empty backroads, take a train along the Hereward Line or walk through some of the flattest countryside in England.

To understand the Fens, it's essential to delve into the past – this was once the largest wetland in England, alive with croaking frogs, whispering reeds and screeching wildfowl. Rising a few feet above the swamps were low-lying islands where early settlers built villages on stilts, hermits sought solitude and towns like Ramsey (page 201) grew around some of the wealthiest abbeys in England. The Cambridgeshire Fens also had a coastline – a ridge of higher ground to the west and south where settlements like Peterborough (Chapter 3) and Waterbeach (Chapter 5) developed along the fen edge.

The people of the Fens lived in tune with their drowned world. They travelled using boats, stilts and ice skates; they built homes from reeds and mud; and they lived off eels, fish and wildfowl, using fertile patches of fen that dried out in summer to graze their livestock. But it was this fertile land, which lay submerged in water for much of the year, that sealed the fate of the wild fens. The great drainage operation began in the 17th century and hasn't stopped since, transforming the swamps into vast swathes of productive agricultural land (see box, overleaf).

THE GREAT DRAINAGE OF THE FENS

There were several early attempts to drain the Fens, first by the Romans and then by the monks of the fenland abbeys, but it wasn't until the 17th century that drainage took place on such a vast scale that life was changed forever. In the 1630s, Charles I gave the go-ahead for one of the reatest engineering projects of the time. The fourth Earl of Bedford and his Company of Adventurers (investors) took on the project, hiring Dutch engineer Cornelius Vermuyden. The River Nene was widened, a network of dykes and ditches were cut by hand, and a new river channel, now known as the Old Bedford River, was created to divert the River Great Ouse directly to The Wash. Despite these efforts, the Fens still flooded, so a second channel – the New Bedford River (also known as the Hundred Foot Drain, owing to the distance between the embankments on either side of the river) – was cut parallel to the Old Bedford River in the 1650s. This created two mighty channels and a large flood storage area known as the Hundred Foot Washes or, in more recent times, as the Ouse Washes.

By the end of the 17th century, the Fens were unrecognisable, with marshes, meres and meanders replaced by a grid pattern of fields and drainage channels. Yet there was one more hurdle to overcome: as the land drained, the soil shrank so much that it contracted below river-level and flooded. Channels were dug deeper, embankments were built higher and a new course for the River Nene was cut between Peterborough and The Wash via Wisbech. Around 700 windmills were also installed to pump water off the land and, in the 1800s when wind power was replaced by steam, full-time drainage took hold.

With the wild swampland tamed, the loss of wilderness was catastrophic – otters, beavers and bitterns were shot, eel populations plummeted, storks fled and endemic species like the large copper butterfly became extinct. Along with the loss of wildlife was the devastation of fenland culture. Centuries-old skills and lifestyles were swept away, and the eel catchers, wildfowlers and fishermen of the Fens had no experience of farming in the modern sense. They fought hard to resist the changes by sabotaging the drainage work but, eventually, they had no choice but to adapt to the new way of life. Today, almost the entire fenland economy depends on artificially drained farmland, which is maintained by around 300 pumping stations and 3,800 miles of watercourses.

Today, towns and villages like Wisbech (page 175), March (page 209) and Thorney (page 186) still occupy the former islands. The difference is that they're now surrounded by seas of farmland, rather than water. With relatively few people living out here, the settlements of the northern Fens range from 'romantically remote' to 'tired and forgotten'. To see them at their most vibrant, visit on a market day or time your trip around an event like the Wisbech Rose Fair (see box, page 182) or the Whittlesey Straw Bear Festival (see box, page 191). Gatherings like these celebrate fenland culture past and present, with folklore and traditional dancing still alive and jigging.

Rich in natural and archaeological finds, the Fens are a living museum of how lives and landscapes have changed over time. Enormous 'bog oaks', the remnants of prehistoric forests, are often found in the peat, while Stonea Camp (page 213) near March is the lowest-lying hillfort in Britain, and parts of a Bronze Age causeway can be seen at Flag Fen Archaeological Park (page 193). The old ways of the Fens are preserved in several small museums, all of which display fenland tools, like eel nets and turf spades – Wisbech & Fenland Museum (page 177) and Ramsey Rural Museum (page 205) are particularly good. Another good way to delve into the past is to read one of the many novels written about the Fens: Graham Swift's *Waterland* (1983) is one of the best known but my personal favourite is *Fenland Chronicle* (1967) by author Sybil Marshall, who lived in Ely (Chapter 5).

For me, the Fens' trump card is its wildlife. Finding refuge in the Ouse and Nene washlands, and in pockets of ancient marsh like Woodwalton Fen (page 197) and Holme Fen (page 198), are flocks of overwintering swans, Britain's largest birch forest and fragile flowers found nowhere else in the country. Some of these fragments are now part of Great Fen (page 195) – a project that aims to connect and expand these wild areas to create one of the most ambitious wildlife restoration projects of our time, returning a portion of the Fens to the partially drowned world it once was.

GETTING AROUND

When you're cruising along arrow-straight roads surrounded by open farmland, driving around the Fens can feel like a blast of freedom – away from the main towns and busiest roads (the A47 and A141), you'll often find very few cars in sight. But keep your wits about you, as many a careless driver has been lulled into a false sense of security only to come a cropper when they hit a pot-hole, meet a tractor or are taken by surprise at an unexpected bend in the road. With drainage channels running alongside every road, most accidents end up with at least one car in a ditch; my brother-in-law Felix can vouch for that. Other fenland

FENLAND & GREAT FEN

The Cambridgeshire Fens have a unique culture, fascinating wildlife, vast horizons and some of the richest farmland in the world.

1 The Whittlesey Straw Bear Festival is a three-day annual event based around traditional dancing as well as music, poetry and storytelling.

SIMON BUHAM

5

2 The Wisbech Rose Fair celebrates the horticultural heritage of the Fens with flower displays and parades. 3 Molly dancing is thought to be distinctly East Anglian and has a long history in the Cambridgeshire Fens. 4 The Fens are home to incredible wildlife, from rare beetles to Chinese water deer. 5 The Brinks in Wisbech is considered one of the finest Georgian brick streets in England. 6 Great Fen is one of Europe's most ambitious conservation projects and aims to connect two of the UK's last fragments of wild fen.

6

HENRY STANIER/GREAT FEN

roads are so rutted and ruptured (thanks to the unstable peat they're built on), you have no option but to go slow – even cyclists should take it easy to avoid ripping a tyre.

TRAINS

There are three train stations within this chapter: Manea, March and Whittlesea (Whittlesea Station uses a different spelling from the town of 'Whittlesey', which it serves). All three sit on the Ely–Peterborough **'Hereward Line'** (⊘ herewardcrp.org) – a scenic stretch of railway named after Hereward the Wake (see box, page 175), who travelled from Ely in the 11th century to plunder Peterborough Cathedral. The end-to-end journey takes around 40 minutes.

March has links to Cambridge, with regular services taking just over half an hour, and Manea also has a direct line to Cambridge. Most trains between Whittlesea and Cambridge go via Peterborough.

BUSES

With its central position within the Fens, March is the main hub for bus services in the region. Most villages and towns also have bus services to Peterborough (mostly Stagecoach). Stagecoach 31 connects Ramsey, Whittlesey and the surrounding villages, and also stops one mile from Woodwalton Reserve (Chapel Rd stop). Stagecoach 33 connects March, Whittlesey and Chatteris; and bus 56 connects Wisbech, March and Manea. For Holme Fen reserve, number 415 (Dews Coaches) from Peterborough stops in Holme village, roughly 1½ miles from the reserve. Wisbech and Thorney are on First Group's excel cross country line, which connects to Peterborough in the west and Norwich (in Norfolk) in the east. March and Chatteris also have regular services to Ely (Stagecoach 39) and Cambridge (Stagecoach 8).

WALKING

It's no secret that long-distance walks through the Fens can feel monotonous, with little variation in the views other than more fields, drains and dykes. When I contacted a local rambling group to make sure I wasn't missing a trick, they replied, 'the Fens are a bit flat'. Nonetheless, a short walk of a few miles or so is a great way to experience the big skies and sense of remoteness that the Fens are famous for. The walk between Ramsey and Bury (page 207) for example, is a good option.

You could also follow part of the new **Fen Edge Trail** (fenedgetrail. org) – a series of walking routes that roughly follow the 'coastline' of the Fens (where the low-lying fenland meets higher ground) and trace circular routes around the former fenland islands of Thorney, March, Chatteris, Whittlesey and Wisbech. At the time of writing, most of the walks had been mapped, with ten walk guides already published, including that for a 2½-mile loop around Thorney island (page 187), and the others should follow soon. Keep an eye on the Fen EdgeTrail website, which hosts the walk guides with maps and instructions, along with geological and historical information for each walk.

If, however, you possess enough zen to meditate on the same vista for several hours at a time, you could tackle part of the long-distance **Hereward Way**, which runs for 43 miles between Peterborough and Ely, passing through March and Whittlesey (leaflets can be downloaded at visitcambridgeshirefens.org). The **Greenwich Meridian Trail** (greenwichmeridiantrail.co.uk) also passes through parts of this chapter, navigating through Chatteris, Doddington and March, while the **Nene Way** (ldwa.org.uk) makes its final push towards The Wash via Whittlesey and March. My Dad, who completed this walk from start to finish, told me that the fenland section was 'an experience': 'We spent two days walking towards the same tower on the horizon, and we ran out of "I spy" options pretty quickly.'

CYCLING

With a landscape this flat, fenland cycling can be a breeze, and dedicated riders can clock up some serious miles – that said, never underestimate the power of a headwind, which can make contour-free roads feel like mountains. A good source of inspiration for route planning is visitcambridgeshirefens.org/cycling – take a look at the **Cycling in the Fens** download, which has ten rides ranging from 11 to 25 miles. Of these, I can recommend the 13-mile *Apples & ale* route (see box, page 184), which loops past the orchards and village pubs west of Wisbech.

TOURIST INFORMATION

Etcetera Community Hub 7 York Row, Wisbech PE13 1EB 01945 232456
 visitcambridgeshirefens.org

Another good cycling option is National Cycle Network Route 63 (NCN63), which guides you through Wisbech, March and Whittlesey, and links to Peterborough in the west. My favourite section is the 11-mile ride between March and Wisbech, which has panoramic views of open fenland landscapes and leads through Elm village. There's also a waymarked NCN63 'wet weather route' which detours along an elevated track in Rings End Local Nature Reserve.

 BIKE SPARES & REPAIRS

The following all offer repairs and bike sales. Your nearest options for hire are at Wicken Fen (page 223) and Ferry Meadows (page 131).

The Cycle Shop 3 Nene Parade, March PE15 8TD ✐ 01354 656150 ⟁ thecycleshop.uk.com ⊙ Mon & Wed–Sat
Discount Cycles 114–115 Norfolk St, Wisbech PE13 2LD ✐ 01945 474635 ⊙ Mon, Tue & Thu–Sat
Halfords Unit D, Cromwell Rd, Wisbech PE14 0SL ✐ 01945 580756 ⊙ daily

BOAT

The Fens have miles of interlinking rivers and manmade channels to explore by boat. March is the main hub, with the old course of the River Nene running through the town. Here you could hire a day boat and cruise west to Whittlesey or south to Ramsey, or embark on a longer narrowboat holiday and make your way to Peterborough, Ely, Cambridge or beyond. If you'd prefer to paddle, you can hire a canoe at Fourwinds Leisure.

 BOAT HIRE

Fourwinds Leisure (canoe hire) 113 Whittlesey Rd, March PE15 0AH ✐ 01354 658737 ⟁ fourwindsleisure.com
Fox Boats 10 Marina Drive, March PE15 0AU ✐ 01354 652770 ⟁ foxboats.co.uk/day-boat-hire ⊙ Oct–Mar

WISBECH & THE FAR NORTH

Here on Cambridgeshire's northeast tip, the spaces are wide, the skies feel huge and acres of orchards roll towards the horizon. The town of Wisbech is a hub of fenland culture, with fascinating museums and a much-loved brewery, which supplies all the local pubs. History abounds west of Wisbech, with Bronze Age relics on show at Flag Fen Archaeological Park, and the remains of a once-mighty abbey in Thorney. One of the best ways to experience this area is by bike, with quiet backroads, quiet villages and widescreen fenland views.

1 WISBECH

🏠 **Coach House Loft** (page 317), ⛺ **Secret Garden Touring Park** (page 316)

Wisbech, the northernmost town in Cambridgeshire, is dubbed the 'Capital of the Fens'. Lining the River Nene, it nestles against the Norfolk border, just a few miles south of Lincolnshire. It feels well off the beaten track but Slow travellers who venture to this outpost can look forward to some of the most impressive Georgian architecture in Britain, along with fascinating museums and memorials that honour the town's inspirational former residents – the likes of anti-slavery campaigner Thomas Clarkson, philosopher William Godwin and social reformer Octavia Hill. However, it's important to manage expectations: like many fenland towns, Wisbech could certainly benefit from an injection of cash to revamp its buildings and boost employment opportunities. But beyond the peeling paintwork, there's lots to discover, from Peckover House and Octavia Hill's Birthplace House, to Elgood's Brewery and the Wisbech and Fenland Museum, which houses the original copy of *Great Expectations* by Charles Dickens.

HEREWARD THE WAKE

An Anglo-Saxon action man, Hereward the Wake led the English resistance against the Norman Conquest from his base on the Isle of Ely (Chapter 5), with support from the monks of Ely. The waterlogged Fens made a perfect stronghold for Hereward and his mob, with the Normans unable to penetrate the foreboding swamps – those that did often lost their way and perished.

Launching a series of ruthless attacks, which included plundering Peterborough Abbey, Hereward's army held strong for five years (1066–71) in their effort to resist the feudal system and other changes being enforced by William the Conqueror. Eventually, the monks shifted allegiance to William, and Hereward vanished into the Fens. Famed for his exploits (which include fighting a bear), he has been immortalised in stories and poetry, elevating him to hero status and blurring fact with fiction. Dubbed the 'Hero of the Fens', he has come to personify the region's spirit of independence, with everything from train lines to long-distance walks named in his honour.

In medieval times, Wisbech stood at the mouth of The Wash, where a successful inland port was established. The town thrived for several centuries and saw great prosperity in the 1600s when the Fens were drained and the surrounding area became a rich agricultural hub. By the mid 1800s, it boasted one of England's busiest ports, exporting corn and rapeseed oil to London, the Baltic and beyond. Wisbech owes much of its architectural richness to this period, with wealthy families like the Peckovers building fine townhouses and public buildings. Over time, The Wash became clogged with silt and the viability of the port declined, with most functions shifting to the more accessible port at King's Lynn in Norfolk (13 miles northeast). Although greatly diminished, Wisbech port still functions today and the town's ties with the Baltic have remained strong – thousands of eastern European labourers have migrated here over the years and many have settled in the town.

Central Wisbech has two distinct halves: the town centre with its marketplace and Georgian crescent, and the historic Brinks area, which overlooks the River Nene. These two areas are roughly separated by Town Bridge which, installed in 1931, was one of the UK's first concrete bridges. I've given a brief guide to these areas below but, for a more in-depth tour, ✎ visitcambridgeshirefens.org has several town trails you

THOMAS CLARKSON

Instrumental in ending the British slave trade, Thomas Clarkson (1760–1846) helped to lead one of the most important humanitarian campaigns in modern history. Born in Wisbech and educated at the local grammar school, Clarkson went on to study at Cambridge University, where his essay 'Is it lawful to make slaves of others against their will?' inspired his subsequent career and lifelong commitment to abolishing the slave trade.

Through his work as an abolitionist, Clarkson met Granville Sharp and together they helped form the Committee for the Abolition of the African Slave Trade (1787). Clarkson visited slave ships to gather evidence, which he presented to members of parliament. With MP William Wilberforce taking up the cause, the Slave Trade Act was passed in 1807. Clarkson continued the fight into his eighties, by which point he was almost completely blind. He achieved his ultimate goal in 1838 when nearly 800,000 slaves were freed throughout the British Empire. Despite his achievements, recognition of Clarkson is often overshadowed by that of Wilberforce, who is better known for leading the campaign in parliament.

could follow and the National Trust website has a two-mile walking tour – search for 'Octavia Hill Wisbech heritage walk'.

Town centre & The Crescent

Wisbech town centre sits northeast of Town Bridge and has an impressive array of historical landmarks. Near to the bridge, at the junction of Bridge Street and York Row, the **Clarkson Memorial** is a tribute to Thomas Clarkson (see box, opposite), who devoted his life to the abolition of the slave trade. Beneath his 68ft statue are memorials to fellow abolitionists Granville Sharp and William Wilberforce. A few paces east of here on York Row, you'll find a blue plaque outside the Clarksons' family home (number 8).

Branching south off the Clarkson Memorial, Post Office Lane leads to Alexandra Road where you'll find the **Angles Theatre** (4 Alexandra Rd, PE13 1HQ ✆ 01934 474447 ⌂ anglestheatre.co.uk) – first opened in 1792, this arts centre is one of the oldest surviving Georgian theatre buildings in the country. As you face the theatre, the red-brick building on your left bears a blue plaque that marks the birthplace of journalist and political philosopher William Godwin, who was the founder of philosophical anarchism and the father of *Frankenstein* novelist Mary Shelley. Further south on Alexandra Road is the **Luxe Cinema** (⌂ wisbechcinema.com) – an independent, single-screen picture house. Diagonally opposite, Loves Lane leads left to **St Peter's and St Paul's Church** (Church Tce, PE13 1HP), parts of which are 12th century. Unusually for its size, it has two naves and two chancels, plus some impressive Victorian stained glass.

At the west end of the church is Museum Square, home to **The Wisbech & Fenland Museum** (Museum Sq, PE13 1ES ⌂ wisbechmuseum.org.uk ◔ 10.00–16.00 Tue–Sat). One of the UK's first purpose-built museums, 'W&F' opened its door in 1847. Focusing on fenland culture and Wisbech history, the museum is a charming example of a Victorian museum, with original display cases housing its eclectic collections. Photos and artefacts tell stories of fenland farming, drainage, crime and bygone crafts and trades, like peat digging, along with information about key town landmarks like Wisbech port and Angles Theatre. You can also learn about famous residents like Thomas Clarkson – the museum displays the leg shackles, thumbscrews and branding irons that Clarksons' collected in the 18th and 19th centuries to reveal the cruelty of the slave trade.

In addition to natural and cultural heritage displays, the museum houses internationally important literary documents, including medieval works, 15th-century atlases and the original manuscript of *Great Expectations* by Charles Dickens – the novel was bequeathed to the museum in 1868 by Dickens's friend, Reverend Chauncy Hare Townshend.

Walk through Museum Square and you'll arrive at **Wisbech Castle** (wisbechcastle.org), a manor house built by local builder Joseph Medworth in 1816. The site was originally home to a Norman motte and bailey castle, and later a 16th-century prison. Today, it's managed by Wisbech Town Council (01945 461333), who offer pre-booked tours of the house, gardens and vaults – a series of underground passages that were part of the prison.

In the early 1800s, Joseph Medworth also built **The Crescent** – this circus of Georgian terraced houses which surrounds the manor is built

DIGGING TURF

Turning the turf was an agonising, back aching job. Turning all day long – about twelve thousand turf in a day – made the worker feel sick and bad with pain in his back. A good many real old turf men growed to stoop so much that in their later life they looked more like four-footed animals than human beings.

Fenland Chronicle (1967) by Sybil Marshall

When the Fens were drained, agriculture wasn't the only valuable asset to be gained. Cambridgeshire's black peat – called 'turf' in the Fens – was dug out in blocks, dried and burnt as fuel. Fenmen had been burning peat for centuries but drainage vastly increased access to it. Spring was turf-cutting season: the job was carried out using a long-bladed turf knife (for making the initial cuts) and a becket (an iron-tipped, cricket-bat-shaped tool for slicing the peat into shape), along with specially designed turf spades and shovels. The peat was then left to dry in summer and transported along the fenland waterways in autumn.

Turf was a universal fenland fuel until the early 1900s – by which time, many of the peat-digging areas (known as turf pits) had been repeatedly dug over the years and were no longer fit for use. Today, peat is known to be one of the most polluting fuel sources going, emitting more carbon dioxide than coal and almost twice as much as gas. In contrast, undisturbed peatlands are vital carbon reservoirs, which play a crucial role in regulating the global climate – worldwide, peatlands store around 550 billion tonnes of carbon, which is double the amount stored in our forests.

within the Norman castle's old moat. On the northeast side of The Crescent (between Union Pl and Ely Pl), Market Street leads to Market Place, where markets are still held seven days a week.

The Brinks

Southwest of Town Bridge is North Brink, with its elegant sweep of Georgian houses. Described by Nikolaus Pevsner as 'one of the finest Georgian brick streets in England', it has been used as a filming location for period productions, including the 1999 BBC adaptation of *David Copperfield*. This is the quieter part of town, and strolling along and admiring the architecture is a highlight for Slow visitors.

Set slightly back from the main strip of Georgian buildings, the standout landmark is the National Trust's **Peckover House** (North Brink, PE13 1JR; ☉ Mar–Oct 11.00–13.00 Thu–Mon). Built in 1722, this Georgian merchant's house is testimony to the wealth of Wisbech in the 18th century. For 150 years, it was home to the Peckovers – a Quaker banking family that played an important role in the history of the town. To explore the house, it's best to book in advance on the National Trust website – at the time of writing, you could only visit via a pre-booked guided tour, but it's worth checking the website for the latest updates.

During a tour, you'll explore the rooms of the house and learn about the Peckover family history and banking business. You'll discover the door to the vaults, and step inside the candlelit dining room and the library, which once held Alexander Peckover's impressive collection of books. Upstairs are four bedrooms, one of which has been recreated in 19th-century style, while the others show exhibits about the Peckover family and Wisbech town. When the weather's good, the tour finishes on the roof of the house, giving fantastic views over the estate, the River Nene and the town.

The two-acre Victorian-style garden at Peckover House is a wonderful little sanctuary. Once you're standing within its walls, it's hard to imagine that it's surrounded by a town – it feels more like a rural country retreat, and there are lots of benches dotted around so you can enjoy the flowers and fragrant smells. One of the most important surviving town gardens of its era, the Peckovers laid it out in the early 19th century with foreign and British plants, which included more than 50 varieties of roses. They also installed some beautiful orangeries which, when I visited in spring, were bursting with plant life. The croquet lawn has a glorious view of

THE PECKOVER FAMILY

The Peckovers were a Quaker family that greatly influenced the history and wealth of Wisbech. It all began in 1777 when Jonathan Peckover established a local grocery and, with a reputation for honesty, began offering people a safe place to store their money. Jonathan went on to establish the town's first official bank, forming a partnership with Gurney's bank in 1782. His sons, William and Algernon, later joined the family business.

The family moved into Peckover House (known then as Bank House) in 1790 and began using their wealth to support the town. They funded local institutions, like the Working Men's Club and the Wisbech and Fenland Museum (page 177), and they campaigned for improvements in education and the abolition of slavery. The Peckovers also oversaw the development of many buildings along North Brink, with Algernon providing input as an amateur architect.

When Algernon died in 1893, the family's banking business passed to one of his children, Alexander, who was appointed Lord Lieutenant of Cambridgeshire and Baron Peckover of Wisbech for his services to Cambridgeshire – like the rest of his family, Alexander was a great philanthropist. He retired from banking in 1894 and the business was bought by Barclays Bank in 1896. His daughter, Alexandrina, was the last descendant of Jonathan Peckover and, a few years before she passed away in 1948, she bequeathed Peckover House to the National Trust.

the rear of the house, and if you visit the Wilderness Walk area between 11.00 and 13.00 on Mondays, you'll find yourself in a silent space where mobile phones must be switched off – this is in keeping with the Quaker belief of quiet contemplation that was part of the Peckovers' lifestyle. There's also a pet cemetery in the gardens, which remembers the family's beloved cats and dogs.

Other notable buildings include the Town Council building (1 North Brink, PE13 1JR), which was originally a Corn Exchange and Reading Rooms built by Joseph Medworth in 1811. The former White Hart Hotel (5 North Brink, PE13 1JR) was a thriving coaching inn during the town's Georgian heyday; the slogan 'Patronized by Royalty' (a replication of the original) which sits over the filled-in coaching archway refers to the day in 1835 when the young Queen Victoria stopped here in her carriage to change horses. At the far southwest end of North Brink is **Elgood's Brewery** (72 North Brink, PE13 1LW ✆ 01945 583160 ⌨ elgoods-brewery.co.uk ☉ tours May–Dec, check the website for the latest shop opening hours), which sits within a building that was built in 1795 as one of the first Georgian breweries outside London. After changing hands several times, the brewery was bought in 1877 by local maltster John Elgood. Brewing began in 1878 and the Elgood family have continued to craft prize-winning ales ever since.

The visitor centre tells the brewery's story and there's a shop and café where, among other things, you can buy Elgood's beer. For a fuller experience, you could join a guided tour to learn about the brewing process and see the 1910 mash tun. You can also visit the brewery's beautiful gardens, which have a maze and ancient trees that are as old as the brewery itself.

Facing North Brink, on the opposite side of the River Nene, is South Brink, with its shorter strip of regency period buildings. For the best view of South Brink's Georgian buildings (which include Octavia Hill's Birthplace House), take a stroll along North Brink between numbers 1 and 27. To access **Octavia Hill's Birthplace House** and museum (7–8 South Brink ⌀ octaviahill.org ☻ 13.00–16.30 Wed–Mon), cross back over Town Bridge and walk a few paces west of the Clarkson Memorial. This volunteer-run museum was the birthplace of Octavia Hill (1838–1912) – a social reformer who co-founded the National Trust, campaigned to improve urban housing and fought hard to preserve open spaces. She believed in the importance of nature for well-being and wanted to improve the standard of living conditions for working-class people. When she left Wisbech, she moved to London and became shocked at the conditions faced by the urban poor. She began overhauling neglected properties and reducing overcrowding by charging lower rents. In addition to taking good care of her properties, she nurtured the communities that lived in them, providing educational opportunities like music lessons, theatre performances and cultural outings. She also believed that access to nature was key in transforming lives, and so began campaigning to save green spaces from development. In 1895, she helped to found the National Trust for Places of Historic Interest or Natural Beauty, so that nature could 'be kept for the enjoyment, refreshment, and rest of those who have no country house'. She continued campaigning and developing the trust until her death in 1912.

The museum has a pretty garden and 13 rooms, many of which have been decorated in an early Victorian style, typical of the era when Octavia Hill lived here (1830s/40s). The rooms tell the story of her life, her achievements and the people who influenced her. The John

Ruskin Room looks at the impact this writer and philosopher had on her life, and the National Trust Room explains how she helped to found the charity. There's also an Army Cadet Room, which details how she formed this youth organisation to help urban youths socialise and find direction. Down in the basement, you can experience what life was like in the Victorian slums of London through reconstructed displays of squalid living conditions.

¶ FOOD & DRINK

Wisbech has several places to curb hunger pangs or quench your thirst but few truly appeal to the Slow mindset. You'll find most cafés and restaurants in and around the marketplace, or you could visit **The Clock Tearoom** at Octavia Hill's Birthplace House (10–14 South Brink, PE13 1JQ ⊙ 13.00–16.30 Wed–Mon), which serves teas, cakes and sandwiches.

The licensed café/bar at **Elgood's Brewery** (72 North Brink, PE13 1LW ✎ elgoods-brewery.co.uk) serves homemade cakes and light lunches made with local ingredients. Wisbech also has several pubs, most of which serve Elgood's beer. The 18th-century **Red Lion** (32 North Brink, PE13 1JR) occupies a particularly good spot, facing the river. A traditional, no frills pub serving hearty home-cooked food, it was built in 1764 as a hostelry.

2 VILLAGES & ORCHARDS WEST OF WISBECH

Peaceful villages lie to the west, south and north of Wisbech (anywhere on the east side of the town is in Norfolk). Life has a wonderfully gentle pace here, with quiet rural settlements surrounded by open fens, ancient sea banks (relics of the days when the coastline was closer) and hundreds of acres of orchards – some of the apple trees here are more than 100 years old. Come spring, the orchards are heady with the scent of blossom, while autumn sees them heavy with fruit. Exploring the backroads in these parts is an experience in itself – some are so narrow and rutted that car drivers have little choice but to crawl along at a snail's pace, while it isn't uncommon to find the locals strolling or cycling down the middle of the roads, which is testimony to the lack of traffic in these parts. If you have a bike (though note that there are no obvious places to hire one round here), there are lots of quiet routes to explore, including NCN63 between Elm and Wisbech, and the backroads between Leverington, Newton and Tydd St Giles.

Directly south of Wisbech is the pretty village of **Elm**, where the early Gothic church of All Saints has a double hammerbeam roof, adorned with angels, dragons and two rowing boats – a reminder that this village once sat beside a salty marsh, at the mercy of The Wash. A mile and a half south of Elm is **Friday Bridge**, with its pebble-dashed clock tower, 19th-century water tower and lopsided church tower – the foundations of St Mark's (built 1860) have suffered from peat shrinkage but the building is, apparently, stable enough for services to continue. South of here, it's pretty much uninterrupted fenland all the way to March and Manea. West of Elm are acres of apple orchards growing traditional fenland varieties, while the village of **Guyhirn** sits just off the A47 and is notable for its Grade II-listed old chapel. Cared for by the Churches Conservation Trust, Guyhirn Chapel of Ease was built in 1660 during the Puritan Commonwealth of England and has been virtually unchanged since. Its simple and austere style features plain glass windows and narrow pews that were deliberately unsuited to kneeling.

North of Guyhirn is **Wisbech St Mary**, a large village surrounded by orchards. In its centre is the 14th/15th-century parish church of Wisbech Saint Mary with Guyhirn, which contains artefacts collected by the former village vicar Mowbray Smith, including the dented helmet that saved his life at the Battle of the Somme. On the village's northern edge is Fens Falconry (Station Rd, PE13 4RY ⊘ fensfalconry. co.uk) – an appointment-only falconry where you can book in for owl evenings, hawking experiences and bird of prey handling. Two and a half miles northwest of here is one of my favourite places in the Fens: Manor Farm Woodland Walks (344 Main Rd/B1166, Church End, Parson Drove PE13 4LF ⊙ 11.00–15.00 Wed–Sun). The landowner has rewilded parts of the farm for walkers to enjoy, with trails mown through the grass and woodland past wildlife-rich hedgerows and

Apples & ale cycle ride

✿ OS Explorer map 235 *Wisbech & Peterborough North*; start: Elgood's Brewery, 72 North Brink, Wisbech PE13 1LW ♥ TF455092; 13 miles; easy (flat all the way)

O ne of several cycle routes on ⊘ visitcambridgeshirefens.org, this 13-mile loop begins at Elgood's Brewery in Wisbech (or you could set off from any of the villages en route) and leads along quiet backroads past orchards, peaceful villages and pubs (most serve Elgood's beer). It's a glorious route with spectacular views across the Fens. Some of the most impressive orchards lie between Fitton End and Leverington, where neat rows of apple trees reach towards the horizon. You can download more detailed instructions of this route from the website.

1 With Elgood's Brewery on your right, cycle along North Brink for just under two miles, with the River Nene embankment on your left.

2 Turn right on to Bevis Lane, then take the first left on to New Drove, which leads past orchards and farmland. At the end of New Drove, turn right on to Rummers Lane.

3 Turn right into Wisbech St Mary at the end of the lane and then, just after the Wheel Inn, turn left on to Station Road.

4 When Station Road meets the B1169, turn right to cycle along Garden Lane (which runs parallel to the B1169). Cross over the B1169 and turn right, following the signpost for Wisbech. After about 160yds, turn left on to Wolf Lane, following the signpost for Gorefield.

5 At the end of Wolf Lane, turn left on to High Road. Just before St Paul's Church, take the right turn on to Gote Lane, following the signpost for 'Newton 2½'.

6 Turn right on to Fitton End Road at the end of Gote Lane and follow this for a mile, through the hamlet of Fitton End and past farms and huge orchards.

7 At the end of Fitton End Road, turn right, following the sign for 'Leverington 1¼'. After a mile you'll reach Leverington church (on your right); go straight ahead on Church Road here.

8 When Church Road meets the B1169 (Dowgate Rd), you'll have the Rising Sun pub on your left; turn left on to the B1169 (signposted for Wisbech) and stay on it for half a mile.

9 Just before the traffic lights and A1101, turn right on to Pickards Way. At the end of the road, take the right turn on to Harecroft Road and follow it left around the corner to Chapel Road. Just after the zebra crossing and small car park on your right, turn right on to Old Market and

ponds. The farmer will give you a tour himself if he's free, and there's a rustic train carriage which is used as a tea room.

Leverington is northeast of Wisbech St Mary and is home to 13th-century St Leonard's Church and an old sea bank, which once marked

then the first right on to North Brink, just before Town Bridge. Follow North Brink for half a mile back to Elgood's Brewery.

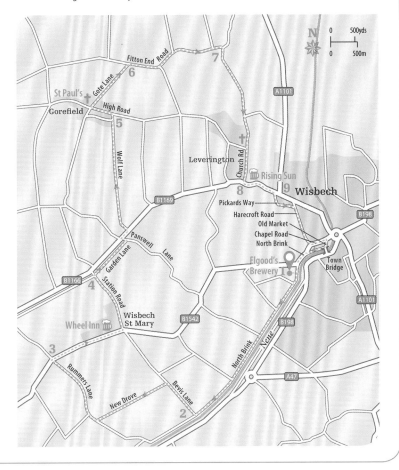

the edge of The Wash. Back then, goods were transported to the village along marshland creeks that linked with the River Nene. When the river was straightened in the 1700s, the marshes were reclaimed and the creeks dried up. Today, the old sea bank has become an elevated footpath between Leverington and Wisbech (half a mile each way). To find the start point from Leverington, head north of the church along Church End and follow the footpath sign for Roman Bank.

Northwest of Leverington is the Early English flint church in **Gorefield** village, while the remote villages of **Newton** and **Tydd St Giles** sit further north still, close to the Lincolnshire border. Cycling or driving along the quiet roads between these villages can feel like a real adventure, with big skies, huge expanses of fenland and roads so ruptured by peak shrinkage that they'll clip the bottom of your car if you're not careful.

¶¶ FOOD & DRINK

All of the villages I've mentioned have at least one pub, except for Newton, whose local boozer closed down. Most serve traditional pub grub and Elgood's beer from the brewery in Wisbech (page 180). Other places to eat and drink include:

Manor Farm Woodland Walks & Railway Carriage Tea Room 344 Main Rd/ B1166, Church End, Parson Drove PE13 4LF ⌀ 07999 510678 ⬛ ☉ 11.00–15.00 Wed–Sun & special events. The casual, ad-hoc nature of this makeshift café sums up the easy-going attitude of rural fenland life. The tea carriage is sometimes open for lunches but, if closed, you can order drinks and fresh baguettes by calling the number on the pinned-up menu by the parking area – the kitchen staff will bring your order out, and you can enjoy it on one of the seats dotted around the farm. The tea carriage also opens for pop-up suppers and private bookings – to find out when the next event is, contact them directly or check their Facebook page.
Orchard Tea Room & Farm Shop Redmoor Ln, PE14 0RN ⬙ theorchardtearoom.co.uk ☉ 11.00–16.00 Fri–Mon. This rustic café sits at the edge of a beautiful apple orchard that has been in the same family for generations. It sells cakes, light lunches and local produce. You can also walk your dog on the orchard trails.
The Potting Shed Bar Mile Tree Ln, Wisbech PE13 4TR ⬛ ☉ 09.00–21.00 Sun–Thu, 09.00–21.00 Fri & Sat. Two miles southwest of Wisbech, this ranch-style bar is part of the Secret Garden Touring Park (page 316). They serve local beers, ciders and their own liqueurs, distilled on site. Food trucks visit on the weekends, and they often have live music (check Facebook for upcoming events).

3 THORNEY ABBEY & VILLAGE

🏠 **Dog in a Doublet** (page 316)

Thirteen miles west of Wisbech, Thorney village boasts the remains of a Benedictine abbey, along with some of the most extensive Victorian cottage architecture in England. In the days of the pre-drained Fens, Thorney was an island, connected to the fen edge by the faintest whisker of higher ground, and would have been surrounded by swamps when water levels were high. Thorney's earliest settlement was a hermitage, which was later developed into an abbey but, unlike the abbeys at Peterborough, Ely and Ramsey, Thorney never had a market or a medieval town. Instead, the island was devoted entirely to religious worship.

With much of the abbey destroyed during the Dissolution (1536–41), the village you see today was shaped by the Dukes and Earls of Bedford – the powerful gents who orchestrated the 17th-century drainage of the Fens. Thorney island and its surrounding fens were granted to John Russell (the first Earl of Bedford) in 1549 and, for the next 350 years, the Russells (successive Dukes and Earls of Bedford) shaped and developed the village as an estate. Many of their employees were French Huguenots who, having fled to England to escape religious persecution, were recruited to help drain the Fens. In 1848, the seventh Duke of Bedford commissioned a 'model village' for his workers and, by the end of the century, more than 300 cottages had been erected, along with schools, a fire station, sewerage system and freshwater supply. The architect was Samuel Sanders Teulon, a Huguenot descendant who also created the Wansford look (page 150).

To get the most from a visit to Thorney, you need to understand its historical context. Luckily, the excellent volunteers at **Thorney Museum** (The Tankyard, Station Rd, PE6 0QE ⌂ www.thorney-museum.org.uk ☺ Easter–Sep 14.00–17.00 Sun or by appointment) are here to help. If you call in advance, they can arrange a guided village tour for a nominal fee. My guide was historian Dorothy, who had an encyclopedic knowledge of Thorney's past. As well as giving me the full backstory to the island, abbey and model village, she pointed out local quirks, like the worn-down stone outside the girls' school where the boys used to climb up to peer through the window. The museum itself is full of local history, telling Thorney's story from fenland hermitage to model village. It includes a scale model of Thorney Abbey and a 14ft-long copy of Teulon's town plan.

If you fancy stretching your legs with a walk through the countryside, Thorney has a 2½-mile stretch of the Fen Edge Trail (⌂ fenedgetrail. org), which starts and finishes at Thorney Abbey, following parts of the

THE FEN FIVE

During the medieval period, the remoteness of the wild fens attracted Christians seeking solitude. Hermitages were built on the fenland islands and, over the years, they were developed into monasteries. By the 11th and 12th centuries, the Fens were home to five of the wealthiest monastic houses in England: Ely, Thorney, Ramsey, Peterborough and Crowland. Collectively known as 'the Fen Five', these mighty monasteries had a huge influence over the region's land, resources and wealth, not to mention its devotion to God.

Today, you can experience the fabric of these former monasteries at Peterborough Cathedral (page 134) and Ely Cathedral (page 228) but, sadly, the other three sites fell victim to the Dissolution and were almost completely destroyed – at Thorney (page 186), the old west porch is now part of the church of St Mary and St Botolph, while a fragment of an old gatehouse still stands at Ramsey (page 201). Crowland has a little more to show but sits just over the Cambridgeshire border in Lincolnshire.

island's old perimeter. You'll find a map and instructions on the Fen Edge Trail website, or you could ask at the museum about guided walks, which include historical and geological commentary.

A mini tour of Thorney

If you haven't arranged a tour with the museum, a self-guided wander around the village will reveal the main sights. **Thorney Abbey** on Abbey Place (B1040) is the obvious place to start – it's officially known as 'the Abbey Church of St Mary the Virgin and St Botolph' but most people call it Thorney Abbey, in reference to the Benedictine abbey that once stood here. Built on the site of a 7th-century hermitage, the abbey was founded in 972 and grew to become one of the largest of its time, with its abbots holding great power and wealth. Following the Dissolution, only the west porch and nave survived, while much of the stone was used to build the Cambridge colleges of Trinity and Corpus Christi. The nave and porch were restored in the 17th century (note the date 1638 engraved in the porch's façade) to create the church you see today, with further restoration work in the 19th century.

For a sense of what the original abbey looked like, stand back and take in the full glory of the west porch. The carved row of Anglo-Saxon saints is testimony to just how important this abbey was, with some of them buried in the grounds. Step inside (it's usually open) and, as you gaze down the nave, try to imagine the original abbey: at around 290ft long, it was two and a half times the length it is today. The blue stained glass at the east end of the chancel depicts the miracles of Thomas Becket and was copied from Canterbury Cathedral.

Back out in Abbey Place, the small green on the south side of the church is surrounded by stone houses that were partly built from the abbey's stone. The building opposite the West Porch is **Abbey House** – the oldest house in Thorney (some parts are 16th century), it was originally home to the Dukes of Bedford but has seen many alterations since.

Turn to face the church again and walk left through the graveyard (around the church's north side) to peer over the wall on to **Church Street**. The gabled stone building with diamond leaded windows was the original **girls' school**, designed by Teulon for the model estate. The weather-worn shield on the wall is the Earl of Bedford coat of arms. Continue around to the east end of the church and follow the path to the church gate, which leads to a park. Turn left and follow the path to Wisbech Road (B1167), where you'll be faced by a string of terraced houses that appear suspiciously uniform. These are some of the original **Victorian cottages**, where the estate workers lived. Dorothy from Thorney Museum informed me that, in addition to receiving a house, the estate workers were also given a third of an acre of land to grow their own veg and raise a pig. If you walk right (east) along Wisbech Road, you'll find plenty more of these cottages, all in a similar style but with slightly different windows or bricks for variety. Once you'd had your fill, walk west along Wisbech Road to the B1040 and turn right (this part of the B1040 is called Station Road).

Ahead, you'll see a 96ft brick tower on your right. This is Bedford Hall, part of the Jacobean-style Tankyard built by Teulon in 1855. The tower provided water storage for the model village, with water pumped from the River Nene via Thorney River. Teulon's Tankyard also featured a sawmill, smithy, craft workshops and the engineer's house, which is now the museum. To return to Thorney Abbey, retrace your steps down Station Road and cross to Abbey Place.

FOOD & DRINK

Tea at 18 18 Wisbech Rd, PE6 0SB ⊙ 10.00–16.00 Tue–Sat. Traditional little tea room serving good-value sandwiches, cakes and homemade milkshakes. There's a garden at the back.

4 RSPB NENE WASHES

Eldernell Ln, Nr Coates PE7 2DD

Part of a large washland (flood storage area), this RSPB reserve is the most important breeding site for black-tailed godwits in the UK. One of our most threatened species, around 50 pairs breed on the wetland each spring – to spot them, look for brown wading birds with long black legs and bills. The winter floods bring more excitement, with thousands of Bewick's and whooper swans visiting the washland. Common cranes, the UK's tallest bird (up to 4ft), are another winter spectacle. Having vanished from the UK in the 17th century, record numbers can now be seen at the reserve. In summer, you can also see warblers near the car park, or hear the haunting call of corncrakes, while autumn is good for osprey, marsh harriers and other birds of prey on the hunt.

On arrival, you may be surprised to find nothing more than a car park and an information board. You are indeed in the right place but there's no trail network, no bird hides and not even any toilet facilities here. Instead, the elevated car park gives uninterrupted views from the reserve's southern barrier bank – it's an exceptional vantage point, with little to obscure your panoramic view. Even in summer, when birdlife is less forthcoming, I enjoyed a lovely afternoon with a deckchair, a flask of coffee and serene views over the washes. If that sounds too sedate, you can follow the Nene Way footpath along the south bank, bird spotting as you stroll. To venture down into the washland itself, you'll need to join one of the RSPB's occasional guided tours (⊘ rspb.org.uk), which in the past have included evening bird walks and 4x4 safaris.

5 WHITTLESEY

Directly south of Thorney, Whittlesey (sometimes spelt 'Whittlesea') is a typical fenland town. It began life as an island settlement, back when a few feet or so of elevation made the difference between swamp and dry land. The town has a train station, a 27-acre local nature reserve (Lattersey LNR, New Rd, PE7 1SZ) with wetlands and boardwalks, and a heritage museum but there otherwise isn't a whole lot more for visitors, and it's no secret that the town can feel rather tired, with youngsters bemoaning 'there's nothing to do'. However, this complaint is flipped on its head for three days each year when the quirkiest festival in Cambridgeshire makes its annual debut – the Straw Bear Festival (see box, opposite) is an absolute must if you're visiting the Fens in January.

THE STRAW BEAR FESTIVAL

strawbear.org.uk

My favourite fenland festival, the Straw Bear takes place on the second weekend in January. It's a three-day event of music, drinking, poetry, storytelling and, most of all, dancing – hundreds of morris, Molly, clog and sword dancers flock to Whittlesey to hey, cast and polka in the streets. It really is good fun, and you can't help but jig along as you watch groups of costumed dancers performing in the town centre. The centrepiece is the straw bears themselves – a local man and boy dressed from head to toe in straw and led through the streets by their 'keepers', followed by a merry crowd of festivalgoers.

The custom is centuries old, harking back to a time when, on Plough Monday, a man or boy dressed in straw would dance from door-to-door for money or food. Nowadays, the festivities kick off with a Friday night concert, followed by a parade and dancing on Saturday, and a bonfire on Sunday to 'burn the bear' (with said man and boy safely removed from the costume). If you can only make one day, come on Saturday. The parade and dances are free to watch (donations optional), and it's best to arrive early, as trains, roads and parking spaces are always filled to capacity. If driving, see the website for parking options and use the festival's shuttle-bus service to travel into the action.

The Whittlesey Summer Festival (September) is another annual highlight of the town, with a parade, music, marching bands and kids' entertainment, plus a display of classic cars. Details are posted on whittleseytowncouncil.gov.uk.

At the heart of Whittlesey is the market square and **Buttercross** – a 17th-century market house. A few attractive buildings stand around the square, including the 18th-century George Hotel (currently a Wetherspoon pub) and, on the corner of Market Street, a 17th-century thatch with a miniature straw bear dancing on the roof. Scraping the sky behind the George Hotel is the 173ft spire of **St Mary's Church** (Station Rd); inside the church is a memorial to local celebrity Sir Harry Smith – the Hero of Aliwal – who you can learn about at Whittlesey Museum. The church is often locked but you can visit for services – see wpcteam.co.uk for details.

A short walk from the Buttercross, **Whittlesey Museum** (Market St, PE7 1BD whittleseymuseum.co.uk) occupies the 19th-century Town Hall, which once housed a horse-drawn fire engine. A tribute to fenland culture, it is full of local treasures, including old toys, a funeral cart, an old forge and a display about Sir Harry Smith, the 'Hero of Aliwal' – a Whittlesey-born lad, Harry Smith became a commander in

SCUBA DIVING & OPEN-WATER SWIMMING

When I was a teenager, I used to visit Whittlesey to go scuba diving at **Gildenburgh Water** (Eastrea Rd, PE7 2AR ✆ 01733 351288 🖱 gildenburgh. com ⏰ 08.00–20.00 Fri, 08.00–16.00 Sat–Thu). Known to regulars as 'Gildy', this former brickworks turned 6½-acre diving lake has a maximum depth of 72ft.

Lurking in the deep, along with giant pike, are a series of sunken objects for divers to discover – my favourite was always the double-decker bus. You'll find scuba divers here in the daytime and after dark, along with freedivers and open-water swimmers. To join them, you'll need to book a slot in advance via the website.

the British Army, leading the 1846 Battle of Aliwal in India. He also became Governor and Commander in Chief of the Cape of Good Hope in South Africa, and the city of Ladysmith is named after his wife. Sir Harry and Lady Smith are buried in Whittlesey Cemetery (Cemetery Rd), and the town has no shortage of memorials to celebrate their hero: a plaque on number 17 St Mary's Street marks his birthplace; Sir Harry Smith Community College is named after him; and St Mary's Church dedicates a chapel to him.

Whittlesey also has 27 surviving sections of **mud wall**, which were built using clay and straw. One of the best examples is on West End (A605), where a long, thatched section leads west of the Low Cross junction. The Whittlesey Mud Walls Group has created a walking tour of the walls, with leaflets available to download on 🖱 whittleseymuseum.co.uk. They also have a Facebook page where they announce occasional guided tours.

Southeast of the town centre, just past Lattersey Local Nature Reserve, is the start of the **Whittlesey Way** – a five-mile circular route that passes through open fenland and the village of Coates. It isn't the most interesting of walks, as it mostly follows rural byways that have the feel of rough country roads, but it would make a good traffic-free cycle ride for families with younger kids. It's easy to follow if you keep your eye on the waymarkers, or you can download a map from 🖱 visitcambridgeshirefens.org.

🍴 FOOD & DRINK

Whittlesey has plenty of places to fill your face but it doesn't have a whole lot in the way of Slow food. A better bet is to head one mile north to **Dog in a Doublet** (North Side, PE6 0RW

✆ 01733 202256 ⌖ doginadoublet.co.uk). This unique pub/restaurant sits amid the fenland beside the River Nene, with many ingredients on their menu sourced from their farm. It's a slightly ramshackle, quirky sort of place, but it's all part of the no-frills fenland charm. Last time I visited, I sat outside on the terrace and tucked into an enormous Sunday roast. It's also a popular brunch spot for wild swimmers who often come here for a dip in the river.

6 KINGS DYKE NATURE RESERVE

222 Peterborough Rd (A605), PE7 1PD ⌖ kingsdykenaturereserve.com

One mile west of Whittlesey, this nature reserve occupies a former London Brick clay pit, which was dug by pickaxe in the 1920s. Now returned to nature, it still sits beside an active brickworks, which you can gaze down on from a viewing point. Of more interest to most are the nature trails, ponds and bird hides, where you can peer at the reserve's wildlife. In 2019, Kings Dyke was named one of the UK's most biodiverse reserves – BBC wildlife presenter Chris Packham led an audit that identified 1,139 different species, from otters and water voles to the *Chrysomeia saliceti*, a new species of beetle for Britain.

You can also go fossil hunting here – the Oxford Clay that the reserve sits on was formed 140 million years ago and, as a result, is riddled with fossils. A purpose-built fossil-hunting area is filled with clay from the surrounding quarry sides, and visitors are free to rummage in the debris to their heart's content. Ammonites are ten a penny – you only have to look down at your feet to find one, while serious fossil hunters will want to take a trowel and chip away at the rocks for a chance of finding evidence of belemnite shellfish, Jurassic sharks and *leedsichthys* – the world's largest fish. You're welcome to take any findings home.

To access the reserve, you'll need to either visit on an open day (see the website for dates) or register (for free) as a member – once you've sent an application, they're usually pretty quick to issue you with a membership card (I received mine within a week) and instructions for the gate code. Membership forms are on the website, which also gives tips on fossil finding.

7 FLAG FEN ARCHAEOLOGICAL PARK

The Droveway, Northey Rd, PE6 7QJ ⌖ vivacity.org ⊖ Apr–Sep

This fascinating archaeology park is the only place in the UK where you can see original Bronze Age remains in situ. Home to part of an ancient causeway that once stretched across the waterlogged fens, Flag

Fen transports you more than 3,000 years back in time, when hunter-gatherers developed small sheep farms on the fen edge and fenland islands. These farmers installed a line of more than 50,000 wooden posts across the marshes between points of higher ground. It is thought that these posts were used as a bridge, a barricade and a ceremonial site for making offerings – hundreds of deliberately buried objects have been uncovered, ranging from swords to silver jewellery.

Archaeology buff or not, I'd highly recommend a visit. The historical weight of this place is astounding and the landscaped site is a serene place to spend half a day, with its meres, wildlife and grassy lawns, which are grazed by horned Soay sheep – the same type of breed that would have been farmed here in the Bronze Age.

After entering through the visitor centre, you can walk through the grounds, following a walking trail that guides you to key sites. These include a reconstructed Bronze Age roundhouse and a preservation

WILDLIFE WONDERS

The Fens are home to vast flocks of birds, rare plants and tiny creatures that are bouncing back from the brink of extinction. Here's a handful of highlights and where to find them.

Bitterns – Once extinct in the UK, Britain's loudest bird hides in the reeds at Woodwalton Fen and Wicken Fen. The male's booming foghorn call is unmistakable.

Black-tailed godwits – RSPB Nene Washes is the UK's most important breeding site (spring) for these waders, which also visit RSPB Ouse Washes in autumn.

Cranes – In 2016, breeding cranes were spotted in Cambridgeshire for the first time in four centuries. Find them at RSPB Nene Washes where they form flocks of more than 30, or on autumn afternoons at RSPB Ouse Washes.

Fen violets – These pale violets are only found at three UK sites, including Woodwalton Fen and Wicken Fen. Spot them flowering between May and June.

Fen Woodrush – Found in the Great Fen reserves and nowhere else in the country, you'll find these honey-coloured flowers in Woodwalton Fen and Holme Fen.

Marsh harriers – A highlight at Woodwalton Fen are the harriers' aerial displays over the northern reed bed. You'll also find them roosting at Wicken Fen and RSPB Nene Washes.

Water voles – These endangered rodents have found refuge in the hundreds of miles of ditches that drain the Fens. Look for their star-shaped paw prints in the mud.

Whooper & Bewick's swans – Two of the most important UK sites for overwintering swans, see them in their thousands at RSPB Ouse Washes and RSPB Nene Washes.

hall, where you can see a section of the causeway preserved in water – as you peer down from the viewing platform, it's incredible to think just how long ago these wooden posts were installed.

The site's floating museum (suspended over a mere) fills you in on the history of the causeway and reveals how the landscape has changed between the Bronze Age, Roman era and modern day. England's oldest surviving wooden wheel is on display along with other objects that have been recovered from the area. You can also learn how the causeway was discovered in 1982 when archaeologist Francis Pryor tripped on a protruding piece of wood.

Two miles south of Flag Fen is another important archaeological site which was part of the same historical landscape. Must Farm is the excavation site of a late Bronze Age settlement, which has revealed some of the most celebrated finds of its kind in Europe, from fish traps and textiles to nine intact prehistoric log boats. Although you can't visit Must Farm, you can learn about it and see some of the log boats being preserved in wax in one of the barns at Flag Fen – the process takes several years, and the boats can be viewed through a glass screen.

GREAT FEN & RAMSEY ABBEY

Here in the western Fens, you can stand at England's lowest point, delve into the story of one of the most important religious powerhouses in England and discover the pioneering vision of Great Fen – a conservation project which is set to transform the long-term future of the Fens.

8 GREAT FEN
⊘ greatfen.org.uk

West of Ramsey is a collection of nature reserves that belong to one of the most ambitious conservation projects in Europe: Great Fen. This 50-year habitat restoration initiative aims to connect two of the UK's last fragments of wild fen – Woodwalton Fen and Holme Fen – by restoring the degraded land between and around them. Once a watery world on the edge of Whittlesey Mere (see box, page 199), this area was, along with the rest of the Fens, drained and transformed into an intensive agricultural landscape. But even after drainage took hold, Woodwalton Fen and Holme Fen were still deemed too wet for farming. Having been left to their own devices, they have since become sanctuaries for threatened fenland species that include bitterns, otters, dragonflies and amphibians, along with the rare fen violet and fen woodrush – plants found almost nowhere else in the UK.

Although Holme Fen and Woodwalton Fen provide safe havens for these fragile species, it is difficult for wildlife to thrive in such small and isolated reserves. Great Fen hopes to change this – the plan, which launched in 2001, is to link the two reserves by restoring 14 square miles of land between them. It's an ambition that is widely supported in Cambridgeshire and beyond – actor Stephen Fry became President of Great Fen in 2006, and the Prince of Wales is the Royal Patron. Other patrons include Tim Smit, who created the Eden Project in Cornwall.

Over the coming years, Great Fen will become a mosaic of wetland habitats that mimic the pre-drained fens. This restoration will also help to reduce peat loss, capture carbon, mitigate flood risks and encourage new economic opportunities that focus on tourism and the environment. The first step involves turning arable fields into grassland, to lock in the remaining peat. Tiny new meres are also being created on the former bed of Whittlesey Mere, reed beds are forming naturally and marshland

BRITAIN'S BREAD BASKET

The Fens are home to England's most productive soils and some of the richest farmland in the world. Despite occupying a mere 4% of Britain's farmed land, they boast 4,000 farms, which produce a third of England's fresh veg, a fifth of our potatoes and enough wheat to bake 250 million loaves of bread each year. The mustard plants that create Colman's English Mustard are grown entirely in the Fens and there's a 50% chance that any British beetroot in your kitchen cupboard was grown here. It's fair to say that fenland agriculture plays a vital role in the UK economy, generating more than £3 billion locally each year and employing around 80,000 people, from carrot and wheat farmers to fruit pickers and factory staff.

Britain relies on the Fens to produce the record yields that fuel our businesses and fill our shopping baskets. It's a huge responsibility and, in order for farming to thrive into the future, several fenland challenges need to be tackled, from peat loss and flooding to environmental sustainability. New technologies are being explored, and many farmers are moving away from intensive farming to models that are more in balance with nature. They're also creating new ponds, reed beds, wildlife corridors and bird-friendly zones that, along with enhancing the natural world, can help to mitigate flood risks, anchor the soil and enrich the land they depend on. For many, this agri-environmental approach is seen as the future of fenland farming.

birds are recolonising the region. And not only is the Great Fen project changing the fate of the Fens, it is now being seen as a model to inspire other conservation projects in the UK and beyond.

There are several different sites where you can experience Great Fen, all of which have mapped walking trails that you can download on ✑ greatfen.org.uk. Woodwalton Fen and Holme Fen are the most scenic and, as they are completely contrasting, it's worth visiting both. You could also experience the Great Fen area at night – it's a designated Dark Skies reserve, meaning low levels of light pollution often give clear views of the Milky Way. Guided stargazing events are sometimes advertised on the Great Fen website.

Woodwalton Fen
Chapel Rd, Ramsey Heights PE26 2RS

The richest fragment of Great Fen, and one of England's first-ever nature reserves, Woodwalton Fen gives a glimpse into the landscapes of the past. Bordered by drains and flood banks, it sits at the end of a lonely road and is surrounded by farmland that will, one day, become part of Great Fen. The reserve has an information stand and three marked trails but no other facilities. It's worth mentioning that dogs are not allowed, even on leads.

Driving or cycling is the easiest way to get to this remote reserve, which has a small parking area beside Great Raveley Drain. Find a quiet spot within the reserve and you'll be immersed in ancient fenland sounds – the whisper of grasses, buzzing of dragonflies and calls of waterbirds. Grassy paths lead around the site, and there are three meres with raised bird hides that beckon you to sit patiently and wait for the wildlife to emerge. Among the highlights are marsh harriers and common cranes, which disappeared from the Fens 400 years ago but recently returned. There's also a chance of seeing water voles and Chinese water deer.

Tucked away in the north of the reserve is a stilted bungalow that, 100 years ago, belonged to Charles Rothschild. A banker and dedicated naturalist, Charles bought Woodwalton Fen in 1910 to ensure that at least one part of the ancient fens wouldn't disappear forever. From his 'safari lodge', Charles and his family would observe the fenland wildlife and head out at night to spot moths by lantern light. You can find the bungalow (which is usually closed, except during public events) by following the ¾-mile Bungalow Trail from the reserve's entrance; extend this by just over half a mile and you'll reach Great Fen View where you can climb on to the flood bank and squint across the horizon towards the treeline of Holme Fen. The land between you and this treeline is part of the Great Fen project, and some of it is already being converted into wet pasture.

Ramsey Heights Nature Reserve
Chapel Rd, Ramsey Heights PE26 2RS

On the road that leads to Woodwalton Fen, you'll pass the entrance to Ramsey Heights Reserve. Compared with the other Great Fen reserves, this one is fairly compact (nine acres) but is a good option for families with young kids – there's a minibeast area, a pond-dipping spot, a den-building site and a bird hide. Carved wooden statues and benches are dotted around the pathways that lead past reed beds, meadows, ponds and streams. As you explore, look for water stick insects, rare beetles and great crested newts, along with brown hares, muntjac deer, woodpeckers and red kites.

Near the entrance to the reserve, the Wildlife Trust Countryside Centre occupies a small brick building which is open during Great Fen events and activities (see ⊘ greatfen.org.uk for announcements). This building was once part of the Victorian brickyard which the reserve stands on – it was one of several in the area that extracted the local Oxford Clay. To fire the brick kilns, peat was dug at neighbouring Woodwalton and Lotting fens, while the finished bricks and tiles were transported along the fenland waterways. The Countryside Centre is housed in the original brickworks building and the pond outside is what's left of the old harbour where barges were loaded up with bricks. To learn more about the reserve's brickmaking past, download the Burning Bricks and Hidden Harbour Discovery Trail (870yds) on the Great Fen website.

Holme Fen & the Holme Posts
Nr Holme village

Holme Fen is unlike anywhere else you'll find in the Fens, or in Cambridgeshire for that matter. It's the lowest point in Great Britain (around 9ft below sea level) and, according to Natural England, the 'finest example of birch woodland in natural Britain'. I absolutely love this place – there's something utterly magical about the slender trunks

WHITTLESEY MERE – THE VANISHED LAKE

Much of the Great Fen area was once covered by Whittlesey Mere – one of the largest lakes in England. Up to six miles long and three miles wide, it had two ports and was an important means of fenland transport. For centuries, it dominated local lives, providing a healthy supply of fish, eels, wildfowl and reeds. The medieval fenland monasteries managed the mere's fishing grounds and, by the 1600s, it was a popular place for leisure activities: summer visitors came from far and wide for regattas and pleasure boating, while winter was the time for skating competitions and ice yachting.

During the early years of 17th-century fenland drainage, the lake remained an important source of fenland produce and a local landmark. But, as more of the Fens were drained, the lake's water level began to shrink. By the 1850s, it was a fraction of its original size and the fertile lake bed was deemed more valuable than water and wildlife. East Anglia's greatest mere was drained by a centrifugal pump and, as the water disappeared, so did local livelihoods, ways of life and unique fenland wildlife. Whittlesey Mere is still named on modern maps, although no trace of the once-great lake remains.

and silvery bark of the trees, and the dappled sunlight filtering through the canopy to the forest floor, which boasts 500 species of fungi. And all this in the least-wooded area in the UK. How then, did this 657-acre woodland come to be? It's a story of natural succession: Holme Fen was once an area of reedy wetlands at the edge of Whittlesey Mere (see box, above) but as the lake was drained some of the surrounding land transformed into a raised bog, which became colonised by birch trees – the seeds of which are easily spread by the wind.

Within the woodland are the **Holme Posts**, which look like two big lamp posts sticking 13ft above the ground. These were the brainchild of William Wells – a local landowner who spearheaded the drainage of Whittlesey Mere. In 1848, Wells predicted that, when the lake was drained, the peat-rich soil left behind would shrink. To test his theory, he drove a timber post deep into the earth and cut the top off at ground level. Sure enough, the soil shrank away and the top few inches of the post were revealed – in these early years, the ground shrank as much as nine inches a year. The post was replaced by a more robust iron pole in 1851 and, when it became so exposed that it started to wobble, a second pole was installed in 1957. As you stand beneath this pair today, it's unfathomable to think that the ground was once level with the top of the posts.

You can visit the posts and explore the reserve via several walking tracks. But don't come here expecting a manicured nature reserve with a car park and café – there's no obvious entrance, the footpaths are narrow and winding, and I almost took the bottom out of my car when I drove down one of the two ruptured access roads that slice through the reserve. But it's all part of the fun. There are several small lay-bys where you can park, and you'll find a network of footpaths weaving through the woods and leading to small meres at the eastern and western edges.

The Holme Posts can be reached without walking far – they stand opposite a parking lay-by on the road that runs parallel to Holme Lode. To find them, head half a mile north of the Admiral Wells pub (see opposite) on Yaxley Road, which becomes Hod Fen Drive. When you see a sign directing you to 'the Holme Posts', turn right down this unnamed road, go over a level crossing and you'll find the posts on your right, around half a mile down the road. There's an information board beneath the posts and a map of the waymarked Discovery Trail – a two-mile path which leads around the woodland. To explore more of the reserve, check out the map on the Great Fen website – I can recommend the 2½-mile loop past Trundle Lookout, a large bird hide next to a partly restored reed bed.

New Decoy
Long Drove (B660), Nr Holme PE7 3PW

A nature reserve in progress, parts of New Decoy are still being farmed while the rest is under restoration. Work started in 2010 and some of the land near the car park has now returned to wet meadow. Admittedly, it isn't the most varied of landscapes and, unless you're an ecologist or hardcore Great Fen enthusiast, you'll find Woodwalton Fen or Holme Fen more rewarding. However, what it does offer are uninterrupted vistas across the open fenland, and a rare insight into a Great Fen reserve in the making. The car park area also displays some fine pieces of bog oak (see box, opposite).

There are information boards to explain the site's past, present and future, plus walking trails to guide you around the meadows, ponds, woods and farmland – the Dragonfly Trail (1½ miles) and Last of the Meres Trail (6½ miles), which link up with the Northern Loop Trail (2½ miles) on the reserve's northern edge. Within the reserve are ancient

BOG OAK

A feature of the fenland landscape, bog oak or black oak is a relic of the ancient forests that once covered the area. It's not certain why the forest disappeared but it's likely to be due to rising sea levels. When the trees fell, they became preserved in the acidic peat bogs, only to be revealed when the Fens were drained and the peat started to shrink. While problematic to the early farmers, who hauled them out by hand, they were also valuable – once dried, they could be used as fuel; larger pieces could be carved into furniture.

Pieces of bog oak are still being unearthed today and, in 2012, a 42ft-long piece of 5,000-year-old oak was found. Some years later, a group of craftspeople decided to embark on a pioneering project to preserve the 'Jubilee Oak' by crafting it into an iconic table that will be placed in Ely Cathedral. At the time of writing, the tabletop was complete and they were in the process of raising funds for the understructure. You can follow their story at ⌗ thefenlandblackoakproject.co.uk.

decoy ponds, old farm buildings and the remains of the Ramsey–Holme railway line. There's also the unique 'Jon's bird hide', which was built using straw bales.

FOOD & DRINK

The Admiral Wells 41 Station Rd, Holme PE7 3PH ⌀ 01487 831214 ⌗ admiralwells.co.uk. Britain's lowest pub, the Admiral Wells was named after a prominent local family – one member (Admiral Thomas Wells) was a high-ranking member of the Royal Navy, while his great-grandson, William Wells IV, spearheaded the drainage of Whittlesey Mere. On the edge of Holme village, not far from Holme Fen, it has a large garden with a small wildflower area. Painted in rich, dark colours, the atmospheric interior has log fires and old photos that tell stories of the Fens. Expect British pub food, plus lunchtime baguettes. Sunday roasts are popular.

9 RAMSEY

⋏ Rivermill Caravan & Camping Park (page 316)
⌗ discoverramsey.co.uk

An unassuming market town, Ramsey was once home to one of the richest monastic buildings in England – Ramsey Abbey owned most of Huntingdonshire (Chapter 2) and the most valuable fishing and grazing grounds in the Fens. Built on a peninsula which sat just off the western fen edge, the abbey was surrounded by eel-filled marshes on three sides and was cut off from solid ground when the winter floods rose – everything from gold to building stone had to be brought here by boat.

The town of Ramsey grew around the abbey, with a market and three-day fair established in the 1200s. But in 1539 the abbey came crashing down, quite literally, when it fell victim to the Dissolution. Today, all that remains is part of the gatehouse and some of the precinct wall, while bits of the ruins have been incorporated into the parish church and Ramsey Abbey House, which was built on the site of the abbey.

Despite its limited ruins, the abbey site is still a focal point of the town, with the gatehouse and several 18th-century buildings clustered around Abbey Green. The rest of the town feels at odds with this historical heart as, although Ramsey prospered with the drainage of the Fens and the coming of the railways, it never again experienced the wealth and importance of its pre-Dissolution days. It also had a rough time of it during the Civil War (when much of the town was destroyed), and the Great Plague (the population was decimated in 1666), as well as during a series of 17th- and 18th-century fires which saw many of the oldest buildings burn to the ground.

The town centre mostly consists of **Great Whyte** and the **High Street**, with the latter leading directly to Abbey Green. Great Whyte is an

RAMSEY THE RICH – A POTTED HISTORY

You see, Ramsey were an island as stuck out above the waters of the fen all round; and eleven hundred year ago some old monk as wanted to get away from everybody else took and built a monastery there. Then the monks kept on getting hold of a bit of land here, and another bit there, till it warn't long afore the Abbott of Ramsey were the richest man in all England.

Fenland Chronicle (1967) by Sybil Marshall

For almost 600 years, Ramsey Abbey was one of the most powerful religious houses in England, so wealthy that it was nicknamed Ramsey the Rich. Its story began with a hermitage founded in 969 by Ailwyn, Duke of East Anglia. When the more powerful St Oswald of Glastonbury heard of the hermitage, he developed it into a monastery, sent Ailwyn some monks and stepped forward as the first Abbot of Ramsey. Vast sums of money and eels (which were often used as currency) were invested in the monastery, which was built from Barnack stone (see box, page 146). With a reputation for order and discipline, the abbey became a respected centre of learning with an impressive library. Many nobles sent their children to be educated here and, in the 11th century, three of the abbey's monks became bishops of Dorchester. With this fine reputation, Ramsey amassed much wealth

unusually wide street (up to 82yds across) and once had a stream (Bury Brook) running along its length, which carried boats through the town and fed into the River Nene. Covered by a tunnel in 1852, Bury Brook still exists beneath the tarmac and trickles out into the countryside at the back of the Ale House Kitchen (65 High St). In the centre of Great Whyte is a cast-iron clock tower that was erected in 1888 as a memorial to Rt Hon Edward Fellowes, the first Baron de Ramsey (see box, page 113). Most of the town's shops cater for local needs rather than tourist interests, although Ramsey Indoor Market (Great Whyte, PE26 1HG), on the corner of Little Whyte Street, is worth poking your nose into – it sells fenland crafts and products that range from jewellery to tea cosies. Ramsey also has a small Saturday morning market (on Great Whyte), as well as occasional artisanal markets which are organised by Ramsey Neighbourhood Trust (see their Facebook page for dates). If you're interested in delving deeper into the town's history or taking a self-guided walking tour, the website ⌀ discoverramsey.co.uk is an excellent resource and includes several downloadable town trails. You could also learn more about the covered stream at ⌀ ramseytunnels.co.uk.

– by 1087 it had become the fourth-richest religious house in England, owning 40,000 acres of land and many other assets, including the lucrative fair at St Ives.

But it wasn't all plain sailing. There were fierce rivalries between Ramsey and the other Fen Five monasteries (see box, page 188) over land, assets and boundaries. The bishops at Ely and Ramsey regularly fought over the ownership of local manors, and Ramsey had to pay Thorney Abbey 4,000 eels to gain access to the stone at Barnack quarry. In 1143, the rebel Geoffrey de Mandeville seized Ramsey Abbey in his revolt against King Stephen (see box, page 268). The damage he caused led to a long period of repair and rebuilding, which continued into the 15th century.

When the Dissolution brought an end to the abbey in 1539, the site was granted to Sir Richard Cromwell (great-grandfather of Oliver Cromwell, Lord Protector), who sold the stone to various churches and Cambridge colleges. The estate passed through the Cromwell family and, in the 17th century, Sir Henry Cromwell used the remaining stone to build a house on the site, incorporating the ruins of the abbey's 13th-century Lady Chapel. Ramsey Abbey House still stands today and is used as a school building, while a remaining part of the abbey's gatehouse is home to a late 13th-century statue, which is thought to represent Ailwyn – the humble hermit who initiated one of the wealthiest abbeys England has ever seen.

Surrounded by pleasant countryside, Ramsey is a good place to start a short walk, with footpaths leading in most directions from the town. The circular loop to Bury's village church is my favourite, or you could download the Countryside Trail or Waterways Trail on ⊘ discoverramsey.co.uk, or tackle a section of the Fen Edge Trail (⊘ fenedgetrail.org), which leads five miles south to Wistow village.

Abbey Green & around

At the eastern end of Ramsey High Street is **Abbey Green**, where crowds of pilgrims once congregated and the site of the abbey's annual fair. It's a pleasant spot to ponder the abbey's story, or to listen to the bands that play on Sunday afternoons in June and July. The remains of the **Abbey Gatehouse** (⊙ Apr–Oct 10.00–17.00 Sun; National Trust) dominate the south side of the green – the gatehouse used to span the road but it was dismantled by the Cromwell family in the 1500s and rebuilt at Hinchingbrooke House (page 89). You can walk through the gatehouse on open days but there isn't a huge amount to see as only the inner gate and porter's lodge (which has an ornate oriel window) remain. The gatehouse is also the entrance to Abbey College secondary school, which occupies Ramsey Abbey House – built in the 1600s by Sir Henry Cromwell (Oliver Cromwell's grandfather) on the site of the abbey church, the house was bought by the Fellowes family (see box, opposite) in the 1800s, who leased it to the school in 1937.

On the eastern side of Abbey Green is the Norman-era church of **St Thomas a Becket**. Dating back to c1180, the oldest parts of this building served as an infirmary for the abbey. It was converted into a parish church in the 13th century, and the west tower was added in 1672 using stone from the demolished abbey. The graveyard bears several headstones belonging to the Cromwell and Fellowes families, including Oliver Cromwell, uncle of the Lord Protector. Other interesting buildings around Abbey Green include the almshouses opposite the gatehouse ruin, which were built for 12 women in 1839 using stone from the abbey. The yellow-brick building next door was built in 1848 as a school, with the bell turret separating the boys' side from the girls'.

Flanking the north side of the church is Church Green – a pretty green with old chestnut trees, a war memorial and a duck pond – last time I visited a heron was perched here, reminding me just how close the Great Fen wildlife reserves are. A strip of old houses and buildings overlook the green, including a former Spinning School (the red-brick building with latticed windows), and the single-storey Ramsey Abbey Estate Office.

Another of Ramsey's intriguing landmarks sits around 500yds south of the abbey gatehouse on Hollows Lane. Here, on the corner of Abbey Road, is a scruffy mound known as **Booth's Hill**. This site is thought to have housed a 12th-century fort built by the rebel Geoffrey de Mandeville (see box, page 268) who seized Ramsey Abbey and used the island as a base for his fenland mob. It was converted into an icehouse in the 1800s. There's an information board to fill you in on the details, plus a bridge across the moat for access – although I wouldn't recommend this (unless anything's changed since I last visited) as it was a mission to scramble through the scrub, with little reward for either myself or the wildlife inhabiting it.

Ramsey Rural Museum & around

On the town's northeast fringe, the award-winning **Ramsey Rural Museum** (Wood Ln, PE26 2XD ⌀ ramseyruralmuseum.co.uk ⊝ Apr– Oct 10.00–17.00 Thu, 14.00–17.00 Sat, Sun & bank hols) occupies several 17th-century farm buildings which were built from abbey stone. Opened in 1988 by fenland author Sybil Marshall, this treasure trove of rural fenland history tells stories that span more than 200 years, with reconstructed shops and rooms that include a Victorian cobbler's, a fully stocked chemist, a schoolroom and, my personal favourite, a furnished

THE FELLOWES FAMILY

The Fellowes family acquired the Ramsey Abbey site in 1736–77, when Coulson Fellowes, who represented Huntingdonshire in the House of Commons, bought Ramsey Abbey House and estate. Since then, the Fellowes have had a major influence on the development of the town, having built many historical properties, including the almshouses and Abbey Terrace on Abbey Green, the Estate Office on Church Green, and the Abbey Rooms on the High Street. As such,

you'll notice their family crest on several of Ramsey's older buildings.

The Fellowes have held the title of 'Baron de Ramsey' since 1887 and have carried forth the family trend of representing Huntingdonshire and serving on national bodies for agriculture and the environment. Although they vacated Ramsey Abbey House and moved the family seat to Abbots Ripton (page 112) in 1926, the Fellowes continue to serve as Barons de Ramsey and as landowners of the Ramsey estate.

fenland cottage, which was built in the 1930s with no running water, mains drainage or electricity. It was dismantled in 2006 and transported to the museum site, piece by piece.

The museum also has an extensive collection of old farming machinery, from tractors and beet harvesters to thistle cutters and pig scales. The Pump Room delves into the history of fenland drainage, and you can see the tools that were used for vital tasks like hedging, ditching and digging turf – trades that, for decades, kept floodwaters in check and local people in work. The Barn Annexe gives an insight into the work of wheelwrights and farriers, and there's a thatched well that was once a source of water for Ramsey Abbey.

Next to the Rural Museum is Ramsey's 19th-century **Walled Garden** (⊘ ramseywalledgarden.org ☉ Apr–Oct 14.00–17.00 Sun & bank hols). A typical Victorian garden within the boundaries of Ramsey Abbey, it produced fruit and vegetables for Ramsey House for more than 100 years. Its last known use was in the 1950s when it was used for growing flowers. Having fallen into disrepair in the 1960s, it was rediscovered in 1996 by the Cambridgeshire Gardens Trust and lovingly restored to showcase the flowers, fruit and veg that would have been grown here in Victorian times. Highlights include a glasshouse and apple tunnel, which is planted with Cambridgeshire varieties.

"Highlights include a glasshouse and apple tunnel, which is planted with Cambridgeshire varieties"

Opposite the museum's entrance on Wood Lane are the **Mortuary Chapels** (⊘ ramseymortuarychapels.org.uk ☉ Apr–Oct 14.00–17.00 first Sun of the month). This pair of 19th-century Gothic Revival chapels are linked by a gabled archway with ornate belfry and spire. The chapels feature some of the only remaining 'contagion' windows in England, which allowed mourners to pay their respects to the dead while shielding themselves from potential diseases carried by the deceased.

Northeast of Ramsey Rural Museum, just off Wood Lane, is The Camp (Wood Ln, PE26 2XB). Every year, over the August Bank Holiday, this former militia camp hosts one of Britain's biggest living history events, **1940s Ramsey** (⊘ ramsey1940s.co.uk). The weekend recreates the sights and sounds of the 1940s, with re-enactments, vintage vehicles, aircraft displays, food stalls and period costumes. Visitors can come for a full weekend of camping or just pay for a day pass.

Ramsey to Bury Church

✳ OS Explorer map 227 *Peterborough*; start: Ale House Kitchen, 65 High St, Ramsey PE26 1YU ♀ TL288850; 2 miles; easy (flat all the way)

1 Walk through the old coaching arch to the back of the Ale House Kitchen and follow the footpath sign southwards. Go through a metal gate and continue along the footpath beside a stream (Bury Brook), passing a couple of little footbridges on your left and a golf course on your right.

2 When the path ends, turn left and cross the footbridge over the brook. At the warehouse, bear right on to a narrow track, then immediately right into a field. Follow the path south along the field edge.

3 When the field ends, the path will spit you out on to the golf course. Cross the course via the raised track, with views of Bury's village church ahead. Continue straight on along a narrow path behind garden fences that leads into the churchyard.

4 Exit the churchyard through the gate and turn left to walk along the B1040, then take the first left along Meadow Lane, which leads to a narrow track and then on to a wider track through open farmland. Follow this track, as it bends left through the fields.

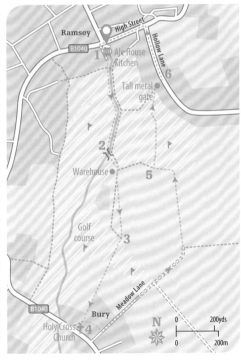

5 Where the farmland ends, enter a narrow path through the trees and take the first right to cross a footbridge back on to the golf course. Follow the path straight across the golf course to a tall metal gate.

6 Go through the metal gate and turn left on to Hollow Lane. Walk north, passing Abbey Green on your right. Turn left on to the High Street and follow it back to the Ale House Kitchen.

╫ FOOD & DRINK

Ale House Kitchen 65 High St, PE26 1YU ✆ 01487 710128 ▓ ⊙ Wed–Sun. Set in the former George Hotel, this large pub serves British cuisine ranging from goats' cheese salad to steak and ale pie. They have a big gin selection, local ales on tap and a terrace at the back. You can find their latest menus on Facebook.

Great Whyte Coffee 28 Great Whyte, PE26 1HA ⊙ Mon–Sat. Family-run coffee shop, serving cakes, toasties and decent coffee. The breakfasts are popular.

The Jolly Sailor 43 Great Whyte, PE26 1HH ✆ 01487 813388 ⊘ jollysailorramsey.co.uk. This 400-year-old pub once sat beside the river that ran through the town centre. Expect a traditional interior with an inglenook fireplace and tankards hanging from the beams. They serve real ales and pub classics.

Ramsey Rural Tearoom Wood Ln, PE26 2XD ⊘ ramseyruralmuseum.co.uk ⊙ Apr–Oct 10.00–17.00 Thu, 14.00–17.00 Sat, Sun & bank hols. The café at Ramsey Rural Museum is open to the public, with courtyard seating surrounded by reconstructed fenland shops and vintage farming machinery. The café is a simple affair, serving teas and homemade cakes, but the setting is unique and you can stroll here from Abbey Green (walk 550yds out of town along Wood Lane, then turn right on the track signed for the museum).

Wild Frost 18 Great Whyte, PE26 1HF ⊙ Mon–Sat. Ramsey's trendiest coffee shop serves speciality cakes and light lunches made with seasonal produce.

Windmill Bakery 34 Great Whyte, PE26 1HA ⊙ Tue–Sat. Fresh bread and cakes are made daily at this traditional bakery.

10 FENLAND LIGHT RAILWAY

Mereside Drove, Ramsey Mereside PE26 2UE ⊘ fenlandlightrailway.co.uk

One for the kids or grandkids: on this 1950s-style narrow-gauge railway you can step aboard a mini train and chug around a purpose-built track. It was created more than 25 years ago by a group of railway enthusiasts, with its current site (four miles north of Ramsey), opened in 2014 by Lord de Ramsey. You can also come for themed events, which include Easter egg hunts, cream teas and Santa specials. On site, there's a gift shop, café and a garden with model trains. To find out when the trains are next running, check the website or their Facebook page.

MARCH & THE OUSE WASHES

The central Cambridgeshire Fens have two towns: March, with its medieval church and riverside setting, and the smaller, quieter town of Chatteris. Beyond them are peaceful villages and vast tracts of farmland,

MOLLY DANCING

People have been Molly dancing in the Fens since the 1800s as a way to earn money when farm labourers were out of work in winter. A form of morris dancing, it's thought to be distinctly East Anglian, with a stronghold in the Cambridgeshire Fens. Traditionally appearing on Plough Monday (the start of the English agricultural year in January), Molly dancers would make their way around pubs and houses, asking for food or money. Their dances were often inspired by fenland folklore about marsh spirits and other supernatural tales.

Molly dancers tend to wear macabre costumes, with elaborate clothes and make-up. Originally, they covered their faces in soot, and men often wore women's clothing – the idea was to disguise themselves from the wealthy landowners they preyed upon, so as not to penalise their chances of future employment. Some sources describe Molly dancing as a 'trick or treat' performance, with 'plough witches' cutting furrows across the lawns of anyone who refused to pay them.

Today, the best place to experience Molly dancing is at Whittlesey's Straw Bear Festival (see box, page 191), when they come out in force. You'll also find dancers at other annual events, like Ely Folk Festival, Thriplow Daffodil Festival (see box, page 306) and Mill Road Winter Fair (page 37). Check out the websites of Pig Dyke Molly (pigdyke.co.uk), Gog Magog Molly (gogmagogmolly.org.uk) and Ouse Washes Molly (ousewashesmolly.uk) to see when they're next performing.

cut through by drainage channels – the largest of which (the New and Old Bedford rivers) skirt the southeast of this section. Between these channels is the Ouse Washes flood area, and the prolific birdlife of a remote RSPB reserve.

11 MARCH

Fourwinds Leisure (page 316)

One of the largest towns in the Fens, March has the credentials of a charming rural settlement, with its riverside setting, handsome Georgian buildings and twice-weekly market (Wed & Sat), yet it never quite lives up to its full potential. Perhaps it's the dwindling market stalls, the tired-looking shops or the lack of enthusiasm I received when asking locals what they thought of their hometown. Or maybe I've just visited on bad days. Don't write it off – but if you're looking for heritage museums and visitor attractions, I'd choose Wisbech over March any day. Having said that, March has a better selection of places to eat, and is popular with narrowboaters, who make use of the free moorings and riverside pubs in the town centre. For a detailed tour and historical backstory to the town's landmarks, you could download the Town Trail or Riverside Trail on ⊘ visitcambridgeshirefens.org.

Like all fenland towns, March was once an island settlement, surrounded by swamps. The church of St Wendreda (now at the southern end of town) had been established by the 13th century but the town developed one mile north, beside the River Nene. For several centuries, goods were transported in and out by boat, with everything from mills and lime works to tanneries and pubs lining the riverbanks. This changed with the coming of the railways in 1847 and, as trade shifted from river to rail, March saw a golden era of prosperity. A major railway junction was established and construction of a marshalling yard began in the 1880s. By the early 20th century, the yard was the busiest in Britain and the second largest in Europe, housing 250 steam engines.

The train station still serves the town today, albeit with fewer lines than it had in its heyday. The marshalling yards, however, are no more – the town's importance as a trading centre declined throughout the second half of the 20th century and the yards were phased out. Part of the old marshalling site is now **Ring's End Nature Reserve** – a 27-acre network of ponds and reed beds to the north of the town, with a raised walking/cycling track that runs along the old railway embankment. Here, the ballast pits which were constructed to supply water for the steam engines have become a habitat for herons, kingfishers, otters and dragonflies. Next to Ring's End, on another part of the old marshalling site, is HMP Whitemoor – one of England's highest-category prisons.

The old course of the River Nene runs directly through the town centre, passing beneath **Town Bridge**, which was built in 1850 to replace an earlier timber one. On the north side of the bridge is a double-width road which was once the village green – this is **Broad Street** (B1101), where you'll find most of the town's shops, along with an 18ft war memorial at the southern end and an elaborate fountain at the northern end, which celebrates the coronation of King George V and the Golden Jubilee of Elizabeth II. A couple of interesting side streets lead off Broad Street and run parallel to the river. West of the war memorial, Grays Lane leads to **West End** – a little alleyway of houses that feels like a glimpse into the past, with its fine 18th- and 19th-century buildings. Southeast of the war memorial, next to Town Bridge, **Nene Parade** leads

ANNUAL EVENTS IN MARCH

St George's Fayre (⌂ marchtown-events. co.uk) is an annual April event that takes place in the town centre, with a street market, funfair, parade and live performances that can include anything from Viking warriors to dance and magic shows.

Typically held in June on West End Park, the **March Summer Festival** (⌂ marchsummerfestival.co.uk) is a weekend event that includes Friday evening bands on the open-air stage, a Saturday parade with classic cars and a Sunday 'picnic in the park' with music, acts and a dog show. Visit in December for the **March Christmas Market** (⌂ marchtown-events.co.uk), which also includes a Christmas parade, funfair, Santa's grotto and stalls selling homemade gifts, mulled wine and hot food.

You can also search for the latest on these events on ⌂ fenland.gov.uk.

eastwards along the riverfront and has a handful of places to eat and drink with direct views over the water.

On the southern side of Town Bridge is the **High Street** (also B1101), where you'll find more shops and the **Market Place**. March's finest building (in my opinion) watches over the market square – built in 1900, the Renaissance-style Corn Exchange is topped by a 10ft clock tower and crowned with a statue of Britannia that celebrates Queen Victoria's Diamond Jubilee. It was previously the Town Hall and Magistrates' Court but is now a community arts venue and café. Diagonally opposite, on the corner of the High Street, is Ye Old Griffin Hotel – a former 16th-century coaching inn that welcomed Charles Dickens and Samuel Pepys. Also on this side of the river is **West End Park** where you can stroll beside the river or have a picnic on the grass.

Further south on the High Street is **March Museum** (PE15 9JJ ⌂ marchmuseum.co.uk ◷ Wed & Sat; free entry), which opened in 1976. Set in a former girls' grammar school (built 1851), it showcases the town's history with displays about the railway and Victorian era, along with a reconstructed fenland cottage and forge. You'll also find original fenland drainage tools and military displays from the Boer War and World Wars I and II. On the opposite side of the High Street is **Fossils Galore** (60 High St, PE15 9LD ⌂ fossilsgalore.com ◷ Mon, Tue morning & Wed–Sat), which displays stacks of fossils – some of which were found nearby at Kings Dyke Reserve (page 193). They also have a preparation laboratory where the fossils and other finds are examined.

The church of **St Wendreda** is almost a mile south of the town centre, just off the B1101 on Church Street. This is the only known church dedicated to the Anglo-Saxon nun St Wendreda, and was famously described by the Poet Laureate Sir John Betjeman as 'worth cycling 40 miles in a head wind to see'. The church's standout feature is its double hammerbeam roof, which features 118 carved angels carrying musical instruments, shields and emblems – it really is quite astounding. The door is usually locked but, to see inside, you could visit during a service (visit ⊘ stwendreda.co.uk for times), or follow the instructions on the church door which tell you who to call for the key.

To explore the countryside around March, a good circular walking route (which starts and finishes at St Wendreda's Church) is the waymarked **Woodman's Way** (6½ miles). It leads south to the village of Wimblington, passing through ancient patches of woodland that add welcome variety to the typically treeless landscapes of the Fens.

⊺⏐ FOOD & DRINK

Although it doesn't have a reputation for Slow food, March has plenty of places to meet your needs, from international coffee chains to atmospheric pubs.

The Acre 9 Acre Rd, PE15 9JD ⊙ Tue–Sun. This Greene King pub has a pleasant setting beside West End Park. They do Sunday carveries and generous portions of pub grub – think burgers, mozzarella fishcakes and vegan shepherd's pie.

The Exchange 1 Market Pl, PE15 9JF ⊘ theexchangemarch.co.uk ⊙ 11.00–22.00 Fri & Sat, 11.00–15.00 Sun–Thu. Tea room by day, restaurant and bar by night; come here for lunch, afternoon tea, pina coladas or evening tapas.

The Hippodrome Dartford Rd, PE15 8AQ ⊘ jdwetherspoon.com. I wouldn't normally recommend a Wetherspoon pub but this one is special. You can't miss the old hippodrome, which opened in 1929 as a 900-seat cinema. Although now a budget chain pub, it has retained lots of original features, including the balcony seating area and boarded-up screen which is decorated with fenland scenes. The food is unremarkable but it's worth stopping by for a drink and a snoop around.

Panini's Market Sq ⊙ Mon–Sat. With a spot by the market square, this little café serves good-value breakfasts and lunches which, of course, include a choice of paninis.

The Ship Inn 1 Nene Parade, PE15 8TD ⊘ 01354 607878 🅵 ⊙ noon–23.00 Mon–Thu, 09.00–23.00 Fri–Sun.) Beautiful riverside building with a thatched roof, ancient beams and contemporary furnishings. Expect real ales on tap and a good range of gins. They also host regular events, from live music to beer and gin festivals, and their cooked breakfasts (served

MARCH MARCH MARCH

The March March march is a long, flat, pointless walk across the Fens from the town of March to Cambridge, a distance of about thirty miles. It takes place, of course, in March, often but not always on the last Saturday in March. It has no purpose other than to be called the March March march. It was invented by Jonathan Partington in 1979, apparently because it seemed like a good idea at the time.

This quote from ⊘ marchmarchmarch.org.uk sums up an annual 30-mile walk from March to Cambridge that has been attempted almost every year since it began in 1979 – the exceptions being 2002, when nobody completed it, 2007 when nobody turned up, and 2021 when it was cancelled due to the Covid pandemic. The walk begins with an early morning train to March, where the marchers send a postcard to Cambridge University before walking south through Wimblington, Chatteris Longstanton and Girton. Songs, games and date bars are considered essential to kill the boredom of walking through the unchanging scenery of the Fens. Everyone's welcome so, if you fancy joining them for all or part of the route, you'll find more info on the website.

If you can't make it for the March March march, you could try its sister walk, **May Manea** – an annual stomp from the village of Manea (ten miles southeast of March, or seven minutes by train) towards Cambridge. I say 'towards' as the exact route and destination have never been set in stone. Initiated in 1981, the walk typically covers 20 miles. After alighting at Manea train station, walkers tend to head through RSPB Ouse Washes, then continue to the fen edge at Mepal, before heading south to Histon on the outskirts of Cambridge, where successful ramblers are crowned 'Maneacs'.

09.00–11.30 Fri–Sun) are hailed as the best in town – choose from traditional English, smoked salmon and eggs, Mexican havas rancheros or pancakes. At the time of writing, they weren't doing lunches or evening meals but it's worth keeping an eye on their Facebook page for updates.

12 STONEA CAMP

Stitches Farm, PE15 0PE (signed off the B1093 Manea Rd)

England's lowest hillfort, Stonea Camp was built during the Iron Age on a gravel island, just a few feet above sea level. I felt a real sense of adventure when I went to seek out this ancient site, which is reached via a long and rutted road that leads, like a causeway, between a sea of farmland.

When you arrive at the camp, you'll find yourself looking at a sheep-nibbled field and wondering what all the fuss is about. But feel your way to the first information board, near to the makeshift parking area, and the history of the site starts to unfold. These earthworks were once an Iron Age settlement that acted as a headquarters for the Iceni tribe and witnessed a monumental battle with the Romans, led by Queen Boudicca – just imagine that!

This Scheduled Ancient Monument is one of only three Iron Age hillforts known to survive in Cambridgeshire. As you walk around the raised earthworks, a series of information boards describe different phases of construction and help to bring the fort to life, painting a picture of a vastly different fen landscape than you see today – you can climb up to the raised viewing platform for the best vantage point. I had this place all to myself when I visited, so I sat on an embankment, sipped my flask of coffee and pondered on the historical weight of it all. It really is quite incredible.

Two hundred metres west of the turn-off to Stonea Camp is **Skylark Garden Centre** (Manea Rd, PE15 0PE ◌ skylarkgardencentre.co.uk ◌ 09.00–18.00 Mon–Sat, 10.00–16.00 Sun). It proudly announces itself as 'the largest garden centre in the Fens' but it's actually much more than this. In addition to the garden centre, farm shop and a café is a year-round calendar of family events and school holiday activities, from the Maize Maze and fun yard to spring lamb feeding, autumn pumpkin picking and a Christmas cabin. They also have a series of coarse fishing lakes where keen anglers can buy a day ticket and fish for carp. There's a bait shop on site (◌ skylarklakes.co.uk).

THE OUSE WASHES

Also known as the Hundred Foot Washes, the seasonally flooded land beside the New and Old Bedford rivers is the UK's largest washland, running for 25 miles between St Ives and Downham Market in Norfolk. Created in the 17th century to contain floodwater, parts of it provide a habitat for waders and wildfowl, attracting snipe, redshanks and lapwings in spring, and thousands of ducks and swans in winter. Dotted along its length is a scattering of internationally important SSSIs, which include some of the UK's best wildlife reserves for wetland birds: RSPB Ouse Washes (see opposite) and RSPB Welney (just across the border in Norfolk), along with RSPB Ouse Fen and RSPB Fen Drayton Lakes at the Washes' southwest extremity (Chapter 5).

13 RSPB OUSE WASHES

Counter Wash PE15 0NF

Attracting a staggering amount of birdlife, this linear reserve stretches along the banks of the Old Bedford River. Around 460 acres in size, it's the best place in Cambridgeshire to experience the wildlife of the Ouse Washes area. A long, narrow and rutted track leads to the small parking area – car drivers should prepare for a bumpy ride, or you could walk or cycle here from Manea train station (around three miles from the reserve's northeast tip, via footpaths or quiet country roads). The visitor centre, which is often unmanned, sits opposite Welches Dam Pumping Station – built in the 1940s, this red-brick building still operates as a flood defence mechanism.

The reserve is home to some of the best birding spectacles in eastern England. It's a remote and beautiful spot to visit year-round but winter is the time for drama. From October each year, around 100,000 wildfowl and waders pay a visit, with whooper and Bewick's swans arriving en masse from Iceland. Cranes are also regular visitors, and you can often see owls, merlins, hen harriers and peregrine falcons hunting across the surrounding fenland. The reserve is a hotspot for yellowhammers and corn bunting, as well as breeding garganeys, avocets, black-tailed godwits and redshank in spring and summer. To make the most of all this birdlife, stroll along the riverbank and visit the bird hides, which sit north and south of the visitor centre.

14 CHATTERIS

🏠 **The Bramley House Hotel** (page 316), **The Cross Keys** (page 316)

An ancient market town that grew around a 10th-century abbey, Chatteris is one of my favourite fenland settlements. There isn't a whole lot to see here but it's a compact and community-minded little place, with well-kept streets and a welcoming, laid-back feel. High Street and Market Hill make up the town centre, with the 14th-century church of St Peter and St Paul at the southern end of town, where you'll also find the Cross Keys Inn – one of the oldest buildings in Chatteris and where Samuel Pepys stayed when he visited the town in 1663. The town's independent shops mostly cater to local needs rather than tourist interests, and there's a weekly market on Fridays (held on Park St). Popular annual events include the Midsummer Festival (🖉 chatterismidsummerfestival.co.uk) which is held in June, and

FAMILY DAYS OUT

Families have plenty of options for days out in Cambridgeshire, from heritage train rides and fascinating museums to easy bike rides and up-close wildlife encounters.

1 Skating on the frozen Fens was once a regular winter activity and, although rare these days, can still be enjoyed if temperatures stay low enough. 2 Dray rides are just one of the activities at Thriplow Daffodil Weekend – a country fair with thousands of daffodils on show.

6

3 At Nene Valley Railway you can ride a steam train through a glorious part of the Cambridgeshire countryside. 4 The Imperial War Museum (IWM) showcases more than a century's worth of aviation and is based at one of the most important airfields of the WWII Battle of Britain. 5 At Fens Falconry you can book one of several bird of prey experiences. 6 Go pond dipping in Cambridgeshire's lakes and waterways and discover a miniature aquatic world. 7 St Neots Museum is housed in the town's original prison cells and delves into the history of St Neots Priory.

MACIEK PLATEK/ST NEOTS MUSEUM

the Christmas Lights (⊘ chatterischristmaslights.co.uk), which are considered some of the best in the Fens – the 1 December switch-on is a big event, with food stalls and live music.

Like all fenland settlements, Chatteris started life as an island. A hermitage was established by St Huna in AD679, with the abbey of St Mary founded 300 years later – the town and marketplace developed around this abbey. The Dissolution saw an end to the abbey, and only a fraction remains today – the four Park streets (Park St, West Park St, South Park St and East Park St) mark the abbey's former boundary, and you can see the remains of an original wall on the corner of East Park Street and South Park Street.

Southwest of the church, **Chatteris Museum** (2 Park St ⊘ chatterismuseum.org.uk) reveals stories about local events, characters and archaeological finds, like the town's Bronze Age settlers, the founding of Chatteris Abbey and the impact of the fenland railway boom, along with a wider history of the Fens. At the time of writing, the museum was in the process of moving from Church Street to Park Street with plans to reopen in February 2022. Check the website for the latest information on opening times. Other pieces of history dotted around the town include the remains of Victorian-era catacombs in the car park behind the church, and an ancient mortuary stone that was used to

THE CARROT KING & FEN TIGER

Chatteris is proud of its local residents, and rightly so. With a colourful history of carrot farming and boxing, its most famous folk have gained national and international acclaim. In the mid 1900s, Chatteris became England's 'carrot capital', producing bumper crops of 'red gold'. Almost every local was involved in the industry, from hoeing and hand digging to cleaning and topping – the town produced so many carrots that local farmer Arthur Rickwood was nicknamed 'the Carrot King' by King George VI. Chatteris also lays claim to the UK's first-ever carrot washing machine, which was created by resident Charles Cole.

A century later, professional boxer David Robert Green MBE, who fought between 1974 and 1981, was also raised on carrot farming. In his early days, he hauled carrots by day and trained in the ring after work. Known as Dave Boy Green, or the Fen Tiger, his signature shots were dubbed 'the muck spreader' and 'the carrot cruncher'. Dave won British and European titles and, at the height of his career, he fought world legend Sugar Ray Leonard for a shot at the world title. A Chatteris boy through and through, he still lives in the town and has a pair of red boxing gloves cast in concrete on his driveway.

prepare bodies for burial – you'll find it built into a brick wall on Station Street, behind the Cross Keys Inn.

There are several options for self-guided town tours, with a choice of themed walking trails on ⚲ visitcambridgeshirefens.org. You can also download the five-mile Chatteris Circular Walk – this waymarked loop guides you through the town, along the old railway line (closed to passengers in 1967) and into the surrounding fens on byways and bridleways.

ⵌ FOOD & DRINK

Chatteris has plenty of cafés, restaurants and take-aways. Slow travellers may be tempted by **The Cross Keys** (12–16 Market Hill, PE16 6BA ⚲ 01354 692644 ⚲ crosskeyschatteris.com), which sits opposite the church. This 16th-century pub has an open fire, traditional pub grub and monthly folk music performances. Two doors down, **Pera Palace** (8 Market Hill, PE16 6BA ⚲ 01354 669933 ⚲ perapalace.co.uk) occupies the former Palace Ballroom which, in 1937, had the first sprung floor in the country. Now a Turkish restaurant, you can sit beneath the ballroom's high ceiling and tuck into Turkish classics, cooked on an open grill.

Opposite the old ballroom, **The Old Bakery** (3 Market Hill, PE16 6BB) is a family-run tea room and restaurant in a former bakery. They serve homemade cakes, sandwiches, afternoon teas and Sunday roasts.

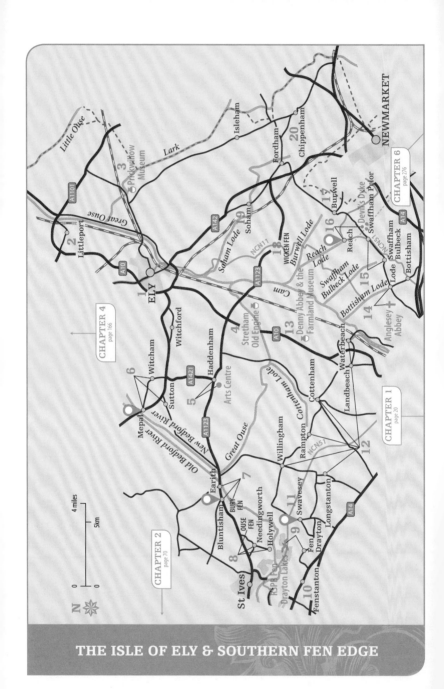

THE ISLE OF ELY & SOUTHERN FEN EDGE

5
THE ISLE OF ELY &
SOUTHERN FEN EDGE

The earliest settlements in the southern part of the Cambridgeshire Fens were built on either the fen edge or the Isle of Ely – this low-lying island was surrounded by eel-filled waters and crowned by a medieval abbey which, from afar, appeared to sail upon the swamps that surrounded it. The Fens were drained for agriculture in the 17th century and the island is now indistinguishable from the land that surrounds it. However, the former abbey site (now Ely Cathedral), remains a formidable one, while the city beneath it is a hub of fenland culture – the riverside arts centre, annual Eel Fayre and excellent markets are just some of Ely's charms.

South of the Isle of Ely, the southern fen edge has a character all of its own, with thriving villages, ancient waterways and abundant wildlife. Once a marshy coastline, lapped by fenland waters, this was the first (or last) promise of mainland, and many villages grew around hythes (landing places) and lodes – navigable waterways dug by the Romans. Today, the lodes have become bucolic waterways to paddle along or stroll beside. The fen edge was also a place to be defended from attackers who could approach along the lodes, concealed by fenland mists – reminders of this include the castle sites at Burwell (page 268) and Rampton (page 258).

It is here on the fen edge that the great drainage of the Fens (Chapter 4) began with the cutting of the Old and New Bedford rivers in the 1600s. From the village of Earith, much of the River Great Ouse is diverted northeast along the Bedford rivers, while its depleted old course wiggles east to meet the River Cam before flowing north to Ely – today, you can boat along this artery or walk beside it on the Ouse Valley Way.

As well as being navigable, the fen-edge waterways are magnets for birdlife, with wetland reserves flanking the Great Ouse and Cam. Southwest of Earith, the Great Ouse meanders past the lakes and walking trails of RSPB Fen Drayton (page 250) and RSPB Ouse Fen (page 248)

– a new reserve which, when complete, will boast the UK's largest reed bed. Nearby, Berry Fen (page 244) – once a Victorian ice-skating rink – is now a haven for birdlife.

Scattered around Ely and the fen edge are oodles of other charms, from working windmills and old fenland pumping stations to art galleries and other former abbey sites – 12th-century Denny Abbey (page 260) is now a farming museum, while Anglesey Abbey (page 261) is an ode to the early 1900s. You could also visit the resting place of Lancelot 'Capability' Brown in Fenstanton village, or lace up your boots and discover the western extremity of Devil's Dyke – an ancient earthwork and walking route with rare chalkland wildlife.

But if I could only visit one place in this chapter, it would have to be Wicken Fen, which sits between Ely and the southeast fen edge. Here, in this ancient fragment of fen, you can follow the boardwalks through a lost world and imagine what life was like when fenmen walked about on stilts, wildfowl screeched through the reeds and eel catchers lay their handwoven traps in the rich, peaty waters.

GETTING AROUND

The southern fen edge sits a couple of miles north of the A14, with Fenstanton in the west and Chippenham in the east. The (often busy) A10 slices north–south through the middle of this chapter, linking Littleport, Ely and Waterbeach, and connecting with Cambridge to the south. But, as ever, it's on the backroads where you'll find all the charm – if you enjoy being behind the wheel, you could follow Burwell Museum's driving route (see box, page 270) and tour the region's many windmills.

TRAINS

Ely, Waterbeach and Littleport all sit on the London–King's Lynn railway line, which connects with Cambridge to the south. It takes around ten minutes to travel between Ely and Waterbeach, and around seven between Ely and Littleport.

Waterbeach station is only ten minutes from Cambridge, and the fastest Ely–Cambridge trains take around 15 minutes. For wetlands and villages in the southwest, your nearest train station is Huntingdon, while the villages in the far east of this chapter are closer to Newmarket station in Suffolk.

BUSES

Bus services aren't too bad in these parts, with Cambridge, Ely, St Ives and Newmarket acting as hubs in all four compass directions. The villages in the southwest benefit from the guided busway (⊙ thebusway.info) – Longstanton, Swavesey and Fen Drayton Lakes are designated stops on the Cambridge to St Ives section, while Fenstanton, Needingworth and Earith can be reached via connections from St Ives.

Settlements that sit just off the A10 (including Waterbeach, Ely and Littleport) are on Stagecoach's Cambridge–Littleport route 9. The villages in the southeast sit on Cambridge–Newmarket route 10, while Soham is on route 12. Buses to Wicken Fen are few and far between – the only direct service is the Thursday bus from Ely (Lord's Travel 117).

CYCLING

There are some excellent options for cyclists, with scenic sections of the National Cycle Network (NCN) running past pretty villages and wildlife reserves. NCN51 runs along the southern fen edge, all the way between Fen Drayton Lakes in the west and Burwell village in the east, with a central section that skirts past the city of Cambridge. The western half of NCN51 follows the car-free guided busway route.

Wicken Fen is a hub for family cycling, with its cycle-hire centre and network of local routes. NCN11 weaves through the reserve, heading northwards to Ely and south to Anglesey Abbey. Part of this route is waymarked as the Lodes Way – an eight-mile ride through fenland scenery, which can be linked with NCN51 for a circular route (see box, page 271).

 CYCLE HIRE

Cycle Centric 37 High St, Longstanton CB24 3BP ✐ 01954 782020 ⌖ cyclecentric.com ⊙ 09.30–1630 Mon–Fri, 09.00– 13.30 Sat. Tandem and triplet hire only. Telephone ahead to arrange hire.
Wicken Fen Lode Ln, Wicken CB7 5XP ✐ 01353 720274 ⌖ nationaltrust.org ⊙ 10.00– 13.30 Tue, Thu, Sat & Sun

WALKING

The nature reserves and wetlands in this chapter are ideal for family walks and pub strolls, with wildlife-rich routes leading through RSPB Fen Drayton Lakes, RSPB Ouse Fen and Wicken Fen. You could also

DAVID1968WS

1

THE ISLE OF ELY & THE SOUTHERN FEN EDGE

The Isle of Ely and Southern Fen Edge have a diverse landscape of manmade waterways, ancient earthworks and rich wildlife, along with pretty villages and stunning architecture that includes Anglesey Abbey and the mighty Ely Cathedral.

2

STEPHEN KELLY/A

3

1 Fen Drayton Lakes is a tranquil world of lakes and birdlife at the southern end of the Ouse Washes. **2** Devil's Dyke is an ancient landmark, thought to date back to the 6th or 7th century. **3** Oliver Cromwell's House was once the home of the Lord Protector and is now an interactive museum that explores his life. **4** The lodes are a series of manmade waters, thought to have been dug by the Romans. **5** The octagonal tower of St Mary's Church in Swaffham Prior pre-dates that at Ely Cathedral.

4 5

explore the arrow-straight footpaths that lead beside the lodes (see box, page 258), or take in the views from Devil's Dyke (page 266). For a taste of true fenland countryside, with its big skies and manmade waterways, you could follow a circular route from Mepal on page 242 or, to discover one of the region's famous skating grounds, try my suggested route past Berry Fen (see box, page 246).

You could also explore some of the Fen Edge Trail – one of the most scenic sections is the six-mile stretch between Witcham and Sutton (page 241). The walks, which range from around four to six miles, can be downloaded at ⊘ www.fenedgetrail.org.

If you fancy tackling a long-distance river walk, you could follow the **Fen Rivers Way**, which traces the rivers Cam and Great Ouse for 48 miles between Cambridge, Ely and King's Lynn. Waymarked with an eel symbol, the 12-mile stretch between Waterbeach and Ely (see box, page 260) gives glorious views of Ely Cathedral. You'll find a leaflet with more information at ⊘ visitcambridgeshirefens.org. Alternatively, you could walk east–west beside the River Great Ouse on the **Ouse Valley Way** (⊘ ldwa.org.uk) – within the boundaries of this chapter, this long-distance route follows the river for around 25 miles between Holywell and Littleport.

BOAT

Cruisers, kayakers and paddleboarders have some lovely waterways to explore, with the River Great Ouse meandering past the wetlands at Ouse Fen and Fen Drayton Lakes. At Earith, you could either navigate the tidal New and Old Bedford rivers, or follow the old course of the Great Ouse to Ely and Littleport. Ely is the main boating hub, with its boatyard and free 48-hour visitor moorings. If you set off from the city, you could cruise south to Cambridge, southwest to Huntingdonshire, northeast to Norfolk, or explore tributaries like the River Lark, and ancient channels like Burwell Lode.

 BOAT HIRE

Bridge Boatyard Bridge Yard, Ely CB7 4DY ⊘ 01353 663726 ⊘ bridgeboatyard.com
Cambridge Boat Hire ⊘ cambridge-boat-hire.co.uk. Boats can be collected at various locations, including Stretham and Clayhithe/Waterbeach.
Riverside Marine Services Overcote Ln (next to The Pike & Eel), Needingworth PE27 4TW
⊘ 01480 468666 ⊘ riversidemarine.co.uk

i TOURIST INFORMATION

Ely Oliver Cromwell's House, 29 St Mary's St, CB7 4HF ✆ 01353 662062 ⌖ visitely.org.uk
⊙ Apr–Oct 10.00–17.00 daily, Nov–Mar 11.00–16.00 daily

ELY & AROUND

The city of Ely and its surrounding villages have some fascinating stories to tell, from the founding of Ely Cathedral and the rioters of Littleport to the draining of the Fens and the rise of Oliver Cromwell. As one of England's smallest cities, Ely feels more like a provincial market town and is easy to navigate on foot, while the countryside that flanks it has plenty of footpaths to explore, along with fascinating landmarks like Prickwillow Pumping Station and Stretham Old Engine. If it's culture you're after, put the annual Eel Fayre in your diary, along with Haddenham's Steam Rally and the World Pea Shooting Championships in Witcham.

1 ELY

🏠 **Peacocks Fine B&B** (page 317), **The Old Hall** (page 317), **Poets House** (page 317)
🏡 **The Coach House at Cathedral House** (page 317) ⛺ **Mad Hatters Campsite** (page 317)

A matchbox-sized city with a big community vibe, Ely is a real unsung gem, with its showstopping cathedral, buzzing arts scene and laid-back river life. It's only 15 minutes by train from Cambridge, yet far too few people make the trip here. Oliver Cromwell loved the city so much that he made it his home for more than a decade. Today, his 17th-century house is a museum (and tourist information centre) that explores the life and times of the uncrowned king.

The story behind the city's name is simple: when it was established on the Isle of Ely, the surrounding waters were writhing with eels, which were caught, sold and consumed in their thousands. Today, the river no longer wriggles with eels, at least not in the numbers that once thrived here, and the last commercial eel catcher hung up his traps in 2016. Nonetheless, the city stays true to its roots by celebrating 'all things eel' during the annual Eel Fayre.

Central Ely has two distinct areas: the city centre and the riverside. To explore both on foot, you could use my suggested route (page 232),

EELS, EELS, EELS

Ely was founded on eel catching. The town was known far and wide for its jellied eels, and live eels were so valuable that they were often used as currency. Today, you can explore this heritage via eel-themed events and attractions:

Eel Art Look out for the five pieces of eel-themed modern art installed around the city, from the eel lifecycle on the Babylon Gallery's door to the eel mosaic in Jubilee Gardens.

Eel Cuisine The restaurant at Old Fire Engine House (page 235) often has eel on the menu, while Oliver Cromwell's House serves up traditional eel dishes several times a year.

Eel Fayre Held each summer (check ⊘ visitely.org.uk for the latest dates), expect everything from an eel parade to the World Eel Throwing Championships and an eel food safari, where you can try the likes of eel curry and eel pâté.

Eel Trail Waymarked with bronze eel plaques, this town trail guides you around some of Ely's highlights and art installations. You can download the trail leaflet at ⊘ visitely.org.uk or pick up a copy at the tourist information centre.

follow the city's waymarked Eel Trail (see above) or join one of the tourist information centre's guided weekend walks (see their website for more details; see box, page 227). If you'd prefer to simply wander, you'll find the Market Square and most of Ely's shops and restaurants on the north side of the cathedral. Downhill of Market Square, the riverside is busy with boat life and has an arts centre, plus a handful of places to eat and drink. From here, you could take a boat trip with Liberty Belle (Quayside, Ely CB7 4BA ✆ 07927 390380), who offer regular half-hour tours (13.00–17.00 daily) – there's no need to book, just turn up on the quayside near Waterside Antiques or The Maltings.

Ely Cathedral & monastic buildings
⊘ elycathedral.org

With its 215ft tower visible for tens of miles across the Fens, Ely Cathedral – the 'Ship of the Fens' – is an iconic Cambridgeshire landmark and, up close, it's even more magnificent. When you're standing in the cathedral grounds it's the intricacy of the stonework that strikes you – the cathedral's vast, ornate façade will give you both neck cramp and eye strain as you try, in vain, to take it all in. Once you've marvelled at the exterior, step through the Great West Door and Gothic Galilee Porch, and it's the 245ft-long nave that first catches your breath, with its painted ceiling depicting the ancestry of Jesus. Beneath your feet are the patterned tiles of a Victorian labyrinth – follow its path and you'll walk the same distance as the height of the West Tower, which rises above you. This is as far as you can get without paying the entrance fee, which is too steep for a quick nosey around. To make the fee worthwhile, set aside at least half a day and take advantage of one of the inclusive hour-long guided tours. If you'd prefer to self-guide, the Ely Cathedral app has a choice of trails, including one for children. Your ticket gives all-day access, so you can always take a break for lunch and come back for more – not a bad idea, as there's a colossal amount to digest here. It also pays to give yourself a head start with a bit of background into the history that hangs this epic piece of architecture together.

With an entry ticket in hand, you can walk the length of the nave and gaze up to the 142ft-high, 74ft-wide **Octagon Tower**, which is topped with a 200-ton lantern. Below the lantern, Etheldreda's story is told in a series of 14th-century pillar carvings – some of the few medieval carvings that survived the Dissolution. To find the site of **Etheldreda's shrine**, continue north of the Octagon Tower and behind the stunning

ELY CATHEDRAL – A POCKET HISTORY

The cathedral's story begins with Etheldreda, daughter of the King of East Anglia, who was gifted the Isle of Ely by her first husband, Tonbert. When Tonbert died, she married Prince Egfrid of Northumbria. Although Egfrid was keen to consummate their marriage, Etheldreda became a nun, fled to the isle and founded a monastery in AD673. When Etheldreda died of a neck tumour in 679 she was buried in a simple wooden coffin but, when she was exhumed 16 years later, her body was undecayed – one of the hallmarks of a saint. She was reburied in the church, her shrine became a place of pilgrimage and the monastery flourished for 200 years until it was destroyed by the Danes in 869 and was refounded in 970.

It wasn't until the late 11th century, however, that the magnificent building you see today started to take shape. It was Ely's first Norman abbot (Abbot Simeon) who began to rebuild the monastery on a larger scale and, in 1109, the monastery's church became a cathedral – a status which saved it from destruction during the Dissolution (1536–41). Instead of being pulled down, the cathedral's doors were closed and 'only' the most ornate statues and decorations were damaged. A century later, it was closed again during the Civil War (1642–46) but was fortunate to avoid the level of destruction wrought on other cathedrals – it's thought that Cromwell, as an Ely local, may have spared it.

Gothic Choir to the presbytery, where it's marked by a commemorative block in front of the High Altar. To the west of the shrine is a walkway to the Lady Chapel, known as **Processional Way**. Dedicated in 2000, this walkway replaces a former medieval passageway and is the first major addition since the 15th century. The **Lady Chapel** is the largest of its kind attached to a British cathedral and contains the widest stone vault (40ft span) of its era in England. Completed in 1349, the original chapel was decorated in rich colours, with fine statues and stained glass. Much of this was destroyed during the Dissolution but, if you look closely at the fragments of glass and hints of colour on the walls, you'll see glimmers of its former splendour. The modern statue of Mary above the altar was installed in 2000.

The stories, history and architectural intricacies of the cathedral could fill a whole book (there are several in the cathedral shop) and there's a mass of treasures to discover, from 11th-century transepts (the oldest parts of the building) and the magnificent ceiling in Bishop West's chantry, to beautiful organ pipes and 14th-century misericords. If it's drama rather than detail you're after, book on to a Tower Tour (via the cathedral's website) and climb the 288 steps to the top of the West Tower for a dizzying view across Cambridgeshire. Ely Cathedral also boasts the UK's only **Stained Glass Museum** ($\oslash$ stainedglassmuseum. com), which features more than 125 British and European stained-glass windows that span an 800-year period. The cathedral also hosts regular exhibitions and events – last time I visited they were showcasing outfits from Hollywood movies that had been filmed at the cathedral: *Elizabeth: the Golden Age* (2007), *The Other Boleyn Girl* (2008) and *The*

MARKET MANIA

To see Ely at its best, visiting on a market day ($\oslash$ elymarkets.co.uk) is essential – this isn't difficult, with markets held in Market Square six days a week.

Mini Markets (Tue, Wed, Fri) Small selection of stalls selling essentials and Ely produce, such as cakes, bakes and locally roasted coffee.

Charter Market (Thu) Traditional stalls, from local veg to meat and pastries.

Craft, Food & Vintage (Sat) International street food, handmade crafts and artisan produce, along with antiques and books.

Farmers Market (2nd & 4th Sat of the month) Cambridgeshire fruit, meat, plants and more, plus a vegan alley of plant-based produce. Held in addition to the craft market.

Sundays & bank hols Street food, gifts, plants, kids' games and more.

King's Speech (2010) to name but a few. And, of course, the cathedral is also a working building with regular services that include Choral Evensong (17.30 Mon–Sat, 16.00 Sun) and Christmas carol services.

Outside, there's more to discover. Home to England's largest cluster of continuously inhabited **monastic buildings**, the grounds include the Prior's House, the roofless 12th-century Infirmary and Prior Crauden's 14th-century chapel – you can ask at the cathedral's main desk for access to the last, which harbours wall paintings and the remains of a medieval tiled floor. To learn more about the cathedral grounds, ask for a map of the Monastic Trail or find it on the Ely Cathedral app.

Oliver Cromwell's House
29 St Mary's St olivercromwellshouse.co.uk

Doubling up as a tourist information centre (see box, page 227) and museum, this half-timbered building was once the home of Oliver Cromwell and his family, who moved to Ely in 1636 and stayed for ten years. Two of Cromwell's nine children were born in this house and the youngest was baptised in St Mary's Church, which you can see through the kitchen window.

Giving an immersive introduction to Cromwell's life, the museum guides you through his story, from local MP to Lord Protector of the Commonwealth – King of England in all but name. As you progress through each room, kitted out with an audio guide, you'll learn about Cromwell's early life, how his family lived and what they cooked in the kitchen (note the recipe for Mrs Cromwell's eel pie). Upstairs, kids can experience 17th-century Puritan life by trying on costumes and learning about medical treatments like leeches and unicorn horns. The last two rooms delve into the Civil War and track Cromwell's rise through the ranks.

Ely Museum
Market St, CB7 4LS elymuseum.org.uk 10.30–17.00 Tue–Sat & bank hols, noon–17.00 Sun

Before the Fens were drained, the Isle of Ely was cut off from the mainland and ruled by a bishop who had the power to summon an army and lock up lawbreakers. The Bishop's Prison, the Old Gaol, is now Ely Museum, which first opened in 1997. Between 2019 and 2021 it underwent a major renovation which transformed it into one of the most impressive local history museums I've seen anywhere. Alongside the exhibits, the fabric of the old building has been cleverly preserved, with an original fireplace and Tudor doorway, and prisoners' names carved into sections of the old walls.

Roughly set out in chronological order, the exhibits start with the Fens' earliest settlers and continue to Roman-era artefacts, which include fragments of Nene Valley Colour Coated Ware (page 155) and a skeleton unearthed in the Fens. You can also learn about the history of Ely Cathedral and the story of the Littleport riots (see box, page 237), while children can listen to folk stories in the video room. A timeline of fenland drainage is printed on the walls, and the museum's second floor includes displays about prison life, contemporary fenland farming and more. There's also a research hub with public computers, where you can delve deeper into Ely's past.

A town & riverside tour

Understandably, most visitors make a beeline for **Ely Cathedral** (page 228), so it makes sense to start here. Standing outside the West Door (main entrance) with your back to the cathedral, the building to your left is the **Bishop's Palace**. Built in the 15th century by Bishop John Alcock, Cambridgeshire's only palace was remodelled by successive bishops until 1941. Like many of Ely's former monastic buildings, it is now occupied by King's School. Keeping the palace on your left, follow the footpath west through Palace Green (Ely's original village green), which brings you to the **Russian Cannon**, on the right. This Crimean War relic was gifted to Ely in 1860 by Queen Victoria. Exit Palace Green through the gap in the wall, which places you on Church Lane. To your right is the 18th-century **Old Fire Engine House** (theoldfireenginehouse.co.uk) – now an art gallery and restaurant, this former farmhouse was once home to Ely's horse-drawn fire engine, which you can see in a photo above the bar. To your left is **St Mary's Church** (mostly 13th century with a 14th-century spire). Walk into the graveyard and turn right to walk around to the church's southwest wall, where a tablet commemorates the five men who were executed for the 1816 Littleport riots (see box, page 237). Retrace your footsteps out of the churchyard and turn left towards a timber-framed black-and-white cottage, **Oliver Cromwell's House** (page 231), where the man himself lived with his family. Notice the circular bench outside, which is inscribed with Mrs Cromwell's recipe for roast eels.

With your back to Oliver Cromwell's House, cross St Mary's Street and turn right to walk northeast (heading back towards the cathedral). On your left, you'll pass Poets House, a hotel, restaurant and the former home of fenland author Sybil Marshall. Continue past Angela Mella Studio and the Bake Shop to reach **Bedford House** (28 & 26A St Mary's St). This was once the headquarters of the Bedford Level Corporation – the company responsible for the 17th-century drainage of the Fens. Notice the coat of arms above the door of 26A, which shows two men with a spade and scythe. The motto 'arridet arridum' translates as 'dryness pleaseth'. As you continue along St Mary's Street towards the town centre, you'll pass the old **Ely Dispensary** on your right, with the words 'heal the sick' engraved above the door. Towards the end of St Mary's is a small antique shop, a sweet shop and a gallery. Ahead is the Lamb Hotel – a former 15th-century coaching inn. Cross Lynn Road and skirt around the right of the Lamb Inn to pedestrianised High Street, where you'll find the excellent **Topping & Company Booksellers** (page 236) on your left, followed by the Tudor-era **Steeple Gateway** on your right. This timber-framed gateway is thought to have been a pilgrimage route to the monastery – peer through and you'll see the cathedral.

Continuing east along High Street, on your right is a series of adjoining monastic buildings, their weathered stone in contrast to the modern shopfronts that surround them. Dating back to the 1320s, these buildings were the sacristy (where sacred vessels and vestments were kept) and almonry (where alms were distributed to the poor). The first tower you come to in this line of buildings is **Goldsmith's Tower**, which once contained the goldsmith's workshop. Next in line is the elaborate **Sacrist's Gate** (a tradesman's entrance) – marked by a plaque, it provides a passageway to the mason's yard and buildings of the sacristry. The adjoining almonry is now a tea shop and restaurant. Further down High Street is **Market Square**, where goods have been bought and sold for more than 800 years.

Exit Market Square on Fore Hill, passing Ely Fudge Company and the entrance to Three Cups Walk on your right (home to a jewellers and craft beer café). Fore Hill leads 430yds downhill to **the riverside**, passing several shops, including Drayman's Son micro-brewery (on your left). At the junction with Lisle Lane, continue straight on to Waterside. When the **River Great Ouse** comes into view, you'll see **Waterside Antiques** (watersideantiques.co.uk) on your left (the largest of its kind in East

Anglia). Continue straight ahead to the bridge and you'll arrive at the **independent cinema and Babylon Gallery** (⟨⟩ babylonarts.org.uk ⊙ noon–16.00 Tue–Sun), which exhibits local artists. Peer down the cul-de-sac between the gallery and the Peacock Tearoom, and you'll spot an unusual resident gazing over the rooftops: **Safara, the Ely giraffe,** woven from 230m of measuring tape.

The riverside itself is a joy. Busy with birdlife and boat life, there are scenic spots to sit, eat and stroll. Walking away from the Babylon Gallery (southwest), follow the river for 150yds to the **Maltings** – this Victorian brewery is now a theatre and cinema with a glass-fronted riverside bar. On the grass outside are two modern artwork. The first is the **Sluice**, which celebrates Denver Sluice – a complex of sluices located downstream in Norfolk, which sit at the junction of five waterways and are vitally important to flood control. The second is a stainless-steel sculpture of spear-like tools represents the gleaves used for eel fishing. Continue along the riverside path to **Jubilee Gardens** – the site of this landscaped park would once have been busy with barges, loading and unloading their wares at waterside warehouses. From here, you have the option to wander a little further beside the Great Ouse to soak up the river life.

When you've had your fill of the riverside, take the path up through Jubilee Gardens to Broad Street. Cross the road and go through the gateway into **Ely Park**, following signs for the tourist information centre. As you walk through the park, look right for a fantastic view of Ely Cathedral. The park's exit brings you to **Ely Porta**. This 14th/15th-century gateway was the main entrance to the monastery, with the smaller arch for people and larger one for carts. To return to the cathedral's West Door, pass through the porta and turn right. Alternatively, you could loop around the back of the cathedral, past the Almonry café.

¶¶ FOOD & DRINK

Ely has an excellent selection of cafés and pubs. Here are some of my favourites:

3At3 Three Cups Walk, CB7 4AN ⟨⟩ 3at3craftbeer.co.uk. This beer café and bottle shop champions local breweries and traditional techniques. Expect more than 150 different bottled ales, a cold shelf of craft beers and six rotating drafts. The staff are super-knowledgeable, and there's a patio at the back for enjoying beers, coffees and snacks.
The Almonry 36 High St, CB7 4DL ✆ 01353 666360 ⊙ Tue–Sun. This local institution boasts a tea room and restaurant in the cathedral grounds. The tea room's garden has

exceptional cathedral views and is a lovely place for lunch or homemade cake (my sister is, quite literally, obsessed with their scones), while the restaurant occupies the cathedral's 13th-century Undercroft, with its striking vaulted ceiling.

The Bagel Bar by Silver Oak Coffee 4 Buttermarket, CB7 4NY ⊙ Wed–Mon. This little café roasts their own ethically sourced beans, and bagel chef Josh smokes the meats and makes sauces and vegan seitan from scratch. They also have a rig in the Market Place.

Bake Shop 30 St Mary's St, CB7 4ES ⊙ 08.00–14.00 Tue–Sat. The place to splash out on fenland butter, cheeses, natural wines and artisan loaves made by local bakery, Grain Culture.

Drayman's Son 29A Fore Hill, CB7 4AA ✐ 01353 662920 ♂ draymansely.com ⊙ 17.00–22.00 Wed, 16.00–midnight Fri, noon–midnight Sat. This award-winning micro-pub serves real ales and ciders from the barrel, along with bar snacks and Ely Gin. The interior features some cracking vintage posters and memorabilia.

Julia's Tea Rooms 16–18 High St, CB7 4JU ✐ 01353 664731. With great views of Ely Cathedral at the back, this friendly café offers toasties, baked potatoes and afternoon teas. They also have a medieval crypt where they host live music and board game nights – find them on Facebook or call the café for dates.

Lemon Tree 9 Market Pl, CB7 4NP ⊙ Tue–Sun. This licensed café and deli serves filled croissants, flatbreads and pastries, with seating outside in the Market Place. The deli sells specialist pasta, flour, oils and more.

Marmalade & Jam 27 High St, CB7 4LQ ⊙ Mon–Sat. Opened in 2020, it didn't take long for this tiny café to gain a fan base. The owner, Jo, is renowned for her warm welcomes and delicious bakes. Everyone seems to have their favourites, from the cinnamon buns to oversized scones. They also sell local honey.

Old Fire Engine House 25 St Mary's St, CB7 4ER ✐ 01353 662582 ♂ theoldfireenginehouse.co.uk ⊙ Tue–Sun. This Georgian landmark once housed a horse-drawn fire engine. In 1968, it became a restaurant that pioneered the trend for local and seasonal produce. Now doubling as an art gallery, it's open for teas, lunches and suppers. They often have eel on the menu.

Peacocks Tearoom 65 Waterside, CB7 4AU ♂ peacockstearoom.co.uk ⊙ Tue–Sun. Tucked away by the river, this traditional tea room is my favourite place to escape to in Ely. It's decorated with peacock feather wallpaper and its shelves are adorned with enormous tea caddies. The menu includes more than 70 teas, from monkey-picked oolong to gunpowder green. They also serve cocktails, lunches and Isle of Ely pudding – a warm sponge with caramel sauce.

Poets House St Mary's St, CB7 4EY ✐ 01353 887777 ♂ poetshouse.co.uk. A stylish hotel with several public areas – you can order British seasonal cuisine in the Dining Room, sip cocktails in the glass-walled Sonnet Lounge or enjoy afternoon tea in the Courtyard Garden.

Prince Albert 62 Silver St, CB7 4JF ✐ 01353 663494. A short stroll from the town centre, this backstreet pub was once an officers' mess. It has a reputation for real ales, and they host an August beer festival in the garden. Expect British cuisine and popular Sunday roasts.

Truly Scrumptious 35 Forehill, CB7 4AA ⊘ trulyscrumptiousvegan.co.uk ◷ 11.00–15.00 Tue–Sat. Named one of the UK's top 50 vegan restaurants, Ely's first dedicated vegan and gluten-free café serves homemade brunches, lunches and more – think lentil dahl with mint soy yoghurt, followed by vegan chocolate cake.

Unwrapped 13 Lynn Rd, CB7 4EG ✐ Mon–Sat. This café, shop and refill centre is run by Prospects Trust – a charity and organic farm that provides therapeutic horticulture and work opportunities to people with learning difficulties. You'll meet some of these co-workers if you pop by for some homemade cake, dry goods refills, and veg from the farm. Located opposite Ely Museum – drop in for a coffee after you've seen the exhibits.

🛍 SHOPPING

The city has some lovely independent shops scattered between its high street stores. I've highlighted a few below but I'd recommend having a good potter to seek out more, taking care not to neglect the little alleyways that lead off the main streets. In addition to the large antique centre I've listed, there are several small art galleries and antique shops, all of which are worthy of a rummage.

The Eel Catcher's Daughter 28B High St, CB7 4JU. The window to this shop is a mini museum, displaying an authentic eel trap and stake. Inside, you'll find gifts, trinkets and body products.

Ely Fudge Company 31 Market Pl. Step inside to see English fudge being made the traditional way by a mother-and-daughter team who use steel pans and a marble slab. There are loads of different flavours.

Ely Gin Company 2–3 Buttermarket, CB7 4NY. Take your pick of locally made flavoured gins, from liquorice to breakfast marmalade.

Topping & Company Booksellers 9 High St, CB7 4LJ ⊘ toppingbooks.co.uk ◷ 08.30–18.30 Mon–Sat. I could spend all day in this bookshop, which has three floors piled high with books. They host year-round author events and reading groups.

Waterside Antiques 55A–55B Waterside, CB7 4AU ⊘ watersideantiques.co.uk ◷ 09.30–17.30 Mon–Sat, 11.00–17.00 Sun. East Anglia's largest antiques centre, this eclectic emporium covers 10,000ft^2 and sells everything from jewellery to World War II helmets.

2 LITTLEPORT

🏠 **Swan on the River** (page 317) 🏡 **Horsely Hale Farm** (page 317)

The village of Littleport sits five miles north of Ely, just back from the River Great Ouse. It appears a little unloved, with its small and somewhat scruffy strip of budget stores and kebab houses, yet the village is known throughout the Fens for everything from riots and skating to Burberry clothing. Littleport was once a popular place for ice skating, with the river often used as a rink – in 1875, local skaters raced the 12.30 train to Ely, with the skaters taking an easy win. In the early 20th century, the village became a national skating hub, with 40 acres of flooded fen beside the railway line providing the rink. Londoners would arrive by train to watch skaters race for prize money and pigs and, in 1900, the British Amateur and Professional Championships were held here. Littleport's last official races were held in 1912; due to rising winter temperatures, fenland ice skating declined throughout the 20th century. Today, it's a rare event.

At the western end of Main Street, opposite St George's Church, is a full-scale **statue of a Harley Davidson** motorbike, which was erected in 2003 to celebrate the company's centenary. This 1937 Knucklehead is a tribute to the Harley family – William Harley was born in Littleport and emigrated to America in the 1800s where his son, William Sylvester Harley, founded the company. At the eastern end of Main Street is the former **Hope Brothers shirt factory** on White Hart Lane. Built in 1882 by Littleport local and philanthropist Thomas Peacock, the name 'Hope' was chosen to provide hope for poverty-stricken villagers. The factory went on to make the England football kit and was later taken over by Burberry clothing. When a decision was made to convert the factory into flats, a plaque was erected on the wall in Peacock's memory, which you can still see today.

To explore more of the village and delve into its past, you could follow one of three themed walks, created by the Littleport Society. The two-mile 'Skaters Trail' takes you to the site of the former rink and along the

THE RIOT TO END ALL RIOTS

In 1816, when Littleport's men returned from the Napoleonic Wars, they found themselves unemployed and faced with starvation. Furious at the government (and at life in general), they rioted from Littleport to Ely, smashing up shops and barricading themselves in a pub. The military disbanded the mob and made 76 arrests. Of these, five men were hanged, and 19 were shipped to Botany Bay penal colony in Australia. Despite their fate, the rioters were an influencing factor in Parliament's 1824 Vagrancy Act, and you'll find a memorial tablet to the ill-fated five on the tower of St Mary's Church in Ely (page 232).

River Great Ouse, while the two-mile 'Harley Trail' guides you to the Knucklehead statue, William Harley's birthplace and the venue of the 2003 Harley weekend festival. The mile-long 'Riot Trail' leads you along the mob's 1816 route, revealing stories of the shops they looted and the pub they barricaded themselves inside. You can pick up a leaflet from Ely Tourist Information Centre or The Littleport Society (First Floor, The Barn, Main St, CB6 1PH ✐ 01353 861547 ◷ 13.00–16.00 Tue), which also houses a collection of local artefacts that range from teapots and newspaper clippings to fossils and Roman pottery.

⁌ FOOD & DRINK

Habis Café 23 Main St ✐ 07445 831648 ⌀ habis.co.uk. Offers a Mediterranean/English menu that includes falafel rolls, calamari burgers and Sunday breakfasts with local sausages and Spanish black pudding. They also host tapas and paella nights.
Station Café 4b Station Rd, CB6 1QE ⌀ stationcaf.co.uk ◷ Tue–Sat. Once a butcher's shop, this little brick building does breakfasts, gourmet burgers, wraps and salads.
Swan on the River 1 Sand Hill, CB6 1NT ✐ 01353 861677 ⌀ swanontheriver.co.uk. Of Littleport's three pubs, the Swan has the most scenic setting, with tables outside by the river. They serve pub grub and pre-ordered afternoon teas.

3 PRICKWILLOW MUSEUM

Main St, Prickwillow CB7 4UN ✐ 01353 688360 ⌀ prickwillowmuseum.com ◷ May–Sep noon–16.00 Mon & Sun

Beside the River Lark (a tributary of the Great Ouse) on the edge of Prickwillow village, this rustic museum showcases some of Cambridgeshire's finest restored diesel engines, salvaged from old pumping stations – these include the station's original Mirrlees engine and a Vickers Petter, which is thought to be the only preserved engine of its type.

Engineering enthusiasts will find plenty to fill their boots with here. After a ten-minute video that introduces the story of fen drainage, you can work your way around the engines and other exhibits – there's a huge display of handheld drainage tools, turf-digging equipment, eel nets and other fenland paraphernalia on show, plus old photographs and maps to show how the waterways have changed over time.

If you fancy arriving on foot, the museum is a five-mile riverside walk from Ely (see the museum's website for directions). You could also travel here by boat and moor up outside.

4 STRETHAM OLD ENGINE
🏠 **Stoker's Cottage** (page 317)

Green End, Stretham CB6 3LF ∅ strethamoldengine.org.uk ⊖ Apr–Oct 13.00–17.00 Sun & bank hols

Follow the Great Ouse five miles south of Ely and you'll see the 75ft brick chimney of Stretham Old Engine rising above the river (the Ouse Valley Way walking route heads directly past) in a serene and secluded spot, surrounded by fens. Of the more than 100 steam-powered pumping stations erected across Cambridgeshire in the 19th and early 20th centuries, Stretham is the only survivor. Built in 1831, it was installed to drain the 5,600 acres of the Waterbeach Level, replacing the less efficient wind-powered pumps that previously did the job. When floods threatened the farmland, locals would have been relieved to see the smoke rising from Stretham's chimney, reassuring them that the engine was at work. The old engine was operational until 1925, when a more powerful diesel engine (also on display) took over.

Today, the engine is cared for by the Stretham Engine Trust, whose volunteers do an incredible job of maintaining it and sharing its story on open days. When I visited, volunteer Martin Byrne took me on a tour of the buildings, starting with the blacksmith's workshop, which is chock full of old fenland tools. 'It's been left pretty much as it always was,' he told me. A door through the back of the workshop led us to the diesel house, home to the four-cylinder Mirrlees engine, which took over from steam in 1925. This engine last ran in 1941 and hasn't turned since but Martin is determined to get it going again one day. Next to the blacksmith's shop is the 37ft wooden scoop wheel which, with every revolution, would have lifted 30 tons of water off the Waterbeach Level and into the river. 'Wait there and I'll get it going for you,' Martin announced, nipping next door into the engine room, which houses the steam-powered engine – although the old engine no longer runs on steam, it can be brought back to life by electricity. Sure enough, the scoop wheel began to turn and I started to get a sense of what life at the working engine would have looked and sounded like.

To see the steam engine in action, I followed Martin into the engine room where the enormous steel beast spans three floors. The 24ft cast-iron flywheel turns at ground level, there's a beautiful wooden-cased valve chest on the first floor, and the top floor gives access to the 24ft beam, which apprentices used to ride on as a form of initiation – a stomach-churning thought if, like me, you don't have much of a head for heights. Also on the top floor are exhibits of the wooden patterns used to make spare parts for the engine, along with the ice skates and tools that the old engine workers would have relied on. The windows from the top floor also give fantastic views, with Ely Cathedral sailing on the horizon.

Back on ground level, Martin took me into the boiler room, where three enormous coal-powered steel boilers have been beautifully preserved. While Martin pointed out the various working parts of the boilers, he painted a picture of what life would have been like for the workers here: in short, overpoweringly hot in summer but wonderfully warm in winter!

5 HADDENHAM VILLAGE & ARTS CENTRE

South of Sutton, Haddenham is the highest village in the Isle of Ely, sitting 100ft above the surrounding farms and villages. To get a sense of this elevation, exit the village on the A1123 towards St Ives and you'll be treated to sweeping countryside vistas – even a few extra feet gives panoramic views in these parts. But, before you rush through for this rare Cambridgeshire thrill, the village itself has a few charms. **Haddenham Arts Centre** (20 High St, CB6 3XA ⬧ haddenhamartscentre.org.uk ☉ 10.00–16.00 Thu–Sat) is a community-run gallery and café, where you can buy local ceramics, jewellery and sculptures, watch artists at work, or join an art class or workshop. North of High Street, the medieval church of **Holy Trinity** sits on a high point. In the graveyard is a replica of a memorial stone, dedicated to St Ovin – according to legend, the first church in Haddenham was founded in the 7th century by St Etheldreda (of Ely Cathedral fame, see box, page 229) and Ovin, her steward. Ovin's original stone was discovered in Haddenham in the 1700s and is now in Ely Cathedral. The rest of Haddenham village has a scattering of independent shops, including a bead store and a bookshop selling rare books. Every September, the village hosts the **Steam Rally and Heavy Horse Show** (⬧ haddenhamsteamrally.co.uk), with steam engines, heavy horse competitions and an old-fashioned fair. It's a full-weekend affair, with camping.

¶¶ FOOD & DRINK

You can tuck into pub grub at **The Three Kings** (6 Station Rd, CB6 3XD ✆ 01353 749080 ⬧ threekingshaddenham.co.uk), or seek out **The Cherry Tree** (8 Duck Ln, CB6 3UE ✆ 01353 749502 ⬧ haddenhamcherrytree.com), for lunches, ice creams and local ale.

6 MEPAL, SUTTON & WITCHAM

🏠 **The Three Pickerels** (page 317) 🛥 **BoatShack** (page 317)

This trio of villages began life as medieval settlements that stood on the western edge of the Isle of Ely, just a few feet above the fenland swamps. Reminders of these early days include the ancient churches of St Mary's (in Mepal), St Martin's (Witcham) and St Andrew's (Sutton). Today, the villages are surrounded by fields and a network of fenland drains, which thread through the countryside and double up as wildlife-rich waterways – water voles are among the species that hide out here.

Mepal (pronounced 'meepal', like 'people') sits next to the New Bedford River. Cut in the 1650s by Dutchman Cornelius Vermuyden, this 100ft river diverts the main flow of the River Great Ouse and was one of the most significant steps taken to drain the Fens. Also known as the Hundred Foot Drain, it was cut parallel to the Old Bedford River (created in 1637), creating a washland between the two that contains floodwaters and protects farmland.

Mepal's Three Pickerels Pub has a privileged setting beside the New Bedford River, with a choice of rural and riverside footpaths heading directly past – for an easy walk, you could walk one mile southwest to Sutton Gault, cross the bridge and walk back on the opposite bank. For more variety, try my suggested route (the Way of the Drains) on page 242 or follow the waymarked **Mepal Way** (three miles), which is signposted from the pub – I recommend picking up a Mepal Way leaflet at Ely tourist information centre (see box, page 227) and checking the route on OS Explorer map 228 *March & Ely.*

North of Mepal, the little village of **Witcham** bursts into life on the second Saturday in July each year when it hosts the **World Pea Shooting Championships**. Held on the village green since 1971, the championships invites participants to shoot dried peas at a target, with top scores for hitting the bullseye. Regulation peas are supplied but you can bring your own shooter. The prize is the John Tyson Shield, named after the school headmaster who launched the event in 1971 – apparently, he took inspiration from the pea shooters he confiscated from schoolchildren.

Witcham is also the starting point for a six-mile stretch of the **Fen Edge Trail** (page 173), which leads through the countryside to Mepal and along the New Bedford River to Sutton. The Geological Society (who designed the trail) recommended this section to me as one of the best for experiencing the landscapes of the fen edge. I walked this linear

The Way of the Drains

✻ OS Explorer map 228 *March & Ely*; start: The Three Pickerels, 19 Bridge Rd, Mepal CB6 2AR
♥ TL439812; 2 miles; easy (flat all the way)

This circular pub walk leads beside the Hundred Foot Drain (New Bedford River) and stream-like Catchwater Drain, before crossing several smaller drains via little wooden bridges en route back to Mepal with its 13th-century church.

1 Walk out of The Three Pickerels on to Bridge Road and turn right then immediately left. Go through the gate on to a bridleway, signed Mepal Way. Follow this bridleway for around 600yds, with the river on your left.

2 When you reach a metal gate, go through and turn immediately right to pass through another gate on to a footpath that leads beside Catchwater Drain. Walk with the drain on your right for around half a mile until you reach a wooden footbridge on your right.

3 Cross the bridge and stay straight as you follow the footpath through a field. At the edge of the first field, you'll come to a junction of footpaths – do a quick left then right to walk over a little bridge into the next field. Follow the footpath through the field to another wooden bridge. Cross the bridge, go left and walk around the left-hand field edge.

4 Where the field ends and the footpath meets a track, go straight, passing houses on your left. The track becomes a surfaced road (New Rd) with houses on both sides.

5 At the end of New Road, go straight and cross the road (High St) on to School Lane. Just after the grassy island on your right, look for the footpath sign across the road on your right,

route on a sunny August day and can thoroughly recommend it. To return to Witcham from Sutton, take bus 39 (Stagecoach) or walk one mile along the (uninspiring) A142 footpath. For maps and directions, see ◈ www.fenedgetrail.org.

Largest of the three villages, **Sutton** sits two miles south of Mepal. Officially known as 'Sutton-in-the-Isle', its showpiece is the striking 14th-century church of **St Andrew's**, which has a pepper-pot tower with octagonal lantern and Victorian stained glass (east window). This village is one of the few places where you can get a real sense of how the Isle of Ely once stood proud above the fenland swamps – take a walk along The Row in the south of the village and gaze out to the countryside, where you'll notice a sharp drop from the fen edge to the Fens beneath. The Witcham to Sutton Fen Edge Trail guides you along this route.

signed 'Mepal Way' and 'Mepal Church ¼'. This footpath takes you across a wooden bridge and diagonally across a field to the church. Stay left as you walk through the churchyard, passing the church on your right.

6 Exit the churchyard and turn right on to a track, which leads back to The Three Pickerels.

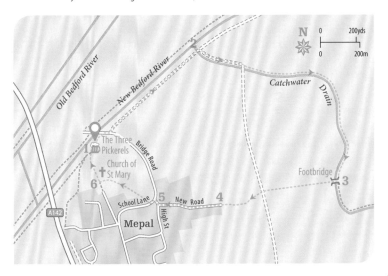

 FOOD & DRINK

All three villages have pubs but **The Three Pickerels** in Mepal (19 Bridge Rd, CB6 2AR ✆ 01353 777777 ⊗ thethreepickerels.co.uk) has the best setting, with a lovely garden by the river. At the time of writing, it was undergoing a major renovation, which included a new conservatory restaurant. Check the website for the latest updates and menu.

THE SOUTHWEST FEN EDGE & OUSE WASHES

Before the Fens were drained, the fen edge was, in effect, the coastline of mainland England, with fenland swamps and islands to the northeast, and the uplands of Huntingdonshire (Chapter 2) to the southwest. The southwest edge sees the last of the River Great Ouse in full flow, before it diverts along the Bedford rivers. Here, the Great Ouse is flanked by birdlife-rich wetlands that form the southern extremity of the Ouse Washes – a chain of internationally important wetlands that stretches 25 miles northeast to Norfolk.

7 EARITH, BLUNTISHAM & BERRY FEN

The neighbouring villages of **Earith** and **Bluntisham** sit north of the River Great Ouse, where the New and Old Bedford rivers begin. These sleepy villages go largely unnoticed to most visitors unless, that is, there's a big freeze: when a rare cold snap grips the county, ice skaters flock here for a spin on **Berry Fen** (also known as Bury Fen), a patch of fenland that sits half a mile south of the two villages.

For centuries, ice skating on Berry Fen was part of local life, and several of the villagers I met here grew up in the days when winter skating was a regular occurrence. In Earith, author Andrew Hunter Blair described how the villagers would gather on the frozen fen, taking mulled wine and sausage rolls to keep warm. The Blairs still have a plentiful supply of ice skates: 'there must be twenty-odd pairs under our stairs,' Mrs Blair

FENLAND ICE SKATING

Cambridgeshire folk have been skating on the Fens for centuries. In pre-Roman times, they attached animal bones to their feet and skated over the frozen washland as a means of winter transport. By the 17th century, metal blades had replaced bones, and skating had become a sport. The Fens boasted the biggest natural rinks in the country, and the world's first official speed-skating race took place here in 1763.

Skating matches were often organised at the drop of a hat, and most of the competitors were labourers who were unable to work when the fields froze over. Thousands would turn up to watch them compete for money, mutton or a bag of flour, and it was as much a social event as a sport – according to an old fenland saying, 'It takes ice to meet old friends'.

Fenland skating entered a golden era in the 19th century. The National Skating Association was established in Cambridge, and Victorian fenmen were renowned for their style, speed and stamina. Their skates, known as 'fen runners', were blocks of wood with blades that were screwed into everyday boots. In 1895, James Smart from the Norfolk border became Britain's only ever world champion speed skater and, in 1924 and 1928, Cyril Horn from Wisbech competed in the Winter Olympics. By the 1940s, almost every family in the Fens had a pair of skates – even city folk in Cambridge would skate along the frozen River Cam.

told me. Similarly, in Bluntisham, Parish Clerk Tracey Davidson told me about her childhood days when the village shop had a ready supply of mismatched pairs of skates to hire. 'If there was ice, you'd skate,' she said. Rewind the clock even further to the 1800s, and Berry Fen's fame went beyond recreational skating – speed-skating championships were commonplace, as were games of bandy (see box, below).

With today's milder winters, ice skating is rare but not forgotten. Earith and Bluntisham's village signs both depict skating scenes, while the little pond on Colne Road in Earith is home to a metal sculpture of a bandy player who skates in vain on a puddle of water. Not to be deterred, the locals are ever hopeful of another freeze and, occasionally, as in the winters of 2010 and 2018, they get a chance for a spin. You can find Berry Fen by walking along the Ouse Valley Way that leads between the two villages – follow the footpath signs that lead south off the A1123, or try my suggested circular walking route (page 246). Berry Fen is part of a Site of Special Scientific Interest (SSSI) that's a haven for birdlife – when I last visited in spring, it was alive with lapwings, herons, black-headed gulls and a host of other birds that were nesting,

THE BIRTHPLACE OF BANDY

Speed skating wasn't the only popular ice sport in the Fens. Bandy has its roots in the Fens, and was formalised by the local players of Berry Fen, near to Earith and Bluntisham. Similar to ice hockey, the game requires a ball, a bandy (curved stick), a field the size of a football pitch and a prolonged spell of freezing weather conditions. Today, it's the last that holds Cambridgeshire back.

In the 1800s, games of bandy were a common sight throughout the Fens, with the Berry Fen bandy team considered the best. Originally, the rules were agreed at the start of each game but in 1822, local player Charles Tebbutt committed them to paper and introduced the game to northern Europe.

The first international match took place in 1891 between Berry Fen and Haarlem in the Netherlands. Who do you think won? Cambridgeshire, of course.

With bandy conditions rare in Cambridgeshire these days, your best bet for seeing a bandy stick is at the Norris Museum in St Ives (page 103), which also displays a pair of fen runners and a copy of Tebbutt's *Bandy Code of Rules*. Bandy is still played throughout eastern Europe, Scandinavia, Russia and the US, with the Bandy World Championship held every two years. The sport is even recognised by the International Olympic Committee, although it's never been officially played at the Olympics.

Ice skates & orchards

❄ OS Explorer map 225 *Huntingdon & St Ives*; start: Rectory Rd bus stop, A1123, Bluntisham
♀ TL367744; 4 miles; easy (flat all the way)

- -

This circular walk leads past RSPB Ouse Fen to the famous skating ground and SSSI of Berry Fen which is abundant in birdlife. You'll then continue into Earith, passing its characterful village sign and bandy player sculpture, before walking past traditional orchards on the return leg to Bluntisham, where you could refuel at the village pub.

1 With your back to the bus stop, walk a few paces west along the A1123 (Rectory Rd). Before you reach the petrol station, turn left on a track signed 'Ouse Valley Way Brownsville Staunch 1¼'.

2 At the end of the track, pass through a metal gate, enter a field and turn right. Walk around the right-hand field edge, keeping straight when the path crosses a drainage ditch into the next field. Walk along the left-hand field edge here and, roughly halfway along the field, you'll pass a wooden gate on your right signed 'RSPB Ouse Fen'. Continue straight and you'll see the River Great Ouse ahead (for a short detour, go through the gate into RSPB Ouse Fen and walk a few paces to the edge of Barley Croft Lake for some bird spotting).

3 When you reach a footpath junction, turn left to walk in a northeasterly direction, with the river on your right. To your left is Berry Fen; the SSSI is at the far end, where you'll pass an information board that tells you about the fen's history as an ice rink.

4 When the track splits, stay straight and follow the main path to a metal gate. Go through, with the river on your right, and follow the path as it bends left at Westview Marina. Go through another metal gate, passing an Ouse Valley Way information board on your left.

5 Turn right at the road (A1123/Earith High St) and walk roughly 400yds to Earith's village sign (note the ice skaters) at the junction of Colne Road.

6 Turn left on to Colne Road and walk along the left-hand pavement past a little pond with a sculpture of a bandy player (an information board on the railings tells you more). Continue straight to Whybrows Lane.

7 Turn left on to Whybrows Lane, following the footpath sign to a metal gate. Go through the gate into a field and walk along the left-hand edge to a metal gate that leads to a track, through scrub and traditional orchards. Keep left on the track until it meets a field.

8 Go left at the field and follow the left-hand field edge as it bends right, with woodland on your

wading and waddling across the watery meadow. It's a stunning spot, and is popular with those who sport binoculars and big camera lenses.

left. Continue along the field edge (or, for a prettier route, enter the woodland, and follow the path that leads parallel to the field). When the path bears left away from the field, follow it to a metal gate. Go through and keep straight on to a surfaced road (Mill Ln), passing allotments, houses and a sports field on your right.

9 At the end of Mill Lane, turn right on to East Street and follow the road, which bends left to meet Bluntisham High Street and the village barometer (housed under a little roof, opposite the bus shelter).

10 Turn left on to High Street, passing the White Swan pub on your right, and follow the road south for around 400yds to the A1123. Turn right to return to your starting point.

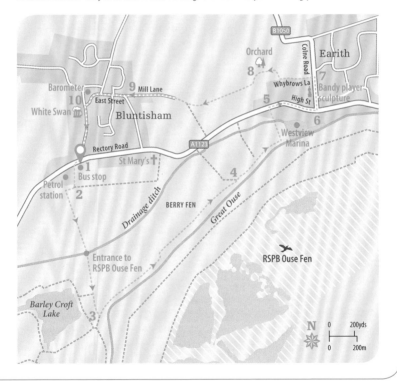

In addition to ice skating and birdlife, Bluntisham and Earith have several traditional orchards, which were once a common sight throughout

Cambridgeshire. You can glimpse some of these by following the walk on page 246, or by visiting the Tony Rowell Memorial Orchard on Colne Road in Bluntisham, where you can sit or stroll beside the apple trees.

In 1973, Earith was at the forefront of a space-age experiment: a hovertrain that was set to revolutionise the travel industry, thanks to £5.25million of government investment. Built in Swindon, Britain's first hovertrain – RTV31 – arrived in Earith and the 73ft-long sci-fi contraption was taken to a test site on the wide, flat area of uninterrupted fenland beside the Old Bedford River, where a mile-long concrete monorail track lay waiting. On 7 February, with sparks flying, RTV31 reached a top speed of 104mph while battling a 20mph headwind. Despite this early success, the government pulled the plug and the hovertrain was abandoned. Fast-forward a few decades and RTV31 was saved from the scrapheap by Railworld in Peterborough (page 136), where you can now see Britain's first and only hovertrain.

¶¶ FOOD & DRINK

Local food and drink options aren't particularly 'Slow', but if you're looking for somewhere to rest and refuel, **The Crown** (48 High St, PE28 3PP ✆ 01487 843490 ⓕ) in Earith has a riverside garden, the refurbished **White Swan** (30 High St, PE28 3LD ✆ 01487 842055 ⓕ) in Bluntisham is north of the church, while **The Lounge** (Station Rd, PE28 3PA ✆ 01487 843088 ⏲ 08.00–15.00 Tue–Sat, 09.00–14.00 Sun), at Bluntisham petrol station, does brunches and lunches.

8 NEEDINGWORTH, RSPB OUSE FEN & HOLYWELL

🏠 **The Pike & Eel** (page 317)

Upstream (southwest) of Earith, on the north bank of the River Great Ouse, are the villages of Needingworth and Holywell, whose secretive charms lie down dead-end tracks. Wander this way and you'll discover riverside pubs, a healing spring and a nature reserve in the making.

The larger of the two, **Needingworth** is the first village you'll come to if travelling by road. At its northern edge is **RSPB Ouse Fen Reserve** (PE27 4TA ⌖ rspb.org.uk/ousefen). Since 2001, this working quarry has been transitioning into a wildlife-rich wetland that, when complete, will boast the UK's largest reed bed. Restoration is expected to take 30 years but you can already experience March hares and 'booming' bitterns in spring, warblers in summer, roosting egrets in autumn, and barn owls gliding over the fields on winter evenings. At the reserve's northeast end, Barleycroft Lake is a highlight in spring and summer when thousands of black-headed gulls nest on the islands – the sound of the gulls can be deafening at times. The trail network includes the five-mile Barleycroft Trail and six-mile Reed bed Trail – see the map board in the small car park or download a guide at ⌀ rspb.org.uk.

Needingworth village is largely a modern creation, thanks to a devastating fire in 1847 which destroyed many of its oldest buildings. Visitors should make a beeline for the marina, set away from the main village down a rough track: follow the sign for 'The Pike & Eel' from the war memorial on Overcote Lane, continue on to a track and, one mile later, you'll arrive. Here, you can eat and drink at The Pike & Eel pub/restaurant (page 250), go for a riverside walk, hire riverboats (⌀ riversidemarine.co.uk) or pick up handmade gifts at Pebble & Pier giftshop (⌀ pebbleandpier.com).

Heading south out of Needingworth, Mill Way takes you to **Holywell** (one mile) – and nowhere else. One of Cambridgeshire's three Saxon ring villages (built on a circular track with houses facing outwards), Holywell is a real delight and would make a scenic stopping point on a river cruise or ramble, with the River Great Ouse and Ouse Valley Way snaking past. On Holywell Front, a beautiful row of thatched houses sits raised above the river, enjoying uninterrupted views over the flood meadows. At the western end of this street, the Early English church of **St John the Baptist** sits on the highest ground. In front of the church (south side) is the holy well. A 'healing' spring and the village's namesake, this pre-Christian well has been a place of pilgrimage for several centuries and is thought to be the oldest landmark in the village. Time your visit for the nearest weekend before 24 June and you'll coincide with the Well Dressing ceremony, when festivities are held at the church.

At the eastern end of Holywell Front is the Old Ferry Boat (page 250). Said to be Cambridgeshire's most haunted inn, this is the domain of Juliet Tewsley who died by suicide in 1050. Inside, her grave is marked by a floor slab, and the pub's chalked-up tale describes her fate. She is said to appear annually on 17 March, the anniversary of her death. The stretch of river outside the pub is popular with wild swimmers, kayakers and paddleboarders (there's a little slipway to launch a vessel), while riverboats can make use of the free 48-hour moorings. The pub used to operate a river ferry here, following the route Hereward the Wake (see box, page 175) apparently used when he escaped from William the Conqueror in the 11th century. Today you can only cross the river if you have your own boat.

Pub walks from Holywell & Needingworth

The Ouse Valley Way footpath goes directly past The Pike & Eel (Needingworth) and the Old Ferry Boat (Holywell), which sit one mile apart along this path. From Holywell, you could follow the footpath two miles west to St Ives (page 101); from The Pike & Eel, you could head east to RSPB Ouse Fen: walk one mile to a lock and a footbridge, which leads to the reserve's eastern lagoon area. Alternatively, continue past the lock for around 600yds to where the Ouse Valley Way forms a junction with the Pathfinder Long Distance Walk. Follow the Pathfinder footpath (leading north, away from the river) for around 200yds to a gate and sign on your left for Ouse Fen – this takes you to Barley Croft Lake. Alternatively, you could visit Berry Fen (page 244) by heading right at the footpath junction. Use OS Explorer map 225 *Huntingdon & St Ives* to plan your route.

¶¶ FOOD & DRINK

The Old Ferry Boat Back Ln, Holywell PE27 4TG ✆ 01480 463227 ⌀ greenekinginns.co.uk/hotels/old-ferry-boat. Said to be one of England's oldest, records of this thatched inn go back to AD560. The terrace overlooks the River Great Ouse and the rustic interior has wobbly wooden beams and an inglenook fireplace. The 'pub classics' menu is mostly pies, steaks and burgers, plus lunchtime sandwiches and jacket potatoes.

The Pike & Eel Overcote Ln, Needingworth PE27 4TW ✆ 01480 463336 ⌀ pikeandeel.com. This refurbished restaurant/pub/hotel sits within a marina, next to the River Great Ouse. The pub has a 200-year-old copper bar, and the contemporary restaurant has been renovated using reclaimed wood from the marina. Both serve modern British menus with an emphasis on Cambridgeshire fare. Outside is a glass-fronted terrace, plus lots of picnic benches on the riverfront lawn – it's a fantastic setting on a sunny day.

9 RSPB FEN DRAYTON LAKES & FEN DRAYTON VILLAGE

⌂ **Thornhouse B&B** (page 317)

Fen Drayton Rd, CB24 4RB ⌀ rspb.org.uk

On the southern bank of the River Great Ouse, **RSPB Fen Drayton Lakes** is a master of the unexpected – don't be surprised if a heron bursts out of the reeds, an orb of starlings performs a mesmerising dusk display, or a bus on rails glides past while you're birdwatching. The reserve, with its network of lakes, sits at the far southwest end of the Ouse Washes wetland system. Habitats like this once covered vast areas of East Anglia, but by the mid 20th century the landscape had become an industrial one of sand and gravel pits. It is now being returned to nature, with weed-dancing grebes, raft-nesting terns and acrobatic hobbies (small falcons) that dart above the water. Dragonflies and damselflies are prolific, with almost half of all UK species found here – to distinguish them, notice how dragonflies rest with their wings open, while smaller damselflies tend to close them.

Ten miles of trails skirt the lakes and riverbanks but don't expect shoreline views all the way. Many sections are shrouded in vegetation, giving wildlife the privacy it needs. There are three colour-coded walking trails, ranging from one to three miles, plus hides and viewing platforms to watch for wildlife. Footpaths lead to and from the villages of Fen Drayton, Swavesey and Fenstanton, while the guided busway stops in the reserve. There are no permanent facilities and the main car park is more than a mile from the nearest road. 'Keep going! Nearly there!' read the signs on the access track, which is signposted as 'RSPB Nature Reserve' off Fen Drayton Road.

"It is now being returned to nature, with weed-dancing grebes, raft-nesting terns and acrobatic hobbies"

The tiny village of **Fen Drayton**, within walking distance (less than half a mile north) of the reserve, is a bucolic gem with its old houses, village lock-up and thatched pub. The **Three Tuns** (High St, Fen Drayton CB24 4SJ ✆ 01954 230242 ⌖ threetunsfendrayton.co.uk) has an inglenook fireplace which is adorned with brasses that belonged to the old village smithy, and the pub also has a set of 15th-century carvings that reveal how Danish tradesmen sailed up the village brook en route to the inland port at Swavesey (page 253).

Other reminders of Fenstanton's agricultural heritage and history of Dutch settlers (engineers who came to drain the Fens) include the distinctive farmhouses that line the High Street – look for 16th/17th-century buildings like the red-brick Old Manor Farm and half-timbered Home Farm. Sitting on the highest ground in the village, elevated above the surrounding fenland, St Mary's Church (on Church St) dates back to the late 13th century.

10 FENSTANTON

🏠 **The Blue Cow** (page 317)

Two miles west of Fen Drayton is Fenstanton, which means 'stony place by the Fen'. This village has greatly expanded over the years and first impressions very much depend on which part you find yourself in. The oldest (and prettiest) bit is in the northwest, where Chequer Street leads to the narrow lanes of the old village. Here, a cluster of thatches lines Honey Hill; 17th-century cottages sit pretty on Church Lane; and **Ron's Farm Shop** (Honey Hill, PE28 9JP ⊘ Tue–Sun) adds to the rural village idyll. It's possible to walk here from Fen Drayton Lakes, which sits half a mile or so northeast along The Fen (a track just off Honey Hill and School Ln).

Surrounded by a tangle of lanes, the 13th/14th-century church of **St Peter and St Paul** has the 18th-century garden designer **Lancelot 'Capability' Brown** buried in its graveyard. Brown bought the Manor of Fen Stanton and Hilton in 1767, was appointed High Sheriff of Cambridgeshire and Huntingdonshire in 1770, and resided at the Manor House on Chequer Street. Fenstanton wasn't his permanent home (Brown lived mostly in London), but he was very fond of the area and requested to be buried here. You'll find his modest headstone in the graveyard, plus a grander memorial and more information inside the church. The church also has a tribute to former Fenstanton resident **John Howland**, one of the Pilgrim Fathers who set sail on the *Mayflower* in 1620 and landed in New England.

South of the old village is Fenstanton High Street, where a 17th-century clock tower sits atop the village lock-up. The High Street is

LANCELOT 'CAPABILITY' BROWN (1716–83)

'England's greatest gardener', Brown was responsible for changing the face of British landscapes by sweeping away formal gardens and introducing a naturalistic style with streams and hills. His clients included King George III, six prime ministers and half of the House of Lords. Today, Brown's legacy lives on at more than 250 estates across England and Wales, including Burghley House (page 147)

and the Wimpole estate (page 296). It's likely that his nickname 'Capability' came from his tendency to describe British estates as having great 'capabilities' for improvement.

The Cambridgeshire Gardens Trust have created a series of four Capability Brown-themed walks, which include a two-mile trail in Fenstanton. To download the leaflet, visit ⊘ cambridgeshiregardenstrust.org.uk.

mostly Georgian, with a handful of independent shops that include **Fenstanton Family Butchers** and **Barkers Bakery** (a Cambridgeshire favourite). In the 19th century, Fenstanton boasted 15 inns, thanks to its position on a drovers' route between rich grazing lands and St Ives's cattle market (see box, page 102). Today, only two pubs survive: **The Crown & Pipes** (a 'proper' local, serving drinks only) and **The Duchess** (🕾 01480 350859 🖱 theduchessfenstanton.co.uk ⊙ Wed–Sun). The latter boasts a 300-year-old bar and serves traditional British food.

🍴 FOOD & DRINK

Fenstanton High Street is home to the village pubs and bakery but, for a truly Slow experience, head to **Carriages of Cambridge (**Capability Barns, Huntingdon Rd, CB24 4SD 🕾 01954 233279 🖱 carriagesofcambridge.co.uk ⊙ noon–15.00 Tue–Sat), which sits just outside the village's southeast end. Here, you can travel back to the romance of the 1920s and the golden age of luxury rail travel just outside of Fenstanton. Carriages of Cambridge serves afternoon teas in three Pullman-style train carriages. Fully embracing the spirit of the age, the carriages sit in a purpose-built railway station, complete with a platform and heritage signal box. Most ingredients are locally sourced or home-grown, including eggs from the owner's chickens. It's a popular place, so you'll need to book – although they sometimes offer walk-up spaces for summer seating on the platform.

11 SWAVESEY

Two miles east of Fen Drayton, Swavesey sits at the eastern end of Fen Drayton Lakes. Once a busy inland port, the village's name means 'landing place.' It gives a fascinating insight into the old ways of the fen edge, with the best bits at the northern and eastern ends, where you'll find the earthworks of Swavesey Priory and the heart of the original village. Information boards dotted around the village tell you about its history, while footpaths lead northwest to Fen Drayton Lakes (less than a mile from the church). Swavesey is easy to reach by public transport or bike, as the village has a stop on the guided busway route (🖱 thebusway. info) which has a cycle track running along its length.

A stroll around Swavesey

This walking tour of historical highlights sets off from the guided busway stop at the crossroads of Station and Over roads (next to the MG Owners Club HQ, where you can ogle the classic cars). If you're travelling by car, you could park on Market Street and follow this route in reverse.

Route 51: cycling the busway – the Swavesey & St Ives Loop

✳ OS Explorer map *225 Huntingdon & St Ives*; start: White Horse Inn, 1 Market St, Swavesey CB24 4QG ♀ TL361689; 9 miles or 14½ miles with Longstanton extension; easy (flat all the way).

The guided busway is a network of car-free bus routes which mostly follow sections of old railway lines. Cycling and walking paths run beside the bus lanes, with NCN51 covering the 14-mile section between Cambridge and St Ives. Several villages sit just off the track.

The most scenic section lies between Swavesey and St Ives, with the busway passing through RSPB Fen Drayton Lakes. For a scenic nine-mile loop, you could set off from Swavesey and combine NCN51 with NCN24, which passes through several villages.

If you fancy attempting the route on a tandem or triplet, you can hire one through Cycle Centric (⊘ cyclecentric.com), based in Longstanton (four miles east of Swavesey). It's also possible to start the route from here, picking up the NCN24 to Swavesey and then continuing on to Longstanton on the busway cycle path on your return.

1 From the White Horse Inn head up to High Street and turn left, following the road south for a quarter of a mile.

2 When you reach a mini roundabout with a playing field on your left, turn right on to School Lane, following the cycle route sign for 'Fen Drayton 2'. You are now on NCN24.

3 When you meet a T-junction, turn right for Fen Drayton village.

4 At the next T-junction, turn right on to Honey Hill, following signs for NCN24 as you enter Fen Drayton village. Follow Honey Hill as it bends sharp left and becomes Horse and Gate Street.

5 When you reach the Three Tuns pub (on your right), continue on NCN24, going right at the mini roundabout, then first left on to Cootes Lane, which bends left and becomes Mill Road.

6 At the end of Mill Road, turn right on to the NCN24 cycle path. Continue straight when the cycle path drops on to the road and leads to the High Street, which guides you all the way through Fenstanton village. At the mini roundabout, stay straight and continue on Huntingdon Road, using the NCN24 cycle path signed for St Ives.

7 When you exit Fenstanton village, turn right on to Low Road, staying on the NCN24 to meet the A1096 roundabout. ▶

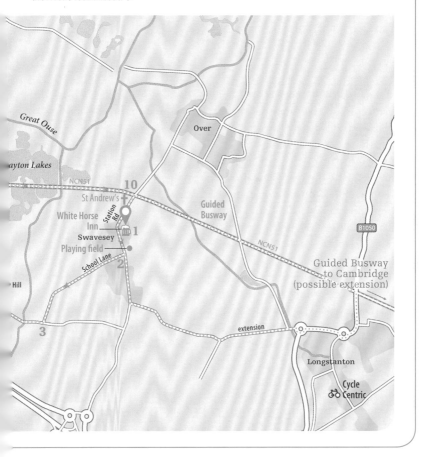

Swavesey to St Ives loop (continued)

8 Go straight ahead at the roundabout (use the cyclist's crossing point). Pass through the signs into Hemingford Grey and take the first right on to London Road. You are now on NCN51. Continue straight into St Ives, crossing the bridge over the River Great Ouse on to Bridge Street. Turn right at the end of Bridge Street, pass the Oliver Cromwell statue on your right, and continue on to Station Road.

9 When you meet the A1096, cross at the traffic lights and go straight ahead into the guided busway car park. Follow the NCN51 cycle route signs through the car park to the guided busway route. Turn left on to the busway cycle path (following signs for Cambridge) and ride east for 2½ miles to Swavesey, passing RSPB Fen Drayton Lakes on the way.

10 As you near Swavesey, you'll pass St Andrew's Church on your right before meeting a set of traffic lights. Turn right at the lights on to Station Road, which merges with the High Street and takes you back to the White Horse Inn.

From the bus stop, walk west along the busway footpath and across Station Road. On your left is an information board that overlooks the site of **Swavesey Priory**. The village and priory sat on separate fenland islands, separated by water. While the village grew into a prosperous market town, the priory was less successful. Founded in 1086 by Count Alan of Brittany, it only ever held a maximum of four occupants and was abandoned in 1539 during the Dissolution of the Monasteries. From here, you'll have a good view of **St Andrew's**, which started life as the priory church. Little is left of the original building, save for some Saxon work in the nave and chancel arch. Inside is a grand monument, commissioned in 1631 by the Lord of the Manor of Swavesey to commemorate his first wife. For a closer look at the church, walk down Station Road, passing the church entrance on your right.

Continue past the church on Station Road to a grassy island, known as **Swan Pond** – this was part of a medieval waterway network that connected to the Great Ouse. Eels and other fenland produce were exported from here, while coal and building materials would have been unloaded on to a cobblestone causeway. To get a sense of how it once looked, notice how the nearby houses are raised above street level – which would have been the water level in medieval times. An information board on the island tells you more.

Follow Station Road as it curves left and becomes High Street. When you reach the White Hart pub, turn left on to **Market Street**, with its pretty green, pub and nostalgic shop which, according to the sign, sells everything from 'pipes' to 'views'. This was the site of the medieval marketplace and docks, which connected to Swan Pond. Before the Fens were drained, Swavesey's direct access to the fenland waterways and River Great Ouse made it ripe for trade between The Wash and the rest of England. Wise to this, the prominent la Zouch family developed the settlement in the 12th century, establishing an eight-day fair that helped Swavesey to become one of the largest medieval towns in the area. Stroll down to the green, where an information board tells you more, then reward your wanderings at the pub or café.

FOOD & DRINK

The Nook 12 Market St ⏱ 09.00–13.00 Mon–Sat. The perfect way to describe it, this 'nook' of a café serves top-notch coffee, cake, flatbreads and breakfast rolls. Dogs are made to feel at home and can add their photos to the Doggy Wall of Fame. My favourite spot is the sofa at the back.
White Horse 1 Market St ✆ 01954 231665 ⏱ thewhitehorseswavesey.com ⏱ Tue–Sun. A traditional village pub with an open fire, book corner and pub games, plus a garden with children's play area. Expect cask ales and home-cooked food, which includes burgers and lunchtime snacks.

THE CAMBRIDGESHIRE LODES

East of the Great Ouse, the fen edge dips south to Cambridge before arcing east towards Suffolk and Newmarket. This southern stretch of fen edge is notable for its lodes – fingers of manmade waterways that connect to the rivers. The area is also home to Anglesey Abbey (a beautiful National Trust estate) and the tranquil Wicken Fen Nature Reserve.

12 THE FEN EDGE FIVE & LONGSTANTON

🏠 **Old School House Rooms** (page 317)

Just a few miles to the north and northeast of Cambridge is a chain of villages that celebrates their fen-edge identity more than most. Willingham, Rampton, Cottenham, Landbeach and Waterbeach are known collectively as the Fen Edge Five, and are united via social events, clubs and a local magazine, the *Fen Edge News*. None are chocolate-box pretty but they have a handful of highlights if you're passing through.

GET A LODE OF THIS

Resembling short stretches of narrow canal, the lodes connect several fen-edge villages to the rivers Cam and Great Ouse. It's thought that they were cut by the Romans around 2,000 years ago and were used as transport routes for several centuries. Each had their own particular uses over the years, with Wicken Lode transporting medieval sedge from Wicken Fen, and Reach Lode exporting Cambridgeshire clunch (limestone) to the Norfolk coast, while Burwell's lode became the busiest, thanks to the village's thriving fertiliser and brick industries.

Today, life on the lodes is more peaceful. Some sections are navigable for pleasure craft, and all have footpaths and/or bridleways leading along their banks. You could, for example, ride a horse or bike beside Bottisham Lode, launch a canoe on Reach Lode, or walk between Wicken Fen and Burwell village on the interconnecting Burwell and Wicken lodes.

Willingham would make a good pit stop on a cycle ride or road trip, with its independent cafés and pubs, which include Cambridgeshire's first micro-pub. The village's church is also of note – the medieval wall paintings at St Mary and All Saints' (Church St, CB24 5HS) include a depiction of St Etheldreda, who founded the abbey at Ely.

Two and a half miles southeast, **Rampton** hosts the annual Rampton Horse Show (⊘ ramptonhorseshow.org) in September and is the site of an ancient castle. From the Church of All Saints' (15 Church End, CB24 8QA), a footpath leads out of the churchyard and across a bumpy field (a former medieval settlement) to Giant's Hill, home to the remains of Rampton Castle. The caste was built in the 1100s at the same time as Burwell Castle (page 268) in defence against Geoffrey de Mandeville (see box, page 268). Wooden boardwalks lead to the castle's site on Giant's Hill, where an information board tells its story.

All Saints' Church itself is also of interest, being one of Cambridgeshire's two thatched churches. Records of worship here date back to around 1092 and the north wall of the nave displays the remains of colourful medieval wall paintings. Cambridgeshire's second thatched church sits three miles south in **Longstanton**. A characterful little church with a 13th-century double bell tower, St Michael's (on St Michael's Ln) has inspired several in America – Google 'St James the Less in Philadelphia', and the resemblance is uncanny.

East of Rampton, **Cottenham** is the largest of the Fen Edge Five and is watched over by All Saints' Church, which sits at a high point on the

High Street. Fragments of this perpendicular church are 12th and 13th century but most of the building dates to the 14th and 15th centuries, with various additions and alterations. Running past the northeast edge of the village is Cottenham Lode, which you can access via Broad Lane or Lockspit Hall Drove. Footpaths lead beside the waterway, which links to the River Great Ouse (two miles northeast) and Giant's Hill in Rampton (1½ miles west).

Two and a half miles southeast of Cottenham, **Landbeach** is the smallest of the Fen Edge Five. Here, the medieval-era Tithe Barn (2 Waterbeach Rd, CB25 9FB ⌂ tithebarntrust.org.uk) is a highlight, with its thatched roof and striking black timbers. To see inside, plan your visit around one of its exhibitions or performances.

Finally, a hop over the A10 leads to **Waterbeach**. 'I never thought I'd see Waterbeach in a guidebook,' was the response from my sister, who has lived here for more than a decade. She's right, it isn't worth coming out of your way for, but you may well find yourself here if you're exploring the Fen Rivers Way (page 260) which trails past the village, or the riverside cycle track that leads between here and Cambridge. In the centre of Waterbeach is a small green, surrounded by old cottages, yellow-brick houses (typical of Cambridgeshire) and village amenities (a shop, post office, pharmacy, café and two pubs). You'll find a few more shops, including a bakery and butchers, north of the green on the High Street. The rest of the village is a mixture of old and modern housing developments, with lots more housing planned for the future. Waterbeach is also worth mentioning for its half-mile stretch of the Car Dyke, which is hidden behind playing fields, west of Waterbeach train station. One of the greatest engineering feats of the Roman Empire, this weedy ditch was once a 21yd-wide hand-dug waterway that ran for 85 miles along the fen edge.

 FOOD & DRINK

All Fen Edge Five villages apart from Landbeach have pubs and independent cafés. Those that appeal most to Slow travellers are in Willingham, Rampton and Waterbeach.

In Willingham, **The Bank** (9 High St ⌂ thebankmicropub.co.uk ☺ Tue–Sat) is a one-room micro-pub that's a must for ale-lovers, while **The Porterhouse** (1 Station Rd ✆ 01954 488080 ⌂ theporterhousepub.com) has an extensive gin menu and homemade pizzas, and the **Duke of Wellington** (55 Church St ✆ 01954 261622 ⌂ dukeofwellington-willingham. co.uk) has been serving 'famous' pies and mash for more than a decade. For breakfasts

The Fen Rivers Way: Waterbeach to Ely

✳ OS Explorer map 226 *Ely & Newmarket*; start: Waterbeach train station ♥ TL500650; 12 miles; easy (flat all the way)

The Fen Rivers Way runs for 48 miles between Cambridge and King's Lynn, following the rivers Cam and Great Ouse to The Wash. One of the most scenic sections is the 12-mile stretch between Waterbeach and Ely – it gives glorious views of Ely Cathedral, while the train stations at either end make it easy to travel between the two. From Waterbeach, you can follow the waymarked route along either riverbank – both sides are pleasant but the east bank has the advantage of going directly past the pub in Upware.

To access the start of the east bank route, walk east of Waterbeach train station (away from the village) for 150yds along Clayhithe Road. Just after passing the train station car park on your right, you'll see a footpath sign with an eel symbol on your left (signed 'Bottisham Lock 1, Dimmocks Cote 6, Ely 12'). For the west bank route, continue along Clayhithe Road for another 400yds to The Bridge Inn (CB25 9HZ), then cross over the road bridge and take the footpath on your left, which is marked with the eel symbol and signed 'Upware 4½, Ely 12'.

and lunches, **Willingham Auctions Café** (25 High St ⌂ willinghamauctionscafe.com ◷ 09.00–16.30 Mon–Sat, 10.00–16.00 Sun) is next to the auction house and, part of the same business, **LOT 25** (⌂ lot-25.com ◷ 17.00–22.00 Thu–Sat) is a courtyard bistro with open-sided barns. On the outskirts of the village, the **Book Warren Café** (Highgate, Over Rd, CB24 5EU ⌂ thebookwarrencafe.com) serves coffees and lunches surrounded by shelves of books and playthings for kids.

Rampton has the **Black Horse** pub (6 High St ✆ 01954 251867 ⌂ theblack.horse), where you can enjoy gin-cured salmon and beef fillet with pomme purée. And on the edge of Waterbeach, the **Bridge** (Clayhithe Rd, CB25 9HZ ✆ 01223 860622 ⌂ chefandbrewer. com) has a lovely spot by the river, while the **Pharmacie** café (I'm a fan of their spicy wraps) overlooks the village green, along with a couple of other pubs.

13 DENNY ABBEY & FARMLAND MUSEUM

Ely Rd, Waterbeach CB25 9PQ (signed off the A10) ⌂ dennyfarmlandmuseum.org.uk ◷ 11.00–17.00 Tue–Sun & bank hols; English Heritage

Standing on the site of a 12th-century abbey, this rural museum guides you through 850 years of fenland life. It started out in the 1960s as a shoebox of broken pottery, collected by four-year-old Craig Delanoy.

When Craig's collection grew too big, it was moved to Denny Abbey, where the land has been farmed since Roman times.

Housed in restored heritage buildings are more than 10,000 objects, all made or used in Cambridgeshire. Highlights include the 17th-century threshing barn, a 1940s village shop and a traditional fenman's hut that houses rat traps, eel nets and more. There's lots for kids to get immersed in – my niece and nephew, who are regular visitors, love the farmworker's cottage, where they can dress up in 1940s attire.

The abbey itself has stood here since the 1100s. England's only religious site to be occupied by three different monastic orders, it first housed Benedictine monks, followed by the Knights Templars and Franciscan nuns, who added several buildings, including a new church, dormitory and the refectory which still stands today. Religious life at Denny ended with the Dissolution in 1536 and it later became a farm.

14 ANGLESEY ABBEY & LODE VILLAGE

Quy Rd, Lode CB25 9EJ ☺ gardens & café daily; house Thu–Tue; mill Fri–Tue; National Trust

Contrary to its name, **Anglesey Abbey** is not an abbey at all. Built on the site of a 13th-century Augustinian Priory, this stately home and gardens rose from the ruins, with its transformation to country house beginning in 1609. It was the last owner, however, who turned it into the remarkable home you see today. Lord Fairhaven bought the house in 1926 and added everything from the spiral staircase to the service wing, filling its rooms with treasures that span the Tudor period to the 20th century.

When Fairhaven passed away in 1966, he left his home to the National Trust, asking that they '…keep the abbey, inside and out, and the gardens arranged as they are at the date of my death', as he saw his home 'as a representation of an age and way of life that is quickly passing'. Hats off to the National Trust, as they have filled the brief exceptionally well – as I wandered through the house, I felt like an intruder, snooping around while the owners were away. The most impressive rooms include the medieval dining room and the library, where royal visitors have engraved their names on the window using a diamond-tipped pen. My favourite area is the service wing, where the keys to the Rolls Royce hang next to the daily schedule of Fairhaven's chauffeur, Claude Grimes. For kids, there's a list of chores to attend to, such as brushing the tweed jacket left behind by a guest, and turning the tins of sardines in the larder to stop the oil from settling.

The 114 acres of garden are largely Lord Fairhaven's creation, designed to entertain his guests. Each zoned section shines at different times of year: the Spring Garden boasts daffodils and hyacinths; the Rose Garden blooms from June to October; the trees on Riverside Walk glow red and golden in autumn; and September reveals one of Fairhaven's showpieces – the Dahlia Garden. If you feel inspired to recreate one of the seasonal garden scenes you see, head over to the on-site plant centre and shop.

Also within the grounds is a working watermill. Lode Mill sits at the junction of Bottisham Lode and Quy Water – a clear stream, which runs along the estate's boundary. Venture inside the mill and you can climb the wooden staircase to see the machinery, which often mills corn (usually at 11.00, 13.00 & 15.00 Tue–Sun).

Next to Anglesey Abbey, the little village of **Lode** has a mixture of modern and thatched houses, plus lots of lovely footpaths leading south beside Quy Water and west across Quy Fen – a 70-acre pastureland and SSSI. The village website (⊘ lode.org.uk) has a downloadable pamphlet with walk suggestions, while the National Trust website features the 4½-mile Beyond Anglesey Abbey walk which explores Quy Fen. To fuel your walk, you could try the National Trust café at Anglesey Abbey, or **The Shed** in Lode (45 Lode Rd, CB25 9ET ⊘ 01223 812425 ⊘ the-shed-pub.co.uk ⊙ closed Mon), which rears its own rare breed cattle and pigs.

15 THE SWAFFHAMS

⚑ St Cyriac's, Swaffham Prior (page 317)

The villages of Swaffham Prior and Swaffham Bulbeck sit a mile and a half apart on a fen-edge escarpment. **Swaffham Prior** is quite striking, with its two windmills and pair of churches with twin octagonal towers. Sitting just off the Devil's Dyke footpath (see box, page 266) and the waymarked Earthworks Way, the village is also popular with ramblers.

Sharing the same churchyard, **St Mary's** and **St Cyriac's** have gazed across the fen edge for centuries. They have colourful histories, with one having been abandoned for the other at various points over the years, and windows and bells being switched between the two until, finally, St Mary's was chosen as the favourite and St Cyriac's was left to rot. Luckily, it was saved from ruin and restored in the 1970s, meaning that the village's 'double church skyline' is here to stay. St Cyriac's has a beautiful Georgian interior, and St Mary's boasts some stunning stained glass (some of which was originally installed at St Cyriac's), but it's the Norman tower at St Mary's that is the standout feature – its octagon stage pre-dates that at Ely Cathedral. St Cyriac's (⊙ 10.00–16.00 daily), is used for exhibitions, performances and overnight 'champing' accommodation. Below the churchyard, you'll find some historical houses and the 17th-century Red Lion pub (✆ 01638 745483) lining the High Street.

The **Earthworks Way** is an eight-mile circular route that links Swaffham Prior with the neighbouring villages of Reach and Burwell. To get started on the walk, head to the northeast edge of the village on Swaffham Road and, diagonally opposite the village entrance sign, you'll see a footpath signed 'Earthworks Way, Reach via Barston Drove 1½ miles'. You can pick up a leaflet with a route map from Ely Tourist Information Centre.

East of the churches are the windmills on Mill Hill. With its jet-black tower and snow-white sails, **Fosters Mill** is in full working order, having been built in 1857 on the site of an earlier mill. Back then, you could, apparently, see 40 windmills from the top of Fosters', either milling corn or draining water out of the Fens. The mill is open to visitors on the second Sunday of each month (14.00–17.00), when you can see it in action and buy freshly milled flour. Its sister mill sits across the road and has been converted into a private house.

BATTLE OF THE TWIN CHURCHES

Before the Civil War (1642–51) it wasn't unusual for villages to be split between two parishes and, therefore, have two churches on the same site. Sitting on the highest ground, St Cyriac's in Swaffham Prior is thought to have the earlier foundations, although subsequent rebuilding means that St Mary's has the older architecture, dating back to the Norman era. Damaged during the Civil War, St Cyriac's fell into disrepair in the 1600s, by which time the village's two parishes had become one. More than 100 years later, a decision was made to revive the site at St Cyriac's, with a Gothic-style church designed by Cambridge architect Charles Humfrey (1772–1848). Following the rebuild, St Cyriac's became the sole parish church.

Fast-forward to 1903 and St Cyriac's met an unforeseen fate when critics attacked Humfrey's mock-medieval architecture as inauthentic – the vicar at the time called it 'an almost grotesque travesty of a church'. And with that, St Mary's was restored and St Cyriac's became redundant once more. A rescue mission arrived in 1973 when the Churches Conservation Trust (CCT) bought St Cyriac's and set to work repairing seven decades of neglect.

A mile and a half southwest of Swaffham Prior is **Swaffham Bulbeck**, with the B1102 wiggling past the village green and Black Horse pub (✆ 01223 811366). You'll pass through this village if you're travelling between Bulwell and Anglesey Abbey, or if you're cycling through on the NCN51 (which links Cambridge with Newmarket). Fans of opera could time a visit around the annual summer performance – almost every year since 1982, the Swaffham Bulbeck Summer Theatre (⊘ sbsummertheatre.com) has performed a Gilbert and Sullivan opera at Downing Farm. South of the green, the 13th-century tower of **St Mary's Church** rises above the High Street and, inside, has 15th-century pew ends carved with dogs, fish and mythical beasts.

At the northern edge of the village is Swaffham Bulbeck Lode and the houses of Commercial End. Once a medieval port, river trade thrived here between the 17th and 19th centuries, and you can still see the old workers' cottages, malthouse and Merchant's House that grew around this industry. Footpaths lead along both banks of the lode, so you could stroll or jog three miles on one side to meet the River Cam, then cross via the bridge and wander back.

16 REACH VILLAGE & DEVIL'S DYKE

The heart of this ancient village has a real sense of yesteryear, with its thatched cottages, old farmhouses and a nostalgic pub, plus the church and old schoolhouse all clustered around Fair Green. Inhabited for more than 2,000 years, Reach was once (like many fen-edge villages) a port. Medieval merchants accessed the village via Reach Lode, and there were busy wharves and quays along the Hythe. The main exports were peat and 'clunch' limestone, cut from Reach Hill at the village's southern edge – you can still glimpse the white cliffs of the clunch pits today if you follow the footpaths leading southwest off Swaffham Road.

Today, most visitors are drawn to Reach for one of two reasons: to walk along Britain's finest Anglo-Saxon earthwork, Devil's Dyke or to visit one of the oldest festivals in England (Reach Fair). Hosted on Fair Green, **Reach Fair** (⊘ reachfair.org.uk) was first mentioned in 1201. Back then, the focus was iron and timber, followed by horses in the 15th century, and entertainment in the late 19th century, with a photographer drawing the crowds. Today, this one-day event takes place on the early May Bank Holiday, hosting craft stalls, live music, fairground rides and performances from the Devil's Dyke Morris Men. The annual **Reach Ride** also takes place over the weekend – this organised bike ride sees troops of cyclists riding from Cambridge to Reach, arriving for the opening of the fair. The full ride is 14½ miles each way but you could join at any point along the route – ⌀ camcycle.org.uk has more information. At other times of year, you can cycle between Cambridge and Reach on NCN51, via Bottisham and the Swaffhams.

North of Fair Green, **Reach Lode** meets the edge of the village at Hythe End. From here, it's possible to walk three miles along the west bank to Upware's lock and riverside pub (⌀ fivemilesinn.com). Reach Lode is navigable, so canoeists and paddleboarders could make the same trip.

Devil's Dyke is an ancient defensive bank and walking route which runs for 7½ miles between Reach and Woodditton in the southeast. Marked on some maps as 'Devil's Ditch', it's thought to have been built in the 6th or 7th century, while local legend claims it was carved by the Devil's tail as he was chased from a wedding at Reach church. In a county as flat as Cambridgeshire, the dyke rises above the countryside like a mountain ridge, reaching a lofty 34ft in parts. Much of the earthwork is an SSSI, home to precious chalk grasslands that have been lost elsewhere in Cambridgeshire.

Reach sits at the dyke's northwest extremity, where you could either set off for the full length (use OS Explorer maps 226 *Ely & Newmarket* and 210 *Newmarket & Haverhill*), or tackle a shorter section and loop back through the countryside. It's worth mentioning that cycling isn't allowed and, unless you make a detour, the only places to eat and drink are at either end – The Dyke's End in Reach (see below) and the Three Blackbirds in Woodditton (page 295). Returning to Reach from Woodditton by bus can be a bit of a faff, as you'll need to change in Newmarket, so it's better to book a taxi. To find out about walks at the southeast end near Woodditton, see Chapter 6.

FOOD & DRINK

The Dyke's End 8 Fair Green, Reach CB25 0JD ⌀ 01638 743816 ⌀ dykesendreach.co.uk ⌀ Wed–Sun. I'm a big fan of this community pub, which overlooks the green and was saved from closure when the villagers bought the freehold. The stripped-back interior provides a wonderful escape from modern life, with candlelit tables, a crackling fire and no music or TVs. Come for oxtail hotpot, battered cod or pulled pork and apple sandwiches.

Devil's Dyke West & the earthworks

※ OS Explorer map *226 Ely & Newmarket*; start: The Dyke's End pub, Reach ♀ TL566661; 3 miles or 4½ miles with optional detour; easy (mostly flat)

A circular route from the pub in Reach, this scenic walk leads along the northwest extremity of Devil's Dyke before following part of the waymarked Earthworks Way.

1 With your back to The Dyke's End pub, turn left and walk along the green to the Devil's Dyke information board. Continue straight, following the Devil's Dyke footpath sign for 'Woodditton 7½ miles' and take the little track on your left which leads up through the trees and on to the dyke, which is lined with trees and scrub. When the shrubs clear up ahead, you can see the twin churches and windmill in Swaffham Prior to your right, with Burwell's church to your left. Continue along Devil's Dyke for roughly half a mile to a set of steps on your left. Turn around here for a view of Ely Cathedral but do not go down the steps. Instead, continue a little further along the path as it bends to the right and drops down to a second set of steps.

2 Walk down the steps, following the signpost for the Earthworks Way, which guides you to a field. Walk along the left-hand field edge (you'll see an old railway bridge ahead) until a sign for the Earthworks Way directs you left, then diagonally across a clearing (site of a dismantled railway). Cross to a set of steps, which leads into a field. Follow signs for the Earthworks Way along the right-hand field edge and into a woodland, passing farm buildings on your left.

3 When you meet Swaffham Road, go left, following the Earthworks Way sign. Just before the Swaffham Prior village sign, cross the road and take the track on your right, signed 'Earthworks Way, Reach via Barston Drove 1½ miles'. Continue on this route until you meet a road.

   (Optional 1½-mile detour into Swaffham Prior: at the Swaffham Prior village sign, continue along Swaffham Road into the village, past the pub and up to the twin churches on your left. To return, take the footpath that leads northeast out of the churchyard. The windmill is signed off this path, which also leads back to Swaffham Road and the signpost for Barston Drove.)

4 At the road, continue straight, then turn off the road on to the public bridleway signed on your right. Follow this bridleway with a hedgerow on your left for around 160yds. When the hedgerow ends, take the footpath on your left signed 'Earthworks Way, Reach ⅓'. Continue along this footpath for around 330yds until you see a woodland (Reach Wood) ahead to the right (the entrance is behind a row of wooden posts).

5 Turn right off the path and walk through the posts, taking the left-hand path into the wood. Stay left through wood until you reach a large wooden gate. Exit the wood at this gate and go left, following a track which bends right, then left, then right again at a set of farm buildings. Follow the Earthworks Way sign to the road, with The Dyke's End pub visible ahead.

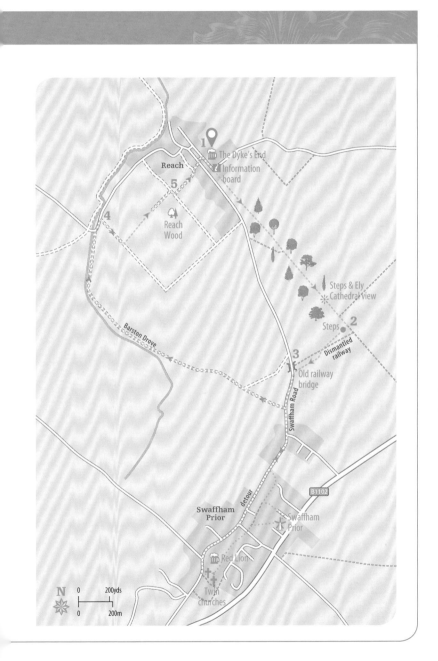

1 The Dyke's End

Reach

Information board

5

4

Reach Wood

Steps & Ely Cathedral View

Steps

2

Barston Drove

3

Old railway bridge

Dismantled railway

Swaffham Road

detour

B1102

Swaffham Prior

Swaffham Prior

Red Lion

Twin churches

N

| 0 | 200yds |
| 0 | 200m |

17 BURWELL

With a working mill, former castle and 'living' museum, Burwell village has lots of history to fill your boots with. It's also a short walk (one mile west) from Devil's Dyke (page 265). This elongated village has three main interlinking roads: High Street, the Causeway and North Street. The High Street area (south end) is home to the village's big hitters – the castle, church and museum – while the Causeway and North Street give access to Burwell Lode.

The earthworks of **Burwell Castle** include a seemingly haphazard collection of hillocks rising above the old moat. Built on the site of a Roman villa, it was one of two unfinished Cambridgeshire castles (the other is in Rampton) that King Stephen commissioned in defence against Geoffrey de Mandeville (see box, below). Information boards tell you about the pair's feud and help you to visualise the layout of the castle, which included tofts (houses) and crofts (smallholdings).

Next to the castle site, **St Mary's Church** (15th century) was described by the art historian Pevsner as 'the most perfect example in the country of the Perpendicular ideal of the glasshouse'. He was referring to the huge windows, which give the interior its fantastic feeling of light and space. Outside, the graveyard features a memorial to 78 villagers who died in the Great Fire of 1727, when they were trapped inside a burning barn – pay your respects at the flaming heart headstone.

Behind the High Street, on Mill Close, is **Burwell Museum & Windmill** (CB25 0HL ⬧ burwellmuseum.org.uk ⊘ Easter–Oct 11.00–

GEOFFREY DE MANDEVILLE

In 1143, England was in anarchy, with King Stephen having seized the throne from its rightful heir, his cousin Matilda. This kicked off 18 years of civil war, with barons like Geoffrey de Mandeville, Earl of Essex, fighting their own battles. Having switched allegiance from Stephen to Matilda, Mandeville fled to the Fens, drove the monks out of Ramsey Abbey and made his base in the swampy fenland underworld. Having amassed a ruthless mob of supporters, he began a series of raids on Cambridgeshire's villages and towns. King Stephen, struggling to penetrate Mandeville's stronghold in the Fens, began fortifying the fen edge with castles. Mandeville attacked the part-finished Burwell Castle in 1143 but was fatally wounded in battle. After his death, the rebellion ended, the castles were left unfinished and East Anglia breathed a sigh of relief. Elsewhere in England, the anarchy raged on for another decade.

17.00 Thu, Sun & bank hols). It tells the story of Burwell through the ages, with different eras and aspects of village life displayed in former farm buildings. You can visit the rooms of an old house, see farm machinery in the Wagon Sheds, and there are World War II uniforms and a serviceman's bed in the Nissen Hut. There's also a working windmill and a tea shop.

In the northern half of the village, the Causeway branches west off the High Street (B1102) and leads to North Street. This is where fleets of fen lighters (boats) would have loaded and unloaded goods at the hythe (now the end of Hythe Ln) and ferried them along **Burwell Lode** and Reach Lode to the River Cam, with trade thriving well into the 20th century. Burwell Lode is still navigable today and can be accessed behind The Anchor pub on North Street.

FOOD & DRINK

Burwell's pubs are dotted along the High Street, Causeway and North Street, along with a few independent cafés and shops that include **Elk Coffee** (105 The Causeway ⬠ www. elkcoffee.co.uk ⬣ Tue–Sun) and **Lanes Bakery** (20 High St) for take-away sandwiches. **The Five Bells** (44 High St ⬠ 01638 741404 ⬠ fivebellsburwell.co.uk ⬣ Thu–Sun) is a traditional pub with a modern menu (think pizzas, pulled-pork burgers and buffalo cauliflower bites), **The Fox** (2 North St, CB25 0BA ⬠ 01638 741267 ⬠ thefoxburwell.co.uk) is a 300-year-old pub with a wood-panelled bar and weekend street-food vans, and **The Anchor** (63 North St ⬠ 01638 743970 ⬠ theanchorburwell.net ⬣ Wed–Sun) cooks much of its menu over open coals and wood – try smoked partridge, fire-steamed mussels and local muntjac.

18 WICKEN FEN (NT) & AROUND
Lode Ln, Wicken CB7 5XP; National Trust
⬥ **Wicken Fen Back to Basics Campsite** (page 317)

Ah, the lovely Wicken Fen – just the thought of the breeze whispering through the grasses of this reedy reserve fills me with a wave of calm. The National Trust's oldest nature reserve, the initial two acres were bought from Charles Rothschild in 1899. Now spanning more than 1,975 acres, this is one of the few places where you can see, hear and feel what the pre-drained Fens may have been like – a landscape so rare that it's internationally protected.

A mosaic of fenland, meadows, reed beds, waterways, meres and ditches, the reserve claims to have more species of flora and fauna

THE MILL TRAILS

Although many of Cambridgeshire's windmills have been lost over time, several still survive and some have been restored to full working order. Burwell Museum has created a driving route and cycle trail that takes in many of the local mills, with maps and details available on their website (⟨ burwellmuseum.org.uk). The **cycle trail** gives you the option of a 26-mile circuit or two shorter loops, and the **driving route** covers 46 miles. For the best chance of stepping inside the mills and seeing their sails turning, try to time your visit around National Mills Weekend (⟨ spab.org.uk), which takes place each May.

than anywhere else in the UK. More than 9,300 different species have been documented here, from cranes, kingfishers, nightingales, bitterns, butterflies and otters to great crested newts, fen violets and the rare reed leopard moth. Some species are considered new to science or have never before been recorded in the UK, like the *Silvanus recticollis* beetle. To safeguard the survival of the reserve's precious wildlife, plans are afoot to expand the reserve and extend the wildlife habitats towards the fringes of Cambridge.

A network of boardwalks leads through the wetlands and reed beds, with elevated bird hides gazing over a sea of golden grasses. Helping to sustain this landscape are herds of highland cattle and Konik ponies, plus a restored windpump, which was originally used for drainage. Ironically, it now pumps water back into the land to stop it drying out.

Before you disappear along the reed-fringed walkways, be sure to pay a visit to the Fenman's Cottage (at the reserve's entrance), built from local peat, reed and clay. Next door is his workshop, complete with an eel basket, foot iron, scoop shovel and becket. There's also an excellent exhibit about traditional fenland life – learn about the osier, sedge and peat that people depended on, and how they used ice skates and flat-bottomed boats to travel.

"Before you disappear along the reed-fringed walkways, pay a visit to the Fenman's Cottage"

A series of mapped trails lead around Wicken Fen and into the surrounding fens – see the information boards or the National Trust website for the three-mile Adventurers' Fen Trail, the two-mile Monk's Lode walk, or the six-mile Octavia Hill Trail via Upware village (and pub). Cycling is popular here too – you can hire bikes at the visitor centre and ride through the reserve on the Lodes Way (see box, opposite), cycle north on NCN11 to Ely, or follow one of the other suggested routes on the website. In the warmer months (Mar–Oct) the reserve runs 50-minute guided boat tours along Wicken Lode.

Little **Wicken** village sits at the entrance to Wicken Fen on the A1123. This pretty settlement has three greens, a pub and the only 12-sided smock mill in the UK. Fully functioning, Wicken Windmill (CB7 5XR) still mills flour and is open to visitors on the first Saturday of each month – if the sails are turning on other days, however, it's also worth dropping by.

FOOD & DRINK

In Wicken Fen, sandwiches and snacks are served from the Docky Hut café. If you fancy something more substantial, try the **Maids Head** in Wicken village (12 High St, CB7 5XR ☎ 01353 727762 ⌂ themaidsheadwicken.com ⏱ Wed–Sun) which serves tapas, grills and hearty meals. If you're walking west of the reserve, you could visit Upware's riverside pub, **Five Miles from Anywhere No Hurry Inn** (Old School Ln, CB7 5ZR ☎ 01353 721654 ⌂ fivemilesinn.com).

Cycle the Lodes Way

�֎ OS Explorer map 226 *Ely & Newmarket*; start: Wicken Fen Visitor Centre ♀ TL563705; 16 or 18 miles; easy (flat all the way)

M y favourite fen-edge bike ride, the eight-mile Lodes Way is a linear route between Wicken Fen and Lode village, next to Anglesey Abbey (page 261), crossing four lodes along the way. You can hire bikes at Wicken Fen (page 223), and there are waymarkers to guide you along traffic-free cycle tracks and quiet country roads, which follow part of NCN11 through Adventurers' Fen, Tubney Fen and White Fen. Along the way, you could lay out some lunch on a picnic bench or detour to one of the villages that sit at the end of each lode. You can download a Lodes Way cycle leaflet from ⌂ visitely.org.uk or the National Trust website, or pick up a copy at Wicken Fen bike-hire centre.

For the return route from Anglesey Abbey, you could either retrace the same route or loop back through the villages of Bottisham, the Swaffhams, Reach and Burwell, following the NCN51 as far as Burwell, where you can branch off on to one of several countryside tracks to rejoin the Lodes Way (around 18 miles total). If you fancy a shorter ride, or you've got young kids in tow, I'd suggest doing a there-and-back route from the Wicken Fen end (the quietest and most scenic section).

NICK BEER 2

THE GREAT OUTDOORS

Cambridgeshire's vast open spaces, serene waterways and wildlife-rich reserves are ripe for exploring by boat, foot, bicycle or horse.

1 The Lodes Way is a beautiful off-road cycle ride between Wicken Fen and Anglesey Abbey. 2 Horseriders can enjoy miles of bridleways that weave through the countryside. 3 Holt Island Nature Reserve is home to crested grebes (pictured here), herons, cormorants and more. 4 Common darters and a host of other wildlife can be found at Paxton Pits Nature Reserve. 5 The River Great Ouse at Hemingford Grey is a stunning stretching to explore by boat.

3 NIGEL SPROWELL/HOLT ISLAND

4 GRAHAM TAPLIN/PAXTON PITS

5 MARTIN CHARLES/SHUTTER

19 SOHAM

If the name of this small town sounds familiar it is, sadly, most likely due to one of two traumatic incidents: the 1944 rail disaster or the 2002 murders (a quick Google search will fill you in on the details of both). These events have overshadowed Soham for decades but there's more to the town than harrowing headlines, including two restored windmills, a series of waymarked walks and an annual Pumpkin Fair held on the last Saturday in September. An autumn highlight since 1975, the fair is a chance for locals to show off their home-grown veg, and there are vintage vehicles, craft tents, a funfair and more. The windmills sit to the north (Northfield Windmill) and south (Downfield Windmill) of the town centre and are usually open during National Mills Weekend in May (⊘ spab.org.uk) and at various other points throughout the year – you can find more details by searching for the mills on ⊘ teamsmills. org.

Most of Soham's shops (which cater more to local needs than tourist interests) are clustered along High and Churchgate streets. In the centre of town is the cruciform church of St Andrew's, with its medieval hammerbeam roof and, in the graveyard, the tomb of Oliver Cromwell's great-granddaughter Mary D'Aye. Opposite the church, on Churchgate Street, the Fountain Inn is more than 500 years old. Attached to the pub's exterior is one of England's few remaining steelyards, used for weighing agricultural produce.

To delve deeper into Soham life, check out the Soham Heritage and Tourism Community website (⊘ sohamhtg.co.uk), which has information on local history and events. The community have also produced a tourist guide and a leaflet of 'Millennium Trails', which range from 1¾ miles to seven miles. To follow one of these walking routes, pick up a leaflet at the library (7 Clay St, CB7 5HJ) or pavilion (Fountain Ln, CB7 5PL) and look for the colour-coded markers around town. If you fancy planning an alternative countryside walk, you could follow the footpaths beside Soham Lode – in contrast to the dead-straight lodes further west, this seven-mile waterway wiggles through the town like a river. It meets the River Great Ouse near Ely.

¶¶ FOOD & DRINK

Soham has several pubs and cafés, including a couple of authentic Portuguese and Lithuanian cafés. One Soham institution in particular stands out for its Slow ethos:

The Red Lion (17 High St, CB7 5HA ✆ 01353 771633 🖥 redlionsoham.com) has been serving customers since the 1600s and, although refurbished, retains its ancient wooden beams and 17th-century fireplace. The weekly changing menu often includes local meats and Norfolk seafood. When *Guardian* food critic Grace Dent visited, she 'dearly loved' this historical gastro-pub, and enjoyed the homemade sloe gin and 'punchy' mackerel pâté.

20 CHIPPENHAM VILLAGE & GARDENS

East of the lodes, the village of Chippenham sits a few miles from the Suffolk border. This historical village, with its cricket green and pretty cottages, grew around the Chippenham estate. Established in the 17th century by Admiral Lord Russell, Chippenham Hall and gardens were bought in 1791 by the sugar baron John Tharp, and remained with the Tharp family until 1948 when they were inherited by a nephew, Basil Bacon. After a period of neglect, the estate was bought by Mr and Mrs Eustace Crawley in 1985 who set about restoring the farm buildings, parkland and estate cottages at the southern end of the village, near to the entrance of Chippenham Hall.

Today, you can experience the estate by staying in the hall's B&B accommodation or visiting **Chippenham Park Gardens** (🖥 chippenhamparkgardens.info), which are open to visitors on select days throughout the year, usually coinciding with the spring daffodil season, summer roses, autumn colours and winter snowdrops. The 40 acres of gardens were designed in an Anglo-Dutch style, with lakes, canals, woodland, formal gardens, summer houses and ornamental grasses.

⅋ FOOD & DRINK

During Chippenham Park open days, refreshments are served at the **Potting Shed Café**, overlooking the kitchen garden. Expect homemade cakes, soups and free-range hot dogs. Chippenham also has a village pub, **The Tharp Arms** (46 High St, CB7 5PR ✆ 01638 720234) which, at the time of writing, was only serving drinks but had regular visits from food trucks – check their Facebook page for the latest updates.

A couple of miles northwest of Chippenham, **Dojima Sake Brewery** sits within the grounds of Fordham Abbey (39 Newmarket Rd, Fordham CB7 5LL 🖥 dojimabrewery.co.uk). The UK's first Japanese sake brewery, it offers pre-booked tours and tastings, and there are plans afoot for a café and shop.

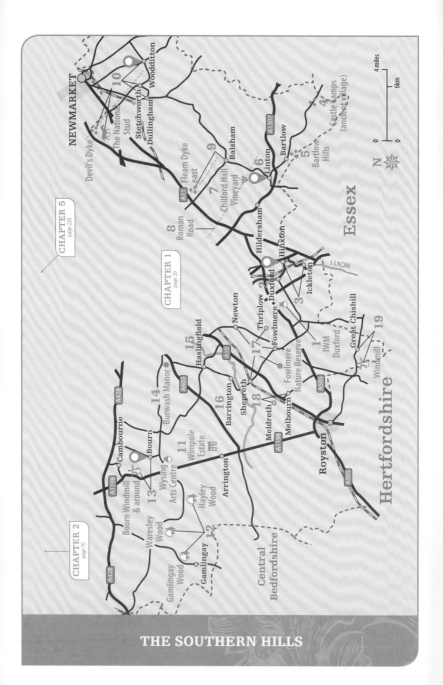

THE SOUTHERN HILLS

6
THE SOUTHERN HILLS

The chalk escarpments that run through southern Cambridgeshire boast the highest points in the county. This high ground builds in the south and east, with the apex teetering on the Hertfordshire/Essex border in Great Chishill (page 313). If you hail from more mountainous terrain, you may well scoff at the subtlety of Cambridgeshire's undulations, but here in one of England's flattest counties even the slightest elevation gives glorious views. Taking advantage of these uplands are some of England's oldest windmills – parts of Bourn Mill (page 299), for example, are thought to be 13th century.

Within these soft peaks and folds are the eastern extremities of mythical earthworks. The high ridges of Devil's Dyke and Fleam Dyke are remnants of Anglo-Saxon defences, while the Bartlow Hills are the largest surviving Roman burial mounds in western Europe. With this combination of uplands, ancient landmarks and rural charm, the southeast offers some of the best walking country in Cambridgeshire. Cyclists are also in for some fun, with gentle gradients to climb up and whizz down.

The landscape softens in southwest Cambridgeshire, where the River Rhee cuts through a high plateau, with pockets of ancient woodland filling the folds, and clear chalk streams trickling past villages like Meldreth. As I explored southern and southwest Cambridgeshire, I stumbled across a handful of villages so quaint and quintessential that I wanted to shrink them and take them home in a box. Hinxton is one such place, with its photogenic watermill, while beautiful Barrington claims England's longest green. Adding oomph to village life is a calendar of events that includes Thriplow's annual Daffodil Weekend, and the biannual Scarecrow Festival in Haslingfield. For many, however, the jewel in the southern crown is Wimpole Hall. Saved from ruin by Rudyard Kipling's daughter, the parklands, farm and hall on this magnificent estate are saturated with stories that span 2,000 years.

GETTING AROUND

Southern Cambridgeshire curves beneath the city of Cambridge and is sliced through by the M11, which heads south to London and meets the A14 north of Cambridge. In the rest of the southern region, it's easy to swap the A roads for quiet country roads and lanes that wiggle past pretty villages. If you explore the county's fringes, you'll find yourself dancing across the borders of Bedfordshire, Hertfordshire, Essex and Suffolk.

TRAINS

Southwest Cambridgeshire is well served by trains on the Cambridge to London King's Cross line, with stations at Meldreth, Shepreth and Foxton. Journey times from Meldreth to Cambridge can take as little as 17 minutes, or less than ten from Foxton. On the county's western edge, you could use the Bedfordshire stations of Sandy and Biggleswade, both of which are on the East Coast Main Line, which continues on to St Neots and Peterborough.

Directly south of Cambridge, Whittlesford and Great Chesterford (Essex) are the nearest stations to Duxford and the villages in southeast Cambridgeshire. For villages further north and east, and for access to Devil's Dyke, your best options are Dullingham and Newmarket stations.

BUSES

Most villages in this chapter have at least one bus a day connecting them to Cambridge, but travel between some villages can be tricky – linear walks between two villages require careful planning.

Stagecoach covers most services directly south of Cambridge and to the southeastern villages around Linton. For the villages in the southwest, A2B run the most comprehensive network.

THE SOUTH CAMBRIDGESHIRE SPIKE

Several south Cambridgeshire churches appear to have swapped their classic spires for needle-like spikes. An intentional architectural feature (which is also seen in neighbouring Hertfordshire), the 'spike' is a short, lead-covered spire, surrounded by a parapet. Hinxton has a good example, as does Gamlingay, Thriplow and Duxford.

CYCLING

Southern Cambridgeshire is a joy to explore by bike. Grab a map, plan a route through the east or west, and tour through an English idyll of village greens, cricket pavilions and thatched cottages. There are no obvious places to hire a bike, so you'll either need to bring your own or hire one in Cambridge (page 23). Directly south of the capital, be sure to explore the idyllic section of **NCN11** between Duxford, Hinxton and Ickleton.

For families, **Wimpole Hall** (page 296) has some of the best options for car-free cycling, with designated tracks leading around the estate. The National Trust website suggests several routes, ranging from 1½ to 4½ miles. More serious cyclists could tackle the 28-mile Wimpole Cycle Challenge (page 298), which starts and finishes on the estate and tours through southwest Cambridgeshire.

The **Roman Road** (page 290) is another good option for traffic-free cycling. This ten-mile track runs west between Cambridge's southeast suburbs (Chapter 1) and Horseheath village. Also in the southeast is the **Icknield Way Trail** (⌗ icknieldwaytrail.org.uk) – this 170-mile bridleway wiggles through southeast Cambridgeshire for around 30 miles, waymarked with an axe logo.

WALKING

Southern Cambridgeshire has lots to offer walkers, from ancient trackways and modest hilltop climbs to riverside strolls and woodland walks. You could explore the 7½-mile **Devil's Dyke** (page 293) footpath, the three-mile path on **Fleam Dyke** and the **Roman Road** (page 292), or tackle the 25-mile **Fleam Dyke and Roman Road Walk** (see box, page 292). There's also Rivey Hill to climb (see box, page 289), the ancient windmill at Bourn to visit (page 299) and several pockets of ancient woodland to explore in the southwest. The footpaths at Wimpole Hall give more options, and the estate marks the end of the 13-mile **Wimpole Way** and the start of the 11-mile **Clopton Way**.

Several long-distance trails pass through this chapter. The aforementioned **Icknield Way Trail** wiggles through the east, while the **Greenwich Meridian Trail** (⌗ greenwichmeridiantrail.co.uk) follows the Prime Meridian in the west, through Meldreth and a few miles east of Wimpole Hall. You could also explore part of the **Harcamlow Way** – a 141-mile figure-of-eight walk through Cambridgeshire, Essex

THE SOUTHERN HILLS

Southern Cambridgeshire is the most undulating part of the county, with charming villages and ancient landscapes sitting within a landscape of subtle peaks and folds.

1 Rivey Hill rises above Linton village, with spectacular views from the top. 2 Linton's High Street has independent shops and colourful listed buildings. 3 Barrington has a thatched school and one of the longest village greens in Europe. 4 Chilford Hall Vineyard offers seasonal tours and tasting sessions. 5 Thriplow Daffodil Weekend is a popular annual event, with thousands of daffodils blooming in the village.

and Hertfordshire. It links Bartlow, Horseheath and Fleam Dyke in the east, and Meldreth, Melbourn and Wimpole Hall in the west; pick up *Harcamlow Way 2 – Country Walks Around Cambridge* (2015) by Phoebe Taplin for a guide.

ALONG THE RIVER CAM

Directly south of Cambridge are the idyllic River Cam villages of Duxford (and the nearby Imperial War Museum), Hinxton and Ickleton, which you can explore on local pathways. I can also highly recommend the NCN11 cycle route, which weaves through all three – just don't make the mistake I did and attempt to ride through the ford: after a graceful swan glide on the slime, I was left chasing my bike down the river.

1 IWM DUXFORD
Duxford Airfield, Building 425, CB22 4QR ⊘ iwm.org.uk ⊙ 10.00–16.00 Wed–Sun

Europe's largest air museum, the Imperial War Museum (IWM) at Duxford showcases more than a century's worth of aviation. This vast site occupies Duxford Aerodrome, which was one of the most important airfields during the Battle of Britain. Here, you can submerge yourself in aviation history and see over 200 aircraft and military vehicles displayed in walk-through battle scenes or suspended in flight. My Dad, who has visited twice, is a big fan, so I asked for his thoughts:

> Visiting Duxford once is not enough! The site covers a huge area; not surprising as it was a major airfield during World War II. On my first visit I tried in vain to see everything, starting with the British war planes, moving on through the American planes, the land war exhibits... And then I stopped. Coming over the field was the unmistakable sound of a Spitfire fighter plane. After watching the landing of that rare two seater version I headed for the commercial plane hangar and the 'big draw': Concorde.
>
> My second visit was more leisurely. I chose my targets and spent more time getting immersed in each exhibition – best for me was the restoration workshop. My third visit is yet to come.

With several aircraft still flightworthy, the annual **air shows** are a highlight. They usually take place three times a year, with themed events in May and July, followed by the main Duxford Air Show in September. Even if you don't buy a ticket, you can catch glimpses of the flight displays from miles around – I've enjoyed many dramatic displays of Spitfires, Lancasters and Hawker Hurricanes while driving past on the M11. But, of course, ticket holders get a lot more bang for their buck with everything from vintage bands and dancing, to movie re-enactments and a chance to meet the lucky engineers who maintain and fly the aircraft; probably my Dad's dream job.

2 DUXFORD VILLAGE

🏠 **The John Barleycorn** (page 317)

Duxford village has a charming old core with tiny thatches, red-tiled cottages and some decent places to eat and drink – this pleasant package makes it worthy of a visit after a day at neighbouring Duxford Airfield.

You'll find the prettiest bits on the little roads and lanes surrounding the village's two Grade I-listed churches, St John's and St Peter's. St John's (10.00– 16.00 daily), tucked away by the village green, ceased operating in 1874 and is now cared for by the Churches Conservation Trust. This unspoilt relic boasts graphic wall paintings, Latin graffiti and medieval markings where arrows were sharpened on the stone walls. When St John's closed, its bells were moved to the parish church of St Peter's, sitting pretty at the junction of Chapel Street, Hinxton Road and St Peter's Street, and gazing over the war memorial and village pump.

"This unspoilt relic boasts graphic wall paintings, Latin graffiti and medieval markings where arrows were sharpened"

🍴 FOOD & DRINK

Graystones 4 St Peter's St, CB22 4RP ☺ Wed–Sun. This coffee shop has a pared-back interior and big garden with kids' playthings. Take your pick from filled ciabattas, Italian salads and handmade pizzas, along with luxury hot chocolates and flavoured lattes.

The John Barleycorn 3 Moorfield Rd, CB22 4PP ✆ 01223 832699 ◌ johnbarleycorn.co.uk. Thatched and shuttered, the village's oldest pub looks more like a pretty cottage. Bearing the date 1660, it is undeniably quaint, with hanging baskets, air-force memorabilia and a seasonal menu that ranges from pies and steaks to seafood linguine.

The Plough 57 St Peter's St, CB22 4RP ✆ 01223 833170 ◌ theduxfordplough.co.uk. A traditional thatched pub, serving real ales, craft beers and draught ciders and perries, plus homemade pub grub with daily specials.

3 HINXTON & ICKLETON

🏠 **The Red Lion** (page 317)

Small but incredibly photogenic, **Hinxton** is storybook-pretty, with its thatched cottages, 17th-century pub and white watermill. Several houses on High Street are 16th century, including the red-roofed Old Manor House. Church Green is a particularly pretty pocket, home to the village pump and the medieval flint-and-rubble church of St Mary and St John.

Hinxton Watermill (🕑 Jun–Sep first Sun of the month) sits just off Mill Lane, next to the River Cam. A 17th-century corn mill with adjoining 18th-century cottage, milling ceased here in 1955 and the building fell into disrepair. Luckily, it was restored in the 1980s. Even when it's closed, this riverside beauty is certainly worth visiting – the picnic bench outside is a lovely spot for a picnic lunch or flask of coffee.

One mile southwest is the larger village of **Ickleton**, with a shop, pub and a rather special parish church. St Mary's dates from the 11th century and is considered one of the most important in East Anglia. The Romanesque exterior isn't particularly striking but it's inside that things get special. In 1979 the church was almost destroyed by fire and, during the clean-up operation, a set of rare and extensive 12th- and 14th-century wall paintings was revealed – the remains of a Doom painting decorate the chancel arch, and there's a four-section arcade painting that includes the Last Supper, the Betrayal, the Flagellation of Christ and Christ carrying his cross. You'll also find the village history recorded on the church kneelers, spanning from the Roman era to the great fire.

Sandwiched between Hinxton and Ickleton, east of Ickleton Road is the **Wellcome Genome Campus** – a world-renowned scientific research campus that specialises in genomics and biodata. The campus occupies the grounds of the Georgian-era Hinxton Hall. It was here that the first draft of the human genome was announced in June 2000.

🍴 FOOD & DRINK

The Ickleton Lion 9 Abbey St, Ickleton CB10 1SS 🖉 01799 530269 🖱 theickletonlionpub. co.uk 🕑 Wed–Sun. A much-loved village pub with a reputation for friendly welcomes and good wine. The hearty pub-grub menu ranges from veggie lasagne to homemade meatballs and local ice creams. Sit outside in the big garden, or inside beneath the wooden beams.
The Red Lion 32 High St, Hinxton CB10 1QY 🖉 01799 530601 🖱 redlionhinxton.co.uk. A sister pub to the Black Bull in Balsham (page 87), this listed building boasts a terraced

garden with dovecote, arbour and church views. The atmospheric interior has low ceilings in the bar and oak rafters in the restaurant. Expect gastro-cuisine, an extensive wine list and micro-brewery ales.

THE SOUTHEAST

As the hilliest part of Cambridgeshire, the southeast offers the most varied walking routes, enriched with charming villages and ancient earthworks. Here, you can explore Fleam Dyke from Balsham village, cycle along the Roman Road, or climb Rivey Hill from Linton and then descend to an English vineyard. Savvy Slow travellers can also catch a glimpse of Newmarket races by rambling along Devil's Dyke, which tracks above the racecourse.

4 CASTLE CAMPS ANCIENT VILLAGE

A quiet village on the Essex and Suffolk borders, Castle Camps boasts pretty cottages and a quaint pub, **The Oak** (thecockerelcastlecamps. co.uk). But what makes it special is the village's namesake: follow the half-mile footpath to Castle Camps Church (signed off Barlow Rd) and you'll arrive at the earthworks of a motte and bailey castle, built in 1068 by the Earl of Oxford. The castle was once the heart of a medieval village, and looming over its earthworks is All Saints Church, with its 13th-century south doorway. Standing alone in empty fields, the earthworks and church make for a superbly atmospheric, if somewhat eerie, sight. And the reason for their loneliness? The Black Death. When the bubonic plague engulfed the village in the 14th century, the settlement was abandoned, and a new village took shape to the northeast. Squint hard and you may just make out the lumps and bumps of the former village, or find a fragment of medieval pottery on your way back across fields to the pub.

5 BARTLOW HILLS

The Three Hills (page 317)

Tucked between the folds of the southern uplands, the village of Bartlow is home to one of Britain's most extraordinary prehistoric sites. The Bartlow Hills are a cluster of ancient barrows and the largest surviving Roman burial mounds in western Europe. The moment you set foot in the village, you'll know you're in the right place – although the hills can't be seen from the road, they're celebrated everywhere, from the village sign to the name of the pub and golf course. And why not? Completely unexpected, and resembling mini volcanoes, I'd challenge anyone not to be impressed by these manmade mounds. To find them, head to St Mary's Church (Camps Rd) and follow the footpath signed 'to Bartlow Hills'; this five-minute walk leads around the back of the churchyard and through woodland to the hills.

It's thought that there were once seven or eight barrows in total but it's the three largest that dominate the scene today. The tallest is more than 42ft high, with 63 wooden steps leading to the top. The summits of the other two are accessed via earth tracks, which turn into mudslides in wet weather.

The barrows were most likely built for respected nobles in the 1st and 2nd centuries AD. When excavations took place in the 1800s, archaeologists unearthed the most impressive hoard of Roman artistic objects found in Britain: wooden chests filled with bronze, glass and pottery, along with incense, wine and lamps, which had been buried still burning. Sadly, most of the hoard was destroyed in an accidental fire.

A QUINTET OF ANCIENT TRACKS

Southeast Cambridgeshire is home to the eastern halves of a set of earthworks that run in parallel, like claw marks scratched across the landscape. Standing proud above the countryside, Devil's Dyke and Fleam Dyke are the most northerly of the set. Further south, the ancient trade routes of Brent Ditch and Bran Ditch have been largely rubbed out by modern agriculture; the former is on private land, while the latter isn't marked on most maps although a small stretch can still be walked.

The parallel positioning of these earthworks is no coincidence. All four once struck across ancient north–south routeways that included the illustrious Icknield Way. It's thought that this quartet of Anglo-Saxon dykes and ditches was used to control these transport routes and defend the East Anglian Kingdom from Mercia. Between the dykes and ditches, the Roman Road adds a fifth 'stripe' to the set – this ten-mile track once connected Cambridge with the Icknield Way.

Today, the dykes and Roman Road provide car-free walking or cycling routes that boast rare chalk grasslands – most of Cambridgeshire's chalk habitats were ploughed for farming but these hardpacked earthworks couldn't be farmed. The result is a cluster of SSSIs (Sites of Special Scientific Interest) that nurture chalk-loving plants, seldom seen in other parts of the county – think orchids, pasque flowers and native juniper bushes – which welcome skylarks, newts and clouds of summer butterflies.

Once you've visited the hills, take a wander back to the church. One of only two Cambridgeshire churches with round towers, St Mary's boasts 15th-century wall paintings and an 18th-century urn in the graveyard. Bartlow also has an excellent pub (the Three Hills) and is a good base for rambling, with the Harcamlow Way (page 279) passing through. The village pub suggests a five-mile loop past the barrows and across the Essex border to Ashdon Mill – you'll find directions on the pub website.

FOOD & DRINK

The Three Hills Dean Rd, CB21 4PW ⌀ 01223 890500 ⌀ thethreehills.co.uk ⌀ Wed–Sun. Set in a 17th-century building, this welcoming pub has been tastefully restored. There's a cosy snug with log fire, plus a sunlit orangery and a landscaped garden by the river. The kitchen holds two AA Rosettes and a Michelin Plate, and meals range from bangers and mash to pulled mushroom tacos.

6 LINTON

⌂ **Pear Tree Inn** (page 317)

With its colourful listed buildings, pretty riverside and backdrop of hills, there's lots to like about the large village of **Linton**. It makes a good base for exploring the southeast, with countryside footpaths, nostalgic pubs, an award-winning vineyard and even a zoo on the doorstep. It also gives access to the Roman Road walking/cycling route.

The high street is a designated conservation area, with half-timbered houses dating back to the Tudor and Stuart times. It's a lovely place to potter, with several good places to eat and drink, plus a scattering of independent shops that includes a gallery, gift shop and a family butcher.

Criss-crossed by footbridges and fords, Linton's stretch of the River Granta is a delight. Wander down Mill Lane and you'll arrive at a white clapboard mill house, parts of which arc 17th century. From here, footpaths lead through waterside meadows and past St Mary's Church to a medieval ford with dabbling ducks. For an in-depth tour of the village, you could follow the waymarked **Linton Heritage Trail**, which reveals stories of the village's leather tanners, millers, Quakers and bygone coaching inns – the former Bell Inn, for example, was frequented by Prince Charles when he was a student at Trinity College. The trail's starting point and map are by the village sign, next to the River Granta bridge (Swan Bridge). You'll need to buy a guidebook from one of the local shops or pubs to get the most from the trail – I bought mine for a nominal price in Darryl Nantais Gallery (59 High St).

On the village's southern edge, across the A1307, is **Linton Zoological Gardens** (Hadstock Rd, CB21 4NT ✎ lintonzoo.com) – apparently, you can hear the lions roaring in the village, although I've never had the pleasure myself. This small conservation park has been owned by the Simmons family since the 1970s, and many species are part of international breeding programmes. Less than two miles northeast of Linton, little **Hildersham** village is home to a 13th-century church and the Pear & Olive Scratch Kitchen, which makes the walk here alone worth it.

Walks from Linton

Rivey Hill (367ft) gazes down on the village and is topped by a 1930s red-brick water tower. As the highest point for miles around, it beckons to be climbed. From the village, two footpaths lead to the top – one follows the Icknield Way Trail (page 279), and the other climbs through the woods. For a circular route, see opposite.

Chilford Hall Vineyard (page 290) is another good walking destination. It sits roughly two miles from Linton on the Icknield Way Trail, just past Rivey Hill. Beyond the vineyard, the Icknield Way continues to Balsham village (another two miles) via a section of the Roman Road (page 51).

Leading west out of Linton is the two-mile footpath to Hildersham. For a circular walk, you could follow the Linton–Hildersham Roman Road Walk (6½ miles). This route guides you along part of the Roman Road, and takes you through Linton's early 19th-century 'clapper stile'. You can download a walk map from the 'Roman Road' link on the village website (✎ linton-pc.gov.uk/tourism), or ask for a leaflet at Linton Kitchen.

¶¶ FOOD & DRINK

Linton has several good places to eat and drink, with the much-loved **Linton Kitchen** (30 High St ✎ 01223 894949 ✎ thelintonkitchen.com ⏲ 09.00–17.00 Tue–Sat) a favourite for homemade cakes and organic lunches (they also sell walking guides); **Jigsaw Bakery** (113 High St ✎ jigsawbakery.co.uk ⏲ Wed–Sat) is the place for freshly baked artisan loaves; and **The Dog & Duck** (63 High St ✎ 01223 890349 ✎ dogandduck-linton.co.uk ⏲ Wed–Sun) is deservedly popular for pints and pub grub – this 16th-century thatched

Linton, Rivey Hill & riverside loop

❄ OS Explorer map 209 *Cambridge*; start: The Dog & Duck, 63 High St, Linton CB21 4HS
📍 TL325564; 3 miles; moderate (one long climb followed by a descent)

This classic walk takes in several village highlights, from the characterful High Street and riverside to the panoramic views from Rivey Hill.

1 Join the Icknield Way Trail by walking down Meadow Lane (left of The Dog & Duck as you face it). Enter the recreation ground and continue straight, turning right to pass the pavilion on your left. Cross the footbridge and road, walk a few paces left and follow the Icknield Way (signed) up a track. Continue past bungalows, turn right out of Crabtree Croft and then left at the footpath sign for Rivey Hill and Icknield Way.

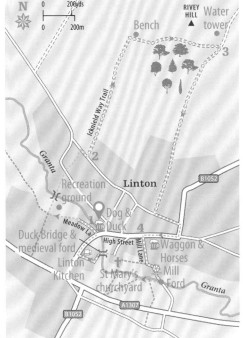

2 Follow the Icknield Way uphill. At the top, turn right at the bench and take in the views, then follow the ridge to the water tower.

3 Just past the water tower and cottages, turn right at the T-junction. Follow the track downhill through the woods and turn left when you meet the road. Continue to a T-junction and turn right, then right again on to High Street. Continue past the Waggon & Horses and the Co-op. When you reach Mill Lane, turn left.

4 Follow Mill Lane to the mill and walk under the gangways to the ford. Cross the ford via the footbridge and turn right along the riverbank. Ignore the first footbridge but take the second one into St Mary's churchyard. Where the paths cross, turn left to leave the churchyard, taking the footpath to the left of the 16th-century Guildhall. Cross Duck Bridge and the medieval ford, and follow the narrow lane back to High Street. Turn right at Linton Kitchen and return to the pub.

pub has old beams and an open fire, while the garden sits above the river. You can also tuck into bistro-style food at **The Crown Inn** (11 High St ✆ 01223 891759 ⌂ crownatlinton. co.uk) or join locals for a pint at Linton's oldest pub, the **Waggon & Horses** (110 High St ☺ afternoons only) which serves drinks only.

Just outside the main village, **Wylde Sky Brewing** (Unit 8A ✆ 01223 778350 ⌂ wyldeskybrewing.com ☺ 17.00–21.30 Thu, 17.00–22.00 Fri & Sat) is tucked away in an industrial estate, next to Linton Zoo. This small-batch brewery throws open its doors three times a week, often with live music and food trucks. They also offer guided tours of the brewing process on Saturdays (13.00–14.00, advance booking required).

In Hildersham village, the **Pear & Olive Scratch Kitchen** (⌂ pearandolive.co.uk ☺ Thu–Sun) has been making waves since it opened in 2018. This intimate restaurant serves farm-to-fork cuisine crafted by acclaimed French chef Gael Lecolley. When I contacted Gael, he was about to launch a supper club, with meals themed to each season. There's also an excellent adjoining farm shop and café (⌂ thepantryfarmshop.co.uk ☺ Wed–Mon), which sometimes hosts summer DJ events.

7 CHILFORD HALL VINEYARD

Balsham Rd, Linton CB21 4LE ✆ 01223 895600 ⌂ chilfordhall.co.uk ☺ wine shop & visitor centre: May–Sep 09.00–17.00 Fri–Sun & bank hols; tours: Mar–May Sat–Sun & bank hols, Jun–Oct Thu–Sun & bank hols

One of England's oldest established vineyards, the very first vines were planted here in 1972. Today, nine varieties are grown across 20 acres, producing over 18,000 bottles of wine each year. This is a gorgeous place to visit on a sunny day; perhaps unsurprisingly, it's also a popular wedding venue.

Ninety-minute tours and tastings are held twice daily on set days (see website). After setting off from the visitor centre you'll wander down to the vineyard to find out about how the vines are nurtured before learning about viticulture at the winery and sampling some red, white, rosé and sparkling wines. To make a day of it, you could walk here from Linton (page 287) or Balsham (see opposite) and stay for a boozy lunch or afternoon tea. Taxi!

8 THE ROMAN ROAD EAST

The Roman Road has been trodden for centuries and most likely actually existed before Roman times. Excavations show that the Romans developed the route by packing chalk rubble on to a pre-existing track, establishing a formal road that connected with the Icknield Way. Today, the chalky ridge they created has become a bucolic bridleway for walkers, cyclists and horseriders.

The road runs for ten miles between Worts' Causeway in the west and a spot called Mark's Grave here in the east (no-one knows who Mark was, or if a grave even exists at this site). Horseheath is the nearest village to the eastern tip, with a 'Roman Road' footpath sign on Audley Way (a street opposite the post office) directing you half a mile across the fields. The footpath leads northwest along the Harcamlow Way to a B road – cross this road and you'll clearly see the wide track of the Roman Road, which is marked as a byway.

With a handful of other villages just off the track, there are several options for exploring the road's eastern half – to plan a route, use OS Explorer maps 209 *Cambridge* and 210 *Newmarket & Haverhill,* and download the Roman Road leaflet from ⟡ frrfd.org.uk. A good focus for a walk from Horseheath could be Chilford Hall Vineyard (see opposite), which sits 3½ miles away, just off the Roman Road. Or you could access the road from the footpaths leading out of Linton and Balsham.

If you fancy walking the road's full length, I'd recommend starting in the west (page 51), which means you can refuel at the Old Red Lion in Horseheath at the end, or even stay overnight. Cyclists could ride the Roman Road there and back in a day, or plan a circular loop through the southeast villages. You'll need off-road tyres, as the road can be dry and rubbly or wet and muddy.

⫴ FOOD & DRINK

Although there is nowhere directly on the Roman Road to stop for refreshments, there are several good pubs and cafés a mile or two's detour of the track, including Chilford Hall Vineyard (see opposite), as well as the pubs and cafés in Linton and Balsham. Horseheath has the **Old Red Lion** (Cambridge Rd, CB21 4QF ☎ 01223 892909 ⟡ theoldredlion.co.uk ⏲ kitchen Wed–Sun; rooms available).

9 BALSHAM & FLEAM DYKE EAST

🏠 **The Black Bull Inn** (page 317) 🏠 **Happenoak Treehouse** (page 317)

Balsham is a great little hub for walkers, cyclists and horseriders, who can often be found refuelling at the village café and pubs. A network of footpaths leads from the village, with Fleam Dyke one mile northeast, and the long-distance Harcamlow Way and Icknield Way Trail passing through. Balsham also sits at the mid-point of the Fleam Dyke and Roman Road walk (see box, below).

In the village itself is the striking church of Holy Trinity, with huge buttresses stabilising its square tower. Inside, you'll find a collection of quirks that includes a matchstick model of Ely Cathedral and an elaborate font cover created by former rector Canon Burrell. The village rooftops are also of interest – look up to see a veritable farmyard thatched into the ridges, featuring everything from a family of ducks to a dog chasing a pheasant.

Fleam Dyke's ridgetop footpath runs for around three miles through open countryside between the villages of Balsham (at the eastern end) and Fulbourn in the west (Chapter 1). From Balsham, you could tackle the full length to Fulbourn (around 5½ miles from village to village), or plan a shorter circular route that gives you a taste of the dyke's eastern extremity, where its slopes are lined with oak, beech and silver birch. When I visited in winter, the bare branches of the trees were decorated in ivy and festooned with berries, while the deep ditch beneath the ridge was obscured with scrub – I could almost imagine a Saxon warrior hiding down there, waiting to attack.

To access the dyke from Balsham village green, walk west along the High Street, turn right down Fox Road and take the footpath on your left, following the signpost for 'Fleam Dyke 1'. When you reach the dyke, climb up on to the embankment to peer into the ditch below. To return

FLEAM DYKE & ROMAN ROAD WALK

Fleam Dyke and the Roman Road run in parallel, less than two miles apart, so a group of local bodies decided to link these linear routes and create a 25-mile waymarked loop. While you could tackle the route as a one-day challenge, splitting it over two days will make it a much more Slow experience, giving you time to take in the scenery, soak up some history and stop off at villages, pubs and attractions along the way – the route skirts past West Wratting, West Wickham and Horseheath,

with Hildersham, Linton, Balsham and Chilford Vineyard just off the track.

Sitting roughly in the middle, Balsham makes a perfect base for tackling the trail in two halves – an eastern loop and a western loop. To plan your route, you'll need a copy of the *Fleam Dyke and Roman Road Walk* booklet, created by the Friends of the Roman Road and Fleam Dyke. You can order one through their website ⌀ frrfd.org.uk or ask in the local shops (try Linton Kitchen or the Old Butchers in Balsham).

to Balsham, turn right along Fleam Dyke and follow the Harcamlow Way, which drops off the end of the dyke and loops north of the village, back to the green.

If walking the full length from Balsham to Fulbourn, you may wish to time your hike around the afternoon Fulbourn to Balsham bus (Stagecoach 16A). Use OS Explorer map 209 *Cambridge* for route planning.

¶¶ FOOD & DRINK

The Bell Inn 2 West Wickham Rd, CB21 4DZ ✆ 01223 892999 ◔ kitchen Tue–Sun. Authentic village pub serving good-value home cooking – pies, lasagne and burgers. There's a separate sports bar and a big garden.

The Black Bull Inn 27 High St, CB21 4DJ ✆ 01223 893844 ♂ blackbull-balsham.co.uk. This thatched 16th-century pub has been refurbished but retains its original charm, with big old beams and an open fire. The tree-lined patio outside was created by a Chelsea Flower Show designer. Awarded several AA Rosettes, the locally sourced menu changes twice a month.

Old Butchers Coffee + Shop 35–37 High St, CB21 4DJ ◔ Mon–Sat. Don't be deceived by the thatched dog running along the roof with a string of sausages – this 300-year-old cottage is no longer a butcher's shop. Today, it's a very welcoming café and shop, with three rooms of gifts and goodies that include fudge made in the village. It's popular with cyclists and hikers and, last time I was there, there was talk of developing this further with regular meet-ups and a collection of route maps.

10 DEVIL'S DYKE EAST & AROUND

🏠 **The Three Blackbirds** (page 317)

Devil's Dyke is the longest, tallest and most northerly of east Cambridgeshire's Anglo-Saxon earthworks. It runs for 7½ miles along its full length (Woodditton to Reach), with a deep trench beneath the embankment. Here, at the far eastern end, the dyke's ridgetop footpath is enclosed by ancient trees. A few miles west, the trees thin as the ridge traces the Cambridgeshire–Suffolk border and bisects the famous horseracing courses at Newmarket – time your walk for a race day and you could be in for a free glimpse of the action.

Woodditton village gives easy access to the dyke's eastern end and, with its excellent village pub, makes a good base. To access the dyke, follow the footpath for 'Reach', signed off Stetchworth Road. This leads you through Pickworth Wood to the earthwork's eastern tip, where kids (and big kids) can swing off a Tarzan-like rope swing. You can also walk to the dyke from **Stetchworth** (one mile west of Woodditton)

A bite of Devil's Dyke

✳ OS Explorer map 210 *Newmarket & Haverhill*; start: The Three Blackbirds, 36 Ditton Green, CB8 9SQ 📍 TL659581; 2 miles; easy, with stepped access to and from the dyke

This circular pub walk starts and finishes at the Three Blackbirds and takes a nibble off the dyke's eastern end. You could walk it in either direction but I think the best views can be enjoyed by following the route as set out below.

1 With your back to the pub, walk right along Ditton Green, which becomes Stetchworth Road. Stay on the pavement past the water tower and follow the road as it bends left. Just after house number 14, take the footpath on the right, signed for Reach. This leads you past private gardens and across a field to Pickmore Wood.

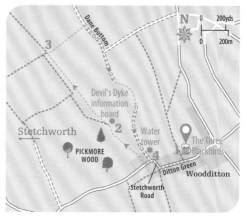

2 Follow the path through the wood to the Devil's Dyke information board. Beyond this, a set of wooden steps leads up on to the dyke. Follow the path along the top of the dyke, passing a rope swing and crossing a wooden bridge. After roughly half a mile, descend the dyke via another set of wooden steps.

3 Turn right at the bottom of the steps and follow the footpath through a field. Climb up the wooden steps at the edge of the field and turn right on to a track (Dane Bottom), which leads back to Ditton Green. Stay straight on the track, which will take you through a metal gate and then leads around some stables and on to a hard track to the water tower on Stetchworth Rd.

4 When you reach the water tower, turn left on to Stetchworth Road, retrace your steps to the pub and reward your efforts with a pint of ale and local Cambridgeshire cuisine.

via the Icknield Way Trail. For information on Reach and the dyke's western end, see page 265.

With Devil's Dyke and its surrounding villages so close to Newmarket, this part of Cambridgeshire is very much 'horse country'.

Take a cycle ride, walk or drive around these parts and you'll find stables and paddocks aplenty. Stetchworth, for example, is the home of Stetchworth Park Stud, where the British showjumping team trained for the 2012 Olympics.

West of Stechworth is the 500-acre **National Stud** (nationalstud. co.uk), where you can book a 90-minute tour with discovernewmarket. co.uk to learn about the history of thoroughbred breeding and see some of the world's finest stallions, mares and foals in the making. Between Stetchworth and the stud is the village of **Dullingham**, with its long village green, two pub/restaurants and a railway station on the Cambridge–Ely line.

FOOD & DRINK

The King's Head 1 Stetchworth Rd, Dullingham CB8 9UJ 01638 507702 kingsheaddullingham.com lunch Fri–Sun, dinner Thu–Sat. An AA Rosette restaurant by the village green, the King's Head uses local and foraged ingredients in creations like hay-baked lamb and squash wellington. Expect wine pairing and impeccable presentation, with prices to match.

The Marquis of Granby 94 New St, Stetchworth CB8 9TG 01638 508383. Traditional village pub with a reputation for good-value meals. Handy for walkers on the Icknield Way Trail, Stour Valley Path and Devil's Dyke.

The Three Blackbirds 36 Ditton Green, Woodditton CB8 9SQ 01638 731100 threeblackbirds.co.uk. Refurbished in 2020 after a devastating fire, this foodie pub has a striking interior, with contemporary décor and pops of colour juxtaposed with old beams and farming memorabilia. The menu focuses on local meats and fenland veg – try the Newmarket sausages, followed by Phil's homemade doughnuts. They even have a menu for dogs, who can slurp Bottom Sniffer Beer or the finest Cambridgeshire tap water.

WIMPOLE & THE WEST

The topography of southwest Cambridgeshire is smoother than the east, with no big hills or ancient ridges to climb. It does, however, boast the county's highest point, as well as one of its best viewpoints, with soul-touching sunsets from Great Chishill Windmill. The villages in this region are some of Cambridgeshire's loveliest, from Barrington with its long green to Thriplow's daffodils. At the other end of the scale is the mighty Wimpole estate, where you can visit the hall and heritage farmyard, or explore Capability Brown's parkland on foot or by bike.

11 WIMPOLE ESTATE

Arrington SG8 0BW; National Trust

Cambridgeshire's largest stately home is one of the county's biggest draws. This working estate spans 3,000 acres, with a magnificent mansion, sprawling parkland, formal gardens and a rare-breeds farm.

There's a vast amount to experience – when I first visited, it took me a good hour to simply stroll around the hall's front garden and take in its mighty façade. Inside, there are sitting rooms, servant quarters and bedrooms galore. Highlights include a library with more than 6,000 books, and a dramatic drawing room that welcomed Queen Victoria in 1843. Don't forget to look up at the ceilings – they're incredibly ornate.

Behind the house, the Walled Garden features a bountiful orchard of plums, apricots, quince and more, plus a kitchen garden which grows 50 types of tomato that are showcased at the annual Tomato Festival (Sep). Much of this produce appears on the menu in Wimpole Hall's café. Over at Home Farm, you can meet Longhorn cattle and white Bagot goats,

WIMPOLE HALL – A POTTED HISTORY

The Wimpole estate sits within an ancient landscape that has been continuously occupied for more than 2,000 years. Early maps show a moated manor that was home to the Chicheley family from the early 1400s and, over the years, the estate has been moulded by a long list of owners, each with a story to tell.

The hall you see today started taking shape in the 1640s when Thomas Chicheley, a Cambridgeshire MP, began building a new home on his family estate; however, when debts mounted he was forced to sell up. Wimpole saw significant changes in the 18th century, when Edward Harley enlarged the house and began making alterations, which were continued by Philip Yorke, the first Earl of Hardwicke. Successive earls carried on

this trend, with the second and third Earls of Hardwicke employing Lancelot 'Capability' Brown (see box, page 252) to redesign the parkland. The fourth earl enlarged the hall and added the stable block.

But it's thanks to Elsie Bambridge, Rudyard Kipling's daughter, that Wimpole is the fine spectacle we see today. When Elsie and her husband purchased the hall and gardens in the 1930s, they were suffering from neglect – the house was almost empty of contents and the rooms and gardens had fallen into decline. Kipling's daughter poured her heart and inheritance into restoring and redecorating the property, filling its rooms with artworks and furniture. On her death, she bequeathed it to the National Trust, who have cared for it ever since.

and kids can pet the rabbits, have a go at milking on artificial udders or ride in a horse and carriage. Even the shops at Wimpole have a scenic setting – you'll find the gift shop and garden shop in the 19th-century stable block.

The rest of the grounds are big enough to give you blisters as you explore the acres of parkland. Dogs are welcome and there's a map by the stables with suggested routes, like the two-mile Folly Walk that leads to a striking Gothic structure. The network of cycle paths makes it easier to cover more ground, and the National Trust's suggested routes range from the 1½-mile South Avenue Trail to the three-mile Victoria Drive woodland track and the four-mile Mare Way Challenge.

Entry costs to the Wimpole estate depend on which bits you want to experience – there's a fee to enter the car park and mansion, plus an extra cost to visit the farm. Cyclists and ramblers without a car can enter the estate via the public path from Arrington village – look for the signs next to the stone gates, across the road from the bus stop.

Wimpole Hall marks the start or end point (depending on which way you walk) of two glorious countryside walks, both of which are linear. My personal preference would be to finish a walk here as, once you've refuelled in the café, you could explore the hall and grounds. Keen cyclists could also tackle the circular Wimpole Cycle Challenge, which starts and finishes on the estate.

Longer walks & cycles from Wimpole Hall

Wimpole Hall marks the end of the **Wimpole Way** – a 13-mile, waymarked walking route that sets off from Cambridge and arcs west then south through rolling countryside, woodland belts and pretty villages. Of course, you could follow the route in the opposite direction, setting off from Wimpole and arriving in central Cambridge around five hours later. Bus number 75 (operated by A2B) takes you between Cambridge and Arrington, just outside Wimpole's walls. To plan your route, use OS Explorer map 209 Cambridge.

The 11-mile **Clopton Way** begins where the Wimpole Way ends. From Wimpole estate, follow the waymarkers west through Croydon village and along a high escarpment (great views) through the walk's namesake: the deserted village of Clopton – now a field of lumps and bumps, this was once a medieval village with weekly markets. The walk continues through Potton Wood to Gamlingay Cinques Nature Reserve, just outside Gamlingay village. Direct bus services linking Arrington and Gamlingay are limited – your best bet is the Thursday-only C2 service (operated by C G Myall & Son).

A fantastic way to explore southwest Cambridgeshire, the **Wimpole Cycle Challenge** is a 28-mile road cycle that starts and finishes at Wimpole Hall – or you could set off from any of the villages along the loop. From Wimpole's stable block, it tours through the county, passing many of the southwestern villages and landmarks mentioned in this chapter, plus a few more. Along the way, you'll visit the ancient mills at Great Gransden and Bourn (see opposite for both), and you'll tackle the Chapel Hill climb near Haslingfield (page 303) before freewheeling past Barrington village green (page 305). There are some great options for refreshments too, with several of south Cambridgeshire's best pubs and cafés on the route. Visit the National Trust website for the map and directions.

12 HAYLEY, WARESLEY & GAMLINGAY WOODS

The quiet corner of southwest Cambridge west of the Wimpole estate is surprisingly rich in woodlands. Scattered between sleepy villages are fragments of a larger wood that once covered much of this area. The most significant of these is **Hayley Wood**, one of the largest patches of ancient woodland in Cambridgeshire. It was in this very place that the British ecologist Oliver Rackham (1939–2015) first developed the concept of ancient woodland. Following extensive research, Rackham wrote his first book, *Hayley Wood: Its History and Ecology* (1975); this research led to his theory of ancient woodland, which he detailed in *Ancient Woodland, its History, Vegetation and Uses in England* (1980). Rackham's work went on to greatly influence British planning legislation, conservation and the practice of traditional woodland management. Rich in fungi (more than 540 species) and wildflowers (spring oxlips are the stars), it's a wonderful place for a walk. The entrance is signed on the B1046 between Little Gransden and Longstowe – park on the verge and follow the lane, which is fringed by an 800-year-old hedgerow. You could also walk here from the parish of Hatley (roughly 1½ miles each way on public footpaths).

Northwest of Hayley Wood, the Gransdens sit on the edge of **Waresley and Gransden woods** – two ancient oak and ash woodlands, bisected by a brook. There are wide rides and leafy footpaths to guide your explorations, and the woods have spectacular bluebells and primroses in spring and, as when I last visited, carpets of crunchy acorns in autumn. The main entrance and car park are signed off the road between Waresley and Great Gransden, or you can follow one of several footpaths leading south and west from Great Gransden and Little Gransden. **Great Gransden** also boasts a 17th-century post mill (ask for the keyholder in the post office on Fox St) and a 15th-century church with a stained-glass window, dedicated to the 801 men of the World War II Royal Canadian Airforce who died flying from Gransden airfield.

Southwest of the Gransdens is **Gamlingay Wood**, which you can walk to from Gamlingay village by following the footpath at the end of Gray's Road. Within this 173-acre wood is the 'Rippengal's Walk', created in memory of a local archaeologist. This two-mile walk leads through ancient ash coppice (at least 450 years old), a historical ring ditch (southern end, nearest to Gamlingay village) and a rare wild service tree (southwest section). In Gamlingay itself, take a gander at the cruciform church of St Mary – in 1954, Nikolaus Pevsner declared this the most impressive church in the area. It's certainly quite captivating, with its 'Cambridgeshire spike' and golden stone walls, built from local stone which was quarried nearby, and some parts date back to the 13th century, including the Early English font. You could also pay a visit to tiny Gamlingay Cinques reserve (Cinques Rd, SG19 3NU), on the village's western fringe. A fragment of an ancient heath, it's filled with wildflowers and you may spot glow-worms twinkling here on summer evenings.

¶¶ FOOD & DRINK

There are several places to eat and drink in the area. Best for ale lovers is **The Chequers** in Little Gransden (71 Main Rd ✆ 01767 677348 ✎ sonofsid.co.uk), where the landlord brews his own beer in the Son of Sid brewery. A finalist in the National Pub of the Year awards, this no-frills drinking hole regularly features in the CAMRA *Good Beer Guide*. Fish and chips are served on Fridays (order in advance). If you're looking for a cooked breakfast, farmhouse lunch or grocery shop, try **Woodview Farmshop and café** in Gamlingay (Potton Rd, SG19 3LW ✎ woodviewfarm.co.uk ◷ from 07.30 Mon–Sat, from 09.00 Sun).

13 BOURN WINDMILL & AROUND

🏠 **The Bull Pen** (page 317)
Caxton Rd, CB23 2SU ✎ cambridgeppf.org

One of the oldest surviving mills in the country, **Bourn Windmill** is a medieval open trestle post mill, with a central pole on which the mill rotates. Earliest records date back to 1636 but it's thought that the mill is far older, potentially 13th century. An information board tells you more and reveals the mill's intricate workings, which you can experience – and even have a go at operating – on scheduled summer Sundays (see website). Outside the open days, you can walk up to the mill from the little car park, admire its black timber cladding and brilliant white sails, and marvel at the changing landscapes and historical events that this ancient mill has witnessed, from medieval serfs to Victorian millers.

Bourn village sits 1½ miles east of the mill. The main pull for visitors is its unique pub/restaurant, The Willow Tree. The village is also home to the world's first IVF clinic, Bourn Hall, which was founded by a trio

Bourn Mill, nature reserve & Roman barrows

❊ OS Explorer map 208 *Bedford & St Neots*; start: The Willow Tree, 29 High St, Bourn
♀ TL325564; 5 miles; easy (flat most of the way)

This countryside loop leads past some of Bourn's prettiest cottages en route to Bourn Mill. Heading on through Cambourne Nature Reserve, you'll pass an impressive solar farm and return to the village via Moulton Hills.

1 With your back to the pub, turn right along High Street, passing the war memorial on your left. At the village sign, turn left (signed Caxton End) and follow the quiet road past pretty cottages. Immediately after the ford, turn left, following the footpath sign for Caxton and Great Gransden.

2 At Brooklands Farm, follow the footpath left over the river, through a gate and across a field. After the second gate, turn right then left, following the brook along the field edge.

3 When you near a footbridge on your left, take the footpath on your right through the middle of the field to the road, walking towards the sails of the mill up ahead (the footpath can sometimes be hard to spot but the farmer assured me you can walk through the field).

4 Cross the road and go through the metal gate to the left of Mill Cottage, following the footpath sign. You are now at Bourn Windmill. Pass the windmill on your right and continue on the footpath through metal gates to a field, walking along the left-hand edge. At the top of the field, veer left at the 'Danger Deep Water' sign and continue to another field. Stay right along the field edge, then cross a footbridge, go through a metal gate and turn right into Cambourne Nature Reserve.

of fertility pioneers who were responsible for the world's first test-tube baby (1977/78). Also of note is the wonky spire on the church of St Helena and St Mary. Parts of the church are 12th century, and it has a memorial to the brother of Nicholas Ferrar who founded Little Gidding church (page 159).

At the northern end of the village is Manor Farm, where a collection of black timbered barns has been converted into business premises. Among them is a butcher's, a yoga studio and coffee shop (The Stove). Behind Manor Farm is Moulton Hills – a Roman burial site with three well-preserved barrows, accessible via public footpaths.

Just outside Bourn, **Wysing Arts Centre** (Fox Rd/B1046, CB23 2TX ⬧ wysingartscentre.org) is a contemporary complex of studios, outdoor

5 Follow the footpath along the edge of the reserve and, when you come to a crossroads of paths, go straight ahead. Pass the solar farm on your right and continue on a meandering track. At the next crossroads, turn right, leaving the reserve to meet the road.

6 Turn right at the road and walk into Bourn village.

7 When you reach The Drift, turn left, following the footpath sign for Cambourne. After passing Townsend Farm, take the byway on your right, which becomes tree-lined. Pass a

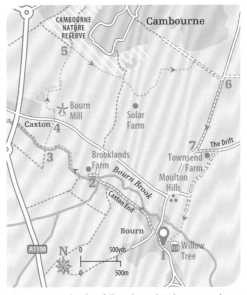

white cottage on your left, and another on your right, then follow the path right to a metal gate into a field – this is Moulton Hills. Keep left along the field edge (or explore the field to see the barrows) and exit through the gate in the left-hand corner. Go left over the footbridge, then right and across another footbridge. Continue along the path to The Willow Tree's garden.

sculptures and galleries. The centre is open to the public most afternoons when exhibitions are on. They also hold courses and workshops.

¶¶ FOOD & DRINK

The Stove 14 Alms Hill, CB23 2SH ℘ 01954 713976 ⑥ thestovebourn.co.uk ⊙ 09.00–16.00 Mon–Sat. Tucked away in the Manor Farm barns, this friendly café serves breakfasts, lunches and homemade cakes, with an emphasis on local ingredients and ethical produce.

The Willow Tree 29 High St, CB23 2SQ ℘ 01954 719775 ⑥ thewillowtreebourn.com ⊙ noon–22.00 Wed–Sun. Bourn's foody pub has an *Alice in Wonderland* eccentricity about it, with its fairy-lit garden and flamboyant vintage décor. It regularly features in the *Michelin Guide*, thanks to the likes of crab seaweed rillette, spatchcock poussin with grapefruit slaw, ox cheek with confit garlic, and blackberry daquiri cheesecake. You can also visit for drinks or afternoon tea.

14 BURWASH MANOR

New Rd, Barton CB23 7EY ⑥ burwashmanor.com ⊙ daily

If pottering around artisan shops, filling your basket with local produce, and tucking into farm-to-fork food in the Cambridgeshire countryside sounds like your idea of heaven, then Burwash Manor will be your new favourite place. Set in converted farm buildings on an organic farm, this collection of independent shops includes a gallery, haberdashery, wine specialist, rug shop, toy store, jeweller, florist and gift shops. The showpiece is **Burwash Larder** (⑥ burwashlarder.com), which sells everything from fair trade teas to local veg and meat. It may not be the cheapest place to do your weekly shop but it's hard to beat in terms of ethical produce and hyper-local food – look for asparagus from Burwash's beds, and pork from their Essex Saddlebacks. When you're all shopped out, crash out at **Flock Café** (⑥ flockcafe. co.uk) for a homemade lunch or snack. Just be aware that Burwash gets busy at peak times so, if you're dreaming of pastoral peace, avoid the weekend brunch rush.

"It may not be the cheapest place to shop but it's hard to beat in terms of ethical produce and hyper-local food"

Threading through the countryside and criss-crossing the 400-acre farm is a series of informative **walks** that showcase the manor's approach to environmental stewardship. There are three colour-coded trails to choose from on the 'Wild Walks' map in the car park, ranging from one mile to almost three. The paths lead between illustrated information boards, which share stories of the landscape and wildlife that inhabits it – owls, sparrowhawks, newts and bats are just a few of the residents. To be brutally honest, I didn't find these the most exciting or varied of Cambridgeshire's walks (they mostly follow field edges), but there's a lot to learn about the history and future of the landscape, from unploughed fields and resurrected orchards to Iron Age earthworks. Wildlife watchers with more patience than me will no doubt find them more rewarding.

15 HASLINGFIELD

This friendly village is best known for its biannual Scarecrow Festival (see box, below). The heart and soul that goes into this three-day event is testimony to Haslingfield's community spirit – you can tell that 'Haslingfielders' are proud of where they live, from the village shop to the children's trail in the churchyard woodland. While it isn't chocolate-box pretty, the village has an interesting history, an excellent coffee shop and lots of rural footpaths that lead to the riverside, old clunch pits and the nearby villages of Hauxton, Harston and Grantchester. The village website (haslingfieldvillage.co.uk) maps out the local walks and rights of way.

A well, weir & village wander

This two-mile tour reveals Haslingfield's historical highlights and hidden charms. Starting at the **Moringa Tree** café on Church Street, cross the road to **All Saints' Church**, entering the churchyard via the gap in the wall (note the old village map here). Follow the path through **Glebe Wood** where wildlife boards have been created by local children.

HASLINGFIELD SCARECROW FESTIVAL

 haslingfieldscarecrowfestival.org

Visit Haslingfield in early September on even-numbered years and you'll be greeted by up to 200 scarecrows. We're not just talking a bit of straw stuffed in an old jacket – these are creative masterpieces, tailored to each year's theme. Previous triumphs have included a giant sausage on a stick, Humpty Dumpty on a wall, and the cast of *Friends* reclining on a sofa. In addition to scarecrow viewing, the three-day festival includes a host of mini events, from open gardens, live music and a treasure hunt, to pop-up jam stalls and plant sales.

Exit the trees and take the footpath on your left. At the end, turn right on to a tree-lined track (Broad Ln), which leads to **Wellhouse Meadow** on your left. This is a fragment of Haslingfield's original Saxon settlement, where you'll also find an old bakehouse and privy (left of the gate), and a restored Tudor well house (diagonally opposite).

"In season, the hedgerows are laden with apples, berries and damsons – relics of Haslingfield's orchards"

Continue along Broad Lane and, at the end, you'll pass the entrance gates to **The Manor** on your left – this 16th-century moated manor was home to Dr Thomas Wendy, personal physician to four Tudor monarchs. Elizabeth I's visit in 1564 is showcased on the village sign, which stands to your right. Walk along High Street with the Methodist Church and an old stone wall on your left – this was part of the manor's boundary wall. At the **village shop**, turn left and follow Fountain Lane to New Road. Turn left, and then shortly after a right on to Cantaloupe Road, following the sign for Grantchester. Where the road bends left, take River Lane on your right.

Soon, River Lane becomes a track beside the River Rhee. In season, the hedgerows are laden with apples, berries and damsons – relics of the orchards that Haslingfield once depended on. Where the track forks, keep left, cross the footbridge and continue to a meadow with the weir on your left. Stop for a picnic or take a wander and look for willow weavings by local villagers.

To return to Haslingfield, retrace your steps along the track and over the footbridge. At the fork, take a left on to Porkers Lane, passing the recreational ground on your right. Turn left at the end of the track, passing River Farmhouse on your left. Then turn right on to **Back Lane**, which was the original perimeter of the Saxon settlement; at the end, you'll see the Moringa Tree up ahead. Treat yourself to coffee and cake, or head back to All Saints' Church for a look inside, where you'll find a memorial to the aforementioned Wendy family, who lived at the manor.

¶¶ FOOD & DRINK

Haslingfield is home to one of my favourite Cambridgeshire coffee shops. Everything is plant-themed (even the loo) at **The Moringa Tree** (11A Church St, CB23 1JE ⌀ themoringatree. co.uk). They have top-quality herbal teas and their lunches include things like Sri Lankan chilli pea wraps, and truffle mushroom toasties. Sit in the secret garden or grab a window seat with church views. Next door, **Country Kitchen** (21 Church St, CB23 1JE ⌾ ckhaslingfield.co.uk) is packed with local produce and gifts, and the deli counter sells homemade lunches – think traybakes, filled rolls, jacket potatoes and more. Further into the village, **The Little Rose** (7 Orchard Rd, CB23 1JT ⌾ littlerosehaslingfield.com) serves paninis and pub grub.

16 BARRINGTON

Claiming to have the longest village green in Europe and one of the last thatched schools in England is the beautiful village of Barrington. The village's 23-acre green is picture-perfect, with thatched cottages, a cricket pavilion and a stream trickling through. Years ago, this was grazing land for livestock.

No matter how many times I visit, I never tire of strolling along the green and picking out my favourite cottages. Some of the prettiest sit opposite the village shop, which sells south Cambridgeshire honey and homemade curries (try the butter chicken and vegetable pakoras). At the eastern end of the green is All Saints Church and, just behind it (on Haslingfield Rd), the thatched school, which is more than 180 years old. At the opposite end is **The Royal Oak** pub (⌾ 01223 870791 ⌾ theroyaloakbarrington.co.uk ⌾ Tue–Sun); sitting pretty in a half-timbered, thatched Victorian building, this freehouse specialises in charcoal-grilled steaks and fish. With black timbers inside, and plenty of outside seating by the green, it's a truly special spot, especially on sunny Saturdays during the cricket season.

Several pathways lead off the green to wooded tracks and countryside footpaths. A finger post by the village shop, for example, points you down Boot Lane, over a pretty bridge and across the fields to Shepreth (one mile) and Foxton (1½ miles).

17 THRIPLOW & AROUND

Arcing around Fowlmere reserve and nudging closer to Cambridge is a horseshoe of little villages, each with a distinct identity. Public footpaths and country roads link these settlements, inviting Slow travellers to embark on pub-to-pub strolls or lazy summer cycle rides. The train stations at Shepreth, Foxton and nearby Meldreth are handy for car-free access.

The best known of these villages is **Thriplow** (pronounced Triplow). Famous for its annual Daffodil Weekend, it has a lovely setting around

THRIPLOW DAFFODIL WEEKEND

Born in 1969, this charity fundraiser began with a few private homes opening their gardens during daffodil season. Today, this annual March event has grown into a traditional country fair, with thousands of visitors flocking to Thriplow for live music, craft stalls, morris dancing, tractor rides, poetry recitals and, of course, daffodils – around 500,000 bulbs are planted in the village, with more than 100 different varieties on show. If you can't make Daffodil Weekend, you can still catch the blooms as late as June – although the best displays are between March and April.

the green and old smithy, which becomes an exhibition space during the Daffodil Weekend. This rural village has a noticeable community vibe, with its award-winning community pub and volunteer-run shop, which sells a bit of everything, from fresh bread and sandwiches, to plants and fishing permits. At the eastern edge of the village is the 12th-century church of St George. Opposite the green, a map of local footpaths provides inspiration for walkers.

A mile and a half north of Thriplow is the tiny village of **Newton**, and one-mile west is **Fowlmere**. Both are small and sleepy but worthy of a visit for their excellent pubs – the Queen's Head in Newton has a timeless charm, and the Chequers in Fowlmere is steeped in history. Fowlmere was home to one of Cambridgeshire's many military airfields during World Wars I and II: RAF Fowlmere opened in 1940 and was used by the USAAF – thanks to its notoriously wet conditions, US airmen nicknamed it 'the Hen Puddle', while nearby Duxford was 'the Duck Pond'. You can find out more about the airfield's history at the tiny Fowlmere Airfield Museum (𝒸 fowlmere-airfield-museum.uk), which opens once a month.

A mile or so west of Fowlmere village on quiet country roads is **RSPB Fowlmere** (Mill Rd, SG8 7SH). Small but very special, this is one of my favourite Cambridgeshire nature reserves. A lush little sanctuary surrounded by open fields, these former watercress beds feel wild and remote. A two-mile circular trail (with optional short cuts) leads from the car park, along boardwalks and leafy tracks that meander through the reed beds, hawthorn scrub and wet woodland. Within the trail network are three hides that give elevated views. Close your eyes and listen for the whisper of reeds and the trickle of the River Shep – a rare chalk stream where water voles scurry, brown trout swim and otters hunt. The trained ear might even pick up one of the ten species of breeding warblers that nest in spring, or the sound of rutting deer in autumn. On summer evenings, look for bats, barn owls and common lizards; in winter, watch out for sparrowhawks and merlins.

North of RSPB Fowlmere, **Shepreth** is best known for its wildlife park which, conveniently, sits next to the train station. A good day out for kids, Shepreth Wildlife Park (Station Rd, SG8 6PZ ⌖ sheprethwildlifepark. co.uk ⊙ Mar 10.00–16.00 daily, Apr–Oct 10.00–17.30 daily, Nov–Feb 10.00–16.00 Thu–Mon) began life as a sanctuary for injured hedgehogs. Today, it's home to everything from meerkats to tigers and has received umpteen awards for its environmental and educational credentials from BIAZA (⌖ biaza.org.uk) and the Green Tourism Business Scheme (⌖ green-tourism.com), among others. Further into the village, opposite the war memorial, is **Docwra's Manor Garden** (⌖ docwrasmanorgarden.co.uk ⊙ 10.00–16.00 Wed & Fri, 14.00–16.00 first Sun of the month), a 2½-acre sanctuary in the grounds of a private house. Once you've pottered around the little gardens, lingered to smell the roses or perhaps whipped up a watercolour, be sure to pop into the tea shop next door (page 311).

One stop east on the trainline from Shepreth is **Foxton**, a little village with a traditional pub, 13th-century church and 300-year-old dovecote. West of Shepreth, on the road to Meldreth, is a unique nature reserve – an unploughed field known as **L-Moor**. Visit in spring or summer to look for wild thyme, blue harebell, purple bugle and fen bedstraw.

￥❘ FOOD & DRINK

The Chequers High St, Fowlmere SG8 7SR ⌀ 01763 209333 ⌖ thechequersfowlmere. org ⊙ Wed–Sun. The Green Man at Thriplow's sister pub, this 16th-century coaching inn is full of history – it used to offer overnight coffin storage, and there's a priest hole above the bar where clergy hid from persecution. Along with meats from Thriplow, they specialise in signature sourdough flatbreads.

The Green Man 2 Lower St, Thriplow SG8 7RJ ⌀ 01763 208855 ⌖ thegreenmanthriplow. co.uk ⊙ Fri–Tue. This community-owned freehouse rears Belted Galloway steers and Berkshire pigs, which regularly feature on the menu. Sit by the fire, in the beer garden or out front by the village green, and tuck into a seasonal meal, washed down with a house cocktail.

The Plough 12 High St, Shepreth SG8 6PP ⌀ 01763 290348 ⌖ theploughshepreth.co.uk ⊙ closed Mon & Tue. A true community hub, The Plough hosts live music and community

1

HOUSES & GARDENS

Cambridgeshire has some of the UK's finest houses and gardens, from National Trust estates to privately owned homes that have been with the same family for generations.

2

ELTON ESTATES CO

1 Anglesey Abbey is a stunning country manor that embodies the spirit of the 1920s. 2 Wimpole Hall is Cambridgeshire's largest stately home with acres of parkland, formal gardens and a rare-breeds farm. 3 Elton Hall has been with the Proby family for 400 years and dates back to the 15th century. 4 Burghley House is the ancestral home of the Cecil family and is widely considered to be England's greatest Elizabethan house.

BURGHLEY HOUSE

5 Island Hall has beautiful grounds with a replica Chinese bridge that connects to an ornamental river island. **6** Buckden Towers was home to the Bishops of Lincoln for more than six centuries. Pictured here, the Knot Garden.

events, and displays work by local artists. The modernised yet rustic interior features a reclaimed timber bar and a piano stage. Expect an experimental menu with foraged ingredients – try the wild hedgerow board with hawthorn hummus, followed by a hogweed seed treacle tart.

The Queen's Head Fowlmere Rd, Newton CB22 7BG ℰ 01223 870436 ☉ Wed–Sun. Step back in time at this unchanged pub, which has stone floors, low beams and traditional games. Expect a warm welcome and simple food, or time your visit for one of the regular pop-up food trucks. There's also an annual beer festival.

Teacake 8 Meldreth Rd, Shepreth SG8 6PS ℰ 07740 264446 ℰ teacakeatshepreth.co.uk ☉ 10.00–16.00 Wed–Sat. Next to Docwra's Garden, this tea room occupies a 17th-century thatched cottage with walled garden. They serve light lunches, homemade cakes and daily specials, with a commitment to local suppliers.

18 MELBOURN & MELDRETH

🏠 **The British Queen** (page 317), **Sheene Mill** (page 317) ⛺ **Guilden Gate Glamping** (page 317)

Although separated by the A10, these neighbouring villages are linked by a charming footpath that follows the River Mel – one of only 161 chalk streams in England, its waters are often gin-clear. Getting here is easy, as Meldreth train station is on the Cambridge–London line. A five-minute walk from the station is the award-winning restaurant at Sheene Mill (page 313).

Fruit farms and mills once shaped the lives and landscapes of these villages, as they did many others in Cambridgeshire. Nine mills were listed in 1066 but only two remain today. The orchards went a similar way – fruit growing declined after a climax in the 19th and early 20th centuries, when Meldreth greengages were known far and wide. One fruit business, however, still thrives: Cam Valley Orchards grows its produce in a heritage orchard that was first planted in the 1900s. Their little shop (27 Whitecroft Rd, SG8 6ND ☉ Aug–Feb 09.00–17.00 Thu–Sat) sells a smorgasbord of seasonal fruits that, of course, includes summer gages.

Melbourn has a narrow High Street with a scattering of shops that includes an excellent butcher's and deli, opposite All Saints' Church. The village also has a heart-warming affinity with its old fire engine station, which it proudly keeps in a beautiful state of repair – look for the Grade II listed shed labelled 'Melbourn Fire Engine', on Station Road. I can only imagine that the engine must have had a busy yet somewhat unfulfilling

MELDRETH – A VILLAGE & RIVERSIDE TOUR

Starting at The British Queen pub, turn right out of the car park and on to High Street. The huge, black-timbered house on your left is the **Gables** which, in the early 20th century, was home to Neville Chamberlain's niece. Towards the end of High Street, you'll pass a grand red-brick mansion on your right, **Meldreth Court**, which was the home of Andrew Marvell, a 17th-century poet who tutored one of Oliver Cromwell's daughters. It later became a courthouse, hence the name.

At the end of High Street is **Marvell's Green** – a grassy island with the village stocks, whipping post and base of an ancient prayer cross. The stocks are likely to have been issued as punishments by Meldreth Court, and records suggest that they were last used in 1860, following a church brawl. Wander over, poke your arms through the whipping post's iron clasps and thank your lucky stars that flogging was banned in 1948. The use of stocks, however, has never been formally abolished.

Turn right on to North End and continue towards the church. On the way, you'll pass the village almshouses (on your right, just after the stocks) and a host of 17th-century thatches (in summer, this is a good place to watch thatchers at work). Notice the ornate bird on the roof of number 29 – this was once the **village smithy**. When you arrive at **Holy Trinity Church**, notice its stumpy 12th-century tower, which looks as if it's been chopped off.

Walk around to the north side for elegant 14th-century windows, then step inside for fragments of a medieval wall painting, a listed barrel and finger organ, and a peal of eight bells that dates from 1617 to 1968.

Cross the road and follow the footpath signed 'Melbourn 1', which leads past **Topcliffe Mill**. Once the property of St Thomas's Hospital in London, the mill closed in 1942. Passing the mill race on your right, follow the footpath through a wooden gate into a field. Keep right along the field edge and, at the far end, veer right into the woodland. You're now following the Meldreth–Melbourn footpath beside the River Mel. Continue for about a third of a mile, passing little bridges and garden fences on your right. Further along, you'll pass an information board for **Melwood Local Nature Reserve**, which is home to kingfishers, water voles, wagtails and spring ducklings. Shortly after, you'll pass a bench on your left followed by a bridge over the river on your right. Cross the bridge into Flambards Close and follow it to High Street.

Turn right along High Street and walk back towards the pub. On the way, you'll pass the wooden-clad village hall on your left and a pink 17th-century thatch (Keys Cottage) on your right. Further up, the thatched cottage opposite the village shop was once the Old Bell pub, which closed in 1910 (Bell Close on your left echoes its memory).

life – Melbourn suffered a series of devastating fires in 1724 and 1915, which wiped out most of its original buildings.

Northwest of Melbourn, **Meldreth** has a cluster of local charms, from its popular pub and village stocks to the enchanting Melwood Reserve

– a patch of mixed woodland that flanks the River Mel. The Prime Meridian strikes through the village, with an engraved stone marking the spot on Fenny Lane – accuracy must have prevailed over aesthetics here, as the stone has a rather uninspiring roadside setting.

FOOD & DRINK

Bookmark Café at The Hub 30 High St, Melbourn SG8 6DZ ⌀ melbournhub.co.uk/cafe/. Based at the Melbourn Hub village centre, this community café has a lending library and play boxes for kids. Come for filled baguettes and all-day breakfasts, plus wine, beer and ice-cream milkshakes.

The British Queen 94 High St, Meldreth SG8 6LB ⌀ thebritishqueen.com. Meldreth's village pub is deservedly popular, with its large garden, stripped-back interior and second-floor balcony with rural views. Their posh pub grub ranges from Meldreth sausages to vegan burgers and handmade pizzas.

Bury Lane Farm Shop & Café Signed off the A10, Melbourn SG8 6DF. This huge food store and garden shop sells East Anglian meats, fresh fish, homemade sausages and pies, cut flowers and pick-your-own strawberries. There's also a café, soft-play barn and an outdoor 'beach' for kids. Customers are encouraged to support the farm's eco-credentials by bringing containers and bags.

Fieldgate Nurseries Farm Shop 32 Station Rd, Meldreth SG8 6JP ⌀ fieldgatenurseries. com ⊙ daily. A family business since 1969, Fieldgate is packed with far more than you'd expect – from local veg, free-range eggs and cut flowers at the front, to an emporium of bric-a-brac at the back.

Leech & Sons 1 & 3 Station Rd, Melbourn SG8 6DX. One of only a few British butchers to run their own abattoir, this family business has been going strong for more than 75 years. Their local meats are fully traceable, and their deli is stocked with cheeses, olives, dips, bread and desserts. They also offer filled rolls and have a second shop at Burwash Manor (page 302).

Sheene Mill 30 High St, Melbourn CB21 4HS ⌀ sheenemill.com. Set by the River Mel, this former 16th-century mill is now a restaurant and wedding venue. The restaurant has achieved two AA Rosettes for six years in a row, thanks to tantalising mains like corn-fed chicken with maple syrup, along with burgers, steaks and classic desserts like Cambridge burnt cream. They also do Sunday roasts and afternoon teas.

19 GREAT CHISHILL & THE WINDMILL

⌂ **Hall Farm B&B** (page 317)

Sitting atop a chalk escarpment, **Great Chishill** boasts the highest point in Cambridgeshire. It may only be 480ft above sea level but it feels like you're on top of the world. The summit is half a mile east of St Swithin's Church on Hall Lane (B1039) but the view from **Chishill Windmill** on Barley Road (also B1039) is far more impressive, with the ground dropping away to the west; it's a stunning spot for sunset. One of seven open trestle post mills in England, and the only one with a fantail, this 19th-century mill ground its last kernel in 1951. A footpath leads here from the main village: from Barley Road, follow the public footpath sign past house numbers 19, 21 and 17. When the track splits, turn right and walk on for half a mile to the windmill.

FOOD & DRINK

King William IV 43 Chishill Rd, Heydon SG8 8PW ✆ 01763 838773 🖉 kingwilliamheydon. com. Neighbouring Heydon village is home to a 16th-century pub known locally as the 'King Bill'. Full of character, it's adorned with farming memorabilia and has a lovely garden with countryside views. The adventurous menu features the likes of lamb rump with aubergine caviar, and cauliflower tagine with black onion rice.

The Pheasant 24 Heydon Rd, Great Chishill SG8 8SR ✆ 01763 838535 🖉 pheasantgc.com ☉ closed Mon. The highest pub in Cambridgeshire, The Pheasant has glorious views from the garden, while the interior has an olde worlde feel, with old beams and mismatched antique furniture. Their pared-back pub grub menu includes fish and chips with local ale batter, and they also offer freshly baked cakes, Friday to Sunday.

ACCOMMODATION

Cambridgeshire has a full spectrum of accommodation options, from simple campsites and traditional B&Bs to trendy glamping options and a handful of luxury hotels. I've included a selection of those that stand out for their uniqueness, green credentials, great location or, in a few cases, convenience to local attractions. You can find a more detailed description of each at ⬧ bradtguides.com/camsleeps.

It goes without saying that this is by no means an exhaustive list. There are many more shepherds' huts, glamping pods and cosy B&Bs that could have made it into this book but, sadly, there simply isn't room to list them all nor time to check them all out. Other good sources for accommodation in the county include ⬧ visitcambridge.org, ⬧ visitely. org.uk, ⬧ visitcambridgeshirefens.org and ⬧ visitpeterborough. com, as well as the Cambridgeshire listings on ⬧ coolcamping.com, ⬧ canopyandstars.co.uk and ⬧ sawdays.co.uk.

1 CAMBRIDGE & AROUND

Hotels
The Crown and Punchbowl High St, Horningsea CB25 9JG ⬧ 01223 860643 ⬧ thecrownandpunchbowl.co.uk
University Arms Regent St, Cambridge CB2 1AD ⬧ 01223 606066 ⬧ universityarms.com

B&Bs
The Blue Ball Inn 57 Broadway, Grantchester CB3 9NQ ⬧ 01223 846004 ⬧ blueballgrantchester.co.uk
Cambridge University Rooms Various locations in Cambridge ⬧ universityrooms.com
Crafts Hill Barn 31 Oakington Rd, Dry Drayton CB23 8DD ⬧ 01954 488534 ⬧ craftshillbarn. co.uk

Camping
Gayton Farm Clayhithe Rd, Horningsea CB25 9JE ⬧ 01223 440905 ⬧ gaytonfarm.co.uk
Highfield Farm Touring Park Long Rd, Comberton CB23 7DG ⬧ 01223 262308 ⬧ highfieldfarmtouringpark.co.uk

Self-catering
The Old Chapel Pierce Ln, Fulbourn CB1 5DJ ⬧ oldchapelfulbourn.co.uk

2 THE HEART OF HUNTINGDONSHIRE

Hotels
The George 39 High St, Buckden PE19 5XA ⬧ 01480 812300 ⬧ thegeorgebuckden.com
The Lion Hotel 44–46 High St, Buckden PE19 5XA ⬧ 01480 810313 ⬧ thelionbuckden.com

The Old Bridge Hotel 1 High St, Huntingdon PE29 3TQ ♪ 01480 424300 ⊘ huntsbridge.com

B&Bs

Eagle Mill Houghton Mill PE28 2BS ♪ 07768 537158 ⊘ eaglemill.co.uk

The Elm Moat Ln, Abbots Ripton PE28 2PD ♪ 01487 773585 ⊘ the-elm.co.uk

The Lodge at Hemingford Grey House Hemingford Grey PE28 9DF ♪ 01480 381457 ⊘ hemingfordgreyhouse.com

Camping

Grafham Water Caravan Club Site Church Rd, Grafham PE28 0BB ♪ 01480 810264 ⊘ caravanclub.co.uk

Quiet Waters Caravan Park Hemingford Abbots PE28 9AJ ♪ 01480 463405 ⊘ quietwaterscaravanpark.co.uk

Waterclose Meadows Campsite Houghton Mill PE28 2AZ ♪ 01480 499996 ⊘ nationaltrust. org.uk

Willows Park & Marina Bromholme Ln, Brampton PE28 4NE ♪ 01480 437566 ⊘ willowscaravanpark.com

Self-catering

The Warren House Kimbolton PE28 0EA ⊘ landmarktrust.org.uk

3 THE UPPER NENE VALLEY & GREAT NORTH ROAD

Hotels

The Bell Inn Great North Rd, Stilton PE7 3RA ⊘ thebellstilton.co.uk

Haycock Manor Hotel Wansford PE8 6JA ♪ 01780 782223 ⊘ haycock.co.uk

B&Bs

The Bluebell 10 Woodgate, Helpston PE6 7ED ♪ 01733 252394 ⊘ bluebellhelpston.co.uk

The Crown Inn Elton PE8 6RQ ♪ 01832 280232 ⊘ crowninnelton.co.uk

The White Hart Main St, Ufford PE9 3BH ⊘ whitehartufford.co.uk

Camping

Nene Park Campsite & Caravan site Ham Ln, PE2 5UU ♪ 01780 740250 ⊘ nenepark.org.uk/ campsite

The Nest Southorpe PE9 3BX ♪ 01780 433509 ⊘ thenestglamping.co.uk

Self-catering

The Arc Cabin Duck St, Elton PE8 6RJ ⊘ thearccabin.co.uk

Lynch Lodge Alwalton PE7 3UY ⊘ landmarktrust.org.uk

Pea Cottage Grange Farm, Main St, Southorpe PE9 3BX ♪ 07432 643872 ⊘ peacottage.co.uk

River Nene Cottages 1 Mill Ln, Water Newton PE8 6LY ♪ 01733 230628 ⊘ rivernenecottages. co.uk

4 FENLAND & GREAT FEN

Hotels

The Bramley House Hotel 15 High St, Chatteris PE16 6BE ♪ 01354 695414 ⊘ www. bramleyhousehotel.co.uk

B&Bs

The Cross Keys 12–15 Market Hill, Chatteris PE16 6BA ♪ 01354 692644 ⊘ crosskeyschatteris.com

Dog in a Doublet North Side, PE6 0RW ♪ 01733 202256 ⊘ doginadoublet.co.uk

Camping

Fourwinds Leisure 113 Whittlesey Rd, March PE15 0AH ♪ 01354 658737 ⊘ fourwindsleisure. com

Rivermill Caravan & Camping Park Mill Drove, Factory Bank, Ramsey PE26 2SB ♪ 07884 436012

Secret Garden Touring Park Mile Tree Ln, Wisbech PE13 4TR ♪ 01945 585044 ⊘ thesecretgardentouringpark.co.uk

Self-catering

Coach House Loft 14 North Brink, Wisbech
PE13 1JR ℘ 0344 809 2654 ♂ www.
nationaltrust.org.uk

5 THE ISLE OF ELY &
SOUTHERN FEN EDGE

Hotels

The Old Hall Stuntney CB7 5TR ℘ 01353
663275 ♂ theoldhallely.co.uk
The Pike & Eel Overcote Ln, Needingworth
PE27 4TW ℘ 01480 463336 ♂ pikeandeel.com
Poets House St Mary's St, Ely CB7 4EY ℘ 01353
887777 ♂ poetshouse.co.uk

B&Bs

The Blue Cow 29 Chequer St, Fenstanton PE28
9JQ ℘ 07877 388301 ♂ thebluecow.co.uk
Old School House Rooms 9 Greenside,
Waterbeach CB25 9HW ℘ 01223 861609
♂ theoldschoolhouserooms.co.uk
Peacocks Fine B&B 65 Waterside, Ely CB7 4AU
℘ 07900 666161 ♂ peacockstearoom.co.uk
Swan on the River 1 Sandhill, Littleport CB6
1NT ℘ 01353 861677 ♂ swanontheriver.co.uk
Thornhouse B&B Church St, Fen
Drayton CB24 4SG ℘ 07870 948313
♂ thornhousebedandbreakfast.co.uk
The Three Pickerels 19 Bridge Rd, Mepal CB6
2AR ℘ 01353 777777 ♂ thethreepickerels.co.uk

Camping

St Cyriac's High St, Swaffham Prior CB5 0LD
℘ 0207 841 0436 ♂ champing.co.uk
Mad Hatters Campsite Clayway Farm, CB7 4UD
℘ 07796 261211 ♂ madhatterscampsite.co.uk
Wicken Fen Back to Basics Campsite Wicken
Fen, Lode Ln, Wicken CB7 5XP ℘ 01353 720274
♂ nationaltrust.org.uk

Self-catering

BoatShack Hammonds Eau Farm, Sutton, Ely
CB6 2BG ℘ 07796 261211 ♂ boatshack.co.uk
The Coach House at Cathedral House 17
St Mary's St, Ely CB7 4ER ℘ 01353 662124
♂ cathedralhouse.co.uk

Horsely Hale Farm Horsely Hale CB6 1ER
℘ 01353 361470 ♂ horsleyhalefarm.co.uk
Stoker's Cottage Green End, Stretham CB6 3LE
♂ landmarktrust.org.uk

6 THE SOUTHERN HILLS

Hotels

Sheene Mill 39 Station Rd, Melbourn SG8 6DX
℘ 01223 891383 ♂ sheenemill.com

B&Bs

The Black Bull Inn 27 High St, Balsham CB21
4DJ ℘ 01223 893844 ♂ blackbull-balsham.
co.uk
The British Queen 94 High St, Meldreth SG8
6LB ℘ 01763 260252 ♂ thebritishqueen.com
Hall Farm B&B Chishill Hall, 110 Hall Ln,
Great Chishill SG8 8SH ℘ 01763 838263
♂ hallfarmbb.co.uk
The John Barleycorn Moorfield Rd, Duxford
CB22 4PP ℘ 01223 832699 ♂ johnbarleycorn.
co.uk
Pear Tree Inn High St, Hildersham CB21 6BU
℘ 07961 690008 ♂ peartreeinncambridge.com
The Red Lion 32 High St, Hinxton CB10 1QY
℘ 01799 530601 ♂ redlionhinxton.co.uk
The Three Blackbirds 36 Ditton Green,
Woodditton CB8 9SQ ℘ 01638 731100
♂ threeblackbirds.co.uk
The Three Hills Dean Rd, Bartlow CB21 4PW
℘ 01223 890500 ♂ thethreehills.co.uk

Camping

Guilden Gate Glamping 86 North
End, Bassingbourn SG8 5PD ℘ 01763 243960
♂ guildengate.co.uk

Self-catering

The Bull Pen 167 Alms Hill, Bourn CB23 2SZ ℘
07712 121777 ♂ thebullpencambridge.co.uk
Happenoak Treehouse Stocking Toft, West
Wickham Rd, Balsham CB21 4DZ ℘ 0117 204
7830 ♂ canopyandstars.co.uk

NOTES

NOTES

322

INDEX

Entries in **bold** refer to major entries.

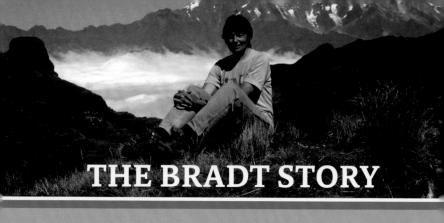

THE BRADT STORY

In the beginning

It all began in 1974 on an Amazon river barge. During an 18-month trip through South America, two adventurous young backpackers – Hilary Bradt and her then husband, George – decided to write about the hiking trails they had discovered through the Andes. *Backpacking Along Ancient Ways in Peru and Bolivia* included the very first descriptions of the Inca Trail. It was the start of a colourful journey to becoming one of the best-loved travel publishers in the world; you can read the full story on our website (www. bradtguides.com/ourstory).

Getting there first

Hilary quickly gained a reputation for being a true travel pioneer, and in the 1980s she started to focus on guides to places overlooked by other publishers. The Bradt Guides list became a roll call of guidebook 'firsts'. We published the first guide to Madagascar, followed by Mauritius, Czechoslovakia and Vietnam. The 1990s saw the beginning of our extensive coverage of Africa: Tanzania, Uganda, South Africa, and Eritrea. Later, post-conflict guides became a feature: Rwanda, Mozambique, Angola, Sierra Leone, Bosnia and Kosovo.

Comprehensive – and with a conscience

Today, we are the world's largest independently owned travel publisher, with more than 200 titles, from full-count and wildlife guides to Slow Travel guides like this one. However, our ethos remains unchanged. Hilary is still keenly involved, and we still get there first: two-thirds of Bradt guides have no direct competition.

But we don't just get there first. Our guides are also known for being more comprehensive than any other series. We avoid templates and tick-lists. Each guide is a one-of-a-kind expression of an expert author's interests, knowledge and enthusiasm for telling it how it really is.

And a commitment to wildlife, conservation and respect for local communities has always been at the heart of our books. Bradt Guides was championing sustainable travel before a other guidebook publisher.

Thank you!

We can only do what we do because of the support of readers like you – people who value less-obvious experiences, less-visited places and a more thoughtful approach to travel. Those who, like us, t travel seriously.